Conscious Consumption

Corporate Social Responsibility and Canada's Grocery Giants

Paul Pellizzari
and the Staff of EthicScan Canada

ETHICSCAN RESEARCH TEAM: Virginia Adey, Jane Dryden, Scott Matter

COPY EDITOR: Virginia Adey, Heather Lang

EDITOR: David Nitkin

TEXT DESIGN AND LAYOUT: Chris Essert, Frank Gubitz

COVER DESIGN: Frank Gubitz

FACT CHECKING: Kristian Galberg, Veronica Pochmursky

PUBLISHER: EthicScan Canada Limited

PRINTER: AGMV Marquis Imprimeur Inc

Publication of this manuscript was made possible by a publication grant from
the United Food and Commercial Workers. The editorial content is wholly that of the
author who asserts the independence of the work.

This independent research is derived from the EthicScan
Corporate 1500 DataBase, which was initiated in 1989. All companies reviewed herein
were contacted for performance updating and, where permission was granted, were
interviewed in the period June-October, 2001. Fact verification occurred in the
period February-August, 2002.

CONTENTS

EthicScan Canada Limited
P.O. Box 54034
Toronto, Ontario, Canada
M6A 3B7

www.ethicscan.ca
phone (416) 783-6776
facsimile (416) 783-7386

ISBN: 0-9731046-0-0

1. Consumer education – Canada – Handbooks, manuals, etc.

2. Social responsibility of business – Canada – Guidebook

3. Corporations – Canada – Directories

4. Shopping – moral and ethical aspects

Printed on paper containing over 50% recycled stock, including 10% post-consumer fibre.

ACKNOWLEDGEMENTS

We extend our gratitude and appreciation to all those who participated in bringing this book to you. These include:

• Virginia Adey, Jane Dryden, and Scott Matter, members of the EthicScan research team, who conducted the research and fact checking, and did the interviews

• Kristian Galberg, Jennie Onyette-Jeffries, Veronica Pochmursky, and Elisa Usher: contract employees who, in doing their DataBase work, supported us enormously

• Chris Essert, Frank Gubitz, Jonathan Howells, and Kanwal Rahim for design, layout, and help with production

• The 60 volunteers from across the country who helped define, through a Modified Delphi Process, the rating and grading schema used to assess corporate social responsibility (CSR) in 2002

• Len Brooks, Lorrie Goldstein, and David Olive, who read and commented on an early draft of the text

• Leslie Dizgun, our legal counsel

• Readers of EthicScan's two previous Guides who took the time to provide us with many constructive ideas

> *The Ethical Shoppers Guide* (1992)
> *Shopping With a Conscience* (1996)

• Company spokespersons, union representatives, government regulators, consumer advocates, and others who consented to be interviewed for this book

HOW TO USE THIS BOOK

Conscious Consumption contains information, much of it never revealed before, about the practices of large companies that produce food, beverage, household and consumer products. The 80 grocery sector corporations reviewed here produce, package, or contract raw ingredients for the vast majority of what Canadians eat, drink, smoke and use as cleansers, cosmetics or household consumables.

Our Readers

This book was written with four basic groups in mind:

Conscious consumers: People who think about what they buy, and want to know more about the companies that make products they use every day.

Progressive business professionals: Anyone who makes procurement or partnership decisions. Executives and managers who manage environmental affairs and employee relations. Compliance officers and board directors concerned with CSR's implications for governance. Charitable foundation development officers. Professionals who need to compare independent information and benchmark responsible business practices.

Non-government organization, government, and organized labour leaders: Civil society leaders and groups undertaking a campaign on a specific issue, or screening prospective corporate partners before accepting funds or co-organizing an event. Have these companies done anything which conflicts with the organization's mandate or principles? Are practices compatible? Do they seem like a strong fit?

Teachers and students: Educators across a wide range of fields—environmental studies, business, human resources, consumer studies, industrial relations, international development— who study the effects of business on the community. Researchers who use independent profiles for case studies, and to see how companies struggle to reduce the gap between espoused values and actual practices.

EthicScan doesn't try to tell anyone how to think or shop. We do provide accurate research about the company behind the name or product. Individuals and groups can choose how and when to apply the details about these 70 enterprises, many of which earn multi-billion dollar sales from Canadian consumers every year.

We don't make decisions for others, or tell anyone how to trade off the virtues of one corporate practice against the warts of another. You must decide, for example, if a company's poor record in an area such as promoting women is offset by positive job creation or demonstrably strong environmental results. The tables, essays, and profiles here illuminate what corporate behaviours exist, which grocery sector companies are forthright about their practices, and how companies can excel.

If you are curious about definitions of social responsibility and how we apply them, the chapter "Measuring Corporate Social Responsibility" (p.35) explains the process EthicScan uses to research and compare companies in eight areas: ethical management and consumer relations, employee relations, equity and family issues, progressive staff policies, sourcing and trade, environmental management and performance, community responsibilities, and candor.

If you want a quick summary of how all companies compare against each other across different categories, the section "Grocery Giants' Ratings" (p.265) is a table that rates each company (excepting private label departments) next to the others.

If you wish to compare a company's details against its peers, turn to "Grocery Company Profiles," (p.58-265) a collection of short reports that reveal the internal workings and practices of each firm according to performance criteria.

If you are uncertain about a specific company, the "Index of Companies and Brands" (p.279) at the back of the book will help to identify and locate page numbers for a familiar banner and its parent company.

Finally, if you want to know how you can influence behaviour and make change happen, three sections at the end of this book will benefit you. "Options for Action" (p.268) suggests what you can do as an individual, employee, student, volunteer, citizen, or advocate. "Sources for Action" (p.271) identifies government agencies, labour unions, environmental advocates, community economic development associations, and other groups worth contacting. Finally, the "Action Report" (p.277) is a form you can fill out to report your actions to others. Send it to us and we will enter it in the EthicScan Corporate Database.

ABOUT ETHICSCAN CANADA

It isn't easy to find regular, credible, detailed information about corporate behaviour, so EthicScan Canada was created to systematically research the social, labour, and environmental performance of Canada's largest companies. As Canada's oldest corporate social responsibility (CSR) research house, we design reports that help people and organizations apply their values to choices they must make, whether they are consumers, investors, donors, fund managers, development officers, or institutions concerned with partnering. Internationally, we work with CSR research groups operating in more than a dozen countries to define measures and to share information on multinational corporations.

EthicScan was established as a fee-for-service business in 1989. Along with conducting original research, we help government agencies, businesses, and non-governmental organizations develop tools for managing their relations and workplaces. With clients, we develop case studies, social and ethics audits, and benchmarking protocols that track business performance and measure different practices. Our extensive library of codes, training materials, and policies assists companies, professional bodies, academic institutions, and industry associations who want to learn about and promote ethical decision-making. For over a decade EthicScan associates have gathered experience conducting confidential staff and stakeholder interviews as ethics trainers, or as facilitators of multi-sectoral dialogues.

EthicScan acts as an independent third party research house. There is no financial or other relationship between it and all of the companies we cover, including those profiled in this book. Nevertheless, we wish to point out what may strike some as a conflict of interest. The consulting side of our business has worked with some of these companies, conducting independent ethics audits or developing corporate ethics codes or training. Likewise, some of these companies are subscribers to our periodical, *The Corporate Ethics Monitor*, while others have commissioned us to prepare Partnership Screening Reports about other companies. No matter what company EthicScan researches in our books and studies, we always ask the same questions every time to every company. We turn to the same critical, independent media and public information sources, and talk to union representatives, activists, community representatives and regulators to see all sides of a corporate performance story. Every company is treated the same way, and all information is independently verified. EthicScan reports on everything that we know or uncovered in our research process. Likewise, we assure corporate clients that no confidential information learned through other work has been disclosed in this book.

INTRODUCTION

WHO WANTS TO CHANGE THE WORLD?

I'm a Protester! I'm Not a Protester

This book starts with a simple but challenging proposition: if Canadians can adjust how we consume, invest, and do business, the world will change for the better.

Sounds wide-eyed and hopeful. Who believes it can or should happen?

Our consumer markets are so sophisticated, they cater to the smallest whim. Most of us get what we need and some portion of what we want. Our jobs create a tax base for social programs, health services, and civic development. Compared to many countries, we are well educated. Generally, Canadians accept that businesses and a market economy will deliver these and other benefits, so most cannot imagine life without them.

Why, then, does anything need to change?

Although economic consumption goes up every year—we like those flashy brands and upsized packages—there are signs of a growing mistrust about a business-dominated world. More than any other institution, the corporation crosses borders and controls resources. Everyone feels its power, and occasionally we glimpse at the undersides of what it can do.

In fact, North Americans gobble up stories about corporate malfeasance. Looking back a decade, American news stories dealing with class action lawsuits against corporations and other organizations rose by a staggering 538% in a single year, and coverage of "white collar" crimes soared by 328%. That was 1991-1992 (the year EthicScan released its first *Ethical Shopper's Guide*). As the nineties wore on, blockbuster films like *Erin Brockovich* and *The Insider* cast companies as villains who waste the environment and toy cruelly with human lives. These stories sell, because we believe that business can perpetrate gross injustice and escape accountability.

By the end of the decade, protests against the ills of global capitalism were regular events in North America and Europe. The anti-globalization movement, as it is often called, clogged the gates wherever the world's leaders met, including the G8 conferences (Alberta 2002, Genoa, Italy 2001), the Free Trade Agreement of the Americas (Québec City 2001), the International Monetary Fund (Washington 2000), and the World Trade Organization (Seattle 1999). By galvanizing the most strident feelings of discontent, protesters drew attention to what they see as problems. These include business's role in perpetuating gaps between rich and poor; the encroachment of corporate interests on environmental and safety regulation; and the proliferation of genetically modified organisms in our food systems, to name three.

But placards and gas masks are only one face of dissatisfaction. Other more moderate expressions also surface. Between 1997 and 2000, a broad sample of Canadians said, through polls conducted by three major research groups, that companies should think about more than money. These people think in terms of brand reputation, their own consumer habits, and how they invest.

Between our need for what business gives us, and a desire to believe it can be more responsible, we are caught by the question: what to do about it? Living in the information age, some turn to what we can know.

Do Canadians want business to just produce profit?
• 90% of respondents believe companies should focus on more than money, by creating jobs, paying taxes, and obeying laws.
• 45% said that companies have a higher responsibility to "exceed all laws, set a higher ethical standard, and help build a better society for all."

What do Canadians notice about a company?
• 60% base their impression of a company in part on its social responsibility reputation.
• 38% could not identify two national companies they thought were outstanding corporate citizens.
• 40% spoke negatively about companies they perceived as lacking social responsibility.

How do we act as consumers or investors?
• 79% always try to buy from good corporate citizens.
• 26% believe that social responsibility is an extremely important part of investing.
• $5.77 billion were invested in socially screened mutual funds in 2000.

Sources: 2000 Millennium Poll, an international survey conducted by Environics International; 1997 Angus Reid survey of 1,500 Canadians on issues concerning corporate responsibility; 2000 Review published by the Social Investment Organization

Much of our day-to-day news comes from the likes of CNN, Internet stock pages, *Fast Company*, *Maclean's* or *The National Post*. But many people who are skeptical about what they learn there need other sources. Every week, research groups like EthicScan Canada get requests for information on the social, labour, and environmental practices of the world's largest companies. Some come from individuals who want to avoid buying from companies that pollute or source ingredients from exploitative countries. Others come from investors and institutions that want to compare ethical management practices across whole industry sectors.

Responsible consumers and investors want to reconcile corporate profits with the costs business incurs on society and the eco-system. Corporate profits are necessary for economic growth, but not at the cost of monopoly, unsafe products, accountability, or predatory business practices. Concerned citizens share the belief that taking action requires reflection, and changing the world requires conscious choices. So they begin their search for facts and perspectives they can use.

How Are We Doing?

How are Canadians actually doing at changing the world? Well, that depends on whom you ask, what you ask, and what you expect. When people say that companies should be socially responsible, they can often name results they want: a more even distribution of wealth, less pollution, well-paying jobs that allow for a family life, less corporate concentration, and fairer trade for developing nations. What is harder to describe is what companies should do to get there.

"Changing the world" often evokes images of impassioned leaders, masses marching, and great leaps of technological progress. The media often use events like the election of Pierre Trudeau, or the end of the Vietnam war, or the advent of personal computers to mark passing decades. But underneath these snapshots, most lives change gradually and quietly. Through many invisible and individual actions, the world changes a little each day, because problems and solutions come from decisions made by millions of people over time.

The world changes when a group of pulp workers at a paper factory discovers how to reduce waste output by a couple thousand kilolitres each year. Or, federal legislation is redrafted, making it easier for a TSX listed company's minority shareholders to circulate questions about its environmental practices. Other investors learn and the company listens. Incremental change is built on events few remember. But it is powerful because it can touch everyone.

Over the last twenty years, corporations have gotten bigger through mergers and consolidation, and gaps have grown between the wealthiest countries and the poorest. Government seems less powerful and independent when setting social and environmental standards, legis-

---

Global Wealth and Poverty

• In the early 1990s, 80% of money invested in developing nations by industrialized nations went directly from government to government.
• By the late 1990s, 80% of investment dollars moved from transnational corporations to governments.
• The number of people living in abject poverty is as great today as the entire human population in 1900.

Source: April 2001, by Ed Broadbent, head of the Canadian Democracy and Corporate Accountability Commission, United Nations Development Program.

---

lating regulations, and enforcing compliance. It has relaxed its traditional roles as monitor and protector of the public good, leaving non-governmental organizations (NGOs) and other civil society groups to gather, share, and report critical information. In this context, groups that want to invest or consume responsibly have sprouted up.

Today, companies must realize that they will succeed only for as long as they enjoy consent of the public, and acceptance from other stakeholders like workers, shareholders, suppliers and regulators. This book tries to show how more than 70 large makers of grocery products "are doing" at managing their responsibilities in society—what they do to communities, their workers, and the environment—and at responding to demands for greater accountability, transparency, and equality of opportunity. Some businesses reviewed here may say they are doing better than the grades in the chart suggests. If this is so, EthicScan may not know about it, because of a lack of corporate candor. That, in part, is what this book is about. It attempts to present and measure how much and what kind of information is available to conscious consumers. We don't evaluate rationale or motivation, preferring to assess only the results of choices and behaviour. For many readers, the Company Profiles will be core information. But we encourage you to look at them in the context of why corporate social responsibility is personally significant to you and your family, as well as how it relates to larger business and social changes. We challenge you to think about how information is generated, circulated, and used through the media, business communications, and interest groups.

WHAT IS CORPORATE SOCIAL RESPONSIBILITY?

Corporate Social Responsibility (CSR) measures the balance between economic realities and the impacts business has on people and ecologies. Generally, the term applies to issues that affect interests beyond a company's shareholders: from employees to people who buy products and services, and from residents who live near factories to national or local charities seeking philanthropic contributions. In broad terms, CSR speaks to anyone who worries about non-economic effects of corporations, while acknowledging that capitalist markets are getting stronger, not weaker. It aims to make individual companies and whole sectors of industry more accountable and susceptible to changing societal demands, as defined by a broad-based set of interests.

CSR is about measurable behaviour. It looks critically at actual corporate practice - good and bad - in very detailed terms, across a broad range of operations. What is CSR not? Good intentions or self-serving platitudes. Or a rigidly defined philosophy; a theory without any practice; a dogmatic group of critics disengaged from the actual workings of the economy.

Who is drawn to CSR? Consumers who are conscious of what they buy and from whom they buy. Employees who want to know how to make their workplaces more humane, supportive and progressive. Job seekers looking for a responsible employer. Personal and institutional investors looking to screen investment portfolios in order to support corporations they believe are "better," and exclude those they see as "worse." Student groups demanding details about companies that supply their campuses with goods and services. Education and recreation administrators, forced by funding cuts to put out their hand to the corporate sector, who want to know whose money they are getting. Union and government leaders who want to compare compensation and working conditions for sector-wide bargaining. Civil society groups that need help deciding how best to lobby, boycott, or partner with particular companies.

This book asks questions that trace corporate activities across many interactions. What does a cheese processing plant do to reduce toxins in releases to the air, ground, and water? Do private label brand products go on sale at the same time in poor and rich neighborhoods, or does the retailer change the schedule, for example, when welfare cheques are released? Do employees at a salt processing factory feel empowered, safe, well-trained, and part of a company that cares about its integrity? Do any suppliers in a spice maker's chain of production use exploitative labour?

Engaging Companies

Many CSR supporters agree that the current global economic order is flawed, especially when geography, power, and money separate wealthy consumers from the conditions of those who produce goods. Where they sometimes part ways with militant anti-globalization agitators is over questions of what to do about it. Fundamentally, CSR takes a reform approach to questions of business and social change, acknowledging that corporate rule is not likely to disappear any time soon. *Anti*-globalization? Globalized trade is already a reality, and despite serious problems, it can bring benefits and prosperity. Unfortunately or not, multinational corporations are the center of the global economy. Even if they have sometimes hurt, in particular, people in South America, Africa and Asia, these regions will not develop without international trade and investment. Successful corporations are capable of incredible organizational feats and administrative acumen: they build and manage vast resources, wield political clout, and leverage global networks.

Again, unfortunately or not, equity assurances and fair terms for less protected peoples are not going to be imposed by existing authorities. Governments and bodies like the United Nations, the World Trade Organization, or the International Monetary Fund have shown that they are not going to increase safeguards against low standards, neglect, and exploitation. Most of what they propose to companies is completely voluntary. To connect demands for social justice with economic prosperity, to make companies look to longer term consequences, CSR gets them to pay attention to issues they would prefer to forget by hitting them where they live, in the market. It defines and influences the resources, labour conditions, public acceptance, and purchasing dollars that companies want.

Corporate Power in the Global Economy

- 500 corporations control 42% of the world's wealth
- 10 companies worldwide effectively control the world's food chain

Source: "Beyond Borders," Frances Caincross. Tomorrow Magazine, Nov-Dec 1999.

CSR can help people make responsible choices. Through mechanisms such as fair trade labels, socially responsible investing, or partnership tests (negative and positive screening), people approach companies in new ways. In turn, CSR encourages progressive managers to enhance workplaces, transform corporate cultures, and empower employees to reduce harm and improve social impacts. CSR uses the logic of business because it is interested in outcomes. If a strong and demonstrable record of corporate responsibility can enhance economic performance, then managers will know that better practices are in their own interests.

This approach to changing how companies invest, manufacture, and trade is not easy, and sometimes it meets with resistance from different stakeholders. Some protesters believe that companies will never do enough, so the entire economic system needs a complete overhaul. Companies disengage from dialogue whenever they think that they cannot satisfy their critics, if (to paraphrase one researcher from the German CSR institute, IMUG) sticking their heads above the parapet will only get them shot. CSR defines engagement according to stakeholders who are affected positively and negatively by business. It also gathers opinions from business leaders who understand day-to-day corporate life.

In the middle are consumers, investors, unions, and other groups, whose choices decide how well CSR mechanisms actually work. For engagement to be effective, and for benefits to be shared, people on all sides must get some of what they want. Corporate accountability and transparency means that companies cannot be authorities unto themselves. Can conscious consumption in the grocery sector be "win-win" for all stakeholders? Companies want to avoid bad news stories and government regulation where none exists. Workers want meaningful jobs. Consumers want healthy, safe, low cost, and reliable products.

Who decides what corporate behaviours are good or bad? Over the last couple of decades, a core set of CSR fields and definitions have emerged across a number of countries, but some general principles abide: information should reflect multiple stakeholder needs and wants; measures should be credible and verifiable; information should be calibrated in ways that allow users to decide for themselves; each person or group should be able to make judgments based on their own priorities, beliefs, and desired results; if a company has a good environmental performance, but a bad equity and diversity performance, the individual should be able to make the choice that matters most to him or her.

To devise its framework for evaluating companies, EthicScan draws upon many stakeholders and reports information based on what our readers tell us (please see the section on the Modified Delphi, p.35).

Who Counts? Corporate Accountability and Engagement

Traditional economic theory says a company should only worry about a few people: its shareholders, customers, and government regulators. While followers of Milton Friedman focus on corporate obligations to shareholders, CSR broadens this spectrum of business accountability by introducing the perspectives of other "stakeholders," defined as any person or group who benefits from, is hurt by, or otherwise affected by a company's activities. This view leads companies to look toward employees, communities, the environment, suppliers, regulators, and competitors.

Devout believers in so-called free markets usually resist the introduction of social considerations, saying that companies cannot spare time and money to deal with the grievances and aspirations of particular interests. If any claim is credible and serious, this perspective argues, it can fall back on legal recourse to deal with a company. After all, that's what law is for. At first blush, stakeholder interests may sound extraneous to the pursuit of profit, but CSR is premised on the belief that no business can exist independent of people or its environment. From this view, business must deal with other concerns as part of its existence. Social and business concerns are inextricable, and corporate accountability must be defined dynamically and from an extended circle of interests, because current approaches of law and the market will never be responsive enough to the myriad effects that corporate activity actually has on the world.

In real terms, companies will always rank demands made on them according to what and who matter most to their interests. Generally, they consider their investors, consumers, and employees first, slotting considerations for the environment and communities lower. But, as CSR proponents know, corporate priorities are driven by marketing and profit expectations, but also depend on what makes a company vulnerable. Those stakeholders who come further down the priority list find ways to get responses, even if they must engage a company for a long time. Not all actions are punitive, but the splashiest cases seem to be ones involving divestment or boycott campaigns aimed at damaging market share or image.

During the first half of the 1990s, an international activist group, People for the Ethical Treatment of Animals (PETA), criticized the Gillette Company over its management of animal testing when developing its consumer products. Gillette had printed a label on its packages claiming that its products were "cruelty-free," and PETA questioned the validity of this claim and other statements about the terms of testing. After years of PETA campaigns, the Gillette Company reported some information: no lab animals were used to test personal care and consumer products, or any of their ingredients, and no animals were used for safety or research testing of cosmetics for three consecutive years. Gillette also donated millions of dollars to the development of alternative tests. Based on this information, PETA said it was satisfied that things had changed, so it ended the campaign against Gillette in November 1996.

Now, the company has repeatedly stated that PETA's actions had no impact on its decisions, and that it will always comply with any government regulations requiring animal tests for any new chemical or ingredient. Whether Gillette responded directly or not is in one sense unimportant. What matters is that information and decision-making processes became public when otherwise they would have remained private. However Gillette made its choices in this case, it would be difficult for any company not to consider being more transparent about its policies, practices, or performance in the face of persistent campaigns from external stakeholder groups. Making knowledge public is a goal of CSR advocates and a consequence of CSR engagement.

Driven to increase profitability, corporate thinking usually separates different goals. "Becoming the most communicative nut-free candy-maker in Canada" sounds trivial and almost silly, a goal that we would not normally associate with higher-pressure priorities, like upping productivity. But smart companies know that key corporate responsibility measures are integral to long-term survival. In 2001, Nestlé Canada announced it would cease producing certain chocolate bars in a nut-free facility, meaning that five popular products would no longer be safe for people with nut allergies. Consumers, thousands of them, wrote and telephoned to complain about the decision, and savvy Nestlé reversed its decision. While this move may appear to be motivated by a straight business concern for disgruntled chocolate buyers, consider that the company probably lost money by avoiding the proposed production switch. It had to trade off efficiency gains from consolidation of the chocolate bar lines against consumer hostility, the health attributes of a product, and perceived non-accountability. Nestlé understood that paying attention to a sensitive health issue, even if it affects a very small pocket of its consumer base, is not separate from the survival of its brand.

Conscientious consumption, or the application of CSR, requires companies to look at what they do and how they treat their stakeholders in order to promote sales, improve production efficiencies, or protect market share. Engagement is complex, costly, and its effectiveness is hard to measure with cut-and-dry stats like a bigger chunk of market share. A multi-stakeholder world means that business must answer to a great number of interests simultaneously. A major multinational may have to partner with an NGO; negotiate with indigenous peoples who have land claims that encumber operations; appeal to value-based investors who screen portfolios; and address consumers concerned about wage and living conditions of workers in Asia. It renders old models for external relations extinct, because direct action and reporting on many company processes, both relatively uncommon a few years ago, are now requisite for transnational business in this century.

Driving Change with Information

Companies influence how we think and feel about them by spending millions on advertising, product information, direct marketing calls, and more privately, with lobbying pitches. As annoying as this visual and audio noise can be, in the end it somehow works on us.

Left to its devices, business would stay silent about the issues covered in this book. This is understandable. After all, who among us would want to answer questions about difficult, sensitive problems if we did not have to? Without information sources outside the company, we would rarely learn about details like children getting poisoned by spoiled ham, the exploitation of workers harvesting cocoa in Africa, or charges of anti-competitive practices. These sad stories besmirch companies, most of whom would like to think of themselves—and have you think of them—as good corporate citizens. Throughout CSR's history, moments of heightened interest in reporting arise because consumers became concerned about a specific issue: tainted food, corrupt monopolist practices, or unsafe working conditions. They were disturbed with what they knew about companies.

If you believe that the world can change, consider another idealistic proposition: *if it were easy for consumers to know how people and the environment were affected by a product, many would change some of their purchasing habits*. To make this happen, we need informed consumers willing to act on the basis of their humane impulses. Opinion polls suggest that they are out there, so the next question is whether consumers will act *if choices are made easy?* This is one of the toughest and most promising frontiers for CSR: converting information into forms, like an easy-to-recognize label or CSR data embedded (and readily scanned) in product bar codes, that make socially responsible decisions quick and ever-present.

Are we there yet?

Currently, EthicScan is one of a few organizations in Canada that systematically track a broad range of social and environmental information on hundreds of Canadian companies. EthicScan's detailed research profiles (used to write the short company reports in this book) are typically 20 to 30 pages in length, and are created using a standard report that organizes information gathered from a variety of outside sources (media articles, advocacy campaigns, government reports, union comments). Spokespeople from every corporation receive a copy of the report created on them, and are asked to add a company perspective and to supplement information. This approach has been developed over more than a dozen years and has received the input of hundreds of others: CSR researchers from other countries, academics, journalists, activists, government regulators, business people, and readers. To better understand our research process, please see the section, Measuring Corporate Social Responsibility (p.25).

REPUTATION MANAGEMENT

From Shame to Responsible Action

Stories that profile celebrity CEOs or celebrate the triumph of corporate behemoths that create "shareholder value" tend to vaunt the importance of business in our culture. As a result, we sometimes need a reminder that corporate power is neither total nor impenetrable nor destiny. Individual companies may wield heavy influence with government, but they do not always call the shots, at least not with impunity. Individual companies may dominate and structure communications media, but they cannot eliminate argument and dissent. PR and marketing muscles flex when brand images get cracked, but they adapt when public values change and perception shifts.

Think all big companies have brilliant strategies for protecting their reputations against bad-news stories? According to surveys cited by management consultants, GPC International, *fewer than 10%* of North American companies have any kind of "crisis communications" plan. They lack procedures that tell staff how to talk to the media, government, and public should something ugly happen to the company. In other words, most *are not* expert at defending themselves against critical reports from say, the Sierra Legal Defense Fund, who might inform us that a battery maker has been seeping waste into a water supply for a decade.

However, consider the emerging field of "reputation management" (made up mostly of communications consultants). It allegedly helps branded companies manage both short-term crises of communications and long term relations with stakeholders. Curiously, consumer advocates and corporate critics understood how to leverage the power of corporate reputations before most companies learned to defend themselves.

When NGOs realized that legislative change was not always the quickest way to change business-social relations, they turned to other tactics. In the article, "The NGO Industrial Complex," Gary Gereffi and others explain how actions that affect markets became very sophisticated in the 1990s. "Market campaigning" learned to focus "protests against highly visible branded retailers," the authors write, a development that was like the discovery of "gunpowder for environmentalists."

When confronted with a serious corporate reputation problem, management can respond in different ways. If the problem comes from one unit or division of a large company with many holdings, the parent may restructure its ownership or divest the subsidiary outright. Usually, this move is aimed at boosting profitable sister companies whose stock values suffer residual damage from the problem brand. For example, RJR Nabisco (USA) separated its food interests from its tobacco operations, Imasco divided up its various interests that once included Imperial Tobacco.

These days, even relatively remote international contract operations can bring headaches to executives. In 1994, PepsiCo (the parent of the company covered here) faced a major crisis over alleged human rights abuses in Burma (now Myanmar). The Shan Human Rights Foundation reported that forced labour was used to dig a canal that would supply water to a Pepsi plant. Pepsi did not directly control the construction site, but when 600 people among the 60,000 forced labourers died on the site in March 1994, the company had a problem. Corporate watchdogs had begun connecting problems in contracted networks associated with global brands, so PepsiCo began disentangling itself from the situation, initially selling off its 40% interest in Pepsi Burma. After trying to maintain franchise agreements for a couple of years, in May 1997, it eventually pulled out of the region entirely.

When boards and executives shift ownership structures to remove accountability, the interests of CSR *do not* advance. In cases of human rights or environmental management problems, accountability compels a company to confront issues, mollify critics, and forge long-term solutions. Unfortunately, a throbbing PR crisis does not always make this happen. For example, despite the Burma situation, Pepsi gave EthicScan little indication about how it manages foreign sourcing and trade issues: there are no codes or human rights protections (at any of the group companies) reported in our profile.

The opposite reaction sometimes comes from a reputation "challenge" created by a controversial product. There, companies sometimes take advantage of every opportunity to demonstrate responsibility. For example, Imperial Tobacco takes the time to provide a great deal of information to research groups like EthicScan. PR alone cannot guide a CSR response, because it does not cut to the quick of responsibility management. All too often, it focuses on keeping stakeholders happy, not doing the right thing. Ethics is not about keeping all stakeholders happy. In fact, if the public believes that a brand is only fighting a PR battle, the strategy can backfire. In the early 1990s, Clorox anticipated the concern of the emerging environmental movement about the chemical chlorine. Greenpeace found out about a PR consultant retained to protect the bleach maker's reputation, leaked the story, and the plan was never used. A Clorox spokesperson explained to EthicScan that "Clorox did not prepare the draft plan, an agency did. When [Clorox] management reviewed it, they rejected it as not in keeping with the Company's standards." Whatever the reasons were for the decision, what is interesting is the corporate spokesperson's distinction between an outsider's plan and practices normally "in keeping with the Company's standards."

Some individual investors, consumers or students tell EthicScan that corporate talk about "standards" or "values," or a desire to incorporate CSR into a "corporate strategy" sounds like a lot of empty PR talk. In some cases they might be right. But it is important to remember that meaningful changes within a company can only start when it sets "standards" *and tries to enact them.* The questions worth asking are: does the company follow up with implementation plans, training, internal information sharing, independent verification procedures, and public reporting? If so, then real accountability is at work.

Public attacks on a brand will not, by themselves, produce long-term actual change in corporate behaviour, as the UK-based research group, the New Economic Foundation has observed. A company hounded by critics might reach the point where the CEO declares, *we want off that "worst of" list once and for all.* If it tackles not only the PR problem, but the root causes, then it proves itself serious about CSR.

Change involves the systems, structures, and response mechanisms of business. While a weak response might be a quick, one-time, highly visible charitable donation to an environmental cause, a forward-looking firm tries to stay ahead of public expectations by adopting high standards, applying and monitoring them, and continuously improving its performance. In other words, "walking the talk". Increasingly, NGOs, labour unions, food banks, and other civil society groups can now act, for example, as independent verifiers of corporate claims about their environmental or human rights record.

A well-known example from twenty years ago demonstrates how a company can solve a problem. In 1982, Johnson & Johnson had been building a responsible corporate culture around consumer issues since the 1930s, when one of the company's flagship products, Tylenol pain reliever, became spiked with cyanide in a tampering scare. Very quickly, the company was able to issue warnings, remove products from shelves, and innovate package safety features (that became industry standards) because it had a system that started with a code of ethics. Serving as the basis of the company's culture, its "Credo" ranks those to whom the company is accountable. Beginning with doctors, nurses, patients, and parents who administer their products, it then lists employees and communities ahead of suppliers and distributors. The last group cited is company shareholders. The company's health-centered response to the Tylenol scare was so effective that market share and reputation were both enhanced.

Knowing Companies Better

Over the last decade, CSR concepts and systems have developed faster than companies have implemented them. Few leading-edge corporate CSR champions come from Canada, in part because we lack articulate and visionary executives who stand up and advance the business case for broad-based change. Although many corporate executives see themselves as ethical, their operational definition of ethics and social responsibility is often within a narrow and insular context that focuses on marketing and legal compliance. Managerial responses fall short of current, ever-changing socially responsible principles that incorporate independent verification of practices.

Many consumers do not read, trust, or believe corporate websites or sustainability reports when they seem facile, uncritically self-praising and entirely self-serving. Communication of regular, credible, and meaningful information about what goes on at individual plants is impeded by corporate reluctance to empower employee whistleblowers, engage stakeholders, spend money on waste reduction, or improve internal and independent external reporting. Many companies first engage CSR in a reactionary or defensive way. Some still actively resist competing on the basis of social and environmental considerations. Our economy and consumer choice suffer as politicians degrade food inspection systems, delay non-compliance penalties, devolve regulatory authority, and ignore corporate accountability as a priority.

There is some good news. Compared with a decade ago, many companies are doing some things better or very well. In specific areas such as employee diversity and work-life balance, change has come quickly and been accepted. Every year, more companies release environmental or sustainability reports (though their quality varies widely). Major stock indices in Canada, the US, and the UK have introduced socially responsible lists, and new mutual funds that screen companies enter the personal investment market each year. (The screens and research are also getting better.) Employees, consumers, unions, and investors are more confidently able to apply choices with greater flexibility, and more institutions will screen their investments and partners. Magazines as prominent as *Fortune* and *Report on Business* conduct surveys of senior executives, directors, and financial analysts that now include reputation criteria "of interest to socially responsible investors." And, most important to this book, companies now report more details about their activities.

Conscious Consumption, EthicScan's third book in ten years, reveals a growing gap between "high-response" companies and the rest. In a sense, this candor gap is part of the story this book has to tell. The best-reporting firms (generally, the most sophisticated multinational brands like Alcan, Bayer, McCain's, or Nestlé) or those that face CSR issues that generate debate, have more incentive to communicate. Such companies demonstrate that CSR measures are understood, measurable, and attainable, or that at least they must be addressed.

The sunlight of corporate transparency can warm consumers' belief in a fair economy. Because society's expectations continually evolve, EthicScan changed its approach in this book. To better present good policies and practices, or how high profile issues affect brands, we have given more space to those that have the fullest stories. Unlike the individual company reports of previous EthicScan guide books—which presented all firms in uniform length—this change allows better use of the information we know.

Will conscious consumers, investors, and community stakeholders begin to exercise unprecedented influence over corporate behaviour? Is this a moment when we can introduce terms of market competition that extend beyond price, quality, and convenience? People and institutions can now make decisions differently than they did twenty years ago. As consumer expectations and definitions of morality change, CSR increasingly bridges the time lags between its definitions and actual corporate performance. Standards rise incrementally, even if companies fail (or seem to fail) to respond. This guide attempts to address the imbalance between what stakeholders want and what companies can deliver. Our information is a realistic and concrete instrument of change, but we must guard against co-optation by keeping it independent and critical, while keeping companies engaged.

Critical Engagement

Our research process has eight stages.

1. EthicScan researchers gathered information on all 70 companies using independent and public sources: corporate reports, industry magazines, newspapers, business magazines, government reports on environmental prosecutions and toxic releases, corporate closure and layoff statistics, court records, provincial health and safety statistics, government employment equity reports, critical advocacy reports, along with the EthicScan Corporate 1500 DataBase. This Database includes reports on companies, interviews with industry associations and regulators, and extensive paper files on companies that have been gathered since 1988.

2. Based on this initial research, we prepared profiles that were 15-25 pages, including all the information we had gathered.

3. We contacted each company and requested that a spokesperson respond in writing to the profiles sent to them.

4. Many spokespeople circulated the profile to different departments within their company in order to update the information, fill in gaps, or gather specialized data before responding. Along with profiles, some companies also sent supplemental materials on environmental matters, internal policies or donations. Others sent back information after our deadlines, some did not get back to us at all.

5. Where appropriate, we contacted union spokespersons, regulators, consumer advocates, and industry association officials. Where possible, we added information for officials or sources where the company operates, including local politicians and local media. EthicScan researchers incorporated these comments into a second-draft profiles.

6. We then sent the revised profile to the company for a second chance to review the data. Some corporate spokespersons did not respond, even to this second draft. Others gave so much detail, that third or fourth drafts were required.

7. Evaluative profiles found in this book were written. These were read over the telephone to the corporate spokespersons to confirm accuracy. In some cases, unions who were quoted also heard by telephone what we were planning to say. At this stage, we were only verifying or updating facts, not trying to elicit company or union approval for our interpretations.

8. Grades were calculated.

This entire process was carried out for all companies by two EthicScan researchers in 1998. To update and fact check the information in 2001 and 2002, two different researchers updated the profiles, following all steps of the process.

GROCERY GIANTS AND CORPORATE RESPONSIBILITY

Corporate Consolidation and Domination

Like most sectors of industry, corporate consolidation has transformed the grocery and consumer products sector as companies swallow each other to compete in international markets. Many companies covered by EthicScan in 1992 were either acquired by or merged with another company, and few have a majority Canadian ownership.

As companies become fewer and larger, tracking what they do can become more difficult. Combined or acquired companies have to reconcile departments and systems, and reporting structures may change. A company that, for example, valued a strong environmental program may get absorbed, and the new management may decide to drop this priority. As more mergers occur, EthicScan hears more stories like this.

Consolidation is the order of the day because large companies try to build on their existing strengths, like solid capitalization, underutilized plant capacity, or expansive distribution and retail networks. Often the quickest way to extend markets or assets, or to forge into new territory, is to buy existing product lines or franchises. This is usually cheaper than having to build anew. There are many consolidation stories in this book. In 1988 two potato chip giants, Hostess and Frito Lay merged, and in 1992 Pepsi Co. Food International bought the merged company. Glaxo-Wellcome and SmithKline Beecham merged in 2000, forming Glaxo Smith Kline, one of the largest pharmaceutical companies in the world. In Canada, a series of acquisitions and consolidations left the sugar sector with only two players, Redpath Sugars, a subsidiary of the British Tate & Lyle plc, and Lantic/Rogers.

New competitors often bring innovative product ideas to market, but when they start getting too big, larger more established players often buy them out. By 1993, when Miss Vickies had garnered 1% of the potato chip market, Hostess-Frito Lay decided it was time to gobble them up. Similarly, Glaxo Smith Kline kept growing in 2001 by adding Block Drug to its Consumer Health Care business. Another common trend throughout the 1990s was for businesses to concentrate manufacturing into regional or continental plants. In the process, a small number of large factories replaced many smaller ones, that were closed. Some companies in this book, including Gerber, General Mills, Cadbury Beverages Canada Inc./Motts, and Gillette, no longer produce here at all. Most maintain a marketing, sales, and consumer support presence, which employ staffs of one or two dozen people, yet their brands still dominate their product categories.

The result? Companies invest substantially in mechanized production, close many smaller plants that were mainstays in local economies, and reduce the number of plants located in union-friendly regions. More production of non-perishables and ingredients move off-shore and consumer choice is reduced, as two or three brands dominate most grocery sectors. Within supplier networks, competition increases to save a few pennies per tonne for a bulk ingredient, and global sourcing of fruits, vegetables and other perishables rewards the lowest cost producers. Is there a cumulative result of these changes? More than ever before, international agri-business effectively consolidates decisions and controls food production and distribution.

The Problem of Getting on the Shelf: A Case Against Exclusivity

Together, Lantic/Rogers and Redpath control 98% of the sugar market in Canada. When a new company, Toronto's Richdale Sugar, entered the market in the late 1990s by introducing a better package, sugar in a gable carton, management thought that replacing the old paper bag with a sturdier container would win customers. Then the upstart company found it could not get its white refined sugar, the industry staple, listed with a major grocery chain.

Frustration led Richdale to file submissions with the Competition Bureau. In one dated 2000, the company claims to have suffered a number of "abuses" including the loss of a contract that could have attracted the mainstream market. Between October 1999 and February 2000, Richdale negotiated a detailed supply contract with a major Canadian grocery retailer that would have put the new brand into the mainstream. Richdale alleged that it was led to believe that this retailer "did not have or did not consider itself bound by exclusivity agreements for the supply of sugar." In other words, the store was in no way obliged to the major sugar companies to avoid listing Richdale's sugar, so it began to make purchase orders. The retail market for consumer sugar is divided into a few large chains such as Loblaws, Sobeys/Oshawa, A&P, and all of their related chains as well as smaller grocery and convenience stores. When the large chains buy directly from the refiners, Richdale claims, they are induced to enter into exclusivity agreements that provide volume discounts and ensure the supply of all forms of refined sugar. In exchange, the retailer agrees to buy all of its sugar from one refiner. These relationships are said to be typical of all products in the grocery business.

On the day prior to shipment in February 2000, the retailer abruptly cancelled the order, informing Richdale that it "had decided to stay loyal to Lantic". It agreed to buy certain specialty sugars from Richdale, because Lantic did not sell these products, but it would not buy the all-important white sugar. Based on this sudden about face, Richdale concluded that the retailer had an exclusivity agreement with Lantic. Furthermore, the complaint to the Competition Bureau also asserts that it assumes that Lantic paid the retail chain money or other valuable consideration for entering into an exclusivity agreement and preventing Richdale from entering that market. To prove these claims, the company wants the Bureau charged with protecting consumer interests to investigate the concentration of power in the industry.

Compared with the U.S., where a typical grocery store carries sugar from a number of suppliers who offer various packaging options, Canadian grocery shoppers are restricted to one brand and one packaging option. Even when two or three different brands are sold, they may all be produced by the same manufacturer. Effectively, markets are divided up with Rogers acting as a monopoly in Canada west of the Ontario/Manitoba border, leaving Lantic and Redpath as the ruling oligopoly in the east. Another strange irony in this case is that retail prices, relative to the cost of raw sugar, are higher in Canada than in the U.S. Because the American government gives financial support to their domestic beet and cane farmers, raw sugar costs about three times as much as the raw sugar available to Canadian refiners. However, the cost of refined sugar in the store is approximately the same in both countries, and the major refiners take a healthy mark-up.

Richdale requested a Competition Bureau review of the competitive practices of Redpath Sugar and Rogers/Lantic and the imposition of appropriate sanctions. No investigation was ever launched. Richdale CEO Martin Richardson believed nothing happened because the Bureau lacks resources. "Every time I call [the Bureau], they tell me that they only have nine investigators and that they're all out chasing planes," he said, in reference to the bureau's attention to the consolidation of the Canadian airline industry.

Private Label Brands: A Case of Growing Retailer Power

Since the 1960s, private label grocery products have undergone a huge transformation. These once low-quality off-price "generics" are today high value gourmet brands that help retailers make money, pump up their images, and gain power when negotiating with food companies who produce the big "name" brands. In Canada, key marketing innovation came from Loblaw's President's Choice, the brand that in the 1980s and 1990s demonstrated how grocery chain products could compete against the most recognized multinational brands, while boosting store recognition among consumers. Today, many divisions or units of the companies profiled here sell anywhere from $300 million to $2 billion worth of private label goods every year across most product categories from chips and frozen foods, to health and beauty, perishable goods and soft drinks, all under retailers' private labels.

Retail grocers do not make their own branded goods. Instead, they contract production from the same major food companies they compete against, and then provide shelf space. Historically, brand name manufacturers earned little profit making private label products for retailers. They agreed to the relationship in order to use up excess production capacity that otherwise would remain idle, and as a way to solidify retailer relations. Contract lengths were irregular, because private label divisions were more interested in price than in product consistency. As the quality of private label products improved, however, many brands developed a loyal customer following, and the economic value of the entire category increased.

A Question of Shelf Space

Grocery retailers began seeking more product quality and longer-term contracts with manufacturers, thus raising competition for prime shelf space. As retailers gave their own goods a higher placement priority, they generally reduced the total number of name brands listed in each category. Grocery stores were in a position to demand better terms, including special placement fees from food makers who wanted to secure contracts, and a number of marketing tactics such as "shielding" (please see the profile on Cott) became common.

To better understand how these relationships work, and what companies do to manage producer-retail relations, EthicScan asked private label divisions and departments about policies, guidelines, and practices (please see the profile on Private Label Brands that includes information on six prominent store brands, p.219). Specifically, how do production contracts affect retail shelf placement for manufacturers' brands?

When asked if any exclusivity arrangements govern relations with manufacturers, most retailers said that they secured suppliers based on quality, service, and price. Three companies (Safeway, Sobeys, Metro-Richelieu) said explicitly that no relationship or preferential treatment connect the producers of its private label goods to the shelf space they allot to brand name products. None reports any formal policy guaranteeing this separation.

EthicScan did discover that contract lengths vary according to the supplier relationship and the product involved. Safeway said that the duration of private label contracts are variable, while Sobeys preferred to sign long-term contracts and avoid switching companies. One spokesperson noted that generally, "the space that a product occupies on a shelf, whether national or retail brand, is dictated by the consumer demand which it generates," meaning that high demand products receive better shelf opportunities. Metro said its private label supply contracts vary according to product type; some may last as long as a year, while others extend for a period of months. Loblaw Brands was the only company to say that it signs no contracts with manufacturers.

While labels may be proliferating, the number of companies are shrinking. The next time you're buying spices, for example, you'll notice that it seems like three or four companies are competing on the shelf, but if you trace the brands back to the factories, you'll discover they all come from the same company. Increasingly, it is becoming harder to attach a brand label to a manufacturer, so consumers interested in applying pressure to companies must focus on high-profile retailers. As the next case demonstrates, they, along with a few best known brand manufacturers, are some of the few giants who are sensitive to challenges of reputation. They are also the ones who can influence decisions made along supply chains.

Genetically Modified Organisms: The Case for Better Information

When health food shoppers picked up their favourite organic products at Loblaws in June 2001, they got a shock. The labels' familiar claim, "free of genetically modified organisms," had been blacked out by magic markers. It looked like some kind of information emergency had been declared for the packages. In fact the "GMO free" label had been deemed too risky for retailers to promote, so Loblaws acted decisively, blotting out the line and informing its natural food suppliers that anyone who objected to the label alterations risked having their products pulled from the shelf.

Chalk up another public controversy for food biotechnology, and for the struggle for good consumer information. Anyone wanting to avoid genetically modified ingredients was left in a muddle. Genetically modified organisms (GMOs) have been called "Frankenfoods" by some food advocates, and celebrated as "the future of food" by biotech champions. Nothing in recent years has mixed food science, industry, politics, and consumer rights quite like the GMO.

What's the problem? One type of biotechnology, a GMO, results when a gene from one plant or animal is spliced into another, in order to create a specific set of biological characteristics. This kind of control excites some farmers and researchers, who see enormous agricultural and consumer benefits in fusion, but it scares other scientists and food advocates who fear long-term risks to human health and agricultural eco-systems. How about multinational food processors? Perhaps their sentiment was best summed up by Harrison McCain, chairman of McCain Foods, when he said that "modified material is very good science, but at the moment, very bad public relations."

In a short span of time, GMOs have become part of our food supply, because the top three GM crops—soybeans, corn, and canola—are processed into much of what we eat. Consumers who worry about food safety want the right to choose "GMO-free" products. At first, marketing savvy companies jumped to help them, knowing a good sales niche when they saw one. But by 2001, a problem lingered. Government and industry failed to agree on a system that could authoritatively declare an ingredient genetically modified, and conversely GMO-free. Because many foods sold as organic claim to be GMO-free, there was a problem in the natural food aisle. Dispatch the magic markers.

For those in the health food world, the problem was big, because any product certified as "organic," according to an independent, non-government standard, must be GM free. Even though this "organic" standard accepts claims that crops are clear of the biotech seeds, no general agreement has ever been reached. What stands in the way of achieving clarity? The costs of keeping GM and non-GM ingredients separate, the costs of verification, and the corporate and government will to protect non-GM products as a viable alternative. For Canadian consumers, stores like Loblaws will not support packages with GMO-free claims until regulators can guarantee that a given food does or does not contain GM ingredients.

What are the implications? Consumers say that they are uncertain about what is in the food they eat. Canadian exporters of wheat, one of our biggest exports, may soon be unable to sell grain in places like the European Union. Individual grocery retailers are introducing their own organic labels. Concerns about food supply and safety go unresolved.

Why Worry?

For centuries, humans have played with the make-up of food. We continue to alter human diets, feed grains to animals, plant new "green" crops, and invent new food. In the process, we change food and make its production more efficient. Today, food biotechnology is often equated with GMOs, 99% of which are modified to render animals, food, and plants more tolerant to herbicides, heat, or drought, or more resistant to insects and viruses. The benefits include greater animal and crop yields for farmers. A second generation of GMOs will delay ripening, or enhance nutritional or functional characteristics by adding so-called nutraceutical and pharmaceutical proteins and enzymes. (We may see, for example, potatoes that help fight viral gastroenteritis, or, bizarre as it may seem, tobacco that produces a therapeutic agent against the herpes virus.)

Canada is the third largest grower of genetically modified crops in the world, after the USA and Argentina. Since commercial development began in 1994, we have grown to account for ten per cent of the world's GMO production. Canada is the leader in GM canola and has approved modification for corn, potatoes, and soybeans. Fish, yeast, and vaccines have also been approved in some countries, and GM wheat is expected by 2003. Almost all scientists agree that current GMO crops have produced no measurable or anticipated risks to human or animal health. Governments in both Canada and the United States say that no evidence of harm has been gathered to date, and that GM food is not very different from traditional food.

Why all the fuss then? Most expert critics of GM food are not fear-mongering opponents of technology. They just worry that new technologies are not tested sufficiently before coming to market. Professor Ann Clark of Guelph University points out that no one knows the long-term effect of these crops on other plants and organisms they encounter. She worries that introducing multi-gene traits might make predicting and assessing a range of side effects more difficult, and she questions what we know about their potential toxicological or allergenic effects. She asks, for example, what serious allergic reactions might result in people?

GMOs have already made their way into approximately 60 per cent of processed food on grocery shelves. Some of this spread comes inadvertently, because plant life is hard to contain. In 1997, for example, the federal government unwittingly allowed the sale of genetically modified canola seeds even though it had yet to be approved safe enough to mix with other seeds. Realizing that this GM "contamination" had occurred, a hasty recall took place, but did not curb the spread. Two farmers had already planted them, creating fields of untested canola with unknown characteristics, and although they destroyed the fields, the contamination proved a harbinger of problems to come.

While many farmers embrace GM technology, the unintentional spread of modified seeds to non-modified crops has turned others decidedly against the technology. In western Canada some canola fields have been infested with "volunteer" GM canola, seeds that pop up without being planted, spread by wind or pollen transmission. Because they are immune to most weed killers, these plants are tough to eradicate. Wary farmers want the option to grow non-GM crops and call for tighter controls and guarantees. Whether markets in the European Union or China will accept exports that cannot be certified remains a serious trade question.

Information Under-load

Relationships between corporations, government, and citizens have changed profoundly over the last two decades. The private sector's control over the economy has increased, as fiscal restraint, government cutbacks, and privatization defined policies since the 1980s. Although the state's capacity and seeming willingness to act as public protector has diminished, the need for independent regulation and monitoring of food has not. In other words, we need governments to do things like verify new ingredient safety, set organic or GMO-free standards, and require companies to report where ingredients come from. When municipal or provincial governments do not maintain the highest levels of public health and safety administration, the consequences can become most dire and stark, as was the case with the water contamination tragedy in Walkerton, Ontario.

While the long-term impacts of GMOs may not yet be known, its critics see risks of information mismanagement in the age of corporate rule. Companies exercise a great deal of control over what is known, and as Professor Mark Winston, a biologist at Simon Fraser University has commented, the complete effects of GM plants on other species have been kept confidential by biotech companies. Looking at questions of natural diversity, for example, what happens when we put the same genes into a range of species? How will this affect the evolution of plants' resistance to various natural elements?

GMO critics worry about blurry roles between government and business, even though some of the confusion we see today may have resulted from good intentions. To boost Canada's competitiveness in the global economy, government and industry teamed up to research and develop the potential of biotechnology. Since 1983, when its national Biotechnology Strategy was formed, the Government of Canada invested hundreds of millions of dollars to advance bio-tech companies, as government web sites boast [www.nrcan.gc.ca/cfs/proj/sci-ech/biotechnology/canadi_e.html]. In one way, this support seems logical and laudable, since Canadians benefit whenever we develop a so-called industry cluster like bio-tech. If we get into biotechnology early, the thinking goes, we would make our farmers, scientists, and food makers leaders in the global economy.

But direct government funding for industry R&D makes the government a less-than-cautious GMO promoter, argue critics like the Sierra Club. This creates a potential "mandate conflict" for those federal agencies that must monitor and regulate biotech advancements for safety issues. Specifically, government officials may have an incentive to exaggerate benefits and underestimate the risks of technology developed by private companies. They may feel pressure to show a return on taxpayers' dollars invested.

Evidence connecting biotech advancement and easier regulation is spelled out in a report commissioned by the federally-funded Canadian Biotechnology Advisory Committee (CBAC). This document states that the government's priority should be "streamlining biotechnology product approvals so that regulatory systems are competitive with our major trading partners" [www.cbac-cccb.ca]. Regulatory systems become "competitive" by expediting approval processes for newly developed technologies, and one way to speed things up is to avoid duplicate testing. As part of its approval of GM ingredients, Health Canada, a government agency responsible for food safety, *has accepted safety claims on toxic factors submitted by industry*, Professor Ann Clark argues.

Although Canadians began growing and eating modified soybeans and canola as early as 1996, the federal government did not assess its systems for regulating GMO food safety until 2000, when it asked the Royal Society of Canada to strike a panel of independent scientists to carry out a review. In early 2001, the Expert Panel on the Future of Food Biotechnology released a report severely criticizing both Health Canada and the Canadian Food Inspection Agency (CFIA), the two regulators responsible for food safety. Chief among the Panel's criticisms: the scientific assessment of GM safety was weak, it lacked independence, and study results were kept secret. Health Canada countered that the Panel did not understand regulation, and some industry-funded researchers, including Douglas Powell and Shane Morris (also at the University of Guelph), commented publicly that the panel members were biased against biotechnology. However, the Panel's claims have not been exhaustively refuted.

What is wrong with this picture? Testing and safety assurance for Canadians are neither the sole nor the principal responsibilities of researchers at biotech companies: it's the job of regulators. When safety claims come only from those who make and sell food ingredients, the public good is no longer kept independent of business interests. Even if GM food is proven safe in every way, there is a problem with how approval takes place, *a problem with the structure that produces the information we get*. Authorities must be - and be seen to be - independent of business. In other words, free to assess and report on the possible effects of corporate activity and communicate them to consumers. As GMOs show, consumers cannot always rely on regulators to create and maintain the informational infrastructure we need. Without this support, we compromise transparency and independent verification (two principles that created the need for CSR research in the first place).

Some may respond by asking, what's the big deal? Cutting a few corners to give Canada an edge in an industry as important as biotech is probably worth it, especially if enough experts agree that problems are likely to be minor. Well, the assurances of "most likely" have different receptions. In Europe, public concern over food safety has a more vigilant tenor. Scares like mad cow disease and dioxins in food have damaged consumer confidence in management at all levels, and they have politicized the issues. Questions surrounding GMOs have brought more robust responses from governments, leading the European Commission, for example, to try to block the sale or growth anywhere in Europe of plants with GM components.

The European Union Parliament has also imposed strict corporate liability and mandatory insurance on companies that release GM organisms into the environment. It has written strong rules on the segregation and labelling of GM foods. For example, two GM cottons marketed in the U.S. were kept out in February 1999, the same month that a British court fined Monsanto $25,000 for "genetic pollution" caused by inadequate farm barriers (a six-metre gap between an experimental field of GM canola and adjacent fields of natural crops). Put another way, vexing health questions produced the political will to give consumers choice.

Canadians have not exerted this kind of pressure, but polls suggest that GMO is on our consumer radar. According to Angus Reid, those who have heard about genetic modification want to know more before making up their minds. They want to make choices based on reliable information and labels that tell them what foods contain GM ingredients and which do not.

Divergent Corporate Positions on GMOs

The idea of a GM-free food choice seems reasonable, but the reality of bringing one to market is difficult. Farmers cannot keep track of seeds in their fields, and neither Canada nor the U.S. supports mandatory labelling that would identify GM ingredients, though Canada says it would support a voluntary label. What about the other end of the production line? What are food processors saying and doing? EthicScan asked each company in this book a few basic questions about how they treat GM ingredients. We wanted to know if they have formal policies on GM content in their products, and for those consumers who want to avoid them, how they ensure the integrity of supply.

The vast majority revealed very little about their attitudes or experience with GM technology. Most gave us no information, while a few said that management was "awaiting government regulation." The most interesting response came from a few companies who rejected GMOs wholesale. McCain and Hostess-Frito Lay say unequivocally that they process no GMO food. Hostess-Frito Lay went so far as to say they had a "zero tolerance" for GM potatoes, and that these crops "do not enter our facilities." McCain Foods Ltd. was also vehement, saying that it does not buy GM potato supplies and that all its sources are "completely GMO free."

On the surface, this militant stance might appear to place their brands in the vanguard of corporations who want lead GMO management. Probe a little further, however, and their responses to more specific questions do not differ from other companies. No details were reported on monitoring systems, verification procedures, or disclosure results. Without these details, how do we know what a GM-free guarantee is worth, especially when no widely accepted standard exists? Perhaps these companies have strong procedures and are taking steps no one else is taking, but how do we know?

GMO management illustrates how a chain of stakeholder reactions can force corporate action: watch-dog scientists raise a public concern, consumers get uneasy, governments create policy, and companies respond. McCain and Hostess Frito-Lay are reacting to pressure generated within chains of purchasing, one of the fundamental areas CSR works to influence. More than half of Canadian agricultural exports go to countries proposing some kind of GMO labelling law. According to a University of Saskatchewan study by agronomists Peter Phillips and Heather Foster, mandatory or voluntary labelling of GM foods has been proposed or adopted by the European Union's 15 members, 16 other countries, as well as 29 manufacturers, 21 retailers, and six restaurant chains. Transnational companies are sensitive to these developments, and watch to see if public concerns, like their products, cross borders.

Emerging protections for consumer choice in Europe might influence Canada. If our government drags its feet on developing a credible system, what happens to individual companies who risk losing exports?

The actions of two European-based food giants, Nestlé and Unilever, suggest that Canada is not treated the same as other markets. In May 1999, Nestlé UK and Unilever UK took strong stands, announcing that they would no longer use GM ingredients due to low consumer confidence in the UK and the EU. Ingredients containing GM ingredients would be removed from the majority of their products where possible, and any ingredients that cannot be avoided would be declared on food labels as required by law. In North America? The Canadian units of these companies did not follow suit with such strict policies, because our consumer and regulatory environments did not require it. Why do Canadian operations avoid the bold declarations of their parents? Why do more Canadian giants like McCain and Maple Leaf not lead?

What is sold and where is revealing. The core ingredients in McCain and Hostess Frito-Lay's flagship products are sensitive—potatoes or corn. In a February 2000 issue of *Marketing Magazine*, McCain spokesperson, Scoop Fredstrom was quoted as saying that McCain's decision on GMOs was based on "commercial issues and trade issues." The company exports to jurisdictions with strict rules on GM screening. "We are a major exporter," Mr. Fredstrom said, "we have been told by a few of our major customers that they're looking at the possibility of going to products made out of GM-free potatoes. We are in the business of supplying what our customers want." Similarly, the American company, Frito-Lay Inc., asked farmers for GM-free corn for its Doritos chips and other snacks, not because the company fears health risks, but because it feared consumers might avoid their products if they contained GM corn.

Talking to Consumers: The GMO-Free Label

Internationally, little agreement exists on how best to label GM foods. Although a number of countries have announced labelling intentions, only a few have developed substantial proposals. Even the EU has had trouble with thresholds and definitions. When it announced a rule in February 2000 that said any food containing more than one per cent GM ingredient should carry the label, "Produced with modern gene technology," critics of mandatory labelling pointed out that no test could consistently determine this percentage.

Similar problems exist in Canada, where the federal government is willing to work with the food industry to develop a voluntary standard that would encourage companies to apply a label when GM content is five per cent or greater for each ingredient. Some groups like the Canadian Biotechnology Advisory Committee support the voluntary approach, arguing that it could lead to the development of a mandatory system, but no plan has been established. Many environmental critics typically reject voluntary schemes, fearing that industry cannot be trusted to regulate itself.

Enforcement is also a question. How quickly could a system of independent auditing be conceived, developed and rolled out? Along with the problems of verifying the separation of GM seeds and ingredients on farms, other business challenges exist. Companies like McCain,

Cavendish Farms, and Hostess-Frito Lay might be able to procure large volumes of GM-free potatoes, because potato crops are not yet dominated by, or "contaminated" with, GM ones. This is not the case with GM canola, where Canada's crop integrity is already corrupted.

Saskatchewan researcher and author, Al McHughen, raises a point about the fairness of targeting GMOs. Other bio-technological processes (cross-mutation and breeding) change our food, but we do not require any kind of labels for these products. As well, the costs of separation are an enormous disincentive for business. Unless companies are convinced that a GMO-free market could sustain itself, by passing along a price premium to consumers, they will resist labels. An Australian study noted that if all foods were labelled, costs could rise three to six per cent, or add $3 billion to the Australian food industry in the first year of a program. As a result, non-GMO products could be entrenched as a niche that only wealthier consumers can afford.

Incidents like the Loblaws magic marker scare send chills into farmers, grain-handlers, and smaller businesses who might prefer to innovate for the natural food market. When uncertainty is sustained by the lack of standards development, the requisite communications tools—like a credible label—are stunted, and the business potential that exists for a GM-free niche is left undeveloped. This is too bad, because a realistic mechanism of conscious consumption, facilitating choice through guarantees and information, could move forward and help change the world shaped by consumers.

Tobacco: A Case for Inclusion in CSR Research

Can Cigarettes Be Socially Responsible?

In 1998, EthicScan decided to apply its standard research profile to Canada's three major tobacco makers and publish the results in our periodical, *The Corporate Ethics Monitor*. It was the first time we reviewed this "reputation-challenged" industry sector, and not all of our readers liked the idea. Some called or wrote to tell us that measuring the "social responsibility" of tobacco makers was absurd: *had we not noticed that their products kill millions of people?*

By assessing these companies, one reader argued, we ran the risk of publicizing a few nice stories about staff policies or charitable donations, which might support their public relations, and undermine the efforts of anti-tobacco public health campaigners. Other readers who strongly opposed big tobacco told us that there was nothing morally ambiguous or redeeming about tobacco, so they expected a research company with "ethics" in its name to take a stand against these companies.

We decided to include information on Imperial Tobacco, JTI MacDonald, and Rothman Inc. in this book, because our position has not changed. EthicScan's mandate is to compile CSR information on businesses that operate legally in Canada, telling all sides of a story and enabling our readers to draw their own conclusions. In the process, we pull no punches thrown by critics of corporate activity, and we include business perspectives in the research process.

In many ways, tobacco is not controversial. The damaging health effects of smoking are certain and well known, with cigarette packages warning it will kill you. But Canada, like other countries, has never let disease and mass death get in the way of a strong domestic industry. Health ministers do not table bills insisting that tobacco products be eradicated. Governments subsidize and profit from tobacco growing. Securities commissions do not bar tobacco interests from trading on public exchanges. Hospitals and the health care system spend fortunes on caring for tobacco-related illnesses.

When will this change? Probably not very soon, because mustering political will against something that makes and spreads around wads of money is very difficult. Our governments collect their tax revenues, citizens work at these operations and buy their products, and until legislation banned sponsorships, many cultural and sporting events readily courted and accepted their charity. In a sense, we are all complicit in the existence of a legalized tobacco industry. Like many individuals smokers who cannot seem to quit, Canadians are stuck in a very conflicted relationship with deadly nicotine sticks.

Instead of the decisive and permanent censure of criminalization, what do we do? Chip away at the companies' ability to compete as businesses in a half-hearted effort to mitigate tobacco's impact on human health, and its impact on our societal conscience. Through "sin taxes" and other measures, tobacco prices are controlled, crimping manufacturers' ability to compete on the basis of price. Meanwhile, the nation reaps a consistently huge tax benefit: tobacco excise taxes, surtaxes, and duties raise at least $5 billion per year.

Because critics consistently accuse tobacco makers of marketing to youth, very specific and wide-ranging laws are written to limit how the product can be advertised, distributed, and sold. On top of that, our governments spend millions on anti-tobacco education campaigns to dissuade kids from lighting up. Since 1994, the federal government has diverted $150 million of tobacco surtax money to anti-tobacco education and advertising. Even consumption is governed, as most Canadian jurisdictions have strict ordinances banning smokers from public places.

Tobacco products are cheap to produce, are addictive, and typically kill off those who die of smoking-related complications before they realize the end of protracted lawsuits. In short, tobacco makers are unlike most other corporations. They face a number of powerful initiatives aimed at reducing consumption of their products, and wresting away their control over key areas of business strategy. Despite all of this, they continue to make enormous profits.

Tobacco and CSR

How then, does a research group like EthicScan treat tobacco companies from a CSR perspective? Critics are correct that we give these companies an opportunity to tell stories about their internal practices that most media sources ignore. And, some companies jump at the chance to score well in our Candor quotients. But the CSR framework also gives us *a very detailed means of critiquing the social and environmental costs that their products and processes bear on the environment and human health*. And according to our criteria the list of CSR problems facing tobacco is not small.

Tobacco companies are ravaged by critics for everything from a reliance on child labour, to paper and tallow filter consumption, pesticide usage, and farm impacts. Despite laws forbidding sales and advertising to children, watchdog anti-smoking groups regularly accuse the industry of surreptitiously attempting to hook kids. And of course, the product - which has been scientifically shown to be addictive and cause a range of lung diseases along with cancer - kills people. In fact, the World Health Organization (WHO) estimates that about three million people (one every ten seconds) die as a result of tobacco consumption each year. At this rate, the absolute number of deaths will rise to about 10 million by 2025.

The Move into Developing Nations: These issues are played out on a global stage, because as new and existing customers shrink at home, multinational tobacco conglomerates aggressively pursue new markets abroad. Approximately 70% of the deaths the WHO projected for 2025 will come in developing nations. According to Rob Cunningham, author of *Smoke & Mirrors: The Canadian Tobacco War*, countries in Latin America and Asia have been targeted since the 1960s. Central and eastern European countries have been blitzed since the fall of communist rule. These countries have a combination of conditions tobacco salespeople like to see: populations and incomes on the rise, where limited regulation or opposition exists. Governments in these places usually lack the means for anti-smoking campaigns, which if they could enact them, would take a long time to change anything, given the widespread popularity of smoking among their citizens.

Environmental Concerns: Many scientists believe that deforestation contributes to global warming, increased flooding, and decreased food output. Without regulatory controls in developing nations, the threat of deforestation looms over certain regions, particularly South America. According to a 2000 report from the San Francisco-based NGO, CorpWatch, an estimated 350,000 tonnes of paper are used worldwide each year for cigarette manufacturing. Put another way, one cigarette-making machine uses four miles of paper per hour to roll and package cigarettes, or one tree is consumed for every 300 cigarettes produced. Wood is also burned to cure tobacco. Rob Cunningham details how small farmers in developing nations cure tobacco in individual barns, drawing on wood that each operation must find individually. Solar or central systems of curing would save wood, but these alternatives are not widespread because they add costs. Diversifying crops to discourage tobacco growth isn't always feasible, because it is usually a more profitable commodity. The industry says it encourages reforestation, but these programs do not always work, since small farmers often use their small tracts to grow subsistence food crops rather than replacement trees.

Another author, Peter Taylor, observes that tobacco cultivation requires copious pesticide usage at all stages of tobacco growth: during the three-month period from seedbed cultivation to seed transplanting in fields, up to 16 applications of pesticide may be recommended (applications vary with climate and local pest problems). Because tobacco depletes soil nutrients at a heavy rate, regular quantities of chemical fertilizers are required. According to a 1995 report by the Food and Agricultural Organization (FAO), fertilizers, herbicides, and pesticides contribute to chronic health problems of farm workers, because they seep into the soil, pollute waterways, and damage ecological systems that affect livestock and food crops.

Cigarette butts are also an enormous consumer waste contributor the world over. In the U.S., for example, butts account for almost half of the items collected in an annual California statewide cleanup. They wash into rivers, lakes, and oceans, where seabirds and aquatic life ingest them. According to Tom Stienstra, an environmental writer, cigarette butts take an average of 25 years to decompose.

Youth and Smoking: The tobacco industry has always asserted that it uses advertising only to garner brand loyalty, not to win over new segments like women and youth (for details on this issue, please see the company profiles for Imperial Tobacco, JTI MacDonald, and Rothmans). While government has enacted many measures to deal with this issue over the years, new corporate-government cooperation is taking place. Two companies, Imperial

Tobacco and JTI MacDonald, support proposed legislation, Bill S-20, which intends to reduce teenage smoking through a $400 million-per-year levy on tobacco products. This industry-specific tax will divert about $1.50 per carton to fund an independent foundation, The Canadian Tobacco Youth Protection Foundation, which will undertake education campaigns.

However, studies show that education and advertising campaigns on their own are not usually enough to curb youth smoking. Only with other polices, like high retail prices, can they be effective. For example, after the Chrétien government allowed cigarette prices to drop dramatically in 1993, youth cigarette consumption rose over subsequent years. Prior to that year, youth smoking had been in decline for over a decade.

The Foundation might direct money at the problem without a full array of policy supports needed to achieve the best outcome. Meanwhile, the companies benefit from the appearance of doing the right thing for youth, and forestalling criminalization. In a September 2001 article, *Globe and Mail* columnist Eric Reguly speculated that the industry supports S-20 because it "does not have the credibility to be the author of its own youth anti-smoking campaign - it would have to be done by a third party. If the campaign failed, the Foundation, not the industry would be saddled with the blame." Should this prove true, we may be see another example of weak government intervention in its role as public protector.

MEASURING CORPORATE SOCIAL RESPONSIBILITY

Evaluating Company Performance: The Modified Delphi Process

At some point, most people who want EthicScan information on the ecological and human impacts of business usually ask how we research companies. Who determines how each one is evaluated? Does EthicScan decide what is right and what is wrong? How can we be constructive yet critical enough to push companies into acting more responsibly? The short answer is that we don't decide any of these questions alone.

Over the last couple of decades, research houses in at least a dozen countries have each tracked CSR information on large companies. Although each house's approach grows and evolves according to forces at work in their respective countries - trade realities, role of governments, societal attitudes, and corporate responses to demands for accountability - most focus on similar areas of concern. By the mid-1990s, EthicScan was working with institutes in England, the USA, Germany, Belgium, Italy, France, Japan, Australia, Sweden, Switzerland, and India to develop the best ways for measuring corporate behaviour. But for almost a decade, EthicScan had been convening a panel of specialists from a variety of areas through our Modified Delphi Process (MDP). The name, Delphi, refers to a place in ancient Greece where citizens traveled to put questions about life and business to an oracle (a source of godly wisdom). Instead of the Greek belief in the power of divine fiat, EthicScan turns to people who debate contemporary definitions of CSR. This process culls collective wisdom from a diverse range of academics, environmental advocates, labour leaders, consultants, corporate executives, and journalists, and their opinions and perspectives determine the criteria we use to evaluate every company in this book.

In 1999, we invited 60 people to take part in our fourth MDP in 11 years. Everyone received a copy of EthicScan's existing criteria, a summary of developments in international CSR thinking, suggestions for likely additions and deletions, and a possible grading scheme. For the initial round, the panel commented on the criteria and grades, and suggested changes. All areas of agreement, disagreement, and uncertainty were summarized in a Draft Two, which was then circulated for the next round—the iteration that effectively "modifies" the initial comments by inviting another exchange. At the end of this process, 24 of the 60 people we approached had participated in both rounds.

Because CSR tries to engage companies to change their practices, the questions in our profiles must strike an important balance. We must raise the bar and demand the tougher standards our panel members want, while keeping companies interested in participating. Put another way, we do not want any corporation that is still trying to catch up to withdraw because it feels as though it can never satisfy what panelists want.

EthicScan tries to expand what it covers to stay current with the latest big issues to emerge (Sourcing and Trading), as it restructures others to match changing social demands (Family and Equity) and refines areas that do not change much (Management Practices, Environmental Management and Performance). Generally, the MDP panel told us to place a heavier emphasis on demonstrable corporate performance, systems of disclosure, and reporting. They asked for more detail and heavier grade weights in these three areas, arguing that we should expect progressive companies to talk about results, not just ideas and good intentions. While the priority ten years ago was to encourage companies to write policy and develop systems for managing the environment, employee relations, and community impacts, the next decade will show us if business can actually change what it does through tougher, more broadly-defined measures of reporting and accountability.

ETHICAL MANAGEMENT AND CONSUMER RELATIONS

Measuring Performance

To some, "management ethics" sets a lofty expectation for people who do the gritty and sometimes cut-throat work of making a profit. Actually, when using the term, EthicScan is referring to a discreet field of real corporate policies and procedures. Used this way, "ethical policies" work to influence and guide employee behaviour with tools like codes of conduct, ethics advisory support, training, internal reporting, and whistleblower protection.

Often responsibility for corporate ethics is assigned to an internal counsel or compliance officer who deals with accountability issues. Although "business ethics" is often confused with "corporate social responsibility," the two are different. CSR deals with corporate issues that focus on external groups and interests. In contrast, "ethics policies" remain a function of the corporation's internal management. Because the same managers responsible for ethics often handle Consumer Relations, issues like advertising guidelines and product recall procedures, these areas are categorized with ethics policies.

As a category of CSR, Ethical Management has been around for some time, and its main components are well known to large companies. EthicScan has always asked companies if they have a formal, written code of business conduct, as well as ethics counsellors, on-going training, and whistleblower protection. In 2000, to ensure that the code was applied outside the home country, we began asking if the code is "translated into the languages spoken in countries of operation." We also want to know if employees receive guidelines for accepting business gifts, or for negotiating a product's shelf space.

The Code Support section increased its proportional value to 40 per cent of the category's total grade, because the Delphi panel said that these elements help separate those companies that talk about ethics from those that do something. To find out which firms are paying attention to what actually happens at their factories and offices, we ask: does the company independently audit its social/ethical performance? Does it report results publicly? Are employees included in the code's creation/evaluation?

Consumer Relations criteria did not change. They still measure what companies do to make their products safe, inform and support the public's concerns, and facilitate recalls. Questions are posed about advertising, marketing, and fair competition practices.

Performance in the Grocery Sector

Ethical management performance has not advanced much in recent years, due mainly to corporate inaction. In Canada, the USA, and the UK, companies seem to be devoting fewer resources to advancing ethical governance tools created in the 1980s and 1990s. While 39 grocery companies said they had established codes and procedures, only 21 reported any kind of ethics training, and a paltry four firms reported any kind of independent ethics advisor or ombudsperson. No company in this book has conducted an ethics or social audit. If it had one, or reported any results, or invited employee participation, it would be doing more than 99.9 per cent of companies in the world.

Some progress shows up in the reporting of ethics policies. Compared with 1992 and 1996, some large branded companies now seem willing to explain their policies and follow-up procedures in greater detail (see Colgate-Palmolive's Business Practices Function, or Coca-Cola's Code of Conduct). That said, none of the few companies who claim to have whistle-blower protection explained the specifics of that program.

A few "hot" problems show up in ethical management. Health and marketing controversies over the selling of infant formula (see Nestlé), tobacco (Imperial Tobacco, JTI Macdonald, Rothman's), and animal testing (Gillette, Procter & Gamble) are well-known to Canadians. Many companies are accustomed to dealing with these matters, have staff to handle external relations, and report some of the actions they take. Gillette has managed to convince persistent advocacy groups like the People for the Ethical Treatment of Animals to cease boycotting their products. Tobacco issues garnered more attention in the latter 1990s, as high profile court cases made once secret documents available to the public.

Most large multinational food giants have a consumer safety assurance process that extends beyond regulatory compliance. These procedures include a comprehensive product recall system, a toll-free consumer phone line, and advertising guidelines. Charges of anti-competitive practices have not gone away since the early 1990s, in part because an ever-shrinking number of large companies dominate food and consumer goods. While the public hears about only a few allegations of exclusive contract arrangements between food producers and retailers (Lantic/Rogers, Redpath, Hostess-Frito Lay), the problem is said to be endemic in the sector.

Business strategies like private label manufacturing provide ways for retailers to make money and alter producer-store relations dramatically (see the Private label section and Cott's). However, all of EthicScan's questions dealing with policies governing food companies' relations with retailers are answered poorly. Many companies say they have a policy in this area, but none verifies or reports on performance. The federal Bureau of Competition remains small and incapable of investigating problems of deep and pervasive exclusivity arrangements.

Honour Roll: best performing companies in the Ethical Management Category.

Coca-Cola Bottling Company (100%)
Kellogg Canada Inc (100%)
Pepsi Bottling Group (Canada), Co (95%)
Alcan Inc (85%)
Maple Leaf Foods Inc (75%)
Alberto Culver Canada Inc (70%)
Schneider Corporation (70%)

EMPLOYEE RELATIONS

Measuring Performance

Fundamental workplace measures such as job creation, strikes, injuries, money spent on skills development, and profit sharing did not change profoundly in 2000. The category did get a new name, as "Labour Relations," became "Employee Relations." The more dramatic social changes that reflect Canadians' concerns with work-life balance show up in the Progressive Staff or the Family and Equity sections, categories that describe the means to achieving worker health and satisfaction.

Changes from the MDP in 1995 were minor, but they reflect shifting employment structures in society. Because most companies now outsource whole areas of production or services like human resources or environment, EthicScan asked what percentages of production are contracted out. We also asked about turnover and absentee rates, two measures commonly used to gauge employee satisfaction. One new subsection, State of Relations, covers events like union de-certification cases and unjust dismissal cases. Questions about ergonomic workplace assessments were added, and we now encourage companies to include incidents of psychological and emotional burnout in their reports on health and safety statistics.

Performance in the Grocery Sector

Work has changed dramatically for Canadians over the last decade. According to the Canadian Public Research Network, "Employment relationships appear to have become more diverse, individualized, implicit, deregulated, decentralized, and generally more tenuous and transitory." Unemployment rates peaked and then declined. The traditional ideas of job security and life-long career loyalty became extinct. Demands for just-in-time delivery systems were compounded by round-the-clock schedules created by e-business.

A greater number of people at the lower end of the employment market found they had to work regular overtime or take two jobs just to make ends meet. At the higher end, the demand for talent made "retention" a priority. Executives and boards learned that businesses lose shareholder value, at least in the short term, when skilled employees leave for better jobs elsewhere. Companies also grappled with the fact that fewer than half of all employees feel any traditional sense of organizational commitment anymore. Consequently, human resources issues like staffing, recruitment, and retraining became a higher priority for CEOs.

Compared with other categories, Employee Relations information is poorly reported. In one way, this is surprising, because companies have most of the data EthicScan wants. One might ask why, for example, so few companies report any Health and Safety statistics. One answer may be that lost-time injuries and turnover rates may be bad news stories for a company, so like any sensitive area of business, companies skip this topic, even when they answer other questions.

Some companies proudly tout employment growth. However, apparent growth is deceiving. As technology helped increase productivity rates in the 1990s, production lines grew larger but the total number of factories were seriously cut. Some plants were acquired, then closed to make other production facilities more efficient. Fewer people were needed to produce more product.

Another structural change thinned the ranks of temporary seasonal workers. Those who harvest crops, process perishables, or help with other seasonal demands lost jobs or found them contracted out to lower cost labourers. Despite widespread, significant layoffs, only 17 corporations report any kind of retraining or relocation policies for alleviating the effects of downsizing.

Public and workplace health issues are receiving more attention. Examples include mad cow disease, fertilizer and animal waste run-off, and union campaigns addressing increases in workplace injuries. Some courts are handing down tougher decisions in cases dealing with workplace negligence and injuries. In 1999, the average fine levied against a company found violating health and safety laws was $51,869, more than double the level of fines issued four years earlier. Why have injuries gone up? Unions argue that a corporate drive to cut costs and boost efficiency have taxed human capacities. In this reasoning, multinational manufacturing strategies dictate that a small number of plants in each country should produce a few, high-volume lines that serve international markets, so factories that survive closures have added extra shifts and 7-day production schedules to meet these new roles.

Regulatory changes in Ontario and Alberta have helped change work culture, by relaxing maximum possible work hours. It is easier for companies to extend overtime shifts, rather than hire new workers. Loss of co-workers, greater job uncertainty, consolidation following mergers, and high turnover can fray companies' ability to deliver effective health and safety training. High-stress work environments result. Union spokespeople (Sifto, Maple Lodge) explain that when, for example, a routine like the frequency of maintenance schedules is lowered, equipment breakdowns increase and employee morale plummets. When working conditions disgruntle people, injuries tend to go up.

Gainsharing, or giving employees a financial stake in the business, is one area that is relatively well-reported. More companies are experimenting with extending share ownership options deeper throughout the ranks, rather than just to officers. Companies change and improve these plans on a regular basis, especially as management devote more attention to "rightaining," or retaining the right employees. Despite the downturn of the economy in 2001, keeping the best and the brightest will likely remain as HR strategy, because of high costs that come with hiring the wrong people and losing the right ones.

Honour Roll: best performing companies in the Employee Relations Category.

Imperial Tobacco Canada Limited (94%)
Campbell Soup Company Ltd (80%)
Alcan Inc (74%)
Gay Lea Foods Co-operative Limited (66%)
Heinz Company of Canada, H.J. (66%)

EQUITY AND FAMILY ISSUES

Measuring Performance

In the 1990s, a generation of working women became more empowered. Ethnic minorities, gays, lesbians, and advocates for the disabled lobbied for recognition and fairer treatment on the job. The politics of identity heated up debates about social justice in many parts of Canadian society, and business did not go untouched. When the 2000 MDP said our assessments needed more and better measures of equity, EthicScan created an entirely new section. Concerns over how people deal with the demands of family also increased, and since these fit logically with equity—desirable or not, women still shoulder more parenting responsibility than men—we created Equity and Family Issues. Previously, many of these criteria were collected in two sub-sections of Progressive Staff. The new section reports hard performance facts, such as the number of women promoted into senior management, human rights cases filed against the company, and policies that deal with managing equity issues. Other measures include programs that provide anti-harassment protection, promote advancement of diverse groups, or guarantee support for the disabled.

Equity and Family expectations increased dramatically between 1995 and 2000. In 1995, a company could be considered a CSR leader if it reported the existence of an equity policy, provided statistics on women in management, and offered same sex benefits. Today, those elements are commonplace. More progressive companies work to implement accountability systems, set goals for the advancement of women, establish audit protocols to evaluate performance, and hold managers responsible for real progress, as well as report results publicly. Anti-sexual harassment policies, less common in the early 1990s, were broadened to protect employees from any kind discrimination, whether based on race, age, sexual orientation, disability, or religious beliefs.

EthicScan tabulates allegations of harassment or wrongful dismissal, but grades are deducted only if a company is fined or found to have violated an employee's rights. The one notable exception arose because some Delphi panel members argued that, in poisoned work cultures, where harassment is unchecked, multiple complaint cases often arise even if a conviction never results. So, the panel agreed that if any company has more than ten separate cases (a very high number) filed against it, even in the absence of convictions, it should receive a grade penalty.

The criteria for assessing assistance to the disabled were increased, and we now gather data on building and facilities accessibility, accommodation, and training. EthicScan now asks whether or not companies track data on visible minorities and disabled employees in management, though this area is not graded.

Performance in the Grocery Sector

Managing equity issues is challenging. The good news is that many companies (36) report some kind of employment equity policy. Most (49) said they have some kind of written anti-harassment policy. However, training and implementation are still works-in-progress. Only nine companies disclose statistics on different "diverse groups" working at the company.

Setting hiring quotas for targeted groups has proven problematic. Although some companies still take this approach, others have discovered greater success with other methods. Some companies whose diversity performance (General Mills) has been publicly recognized by awards from independent groups like Catalyst have equity policies written with language like "the company does not consider a candidate's minority status when hiring." Instead, the company embraces "equality of opportunity in all aspects of recruitment, hiring, employment and advancement." A decade of experience has demonstrated that success in diversity hiring and advancement relies heavily on related policies—such as mentoring, expanding applicant pools through broadened recruitment campaigns, non-traditional hiring and promotion, and ensuring equal access to "success streams."

Honour Roll: best performing companies in the Equity and Family Issues Category.

General Mills Canada Corp (90%)
Bayer Inc (74%)
Pepsi Bottling Group (Canada), Co (72%)
S.C. Johnson & Son Limited (72%)
Campbell Soup Company Ltd (65%)

PROGRESSIVE STAFF POLICIES

Measuring Performance

Work-life stress is increasing. The causes include longer home-to-work commutes, dual-career households, and growth in our grey and baby populations. This puts a time-squeeze on people who must take care of both their children and aging parents. Happiness at work is not increasing and it shows. According to a 2000 report by the Business and Economic Roundtable on Mental Health, lost time due to stress costs North American companies more each year than the costs of back injuries, heart disease, or cancer. Reports from Statistics Canada link longer average working hours with increased levels of depression and other health problems. The World Health Organization predicts that stress, anxiety, and depression will be leading causes of disability in the workplace over the next 20 years.

A decade ago, the MDP stressed dramatic upgrading of environmental criteria. Today human issues tend to dominate the CSR agenda: Progressive Staff Policies, along with Sourcing and Trading, and Family and Equity, received more additions and reconstructions from the year 2000 MDP than other sections.

What are the best ways to reduce stress? A Health Canada report, *Best Advice on Stress Risk Management in the Workplace*, notes that sound human resources management helps tremendously. Its elements are quite basic: proper training for new employees, appropriate rewards and remuneration, decision-making on important questions such as scheduling and introduction of new technology, and various forms of staff empowerment. Smart, socially responsible companies pay attention to the physical, emotional, and psychological health of their employees. They try to accommodate changing as well as individual needs. More workplace uncertainty requires greater flexibility.

Progressive Staff criteria measure the ways that companies help employees deal with the challenges and stresses of balancing work and personal life. This includes health and wellness, empowerment, communications strategies, and skills development. These criteria emphasize voluntary corporate action to help employees and reward those companies that give human resources a high priority.

Three subsections (Formal Employee Assistance Plans, Health Promotion Plans, and Communications) from 1995 remain basically intact, but two others are new fields. The creation of Worklife Policies expands our criteria substantially. Flexible work arrangements include job sharing, flexiplace (working outside the office or from home), flextime (flexible start and finish times), compressed workweek, or variable hours (working less than 37 hours per week). EthicScan asks not only if these types of arrangements are available, but also how many staff participate and in what ways. Most companies are unable or less willing to report this information.

Because the MDP was concerned about overwork, we inserted a question about the "guarantee of compensation for time worked beyond a 40 hour week." Company drug plans are also more important today, so "drug coverage as part of health benefits" entered our measures, along with "workplace wellness," or training programs that help employees strengthen themselves physically or better balance their lives.

Some established criteria remain unchanged: Employee Assistance Programs (EAPs) allow employees to contact third-party counsellors. Guidance for staff and family members is available directly through toll-free confidential phone lines. Flexible health benefits permit employees to mix and match health support to each family's requirements by choosing from a menu of options.

Performance in the Grocery Sector

The food and consumer products sector has improved. Ten years ago, for example, flexible scheduling was reported by only a handful of innovative leaders. This practice is now common. Today, some type of flexible work schedule exists at most companies reviewed in this book. Twenty per cent of companies have some kind of child/elder care support, and 15% have some kind of enhanced "wellness" program, up from almost zero in both categories five years ago.

Internal communications are critical, especially as mergers often leave two or three dominant brands in each grocery product category. Three-quarters of 125 executives, interviewed for their experiences with mergers and acquisitions, said that integrating their "information systems" (including operating philosophies and communications strategies as well as computer systems) was the most serious problem they had. While many companies have built company intranets to help staff communicate internally, few report detailed regular employee satisfaction surveys, 360 degree evaluations, or other measures that demonstrate superior management of the human side of consolidations.

Honour Roll: best performing companies in the Progressive Staff Policies Category.

Kellogg Canada Inc (100%)
Alcan Inc (95%)
Pepsi Bottling Group (Canada), Co (95%)
Procter & Gamble Inc (95%)

Schneider Corporation (95%)
General Mills Canada Corp (90%)
S.C. Johnson & Son Limited (90%)

SOURCING AND TRADE

Measuring Performance

Living in a global economy means that Canadian companies buy ingredients, components, and services from all over the world. While EthicScan's criteria in the late 1980s emphasized sourcing from Canadian companies, the 2000 questionnaire changed to reflect the global trade realities that accelerated in the 1990s. Today western and northern businesses shape the economies in developing nations. Our criteria for Sourcing and Trade address conditions of production and supplier relationships, wherever a company-owned or contracted plant is located.

The 2000 MDP enhanced questions about information disclosure, rectification of code breaches, and options for worker recourse. Our criteria begin with questions about basic labour, sourcing, and safety codes that guide companies in their international transactions. We added detailed questions about guarantees or monitoring of freedom of association (for unions), collective bargaining, and paying workers a living wage.

Verification criteria are more stringent, because EthicScan now asks if the company applies codes, audit systems, and assurance procedures to contractors and licensees. Unions and civil society leaders have introduced systems for monitoring conditions through audits and verification procedures. Such ideas are relatively new for business. There are many ethical trading initiatives, and making any them work is a difficult and taxing process.

Foreign Sourcing was expanded from two simple fields to five larger sections that now comprise 80% of Sourcing and Trade's total grade. Three new criteria incorporate local or multi-stakeholder input into companies' day-to-day business operations. Examples include the translation of foreign sourcing codes into local languages, the inclusion of independent groups in factory audits, and the establishment of apprenticeship or education programs. No company will meet all of these requirements unless it works with people from host communities.

Most processors, in food or any other sector, are not yet equipped to scrutinize sourcing networks. In fact, only a handful of high profile global companies (most in the apparel or toy industries) have even attempted to implement such codes or verification programs. Even if few companies provide information for all fields, we took the MDP's advice and made explicit such expectations. The treatment of workers in the global economy is too important and explosive an issue to neglect by not asking for enough information.

Performance in the Grocery Sector

Many common foods and ingredients are sourced from abroad: coffee, tea, sugar, spices, cocoa, bananas, rice, dates, citrus, fruits, palm oil, to name a few. Other produce, like apples, pears, peaches, and plums, once came predominantly from B.C., Ontario and Québec, but even these are more frequently sourced from the U.S. and other places. The few companies that do supply information on their suppliers (E.D. Smith, Scotsburn) typically get most of their inputs locally.

Even EthicScan's basic Sourcing and Trade questions receive a very low response rate from companies. A policy or foreign sourcing code exists at only seven companies. Six disclosed some detail about foreign operations. Most ignored our request for identification of their offshore suppliers. Given complex and changing commodity prices and supplier networks, managers working at transnational corporate head offices speak about the difficulty gathering or confirming data.

Organizations as large and far-flung as Nestlé, Unilever, and Kraft— each of which produces tens of billions of dollars worth of products in dozens of nations— say that they have a hard time tracking raw materials and ingredients, especially when the channels of origin come through brokers and sources that change on a regular basis. For example, vegetable oil, a basic ingredient purchased by more than 80% of the companies in this book, can change from month to month, depending on fractional shifts in palm, canola, and other commodity prices. Only six companies report any independent monitoring of their foreign sourcing. Only seven have any kind of code at all. Until independent verification protocols become better developed and accepted, and consumers demand more accountability and transparency, response rates will remain poor.

Most Canadian consumers want to avoid a corporate "race to the bottom," a world run by companies that contract ruthlessly with lowest cost suppliers, no matter how exploitative the environmental or human rights situation. If companies and communities can agree to outcomes and principles, why then is changing the human aspect of trade relations so complicated? One answer is that a disconnect exists between social aspirations and economic realities. Another is that many consumers espouse environmental and human rights concerns, but won't act on those principles if it costs more at the grocery check-out counter.

The opportunity to reward more responsible corporate actors would be better if there was more transparency about what big companies do in developing nations. To help fill in some gaps, labour and other civil society groups have devised mechanisms called "contact points." These points are part of larger systems that independently check actual corporate behaviour. They give workers and citizens a safe, anonymous procedure for lodging a complaint against a company in their region.

Implementing these contact points has been difficult. Why? If you assumed it is because big companies refuse to allow them, guess again. Resistance comes from governments in developing nations. In 2000, the Mexican government refused to ratify an OECD protocol that would commit countries to a range of CSR principles and procedures. In particular, this government objected to the use of contact points in its jurisdiction. Likely, it was worried that such a mechanism would scare off foreign investment from companies who do not want the scrutiny.

Government-corporate relationships in developing nations are complicated, and it is possible that companies do not like contact points, but will not say so publicly. Whatever the case, contact points show how the intentions of conscious consumers become thwarted. Without testing and transparency, social justice cannot thrive.

Honour Roll: best performing companies in the Sourcing and Trade Category.

Alcan Inc (100%)
High Liner Foods Incorporated (78%)
Schneider Corporation (56%)
Ocean Fisheries Ltd (50%)

ENVIRONMENTAL MANAGEMENT AND PERFORMANCE

Measuring Performance

Environmental degradation is both easier to understand and more threatening than other corporate impacts on society or labour. Economic growth seems to produce endless streams of waste and pollution. Our consumer habits are inextricably linked to these problems. But like business relationships with workers and communities, environmental effects are determined by choices.

Over the coming decade, industry leaders will make decisions that affect a range of problems: how to reduce greenhouse gas emissions? What sources of food, transportation, and energy will we support? What technologies will prove most eco-efficient? Is it possible to dispose of toxic pollutants safely, or eliminate them altogether? Will all companies be required to receive and treat post-consumer wastes? In what ways should genetically modified organisms be part of our food supply? How can governments and business best inform consumers about products in the market? Can animal testing be eliminated in consumer product testing?

To help with some answers, EthicScan asks companies about their environmental policies, management systems, staff, and training. We assess management systems and environmental stewardship standards across all divisions, even in countries of operation where environmental standards are less stringent than those of the parent company. We ask if companies use third-party auditors to evaluate company facilities, and whether or not they use environmental performance objectives to evaluate performance. Are environmental, health and safety reports published? Do stakeholder representatives from all jurisdictions help set policy and oversee relations with regulatory compliance, public affairs, environment, health, and safety?

Voluntary programs like NPRI, ARET, and the Climate Change Voluntary Registry encourage companies to set, achieve, and report reduction goals for emissions, so consumers can access some comparative data, if not full stories. Unfortunately, participation has not grown dramatically, the individual site data aren't synthesized, and business managers and environmental critics alike have questioned the quality of the data that is reported.

Because environmental management progress will only come with more comprehensive, standardized and verified reporting, the 2000 MDP expands and emphasizes questions that deal with behaviours, results, and making them public. We now ask more exacting questions about packaging reductions, energy reductions, water usage, toxic chemicals, hazardous waste, solid waste disposal, and various types of recycling. Eco-efficiency is explored. Grade or rating penalties for regulatory breaches went up, while the points assigned to environmental awards went down slightly, because the majority of the MDP panel accepted the argument that the rigour of many corporate environmental awards is suspect.

In Canada, little performance information is available through independent sources. Since the early 1990s, provincial governments, which have jurisdiction for most areas of environmental protection, have slashed their resources to report on violations, exceedances, and convictions. Government disclosure of inspection reports, discretionary control orders, and standards reduction is uneven and limited. EthicScan reviewed data voluntarily submitted to the National Pollutant Release Inventory on chemical releases and transfers.

Performance in the Grocery Sector

A majority (at least 48) of grocery companies have some kind of environmental policy, although most do not say if or how their practices are evaluated. Only 24 report said they have conducted an independent audit, and only 17 have any kind of separate environmental health and safety report. At least 44 companies say they do something to reduce their most important waste substances. Few demonstrate environmentally-responsible management for a product's entire "Environmental Responsibility Cycle" during all stages—from conception, manufacturing, and packaging, through distribution and disposal.

Some consumers tell EthicScan that they find it hard to imagine that grocery companies could ever practice environmentally-sound packaging and product stewardship. Such pessimism is understandable. Vast aisles of grocery store products still come in packages that are beyond what is necessary to deliver safe, fresh food. Oft-cited examples include bubble packs used for sugar gum, tea bags packed in individual paper envelopes and boxes, or cookies with layers of plastic and paper. These readers tell us that natural food and environmental products stores sell, for example, laundry detergent in bulk. Why, they ask, can't all companies who sell through stores like Loblaws do the same?

If more eco-friendly formats are still a dream, more companies are using thinner and lighter aluminum and plastic packaging. At least 20 firms report making demands on their suppliers to reduce packaging. For example, conventional plastic bottles were converted to pouches, cutting packaging contents by 80% (Colgate-Palmolive), and rigid polystyrene was replaced with a lightweight package, eliminating 70% of the material used in the box (Aquafresh toothpaste, SmithKline Beecham).

Soft drink makers are particular targets of packaging critics. Even though most if not all cans and bottles are recyclable, the entire production-distribution - recycling journey of a can or plastic bottle requires a great deal of energy and materials. In the early 1990s, the Ontario Environmental Protection Act attempted to force beverage companies to reduce the total non-refillable containers they made, insisting that 30% of all packaged pop be sold in refillable containers. Large companies like Coke and Cott were repeatedly charged with breaching the regulation. By the late 1990s, however, this approach was abandoned as unworkable, after the government realized that no soft drink brand had ever achieved this ratio on an annual basis. No cases were ever prosecuted, and today, less than 2% of soft drink purchases are made in refillable containers.

Some waste reduction has taken place in the sector. In Ontario, Coke realized a 54% reduction in material sent to landfill between 1988 and 1995 (despite a 22% average sales growth across the industry) when it switched from steel cans to aluminum cans and began assuming the cost to recover its own containers. Across the food, beverage and consumer products sectors, some processing waste was cut in labs, plants, and in consumer markets during the 1990s, showing us that improvement is possible. Is it enough? No, but lessons were learned about how change actually takes place, and how governments can constructively influence future initiatives.

Overall, corporate eco-efficiency progress in Canada is inhibited by three factors. First, consumers have been less forceful in demanding corporate responsibility than those in other jurisdictions. Second, voluntary industry-led initiatives have usurped leadership from more exacting, mandatory cross-municipal standards. Finally, traditional corporate accounting still treats pollution and the environment as an externality.

Honour Roll: best performing companies in the Environmental Management Category.
Alcan Inc (79%)
S.C. Johnson & Son Limited (74%)
Kraft Canada Inc (63%)

Honour Roll: best performing companies in the Environmental Performance Category:

Schneider Corporation (58%)
Pepsi Bottling Group (Canada), Co (47%)

COMMUNITY RESPONSIBILITIES

Measuring Performance

Traditionally, "corporate citizenship" meant involvement with charitable activities. While donations are still a big part of this topic, the MDP wanted more information on "community engagement," or how a company deals with a broad range of stakeholders in its host communities. The panel also wanted more details about donations policy and reports on giving, and it assigned higher grade proportions for these areas.

EthicScan looks at the value of money and products donated to community and charities as well as areas of giving. We report whether or not a company pledges to the Imagine Campaign, a fourteen year-old initiative run by the Canadian Center for Philanthropy that recognizes any company that voluntarily pledges to donate at 1% or more of pre-tax profits (over a three-year average) to charities or not-for-profit causes. Our questions include: do employees help determine a company's priorities for charitable giving? Are their personal volunteer efforts supported? Do local offices or locations exercise discretion for community involvement?

A majority of MDP panelists agreed that cash contributions should earn higher grades. Some argued that in-kind donation of products or services are less valuable to not-for-profit groups, because cash gives them the most discretion in how they use resources. As a result, a company that gives 1% of annual pre-tax profit in cash receives a higher grade than one that gives a lot of product donations.

EthicScan also adjusted its analysis of areas of giving, for example, giving to health charities, the economically disadvantaged, or the arts. While our scoring scheme favoured companies that supported a wide range of categories, the MDP participants said that this logic penalizes companies that choose to strategically focus on one or two issues. Single-focus or "strategic philanthropy" companies often tie charity to marketing, advertising, and public relations functions. Some CSR supporters find this unpalatable, in part because companies may demand more from not-for-profit groups. However, this strategy has some advantages for charities. Firms that give strategically may commit more personnel and professional expertise to a charitable group, and help cross-sectoral learning. Health groups, for example, may benefit from knowledge of professionals at a pharmaceuticals company. A majority of panelists agreed that, since both approaches can produce productive results for communities, we should not penalize a company for the breadth or narrowness of numbers of areas of giving.

How, beyond charity, do companies deal with community stakeholder groups? What meaningful input do they solicit from residents or other groups? Do firms formally monitor their impacts on towns where they operate? What impact does, for example, an aluminum foil maker's toxic waste haulage have on the neighborhoods it traverses?

Given the importance of aboriginal land claims and local community economic investment issues across Canada, the MDP added two further questions: What agreements and preferred procurement or employment contracts does a company sign with aboriginal groups? Does the company operate in areas of unsettled aboriginal land claims without aboriginal involvement? If these questions do not affect a company's operations, they are deemed not applicable.

Performance in the Grocery Sector

Some consumers have told us that they believe that corporate charity should not be included in CSR profiles, because this area gives companies too great an opportunity to win public relations points by advertising all the "nice" things they do in order to distract the public from other less savoury aspects of their behaviour. In the age of strategic philanthropy or social marketing, some suggest that charity is another way to promote their brands.

Grocery companies do benefit from their giving, it is true, but so do communities. Desirable or not, more not-for-profit groups now have to form partnerships, alliances, and other relationships with business, as governments cut support for this sector. Many groups in this sector want to know CSR information on companies so that they can more effectively select or screen out prospective partners.

Giving has undergone a considerable shift since EthicScan's last book on this sector. Strategic investment has replaced altruism. Decisions are increasingly made by marketers. Product donations, partnerships, broader marketing support, and special events funding are more prevalent. Drink and snack food makers are signing multi-year deals with school boards and recreation departments. Municipal councils and boards are putting procurement policies and screens in place.

Many companies remain loath to disclose donations details. Only 11 companies told us how much they give. Only 16 report the percentage of their pre-tax earnings they gave to charity. Of those who did so, only eight pledge to the Imagine campaign, a benchmark for the highest corporate donors in the country.

The extent of charitable activities and disclosure are often connected to the type of products a company sells and the marketing strategies it uses. For instance, large multinational consumer products makers tend to report more sophisticated programs and give more information. The most common areas of giving across all of these companies include nutrition and children's health and welfare.

Questions about community engagement did not receive many responses. Due to specific high profile issues—animal rights testing, GMOs, consumer recalls, infant formula, tobacco—a handful of companies engage a number of groups on a regular basis. Only eight reported formal systems for multi-stakeholder dialogues.

Honour Roll: best performing companies in the Community Responsibilities Category.

Imperial Tobacco Canada Limited (76%)
Alcan Inc (70%)
Schneider Corporation (54%)
S.C. Johnson & Son Limited (52%)

CANDOR

Many of the companies in this Guide were not as forthcoming as they could have been. Twenty-one of them had candor quotients of 20% or less - meaning they provided answers to less than one in five questions. Despite public interest in grocery product health and safety, nearly two in three companies (53 of 80) failed to answer 50% or more of questions posed to them. Improvements in candor, transparency, and accountability are possible.

Honour Roll: best performing companies in the Candor Category.

Alcan Inc (86%)
High Liner Foods Incorporated (84%)
Imperial Tobacco Canada Limited (81%)
Gay Lea Foods Co-operative Limited (75%)
Ralston Purina Canada Inc (75%)

GRADING SYSTEM 2002

ETHICAL MANAGEMENT AND CONSUMER RELATIONS

Maximum Total Marks = 100

Criteria	**Grading Breakdown**

Ethical Management Practices   Maximum 25 – 5 each
Written code of ethics
Written/modified for Canadian operations
Employee sign-off
Year of last code update reported
Integrated with Corporate Code of Conduct
Translated into languages spoken in countries of operation
Human rights provision

Ethics Policies   Maximum 15 – 5 each
Whistleblower protection
Guidelines for exchange of business gifts
Privacy of employee records is assured
Other

Ethics Code Support   Maximum 40 – 10 each
Ethics training
Ethics hotline/independent ombudsperson
Independent social/ethics audit
Audit results are publicly reported
Formal employee input into code
Compliance is part of employee evaluation

Consumer Protection Policies   Maximum 20 – 5 each
Toll-free consumer phone line
Product recall system
Consumer safety assurance (beyond regulation)
Formal advertising guidelines

Cases and Convictions

Company reports zero cases/convictions: Deduct 20 per conviction

False advertising
Product recall/safety
Competition Act
Other bribes/kickbacks

EMPLOYEE RELATIONS

Maximum Total Marks = 180

Criteria	Grading Breakdown
Layoffs	Maximum 35
What % of production is out-sourced	5 if company reports number
Formal policies to mitigate downsizing:	
Redeployment	10
Retraining	10
Severance packages exceeding law	10
Any layoffs in last 5 years	10 bonus if no layoffs
Work Stoppages	Maximum 10
No work stoppages in last 5 years	10
Total strikes/lockouts last 5 years	Deduct 10 per stoppage
State of Relations Indicators	Maximum 25
No union decertification cases	5
Employee turnover rate	5 if reported
Absentee rate	5 if reported
Average annual grievances	5 if reported
No unjust dismissal cases	5
Number of unjust dismissal convictions	Deduct 10 per conviction
Health and Safety	Maximum 40
Health and safety statistics	10 if reported
Health and safety training	10
Joint health and safety committee	10
Ergonomic workplace assessments	10
Training	Maximum 40
$ on training per employee	10 if reported
Some training given to all employees	10
Formal employee input into training	10
Tuition/book compensation	5
% of reimbursement	5 if compensation is 75% of costs or greater
Gainsharing Programs	Maximum 30
Employee Share Ownership Plan (ESOP)	10 if available for all staff levels
Profit Sharing	10 if for all staff
Stock Options	10 if for all staff

EQUITY AND FAMILY ISSUES

Maximum Total Marks = 250

Criteria	Grading Breakdown
Women in Management	Maximum 70 marks
Track Minorities/Disabled in Management	No marks
Formal Employment Equity Program	Maximum 20 marks
Family Support Programs	Maximum 30 marks – 10 marks/program
Support for Disabled	Maximum 20 – 10 each
Anti-harassment protection	Maximum 40 – 5 for each issue covered
Accommodation of Diverse Groups	Maximum 20 – 10 for each group covered
Advancement of Diverse Groups	Maximum 50 – 10 each
Human rights cases	If 10 cases deduct 5
Judgement, liability, or conviction reported	Deduct 10 per conviction

PROGRESSIVE STAFF POLICIES

Maximum Total Marks = 100

Criteria	**Grading Breakdown**

Formal Employee Assistance Plan   Maximum 20 - 5 each
Counselling
Retirement planning
Financial planning
Eldercare
Services for children with special needs

Health Promotion Plan   Maximum 20 - 5 each
Fitness subsidy
Smoking cessation program
Workplace wellness training
Drug coverage as part of health benefits

Communications   Maximum 20 - 5 each
Employee Newsletter
Formal incentive reward program
Formal Open Door to Managers program
Formal feedback to employees
Feedback sessions/surveys conducted by external verifiers
Orientation program for new employees

Human Development   Maximum 20 - 10 each
Refund tuition/books for external courses
        is greater than 75% of cost
Employee scholarship for external
        degree/diploma programs
Scholarship for children of employees
Other

Worklife Policies   Maximum 20 - 10 each
Flexible scheduling
Telecommuting programs
Job-sharing program
Guarantee of compensation for time worked beyond 40 hour week

SOURCING AND TRADING PRACTICES

Maximum Total Marks = 100

Criteria	Grading Breakdown	
Canadian Sourcing	Maximum	10
Disclose % of Canadian sourcing		5
Policy on Preferential Canadian Sourcing		5
Significant proportion from Canada	Maximum	10
Over 80% of sourcing from Canada		10
50% to 80% of sourcing from Canada		5
Disclosure of Foreign Activity	Maximum	20
Company lists countries		10
Management System ensures company does not source from:		
repressive regimes & slave/child labour/suppliers/contractors		10

Foreign Sourcing Code   Maximum   30 – 5 each

Applied to contractors, licensees
Translated into local languages
Worker protections guaranteed in all factories and plants:
Child labour standards
Exploitation of women, forced labour
Health & safety standards
Disciplinary practices
Freedom of association and collective bargaining
Maximum work hours
Living or sustainable wages: what is company's definition?
Support apprenticeship/education programs
Company confirms no breach of above list Y/N   Deduct 10 per breach

Audit Verification   Maximum   20 – 10 each

Applied to company operations, contractors, licensees
Independent auditors include NGOs, regulators, union leaders
Rectification procedure
Employee recourse
Publicly reported results
Surprise visits

Follow International Labour Standards Maximum   10 – 5 each
(ILO convention, Fair Labour Association, Ethical Trading Initiative, SA 8000)

ENVIRONMENTAL MANAGEMENT

Maximum Total Marks= 220

Corporate Policy — Maximum 35 marks

Written formal Environmental Code	10
Applicable to all subsidiaries	5
Last update (year)	5 if within the last two years
Employee sign-off	5
Train employees on environmental management	10

Monitoring Results — Maximum 50

Performance Audited:

Externally	20
Internally and externally	15
Internally	5
Company certified by independent standard	10

Environmental Reporting — Maximum 45 marks

Performance results reported by:

external verifier	10
internal verifier	5

Reports set: Maximum 10 – 5 each

principles/standards
targets
progress to date

Separate Health & Safety/Environment report	10
Environment section in annual report	5
Frequency of environmental reports to Board	10

Environmental Organization — Maximum 60

Full-time environmental officer	15
Environmental committee of Board	10
Outside environmentalist on Board	10
Staff environment health & safety committee(s)	10
Full-time environment staff	5
Environment officer at each business unit	5
Community stakeholders on environmental panels	5

Environmental Investments — Maximum 20

Capital expenditures: waste management	10
Number of investments	10
Types of investments	No marks

ENVIRONMENTAL PERFORMANCE

Maximum Total Marks = 190

Criteria	**Grading Breakdown**
Waste Reduction Targets	Maximum 40—10 each
Emission reduction included in product design	
Life cycle environmental systems	
Signatory to voluntary protocols	
Other voluntary environmental system	
Recycling and Restoration	Maximum 70 – 5 marks each
Energy resource conservation program	
List quantities	
Waste reduction programs	
List quantities	
Commodity recycling program	
List quantities	
Packaging and process materials recycling	
List quantities	
Workplace recycling programs	10 – 5 each
Quantities recycled	10 – 5 each
Environmental restoration program	10 marks
Violations, Fines and Awards	Maximum 40
Zero environmental convictions reported	20
Total number of violations	Deduct 5 each
Total number of convictions	Deduct 10 each
Total value of fines	No marks
Total awards	Maximum 20 – 5 each
Stakeholder Relations	Maximum 40 – 10 each

Products called "environment friendly" are verified by independent third party
Reductions/environmental improvements to packaging
Environmental demands made of suppliers' packaging or production
Demands made of suppliers are monitored for compliance
Charitable giving to environmental causes

COMMUNITY RESPONSIBILITIES

Maximum Total Marks = 230

Criteria	Grading Breakdown
Community Giving	Maximum 40
Imagine Campaign commitment	10 marks
% pre-tax earnings to charity	Maximum 20 marks
Annual corporate donations	5 marks (if data reported)
Annual employee donations	5 marks (if data reported)
Employee donations	No marks
Donations Policy and Support	Maximum 70
Cash donations as % of total	Maximum 20 marks
Publish donations guidelines	10 marks
Publish report on community giving	10 marks
Publish itemized list of recipients	5 marks
Employees help set policy	10 marks
Donations committee	5 marks (if data reported)
Individual business units can donate	10 marks
Charitable Community Activities	Maximum 40
Single-focus citizenship program	20 marks
In-kind donation of products/services	No marks
Loan of corporate facilities	5 marks
Paid-time loan of staff	10 marks
Gift matching program	5 marks
Areas of Giving	Maximum 30 – 10 each
(e.g. Health, Education, civic, arts, etc.)	
Community Engagement	Maximum 50 – 10 each
Formal multi-stakeholder dialogues	
Funds to monitor community impacts	
Community development investments	
Consultation during plant closing	
Economic engagement with aboriginal groups	
Company is on unsettled aboriginal land claims	If yes deduct 10

ADM Agri-Industries

Archer Daniels Midland Company (ADM Co.) began as the Daniels Linseed Co. in 1902. This multinational company has recently adopted the tag line "the nature of what's to come" to better reflect the entire company and refer to the unlocking of nature's potential and bringing more value to farmers' crops. With sales of $20.1 billion, ADM Co. procures, transports, stores, processes and merchandises agricultural products and commodities. Based in Windsor, Ontario, ADM Agri-Industries (ADM) is the wholly-owned Canadian subsidiary that operates flour mills, oilseed crushing and refining plants, barley malters, and grain elevators. It also has limited interests in formula feed and pet food plants. In 1997, ADM Agri-Industries bought all the assets of Maple Leaf Mills and absorbed them into existing operations, and in 1999, it formed an alliance with United Grain Growers (UGG) Ltd. by acquiring 45% of UGG. ADM has four flour mills and processing facilities in Alberta, one in Manitoba, eight in Ontario, and two in Québec.

> **2000 Revenues:** $20.1 billion (parent)
>
> **Grocery Store Sales:** No information
>
> **Brands:** ADM, Green Giant, Midland Harvest, Harvest Burgers, Ogilvie Mills, Novasoy ®, Nutrisoy ®, Soy 7 ™
>
> **Corporate Status:** Wholly-owned by U.S. parent.
>
> **Candor:** Neither the Canadian subsidiary nor its American parent corporate offices offered any cooperation. The company has an enormous transport and processing presence between the farm and supermarket, yet has relatively few brands or public profile. Candor quotient is 11%.

Ethical Management and Consumer Relations: The company has never reported any written ethics code, though it claims to adhere to "high ethical standards." The parent company has a five-person Public Policy Committee that addresses certain ethical matters, though no details were provided. A 40-page *Food Ingredient Catalogue* is published for consumers with dietary concerns. Over the last decade, the parent company suffered a number of high profile ethical management problems. Industry watchdogs describe ADM Co. as the "biggest corporate welfare recipient in the United States," because it has received huge government subsidies for ethanol and grain, and benefited from federal protections extended to America's sugar industry. These subsidies have cost the American economy tens of billions of dollars since 1980, including indirect costs to consumers through higher prices and taxes. Beginning in 1995, ADM and other grain processors were investigated for fixing the prices of lysine as well as citrus acid (corn syrup), an acidulent used in soft drinks, chewing gum, flavored teas, and juices. Former Prime Minister Brian Mulroney has served as co-chair of the directors' committee that was monitoring this investigation. In another case, the American Securities Exchange Commission began investigating allegations of fraudulent offshore payments to executives. ADM has vigorously denied the charges and defended its executives in the above cases.

2002 Employees Global: 22,753   **1991 Employees Global:** 13,049

Employee Relations: In 2000, ADM Agri-Industries closed "redundant" facilities, but did not provide any details regarding severance terms or redeployment. ADM employees with at least one year's service are eligible for a savings and investment plan, in which the company matches employee contributions, up to a maximum value of 6% of salary or $9,000. Senior executives and directors are eligible for other stock option plans.

Equity and Family: In 2002, two women sat on the parent's 13 member board of directors, along with two of 30 corporate officers. These proportions improved marginally since 1996, when women held one of 17 directorships and none of 28 corporate officer positions. ADM calls itself an "equal opportunity employer," but provided no details about policy or practice.

Sourcing and Trade: Internationally, the company has joint-venture interests in Chinese oilseed crushing operations, storage facilities, and partial investments in palm oil refining and livestock nutrition. It made no mention of policies supporting human rights or environmental protection in its trade regions. The company actively supported China's entry into the WTO and has publicly stated that it favours ending the U.S. trade embargo with Cuba, arguing that this move would create access to more markets and promote free trade.

Environmental Management and Performance: In 2000, ADM Co. spent US$14.7 million to bring its equipment, facilities, and programs for pollution control into compliance with regulations. In 1996, US$25 million went toward pollution control upgrades and regulatory compliance. Company tankers have been converted to heavier gross weight limits and higher capacities, delivering an aggregate energy saving throughout the company's worldwide transportation network of rail cars, trucks, and ocean vessels. Co-generation plants offer an efficient, low cost source of electricity and steam power for the seven largest ADM Co. operations in the U.S., the U.K., Ireland, Germany, and the Netherlands. No information was reported on environmental initiatives in Canada. ADM reports that its U.S. farmers use no-till farming, which can reduce soil erosion by up to 92%. Three ADM Agri-Industries sites report National Pollutant Release Inventory (NPRI) emissions. Measuring total chemical releases or waste generation in 1999, the ADM Windsor, Ontario facility ranked in the 90-100 percentile for its high waste volume (473,500 kilograms released to the environment, primarily N-Hexane) compared with all existing facilities in Canada. No toxic air releases were reported to the NPRI in 1997 or 1998. A Lloydminster, Alberta plant's 1999 air releases (100,000 kilograms, again primarily N-Hexane) were in the 70 to 80 percentile. The Candiac, Québec, site released only 200 kilograms to the air in 1999, placing it in the 0-10 percentile in terms of total chemical releases for facilities in Canada. After ADM/Ogilvie Mills Ltd of Thunder Bay exceeded its effluent control limits for biochemical oxygen discharged into the city's sanitary system in 1993, it changed its practices. This discharge was found to cause operational problems at the city's sewage treatment plant, so the practice was discontinued. The parent company is potentially responsible for environmental infractions at 25 designated Superfund sites by the U.S. Environmental Protection Agency. Internationally, Brazil's federal environmental authorities issued a notice in 2000, levying a $5.6 million penalty for discharge of industrial wastewater from an ADM-owned facility. The company stated its intent to appeal.

Genetically Modified Ingredients: No mention is made of prohibition or voluntary labelling. The company segregates genetically-enhanced foods in its inventory-management systems when there is consumer demand and where this is possible. ADM has in the past offered a premium on non-GMO soy, when consumer demand has been present, but this premium fluctuates with demand for segregation. No other details on its policy or practice were reported.

Community Responsibilities: No information on charitable donations and community involvement was reported for ADM Canada. In 2002, a new position had been created for breaking down corporate donations, but to date more information is not available.

www.admworld.com

Alberto Culver Canada Inc.

The Canadian subsidiary of Chicago-based Alberto Culver Company makes and sells hair care products, sugar substitutes, and spices. The Canadian operations—an office, plant, warehouse and quality assurance laboratory—are in Toronto. Many of the company's 90 mass-merchandise retailers, wholesalers, and brokers are retained on contract. Sally Beauty Co., the parent company's retail chain of 1,656 stores, operates in 6 countries and is the world's largest international chain of cash-and-carry beauty supply outlets servicing the professional and retail trades. Alberto Culver products are sold in over 100 countries worldwide. Personal care and beauty aids account for over 50% of Alberto Culver Canada's business. Staff in Canada distribute and sell, rather than make, products.

> **Annual Revenues:** US$2.5 billion for Alberto Culver globally
> **Grocery Store Sales:** 30-35%
> **Brands:** Alberto Balsam, Alberto European, Alberto VO5, FDS, Molly McButter, Mrs. Dash, Static Guard, St. Ives Swiss Formula, SugarTwin, TRESemme (not sold in Canada)
> **Corporate Status:** Wholly-owned by U.S. parent.
> **Candor:** The company did not complete EthicScan surveys, but a spokesperson later provided much information during a telephone interview. Candor is 46%.

Ethical Management and Consumer Relations: All Canadian and international operations follow Alberto Culver's *Code of Business Conduct* which is revised each year and modified for regional operations. Officers must sign it annually. Other employees sign off at the time of hire, though they are asked to provide input into the code's amendment. An annual survey asks employees questions related to the ethical standards of their supervisors. To reinforce the code, employees receive ethics training, and Alberto Culver is one of few companies to offer an independent toll-free ethics phone line service run by an external authority. To support its policy on business gift exchanges, the American head office circulates an annual Christmas letter to suppliers and retailers, discouraging inappropriate gifts. The company's consumer safety assurance process exceeds legal requirements and is maintained through internal audits. When prompted about advertising standards, the spokesperson comments that the company believes that standards are not necessary, given the nature of the products it sells, but did not elaborate why.

2001 Employees Global: 15,000   **2002 Employees Canada:** 163

1998 Employees Global: 11,000

Employee Relations: Alberto Culver staff has increased 5% over the last five years, much of it coming from expansion at its chain of Sally Beauty Company stores. While some operations in the U.S. are unionized, none in Canada are. No work stoppages, layoffs, or downsizing have occurred over the past five years. All workers are eligible for a profit sharing plan based on the company's global performance, though no other stock option or purchase plans are offered in Canada.

Equity and Family: No statistics on employment of Canadian women were reported. On the U.S. Board of Directors, two of 10 are women, along with 15% of senior managers, and 30% of managers. About 25% of the American workforce is female. Two women from Alberto Culver's founding family hold senior executive positions and board directorships. The spokesperson said that equity is important to the company, in part because most of its customers are women. As the second largest manufacturer of hair care products for people of colour in the world, Alberto Culver "definitely has a commitment to diversity," but did not elaborate. No formal equity policies exist, and no programs work to advance diverse groups. An anti-harassment section—covering gender, sexual orientation, race and disability— forms part of the general conduct code and standards training. No same sex couples benefits package is offered. Neither daycare referral services nor maternity leave extensions are available in Canada. Personal days and sick days have been combined into a single "personal time" category to be used however the employee chooses.

Progressive Staff: Employee Assistance Plans refer employees and their families to a phone-based network that assists with alcohol and drug abuse counselling. The company publishes a quarterly newsletter for all international operations, in addition to the Canadian office's monthly newsletter. A Group Development committee holds monthly meetings to help employees with career planning. Any job-related training courses are fully reimbursed, when the employee submits a passing grade. Regular surveys gauge employee satisfaction.

Sourcing and Trade: Approximately 27% of the parent's global sales come from outside North America. A corporate policy requires facilities to maximize sourcing and labour resources in the country of operation. Key ingredient sources and plants include Australia, Mexico, United Kingdom, Argentina, South Africa, and Sweden. The company says it neither sources from repressive regimes, nor condones poor labour conditions, but these policies are not codified or formally audited.

Environmental Management and Performance: Alberto Culver's environmental policy applies to all subsidiaries. At least once each year, internal personnel conduct comprehensive audits. In Canada, these teams include at least one member from the American corporate staff. While a Director of Environmental Affairs reports to the global Vice-President of Research and Development, no company environment committees meet at a staff or director level, and no regular reports are made to the board. Alberto Culver did not report to the National Pollutant Release Inventory on any chemical releases and transfers. While CFC propellants have been removed from the company's aerosol products, including Alberto VO5, other ingredients such as propane are still used. In both Canada and the U.S., workplace recycling programs collect fine paper, cardboard and some plastics. Some products returned by customers are donated to charities, but no specific details were provided.

Community Responsibilities: Alberto Culver does not disclose charitable donation details. Generally, it concentrates giving in cities where the company operates, and the

Canadian office has some discretion over philanthropic decisions. Typically, it supports national campaigns, including Canadian Juvenile Diabetes, which receives money in the name of the company's SugarTwin product. Canadian and U.S. offices make regular food and monetary donations to health, cultural, and social groups. Scholarships for children of employees are not open to Canadians unless they study abroad, because the company will not make educational contributions in countries where the majority of costs for post-secondary schooling are government-supported. In kind donations are made of mislabeled products and products released under outdated price plans.

www.alberto.com

Alcan Inc.

Alcan Inc., a Canadian corporation, is the parent company of an international group that generates $13 billion in sales of aluminum and packaging. Alcan has a network of operations in 38 countries, a strong presence in the U.S. and Europe, and a global customer base. Within Canada, Alcan has sales/distribution offices and processing plants in all provinces, six smelting facilities and six hydroelectric generating facilities in Québec, and one in British Columbia. Following a merger between Alcan and algroup/Alsuisse in October 2000, the company's size doubled, and operations were re-organized into four business groups: Primary Metal; Rolled Products, Americas and Asia; Rolled Products, Europe; and Packaging. Global activities include: bauxite mining, alumina refining, power generation, primary aluminum smelting, aluminum fabrication and engineered products, flexible and specialty packaging, recycling of used scrap aluminum, the selling of aluminum and industrial chemicals, as well as research technology. Foil, flexible, and specialty packaging are made in 14 countries.

2001 Revenues: US$12.8 billion
Grocery Store Sales: Less than 1% of revenues
Brands: Alcan Foil Wrap, Alcan Boxed Burner Guards, Bake-King Foil Wear, BBQ Buddy
Corporate Status: Publicly traded, Canadian company.
Candor: Few companies commit as much time and care to EthicScan's research process. Candor quotient is 86%.

Ethical Management and Consumer Relations: Honour Roll. Ethics training, formal input from staff, and an annual sign-off support Alcan's *Code of Conduct*. Alcan is one of the only companies profiled in this Guide to report a manager for its Code, and to have begun using a triple bottom line (profit, social, environmental) reporting process. The company planned to release its first Corporate Sustainability Report in April 2002. The company reports that there have been no cases relating to the safety of its products. An ex-President of Alcan Aluminum Corp, a U.S. operation in Cleveland Ohio, attempted to sue Alcan's Canadian parent after he was allegedly fired for opposing a request to study whether or not the company would save money by avoiding compliance with health, safety and environmental regulations. An Alcan lawyer completed an investigation and stated that the allegations "lacked factual merit." This case, filed in 1995, was settled out of court in 1997.

2002 Employees Canada: 11,000   **2002 Employees Global:** 48,000

1996 Employees Canada: 13,000

Employee Relations: Honour Roll. Following the merger with algroup, the company's global workforce grew by about 35%, but Canadian employment has remained stable (given acquisitions and divestitures) for the last five years. Approximately 60% of Alcan's Canadian hourly-paid employees are represented by labour unions (United Steelworkers, CAW,

Confederation of National Trade Unions, Canadian Association of Smelter & Allied Workers, International Association of Machinists & Aerospace Workers, and La Federation des Syndicats de Secteur Aluminum, Inc.). Four strikes and lockouts have occurred in the past ten years, a drop from 11 (1992-1997) and 12 (1989-1994). Since 1988, Alcan and labour unions at nine Québec plants have operated according to an 18-year agreement aimed at maintaining operations and customer service. Under this framework, management and workers commit to renewing collective agreements and settling disputes without strikes, lockouts, and pressure, while employees gained greater participation in management decisions. Over the last decade, layoffs or mine closings have affected ten locations. When job losses hit Alcan, they typically come from the introduction of new technology (mining, smelting, and distribution functions), the effects of seasonal operations, or the sale of operations. In 1999, Alcan shut down its Isle Maligne plant and transferred all employees to the Alma facility, a state-of-the-art US$2 billion smelter next door, or elsewhere in the Alcan network. Other jobs were cut as part of a corporate restructuring at head office. In 1996, Alcan spent an average of $1,800 training each employee, while in 2000, the company expressed annual training as equal to one week of employee time. Alcan has begun a US$30 million, multi-year global training initiative aimed at management. One of Alcan's incentive pay plans, the Business Unit Award (BUA), applies to all employees and provides compensation based on performance as determined by measurement against objectives.

Worker Safety: Mining and metallurgy jobs are dangerous, with high levels of fatalities and injuries relative to total hours worked. Alcan workers exposed to substances of concern are subject to risk-based assessments and training. The Environment, Health & Safety (EHS) Policy sets targets for the elimination of workplace injury and illness. The company reports incidents according to a Lost Time Injury/Illness Rate (calculated according to the number of cases that occur over 200,000 worker hours, or 100 employees working one full employment year). From 1998 to 1999 case rates dropped from 1.16 to 0.95.

Equity and Family: In 2001, women comprised zero of nine board directors, 3% of senior managers, and 7% of managers. Alcan employs 1,400 women in Canada. These proportions have not changed much over the last five years. In 2001, the company reported an employment equity program and a formal hiring and promotion policy for aboriginal peoples. The company does not assess the cultural composition of its workforce, but part of its *Code of Conduct* commits Alcan to employ local people from the places it operates. In 2000, based on a sample of 218 employees provided by the company, Human Resources Development Canada rates Alcan's hiring and promotion practices as less than average for women, and superior for the advancement of aboriginal peoples and persons with disabilities. HRDC found that there were no members of visible minorities in the workforce sample and the number of aboriginal peoples was less than ten. Alcan offers extended maternity leave and daycare referral, while decisions regarding paternal leave, adoption leave, and child/elder care belong to the direct supervisor or accord with the law. An anti-harassment policy is part of its *Code of Conduct*. The spokesperson stated that a revised Code of Employee and Business

Conduct would be issued in the spring of 2002, and would add an ombudsman function as well as update the previous code.

Progressive Staff: Honour Roll. Employee Assistance Plans are available to most employees around the world, covering family problems, marital problems, alcohol and drug dependency, emotional or personal problems, interpersonal relations, stress and burnout, and a referral service for financial and legal problems. The company conducts a confidential, global employee survey (once every two years) to assess views on company performance, the working environment, and to respond to criticisms.

Recycling Resources: Aluminum is a very recyclable product, because as waste, it requires only 5% of the energy needed to produce a primary product, and because its scrap has a high value. Over 25% of the aluminum consumed in the Western world is produced from recycled metal. Beverage cans represent less than 25% of the worldwide recycling business, and a good deal of metal comes from auto parts, cookware, house siding, and aircraft fuselage parts. In 1995, Alcan recycled approximately 15.5 billion cans purchased from around North America. In 1999, Alcan recycled over 25 billion cans worldwide. Its North American recycling network aims to recycle "every ounce of the aluminum returned to it." Currently 21 Alcan Aluminium Can Recycling Centres are joined by over 300 independent recycling centers. Alcan's U.S. recycling plants processed 40% of all used beverage cans (UBCs) recycled by Americans in 2000. Alcan's Canadian operations process 50% of all the UBCs collected nationally.

Sourcing and Trade: Honour Roll. In Canada, 90% of Alcan's goods and services are sourced locally. Through subsidiaries, joint ventures, and related companies, Alcan has operations and sales offices in dozens of countries, including Brazil, China, Ghana, Guinea, India, Kazakhstan, Korea, Malaysia, Russia, Singapore, Thailand, and Turkey. Alcan has been in China since the 1930s when it established an aluminum rolling operation there. Alcan has a long tradition of hiring and promoting people from the regions where it operates. It invests in local education, funding environmental, health, technical, sporting, and arts programs. Consistent with the terms of the OECD Multinational Enterprise and Investment Guidelines, its *Code of Conduct* pledges the company to avoid: discrimination that infringes human rights and fundamental freedoms; disrespecting individual workers; the hiring of child or forced labour; harassment on the basis of race, gender, national origin or religious beliefs; political coercion or intimidation in the workplace that affects employees' abilities to organize and bargain collectively.

Environmental Management: Honour Roll. Alcan's environmental policy integrates environment, health, and safety. All facilities are audited every three years, and more than 75% are certified through ISO, OHSAS, or equivalent environmental management systems certifications. It works with suppliers throughout the product life cycle, consults with stakeholders on environmental issues, complies with legal standards, and reports environmental management systems. A VP is assigned to environmental affairs, a management business unit is responsible for the implementation of initiatives, and the board has an Environment, Health, and Safety Committee. An EH&S council made up of professionals and operations staff meets at least twice yearly. In addition to approximately 200 employees with full-time environmental duties, environmental efforts receive support from technicians, support staff, operators and staff environmental committees at each operating company. Alcan's Environmental Management System requires that facilities develop clear objectives, targets and budgets in order to improve environmental performance. Research and development expenditures address process improvement at all stages of the aluminum refining process: reduced energy consumption, material consumption, and the elimination or improvement of treatment processes.

Greenhouse Gas Emissions: In 2000, Alcan Inc. joined an industry group with at least seven other companies and associations to lobby the federal government over the ratification of the Kyoto Protocol in Canada. The companies urged the government to wait for a better understanding of the Protocol and its implications on industry and the economy before implementing its terms. Advocacy groups accused the industry group of "sabotaging the national climate change process" and using industry reports to present a one-sided view on climate change and the Kyoto Protocol. The spokesperson stated that the industry association's concern is over implementation of the Kyoto Protocol rather than disputing the truth of global climate change and the link to greenhouse gas emissions. Alcan has a program to reduce greenhouse gas emissions by 500,000 tonnes over the next four years, and has signed a covenant with the Province of Québec that would see emissions in Québec reduced by 200,000 tonnes. Alcan is also a member of the Partnership for Climate Action as well as a founding member of the EPA's Climate Leadership Program.

Environmental Performance: Aluminum packaging facilities have reduced their VOC emissions. Packaging requirements for household foil products are on target to be cut by 27%. Extrusion die cleaning waste is recycled at various plants in Brazil, the U.K., and Canada. A technology allows for the substitution of salts for chlorine gas that will eventually result in a decline in chlorine consumption at processing plants. Between 1992 and 1999, industrial waste landfilled in Saguenay, Québec was reduced by 78%. A continuous system for the reporting of major incidents/issues is in place and monthly reports are issued by most business groups. In 1997, Alcan issued its first environmental progress report, several plants supply their own internal annual reports, and the first company-wide corporate citizenship report will be published in 2002. In Canada, Alcan follows ARET, a federal government program for the elimination of toxins, through which it has reduced its emissions of Polycyclic Aromatic Hydrocarbons by over 80%. It also participates in the Voluntary Challenge Registry Program (VCR), the CIPEC energy efficiency program, and a Pollution Prevention agreement for the Kitimat, BC smelter.

Environmental fines and penalties over ten years total at least CDN$175,000 and US$274,000. Convictions include: the Can Pipe Division in Vernon, British Columbia, for discharging business waste and storing/producing/handling special waste; Alcan Smelters and Chemicals Ltd. for causing discomfort to people near its Ottawa plant resulting from smoke-stack emissions of aluminum powder and sulphuric acid. Emissions from Alcan's mines and smelters have, over decades and generations of operation, affected the health of area residents. Past and present claims have been filed against the company. For example, complaints from Arvida and Jonquierre, Québec have focused on emissions of fluoride and hydrocarbon metabolites (PAHs). In response, the company says that it has invested to improve anode technology and other sources of materials that minimize the emission of PAHs from the smelting process. The company is now using a low-tar pitch, which has reduced PAH emissions by 80%. To address other concerns, its Kitimat smelter and works in British Columbia pioneered procurement policies in 1996 that emphasize stronger safety certificate rules for all potential contractors. Alcan is the only large company in British Columbia that takes part in the Pollution Prevention Plan. The company has instituted a risk-based health check program for employees exposed to substances of concern and uses improved industrial hygiene technology and respiratory protection to protect employee health. Line managers must develop local health and safety programs, and contractors and consultants must receive a certification in safety. Environmental distinctions include an award from the City of North Bay for Alcan's contribution of land to Nippissing University for an Environmental Research Centre. The company recently earned a place in the Dow Jones Sustainability Group Index in 2000, and was cited as Best in Class by Innovest in 2001.

Community Responsibilities: Honour Roll. Alcan is pledged to the Imagine Campaign, and as the company has grown in size, its annual donations have grown commensurately. In 2000 it gave $3.4 million. To set donations policies, a committee brings together corporate executives, regional representatives, and a community investment program officer. Social involvement is extensive and includes the loan of company facilities, employee time donations, student work programs, matching gift programs and scholarship funds for employees' children. The company also funds athletic/sports teams and provides health and medical support. Alcan commits hundreds of thousands of dollars to a variety of projects related to whale research, environmental education, and related projects. In 1999, it announced a three-year sponsorship of the World Wildlife Fund's Endangered Species Recovery Fund intended to assist in research and conservation efforts. Alcan is a supporter of cultural and educational causes, including Vancouver's Science World, the Montreal Jazz Festival, Opera Lyra, the Alcan Quartet and the Alcan Performing Arts Award. Alcan reports working closely with aboriginal groups in regions where it operates to resolve outstanding issues. In Québec, Alcan reports being in close contact with the Montagnais First Nation, and in BC with the Cheslotta First Nation. It has signed protocols of mutual respect and cooperation with both groups. The first contract of the Alma smelter development project was awarded to the Montagnais community.

www.alcan.com

Bayer Inc.

Based on its innovation of numerous applied chemistry products, including acetylsalicylic acid (Asprin) in 1899, Bayer is one of the world's most powerful brands, recognized in 140 countries worldwide. Toronto-based Bayer Inc., the Canadian operating subsidiary of the Bayer Group of Companies, owned by Bayer AG of Leverkusen, Germany, markets and sells products and services in five business segments: Agriculture, Chemicals and Polymers, Consumer Care, Health Care, and Rubber and manufacturing products in Chemicals and Polymers (rubber, tungsten carbide powders, and nickel hydroxide). In November 1993, the German chemical parent merged four Canadian units into one entity, Miles Canada, and in April 1995, Miles Canada became Bayer Inc. Bayer AG also acquired all North American Sterling-Withrop brand over-the-counter pharmaceuticals from SmithKline. Today, the Bayer Group operates all its Canadian interests through Bayer Inc. including life sciences, polymers, and specialty chemicals operations. Bayer has two plants: Sarnia, Ontario and Pointe Claire, Québec.

2000 Revenues: $1.5 billion

Grocery Store Sales: No information

Brands: Adalat, Admire, Advantage, Advia diagnostic equipment, Alka-seltzer, Aspirin, Avelox, Bactine, Bayco, Bugs Bunny Vitamins, Canesten, Cipro, Elite glucometer, Everest, Flintstones vitamins, Gamimune/IVIG, Kogenate FS, Macrolon, Midol, Myoflex, One A Day vitamins and Specialized blends, Ozonol, Phillips Milk of Magnesia, Therban

Corporate Status: Wholly-owned subsidiary of German parent.

Candor: Bayer's corporate spokesperson was cooperative and answered many of EthicScan's questions. Candor is 56%.

Ethical Management and Consumer Relations: In 1999, Bayer AG released its *Guidelines for Legal Compliance and Corporate Responsibility* to all subsidiaries. All employees must review this document, along with Bayer Inc.'s Code. A five-page *Corporate Standards of Business Conduct* also guides staff on issues such as competition, rebates, misleading advertising, illegal payments, entertaining customers, and conflict of interest. Bayer does not have a policy regarding product placement in retail stores, nor one for investing in repressive regimes. All staff must sign-off on the *Corporate Standards of Business Conduct* at the time of hire, and ethics-related training is given to all managers. Although no corporate or health ethicist is retained, the Bayer Foundation supports the Bayer Advisory Council on Bioethics, an independent group that advises on ethical practices related to biological issues. On August 8, 2001, Bayer AG voluntarily withdrew its cholesterol-lowering drug Baycol/Lipobay from markets worldwide. Bayer reports knowing of 52 fatalities linked to the drug. The U.S. FDA reported 31 deaths linked to the drug in the United States. Health Canada had received reports of 32 cases of serious muscle weakness associated with the drug, including ten cases of kidney failure and one death. The spokesperson emphasized that the cases are based on spontaneous reports that have limited conclusiveness. A class action suit filed in August 1997 alleged that Bayer Inc conspired with another company to fix the price of iron oxide pigment dyes used to add colour to bricks during the period 1984-1992. To date, this is the largest ever price fixing class action lawsuit in Canada. The Divisional Court of Ontario in May 2001 overturned, on appeal, the Ontario Supreme Court order that certified the class action. The plaintiff is seeking leave to appeal to the Ontario Court of Appeal.

2002 Employees Canada: 2,421   **2001 Employees Worldwide:** 117,000

1993 Employees Canada: 1,006 (Bayer Canada, not including rubber division)

Employee Relations: Bayer Rubber is the only unionized division in Bayer Inc. Local 914 of the Communications, Energy, and Paperworkers Union represents about 1,000 hourly workers at Polysar Sarnia plant (40% of its total workforce), a location that accounts for 50% of Bayer's total Canadian workforce. No strikes have occurred at any site during the last decade. The most recent layoffs came at the parent company, which cut its workforce by 4%, affecting operations in the U.S. and Europe. The company spends approximately $1800 per employee on training and development. Human development programs also include a 100% tuition and books refund, and a scholarship program for the children of employees. In 1998 Bayer Inc. introduced a variable incentive pay system, allowing employees to qualify for a bonus based on personal and divisional objectives. In 2000, Bayer Inc. offered a stock option program for employees at the senior level, and a stock purchase plan for all employees.

Tainted Blood: Bayer, its laboratories, and three other companies that made blood products in the 1980s that enabled hemophiliacs to clot their blood were part of the 1996 Commission of Inquiry on the Blood System in Canada (the so-called Krever "tainted blood" inquiry). Allegedly these three companies knew as early as 1982 that their blood products might contain the AIDS virus but failed to warn consumers. In addition to charges faced by other pharmaceutical/supplier companies, Bayer was accused of having contributed to the failure to warn Canadian hemophiliacs of the risk of acquiring AIDS from the use of factor concentrates. The company was said to have acceded to requests of the Canadian Red Cross Society not to include warnings on products bearing its own name brand. Bayer was also cited for allegedly failing to provide Health Canada with evidence of the efficacy of its viral inactivation method until February 1985: three months after its heat-treated product had been licensed in Canada. In response to these allegations, the company spokesperson noted that Bayer cooperated fully with the Krever inquiry, presented considerable scientific evidence related to the heat-treatment process employed by its predecessor, Cutter Laboratories, and that Justice Krever made no adverse findings regarding Cutter's heat treatment process. In addition, there has never been a proven case of HIV transmission with a Cutter (later Bayer) heat-treated product anywhere in the world.

Equity and Family: Honour Roll. In 2001, 72 of 257 (28%) managers were women, a slight drop from 1998 (36%), along with five of 23 Vice-Presidents (22%), but neither members of the board were women. In 1998, 31% of senior managers, and 45% of the workforce were women. Bayer offers employees diversity training, flex-scheduling, job-sharing, and telecommuting.

Progressive Staff: Bayer nurtures employee wellness through an in-house Bayer Club, worklife balance initiatives, and a golf/fitness club affiliated with the Sarnia site. It offers alcohol and drug abuse counselling for staff, and a stop-smoking program is part of the firm's extended health plan. Internal communications include regular employee focus groups and formal surveys, an annual management meeting, regular information sessions (covering relevant scientific topics such as Bovine diseases, pesticide use and animal care), a recognition program honoring outstanding employees, and an employee newsletter (four times a year).

> **Worker Safety**
> 2000 Injuries: 31
> 1999 Injuries: 33
> Over the last three years, lost time accidents have been reduced by 87% at the Sarnia site. The above injuries took place during more than 2.4 million human hours worked each year at Sarnia and the other Canadian locations.

Sourcing and Trade: Bayer is one of the 50 founding members of the Global Compact Initiative, a UN project whose objective is to pursue Nine Principles relating to human rights, labour standards and environmental protection on a global basis. Bayer AG has recently been included in the FTSE4GOOD index, a UK-based investment index comprised of companies that meet certain performance standards for human rights, social, and environmental sustainability. Bayer was the only non-U.S. or UK-based pharmaceutical company, and the only European chemicals company, included in the index.

Environmental Management: Bayer's environmental management code, last updated in 2000, is part of employee training. Because it makes a range of pesticides and herbicides, Bayer's operations are also governed by the Canadian Chemical Producers' Association Responsible Care Codes of Practice (a set of principles that guide member companies). The Sarnia plant conducts two or three unit environmental audits annually, covering the entire site every three years. The parent company's first annual environmental report was released in 1993, and Bayer Canada's first Health, Environment & Safety Report came out in 1998. Annual environmental reports are submitted to the board of directors. At the German parent's board, an environmental committee reviews policy and performance. Bayer Sarnia has five central health, safety, and environment staff, including a director of health, safety, and environment, and five EH&S supervisors that manage individual operating units, along with five EH&S specialists and two environment lab support technicians. A Health and Environmental Safety department at the Chemicals and Polymers Division employs three regulatory specialists who screen and evaluate the importation of new chemical products, and two others to ensure full environmental compliance (sewer discharge and hazardous waste disposal) at distribution operations at the Toronto and Pointe Claire sites. An environmental task force runs information sessions, "greening," and recycling projects to educate all employees.

Environmental Performance: For the last five years, Bayer has reported a high level of detail on its waste reduction and recycling performance. Materials include steel, wood, cardboard, paper, plastic, glass, and nickel. While the company monitors its wastes, no explicit reduction targets exist. As the largest Canadian industrial source of air emissions for three substances—Acrylonitrile, Chloromethane, and 1,3 Butadiene—the Sarnia plant is monitored closely by external community groups. (Bayer's 1,3 Butadiene emissions represent only a tiny fraction of the total 1,3 Butadiene emissions in Canada, when non-manufacturing sites, i.e. automobile and forest fire emissions, are considered.) Bayer Sarnia also emits Acetonitrile, Tetra-Butyl Alcohol and Cyclohexane, and it is the only facility in Canada using these chemicals to produce synthetic rubber. Bayer Inc. reports chemical releases and transfers to the NPRI. In 1999, the Sarnia facility (1,704,920 kilograms released to the air, 24,620 kilograms to water, and 2,910 kilograms to land), ranked in the 90-100 percentile in terms of major chemical releases or waste generation for facilities in Canada. For potential human health risks resulting from exposure to chloromethane, it is number one in Canada. The spokesperson noted that the information on NPRI was "wrong and should not be included." Further, she explained that Bayer believes the pollution watch website "uses an incorrect factor to calculate human health risk. [Bayer] is working with the CCPA to have the organizations that run the website correct the mistake."

Breaches and Fines: In 1999, Bayer Inc. was fined $40,000 for an accidental release of lubricating oil to the St. Clair River. The oil was cleaned up and no long-term effect on river ecology is believed to have occurred. The Polysar Rubber site in Sarnia was convicted of discharging 73 kg of benzene into the St Clair River contrary to the Environmental Protection Act, section 14, with a fine of $60,000 in 1995. At sentence, the court accepted the Crown's submission and lifted the corporate veil to find a connection between Polysar Rubber and its predecessor company, Polysar Limited. The company's synthetic rubber plant received an Ontario Ministry of Environment award in 1996 for eliminating benzene emissions and converting one of the rubber-producing units to a safer non-carcinogenic solvent. Awards and Distinctions: The Polymers division of Bayer Inc, then called Miles Canada, won the Etobicoke Environment Award in 1994 for developing CFC-free foam technology. In June 1996, Bayer Inc. received the Canadian Polystyrene Recycling Association [CPRA] Award for Best New Generator of Polystyrene Plastics.

Animal Testing: The parent is in the top 10 companies in the U.S. in terms of number of animals tested, and is on the top ten on an IRRC (an American research group) list in terms of painful tests without anesthesia. In response, Bayer AG parent has issued its *Principles of Animal Testing.*

Community Responsibilities: The company donates at least 1% of pre-tax earnings to charity as a committed member of the Imagine campaign. Total 2000 donations were $949,979 (staff: $156,540). Employees can request corporate contributions to charities where they volunteer. In 2000, contributions of $241,354 went to the United Way (corporate matching of employee donations), and the Bayer Foundation provides financial support to the arts and communities. In 1996, Bayer Inc. made a $300,000 grant to the Heart Institute at the University of Ottawa for a three-year study on smoking and heart disease. Charitable activities include long-term agreements with the Ontario Science Centre, National Chemistry Week, and a school outreach program for elementary levels, the Bayer "Scientists in Schools." Bayer Inc.'s Sarnia site is involved in a local community awareness program (CAP) as part of its Responsible Care initiatives.   As well, Bayer is a member of the Sarnia-Lambton Environmental Association (SLEA) which is an organization that deals with complex issues that arise with the presence of the chemical industry.

www.bayer.com

Cadbury Beverages Canada Inc.

Cadbury came to Toronto in 1919, more than 70 years after John Cadbury first sold tea and coffee in England. Today, Cadbury Beverages Canada Inc. is a subsidiary of U.K.-based Cadbury Schweppes PLC, the world's third largest soda maker and largest non-cola soft drink maker. Its three divisions, Mott's, Carbonated, and Snapple, make and sell various categories of juice, soda pop, cocktails, chocolate powders, and processed fruit sauces. In 1999, Coke's attempted takeover of the carbonated brands of Cadbury failed after extensive negotiations with the federal Competition Bureau did not satisfy its regulatory concerns.

2000 Revenues: No information
Grocery Store Sales: No information
Brands: C Plus, Cadbury Schweppes beverages, Canada Dry, Mott's Garden Cocktail, Mott's Beverages, Ocean Spray, Schweppes, Welch's, Snapple, ReaLime, ReaLemon
Corporate Status: Wholly owned by U.K. parent.
Candor: Answers came only from Mott's in the United States, not from the Canadian Cadbury office. Candor is 20%.

Ethical Management and Consumer Relations: The company follows a *Policy Statement on Business Principles,* and *Purpose & Values,* which new employees must sign when hired. No other details on ethics guidance, training, or reinforcement were reported.

2002 Employees Canada: 120   **1998 Employees Canada:** 180 (beverages)

1998 Employees Worldwide: 40,000 (Cadbury Schweppes)

Employee Relations: The Canadian Auto Workers and the United Food and Commercial Workers represent production and transport workers in Canada. Normal seasonal layoffs of 15 to 20 staff occur every spring. Canadian employees can participate in an Employee Share Ownership Program and are enrolled automatically in a Profit Sharing Program, which pays a 2% bonus if plants meet predetermined quotas. However, the union spokesperson indicated that bonuses are not always paid. In April 1996, Cadbury Beverages Canada Inc. announced plans to close its St. Catharines, Ontario plant and terminate 133 jobs. The loss of a major contract with Ocean Spray, which had restructured its North American operations, forced the closure. Fifty-one workers received jobs in a distribution warehouse, while another 53 workers were placed in other jobs, many at sister company Cadbury Trebor Allen Inc. Another six retired. The United Food and Commercial Workers launched a boycott, endorsed by the Canadian Labour Congress, to protest the St. Catharines closure. The union was upset that production jobs were being shifted to the U.S., where the juice would be processed and then shipped back for sale in Canada. The closure also jeopardized the sole grape juice-processing contract for hundreds of grape growers in the Niagara region. The company agreed to purchase the growers' crops until 2002. In the final fact verification stage of this book, the

2002 spokesperson said that the aforementioned layoffs were "recalled" and that the St. Catharines plant did not close, but provided no further details. Due to the late stage of this information, EthicScan was unable to corroborate the story with the union spokesperson.

Equity and Family: Anti-harassment protection and training are part of unionized workers' collective agreement.

Progressive Staff: Employee Assistance Programs offer counselling advice to staff for substance abuse problems and retirement planning. To assess job performance, the company conducts semi-annual employee reviews. Only office employees are eligible for flex hours and reduced summer hours between May and October. The company newsletter, *Mott's Thoughts*, is distributed quarterly via e-mail. Its format was converted for "MottsNet," an intranet web site accessible to all employees at offices and plants.

Sourcing and Trade: The Canadian company said that it has no international operations, and reported nothing about cross-border shipments for its parent company.

Environmental Management and Performance: Canadian operations follow the parent company's worldwide environmental policy and program. Some operations direct comprehensive audits on an "as needed" basis, but no details were offered. Eight employees share environmental tasks as part of their job descriptions. No single manager or director leads environmental affairs in Canada. Cadbury Beverages did not provide the National Pollutant Release Inventory with information on any chemical releases or transfers. In the late 1990s, the company introduced reformatted packages for Mott's products. The 1998 union spokesperson explained that these PET plastic bottles would be returnable through deposit programs in Alberta, Saskatchewan, Manitoba, Nova Scotia, and New Brunswick, but only be recyclable in other provinces.

Community Responsibilities: In 1998, Cadbury began focusing its philanthropic giving on in-kind product donations to community organizations. The company also supports nutritional causes, the United Way, and local sports teams. Employee contributions to educational institutions are matched by company donations.

www.cadburyschweppes.com
www.motts.com

Campbell Soup Company Ltd

The world's most famous soup maker, which started in Camden, New Jersey in 1869, only set up an operation in Toronto in 1931. By 1911, a condensing process allowed Campbell to become one of the first brands sold coast-to-coast. Today the global company's $7 billion in annual revenues includes vegetable and fruit juices, frozen meals, and desserts for both the retail and food service markets. Soups and sauces are processed in Toronto, frozen foods at Listowel, Ontario, and sales staff work out of offices in Calgary, Dartmouth, Montreal, and Mississauga. During the 1990s, the American parent bought out the 30% of stock it did not own in the Canadian company, transforming it into a wholly-owned subsidiary. Following the appointment of a new CEO in January 2001, Campbell North America was reorganized into two separate business units: North American Soup and North American Beverages and Sauces.

2000 Revenues: $613 million
Grocery Store Sales: No information
Brands: Campbell Soup, Chunky Soup, Habitant, Snack in a Cup, Pace, Picante & Salsa, Le Menu, Pepperidge Farm, Milano, Prego, V8, Goldfish crackers, Godiva chocolates
Corporate Status: Wholly-owned by U.S. parent.
Candor: Corporate spokespeople provided extensive responses throughout the research process. The candor quotient is 68%.

Ethical Management and Consumer Relations: Canadian employees follow the parent company's 16-page code of ethics, the *Campbell Soup Company Worldwide Standards of Conduct*. It covers: conflict of interest, business gifts and favours, insider trading, and workplace discrimination. Since the 1980s, the Canadian company has supplemented this code with its own policy statements: *The Campbell Commitment* and *Vision and Core Values Statement*.

2002 Employees Canada: 1,410   **1996 Employees Canada:** 1,339

1991 Employees Canada: 2,200

Employee Relations: Honour Roll. A decade-long push for efficiency cut Canadian jobs by 38.6% between 1991 and 1996, a loss of greater proportions than experienced at the company's other operations (total employees fell to 40,650 in 1996 from 44,934 in 1991). While total production increased in Toronto and Listowel, eight other plants closed (Ontario, Québec, Manitoba, Nova Scotia, and Saskatchewan) and four mushroom farms were sold. No strike or lockouts have occurred in Canada over the last fifteen years. Employee turnover is slightly greater than 10%, which is average for this sector. No Canadian staff are unionized. From January to June 2001, the Toronto plant reported 17 medical aid incidents (a minor injury for which no days are lost) and one lost time injury, while Listowel experienced 54 medical aids and two lost time injuries. At Toronto in 2000, there were 60 medical aids and no lost-time injuries, at Listowel; 106 medical aids and one lost time injury. A company savings plan offers eight possible options, including share options in which the employer matches up to $850 worth of staff stock purchases. In addition, all non-management employees participate in a gainsharing program based on sales and profit measures, as well as three different reward incentives plans.

Equity and Family: Honour Roll. In 2001, women made up two of nine board directors, 25% of senior managers, and 30% of all managers. Of the total Canadian workforce in 2001 (hourly and salaried employees) 46% were female. At all levels, modest increases were made by women since 1996, when they made up one of nine board directors, 23% of senior managers, 26% of managers, and 37.2% of the total workforce. Employees are trained on the company's anti-harassment policy, but do not sign off on it.

Progressive Staff: Few employees telecommute or job share, but 30% of Canadian employees use flexible scheduling options. About 10% of employees work beyond a 40-hour week and receive guaranteed compensation for the extra time. Training programs are shaped by formal employee input that includes an annual needs assessment process carried out by cross-functional teams.

Sourcing and Trade: No formal policies govern human rights and environmental standards. Guidelines require managers to look "globally for the best quality at the best price." The Toronto plant sources all packaging and ingredient supplies from North American companies (preference given to Ontario suppliers first, then Canadian, then North American), or through North American brokers. The company also utilizes supplier contracts already established by World Headquarters in New Jersey. The spokesperson reported that the Listowel facility has fewer than five direct contracts in Mexico and France. Fourteen per cent of Campbell Canada's sales go to the United States.

Environmental Management and Performance: An environmental code applies to all subsidiaries. According to the 1998 spokesperson, "there is a formal system of monitoring environmental performance and providing regular updates to management." No public reporting exists for environmental performance. Waste audits and reduction plan reviews occur yearly. Useable surplus products go to food banks, while damaged goods are sold for use as animal food. Recycling programs for wood, metal, organic waste, cans, paper, cardboard, and glass have reduced solid waste sent to landfills by 68% over four years. The company participates in an industry association program to voluntarily reduce greenhouse gases, but no performance details were provided. No major environmental effluent exceedances or charges were reported. Environmental sponsorships have gone to industry blue box research groups (Corporations Supporting Recycling), the Harmony Foundation, and to match gifts of employees.

Genetically Modified Ingredients: In 1993, a group calling itself the Pure Food Campaign organized a boycott against Campbell's parent for marketing a soup genetically engineered to last longer on the shelf. The company provided no response to this report, nor any details about its policies or practices on GM ingredients.

Community Responsibilities: In Canada, year 2000 donations exceeded $650,000, almost double its 1995 total of $393,000. Although not pledged to the Imagine Campaign, the company's total giving (including product donations) accounts for 1.2 % of pre-tax profits. In 1995, employee giving equaled about one quarter of all giving. Campbell's funding guidelines target either projects that impact children and youth at risk, or food and nutrition issues. Key areas of support include the employee charitable drive (funds which the company matches), food banks, and youth and education. Employees donate time to fundraising, and gift matching programs double employee contributions to educational institutions. Between 1993 and 1996, the company was Canada's largest (by tonnage) corporate food contributor to the Canadian Association of Food Banks, and recognized by an award from the CAFB. Campbell's Labels for Education program invites participating schools to save labels and exchange them for equipment and materials. Each year, six scholarships—worth $2,000 for each of four years—are given to the children of employees, and other students are hired for co-op education programs.

www.campbellsoup.com

Canada Bread Company Limited

Canada Bread is a group of companies that makes bread and food brands sold from coast to coast. Based in Toronto, 69% of its shares are owned by Maple Leaf Foods. Until 1997 the company was called Corporate Foods, before reverting its name back to the one with which it was founded in 1911. With baking facilities in British Columbia, Alberta, Ontario, Québec, New Brunswick, and Newfoundland, the group is organized into three categories: fresh baked, frozen, and specialty products. In 1995, it bought the Tenderflake Division from its parent. In 2001, Canada Bread signed an agreement to acquire the remaining 75% ownership of Multi Marques Inc. that it did not own, strengthening its position in the Québec market and garnering a national presence.

> **Annual Revenues:** $560 million (approximately)
> **Grocery Store Sales:** No information
> **Brands:** Dempster's, Olivieri, Tenderflake, Multi Marques, Toronto Bagel, CircleT Foods
> **Corporate Status:** Majority owned by Maple Leaf Foods.
> **Candor:** The corporate spokespersons answered questions during the research process and the fact verification phone interviews. Candor is 48%.

Ethical Management and Consumer Relations: The code of ethics, last updated in 2000, receives a sign-off by employees at the time of hire. Integrated into a broader corporate code of conduct, the ethics code is translated into French and contains human rights provisions. Although no policy on negotiating product placement in stores was reported, the company does have guidelines for exchange of business gifts. Consumer assurance policies include a toll-free consumer phone line, and a product safety assurance and recall system (that exceeds government requirements). When the Dempster's division wanted to print nutritional analysis labels (ahead of anything the government had planned) on all its bread loaves, management sought and successfully received a special authorization from Health and Welfare Canada. There is a corporate governance committee of the Board, whose duties include corporate social responsibility, compensation, nomination, and monitoring of ethical policies.

2002 Employees Canada: 3,400   **1996 Employees Canada:** 3,264

Employee Relations: All employees are Canadian, and staff levels remain fairly constant, with modest increases (4%) over the last five years. Approximately 75% of employees belong to the Bakery, Confectionery, and Tobacco Workers union. Layoffs did hit 600 people in the Maritimes, Québec, Ontario and Alberta over the last five years. Anyone affected by temporary or permanent layoffs receives redeployment opportunities, retraining, advance notice of technological change, and severance packages beyond the government minimum. Over the last decade, five strikes have occurred at the Toronto Bagel and CircleT Foods units, and one union local has been decertified. Some training is given to employees at all levels, and input is formally solicited for training programs. The company reimburses course tuition and book costs up to 100%. Beginning in 2001, a new bonus plan, based on team objectives and on operating earnings, was paid out to executives, management and sales staff. A savings plan is offered to general staff. After reviewing the material reported on the company, the union representative gave no comment.

Health and Safety: Workplace injuries have fallen steadily at Canada Bread. When expressed per million hours worked, injuries have fallen dramatically to 35.2 in 2000, from 44.7 workplace injuries in 1996, and 74.3 in 1994. The corporate spokesperson attributed this reduction to a "more active focus on health and safety." Health and safety committees, with employee and management members, conduct ergonomic assessments of workplace conditions.

Equity and Family: At Canada Bread, women hold one of 10 board directorships, three of 14 senior manager jobs, and 69 of 286 management positions. The company has an employment equity policy, an anti-harassment policy which covers sexual issues and orientation, race and disability, and training support. Extended maternity, paternity, and adoption leaves are granted on an individual basis.

Progressive Staff: Employee assistance plans provide help for substance abuse, though not at all sites. Only executives receive fitness club subsidies. Through a formal program conducted by external consultants, employees give feedback on management practices and internal policies.

Sourcing and Trade: The company has no international operations. No information on sourcing of flour, yeast, raisins, or other ingredients was reported.

Environmental Management and Performance: Canada Bread's environmental policies were last updated in 2000. Environmental performance is not audited, nor does any independent standards council certify company procedures. Internal environmental reporting is done three times per year, but results are not made public. Three employees share environmental responsibilities, and a corporate governance committee of the board oversees their work. In the late 1990s, the company invested $886,000 on lighting, effluent treatment, insulation, steam traps, burner adjustments, air leaks, and heat reclamation devices in release stacks. No chemical releases or transfers were reported to the National Pollutant Release Inventory. Canada Bread has an energy resource conservation program, commodity and workplace recycling, and methods for recycling packaging and process materials. It recycles paper, cardboard, cans, bottles, corrugated packaging and plastic, and as early as 1990, was recycling 94% of its solid waste material. Management's target for its "war on waste" in 2001 is a 25% reduction in manufacturing and supply chain waste. The company sells waste food to farmers. Transport schedules and routes were redesigned to minimize total mileage.

Genetically Modified Ingredients: No information and no voluntary labelling exist, despite the company's reliance on grain products.

Community Responsibilities: Charitable giving is directed at a few general areas—the United Way, food banks, and school programs that feed children in need—in communities where Canada Bread operates. The company also grants employees time off to work at not-for-profit agencies and matches their financial gifts.

www.canadabread.ca

Canadian Salt Company Ltd

One of Canada's few salt mining and processing companies, the Canadian Salt Company produces table salts and water softening products. Wholly-owned by Morton International of Chicago, it is headquartered in Montreal, with three rock salt mining operations in Ontario, Nova Scotia, and Québec, and four evaporated salt processing plants in Saskatchewan, Nova Scotia, and Alberta. The company began mining and processing salt as a subsidiary of the Canadian Pacific Railway.

2001 Revenues: No information
Grocery Store Sales: No information
Brands: Windsor, Safe-T-Salt, Crystal 2 system saver (water softener)
Corporate Status: Wholly-owned by U.S. parent.
Candor: The company reviewed our research and then provided comments during a phone interview. Other data came during the final fact verification process. Candor is 12%.

Ethical Management and Consumer Relations: Each year managers and key employees at Canadian Salt must read and sign the parent's five-page policy, the *Morton Code of Conduct and Business Ethics*. It covers issues like the giving and receiving of business gifts, conflicts of interest, insider trading of the parent's stock, and the treatment of company-sensitive information.

2002 Employment Canada: No Information

Employee Relations: Of the 960 people who worked at Canadian Salt's mines, refineries and offices in 1998, 600 belonged to one of three unions: the Canadian Auto Workers, Communications, Energy, and Paperworkers (CEP) and the CSN.

Health and Safety: Hazards in mining include cave-ins, fire, and fume emissions. The company spokesperson said that relative to other mine operations, fire is a low threat with salt, because gas pockets do not build up. Work at the Windsor mine is highly mechanized, solitary, specialized, and often carried out under noisy conditions. The company complies with the safety standards set by the Salt Institute, as well as those of the Responsible Care program established by the Canadian Chemical Producers Association. The Responsible Care program's guidelines require measures such as the creation of rescue teams, and training for evacuation procedures. In 1999, the Special Investigations Branch of the Workplace Safety and Insurance Board (WSIB) laid a number of charges under the Workplace Safety and Insurance Act against the company. The company was fined $500,000 because it misled Worker's Compensation Board (WCB) officials about accidents at two Ontario Salt Mines.

Equity and Family: In 1997, the company drafted an employment equity policy, and training on equity issues is part of orientation training for new hires. Canadian Salt has also stated that it complies with all equity terms required of contractors to the federal government. Training reinforces an anti-sexual harassment policy.

Progressive Staff: All workers are eligible for 100% reimbursement of tuition for any educational course they pass. Any worker can apply anonymously for substance abuse counselling, and some facilities offer fitness club subsidies. The company's quality-based "Inner Circle Awards" recognize employee achievement on the basis of criteria such as customer satisfaction, cost reduction, as well as safety, health, and environmental maintenance. Twice a year, parent Morton International provides other employee awards for continuous improvement. An employee newsletter, *The Salt Licks*, comes out three times a year.

Environmental Management and Performance: Canadian Salt reported an environment code in 1998, but provided no details. Internal personnel in conjunction with a Health and Safety team conduct audits. Public reporting of environmental information is limited to a section of the parent's annual report. A union-management committee, established in 1992, is responsible for recycling, but no Canadian employees have full-time environmental responsibilities. Over the last five years, the company upgraded its airborne emissions collection system, along with a control system for salt dust, and reclamation and purification systems that govern effluent discharges at fine salt operations. Paper, aluminum, and glass are recycled, and pallets re-used. A 102-megawatt co-generation plant, built in 1994, captures steam from manufacturing processes and supplies electricity to its Ontario operations. The Canadian Salt Company reported no NPRI releases from its Belle Plaine, Saskatchewan, or Windsor, Ontario facilities in 1999. Over the past five years, charges for smoke emissions and violations of air and water regulations led to two fines totaling $4,200. Canadian Salt's rock salt operations at the Magdalen Islands site were shut down in 1992 due to a water leakage in the production shaft, but were fully repaired and up to full production by 1997.

Community Responsibilities: While no donation figures were reported, Canadian Salt gives to national charities, such as the United Way, through local offices. Each office receives a philanthropic budget and directs sponsorships through local donations committees. In 1994, the company won a local Innovative Support Award for business and the arts for the salt sculpture competition it ran for visual arts students at the Ojibway Mine.

www.windsorsalt.com

Canbra Foods Ltd

Founded in Lethbridge, Alberta in 1957, Canbra is one of Canada's oldest and largest oilseed processing companies, earning $219 million in annual revenues from the sale of cooking and salad oil, margarine, shortening, canola meal, cooking sprays, popping oil, popcorn topping, and other oil products. There also are bulk sales of edible oils to food manufacturers. Canbra's oil plant and oilseed crushing facility is still one of Lethbridge's largest employers. The last company-owned grain elevator (in Prince Albert, Saskatchewan) was closed in 1997, the year Canbra also sold a packaging plant and warehouse in Butte, Montana to USJet, a Montana courier company. Between 1996 and 1999, the company was 53% owned by Pocklington Financial Corp., which won a $28 million takeover bid. Some minority shareholders criticized the takeover and voted not to sell their shares. In 1999, the Alberta Treasury Branches seized the Canbra holdings of Pocklington Financial's principal, Peter Pocklington, as recompense for his defaulting on loan payments. His stake was subsequently sold to James Richardson International Ltd. The company is now a wholly-owned subsidiary of James Richardson International Ltd, the largest subsidiary of James Richardson & Sons, a privately-owned, family-controlled, Canadian company.

2001 Revenues: No information
Grocery Store Sales: No information
Brands: Canola Harvest, Greensplus, Lakeland, Liquid Gold, Rimini, Romana, Tasty Fry
Corporate Status: Wholly-owned in Canada.
Candor: The company gave no responses in 2001, but answered more than 80% of our questions in 1998. Citing that the company is privately owned, and as such does not make much information publicly available, the 2002 spokespeople gave little specific information, but were forthcoming with information that they could provide. Candor is 19%.

Ethical Management and Consumer Relations: The company has no formal code of responsible business practices, although individual policies guide employee decisions on product placement in retail stores and exchange of business gifts. In the mid-1990s, minority shareholders raised questions in the media about majority shareholder, Peter Pocklington's use of Canbra equity as collateral to finance renovations for arenas and stadiums which housed the three professional sports teams he controlled at the time: the NHL's Edmonton Oilers, minor league baseball's Edmonton Trappers, and soccer's Edmonton Drillers. Media articles critically reported that Canbra paid Mr. Pocklington advisory fees of $240,000 in 1994 and 1995. The company now operates under JRI's policies and procedures, but the spokesperson did not specify what those policies included.

2002 Employees Canada: No information   **1997 Employees Canada:** 257

Employee Relations: Canbra staff levels have been stable over the last decade, though no figures were provided for 2001. About 62% of the workforce belongs to the United Food and Commercial Workers union. In 1995, the latest year Canbra reported training figures, the company spent $50,000 ($200 per employee) on education and skills improvement. It offers 100% tuition refunds for outside courses. Profit sharing is reserved for senior managers. The company covers the administrative costs of transactions for a widely offered profit-sharing program. The spokesperson stated that compensation information is not publicly shared by the company.

Equity and Family: The chair of the parent company, James Richardson & Sons Ltd, is a woman. The spokesperson did not provide any other employment figures. Of Canbra's 257 workers in 1997, 59 were women. One woman worked among the company's eight senior managers, six among 24 middle managers, and none sat on the board of directors. Hiring and promotion policies address women, visible minorities, disabled workers, and aboriginals. Sexual harassment protection is covered by a policy and supported by training. According to the spokesperson, Canbra now operates under JRI's policies, which recognize and comply with all federal and provincial regulations.

Progressive Staff: Workplace programs include flexible scheduling, stop-smoking guidance, counselling for substance abuse, and retirement planning. Two post-secondary scholarships for the children of employees are awarded each year to successful applicants.

Sourcing and Trade: Each year, Canbra spends approximately $90 million buying more than 270,000 metric tonnes of canola from contract growers and commercial suppliers, primarily in North America. Canbra's canola is now sourced through Pioneers Grain, a sister company under JRI. Canbra's spokesperson stated that though the company previously sourced from local farmers, policies had changed due to the purchase of the company by JRI. No specific sourcing guidelines were mentioned. The company reports no international operations, although it has direct sales in approximately 15 foreign markets. No policy governing relations in foreign markets has ever been reported.

Environmental Management and Performance: The spokesperson stated that environmental policies and procedures are in place at all JRI operations. Though no specific policies were discussed, the spokesperson commented that JRI's policies ensure compliance with, and in some cases exceed, government standards. No environmental management system was reported, but a staff committee of eight handles environment matters at the Lethbridge facility. Because canola farmers can only seed on the same acreage every three to four years, they must manage crops for long-term economic sustainability. As a result Canbra diversified its product and customer base by introducing a line of vegetable oil-based lubricants sold through Greenland Corp., a joint venture with Calgary-based Control Chemical. No details on the environmental policies of this operation were reported. The Lethbridge facility placed in the high 90-100 percentile (reporting 562,100 kilograms of air releases) among facilities releasing major chemical or waste. The top-ranked release in terms of potential human health risks was N-Hexane. No air releases were reported between 1995 and 1998. Fine paper, cardboard, wood pallets, and plastic packaging are recycled. In 1995, Canbra won the Canadian Feed Industry Association's Environmental Awareness Award.

Community Responsibilities: Major corporate giving by the parent and subsidiaries is conducted through the Richardson Foundation, which focuses its giving on four categories: the performing arts, youth initiatives, education, and environmental initiatives. Small projects related to local operations are conducted through local operations, which have some degree of freedom in terms of donation and sponsorship decisions. No details on specific recipients or donation amounts were provided.

www.canola.com/canbra

Cargill Ltd

Minnesota-based Cargill Inc. was founded in 1865, and is now the largest privately-held company in the world, with 800 locations in 55 countries, controlling close to 25% of the world wheat trade. Canadian operations began when a grain merchandising business was set up in Winnipeg in 1928. Thirty years later, it built a grain handling facility at Baie Comeau, Québec (its first major Canadian investment), followed by the 1971 construction of a rapeseed (now called canola) cleaning plant in North Battleford, Saskatchewan. Today, the subsidiary Cargill Ltd is Canada's largest merchandiser of farm products, supplying agricultural ingredients to other branded food processors. Its 83 locations help transport 10% of western grain, and another 17 locations move approximately 14% of Ontario grain. Revenues come from the processing of malt, canola, flax, fibre, fertilizer, animal feed, and chemicals. In the U.S., Cargill packs meat, mills flour, crushes soybeans, and produces eggs and animal feed.

Annual Revenues: $3 billion (approximately)
Grocery Store Sales: No information
Brands: Few apparent consumer brands, but unbranded meat products are sold in grocery stores. Cargill Nutrena Feeds, Tendercut
Corporate Status: Wholly-owned by American parent.
Candor: Timely answers were given for both drafts of EthicScan's research questionnaires and the fact verification process. Candor is 37%.

Ethical Management and Consumer Relations: Cargill's ethics code is part of its code of conduct. It is translated into the languages spoken at its operations, and is supported by one-hour training sessions and annual sign-offs. The code forbids the exchange of business gifts. The company's human resources director carries out an ethics ombudsperson function. Unlike its sector rival, Archer Daniels Midland, Cargill's American parent was never charged in the infamous 1995 price collusion case involving major corn processors. In 1994, Canadian beef exports were halted for three days after American meat inspectors stopped a company truck that was carrying meat deemed "fecal contaminated". Following the incident, the company took extra steps to protect its meat from contamination, installing a steam pasteurizing process that produces ground beef that is "99.9% bacteria free." A special Corporate Food Safety department sets and ensures safety standards, and according to the company's "Food Safety Policy," suppliers must meet company requirements for raw materials and ingredient safety. The company trains employees on safety issues, maintains an efficient product recall system, and conducts periodic safety audits, both internal and external.

2002 Employees Canada: 5,000   **1991 Employees Canada:** 2,000

Employee Relations: Since 1991, Cargill Inc.'s global workforce has grown from 61,000 to 85,000. The addition of a Chambly, Québec plant was projected to create 1,500 new jobs by 2000. The plant is due to open in late 2002, and will create 600 jobs in its first phase. Six different unions represent more than half of Cargill's workers. Extra staff—between 50 and

100 temporary workers—are hired during peak seasons. In 1995, about 600 workers staged a strike over wages, closing the Etobicoke, Ontario plant for approximately 10 days. Two years later, in July 1997, 1,600 United Food and Commercial Workers staged a walk-out over wages and working conditions. Until a tentative deal was reached in August, the company used replacement workers to operate at 25% capacity. A 1991 unjust dismissal case ruled in favour of a grieving employee, after the judgment found that Cargill's Nutrena Feeds division failed to prove that the complainant could not perform his job without getting sick. The worker received compensation without job reinstatement.

Equity and Family: Two of eight senior managers are women. None sit on the Board of Directors. Equity policies deal with workplace issues facing women, minorities, disabled workers, and aboriginal people, while a separate policy deals with sexual harassment. According to Human Resources Development Canada ratings, based on data submitted by the company, Cargill ranked "good" for members of visible minorities, "poor" for women and persons with disabilities, and "very poor" for aboriginal peoples. The ratings were based on a small-medium sample of 938 employees in 1999. In 1995, Cargill was graded CC (poor) for hiring and promotion of women and aboriginal peoples, BB (fair) for persons with disabilities and BA (good) for those considered visible minorities (AA is the highest possible grade). Cargill's Canadian president served as chairman for the Manitoba branch of the Canadian Council for Native Business. The company provides 35 weeks for maternity leave and 17 weeks for parental leave, as per federal guidelines, but not extended leaves.

Progressive Staff: Confidential counselling services cover financial planning, stress management, substance abuse, retirement planning, and stop-smoking assistance for staff and employees' family members. Wellness training seminars address, among other topics, eldercare. Employees have access to fitness subsidies and a fitness facility (head office only). The company fully reimburses tuition for external courses that develop employees' skills and education. The Cargill Merit Scholarship program allocates $10,000 in total from the head office to a scholarship for children of employees. The award is often split between 4 or 5 recipients. Some operating locations also create their own scholarships independently of this program. Cargill Ltd, known for its decentralized management, receives little direction from its American parent, and senior positions are often filled by internal promotions. Each division has discretionary power to offer employees incentive rewards. Senior and middle managers can participate in a 100% company-sponsored stock option plan.

Sourcing and Trade: Although the Canadian company has no international operations, the parent's code of conduct deals with issues related to child labour standards, exploitation of women, forced labour, health and safety standards, disciplinary practices, freedom of association, collective bargaining, maximum work hours, and setting a living or sustainable wage. However, the spokesperson did not indicate if audits or independent verification on these standards took place for international operations (which include Canada). Cargill is not voluntarily pledged to the United Nations Global Compact, the Caux Principles, the CERES Principles, or other international protocols related to ethical sourcing and trading.

Environmental Management: Since 1991, all operations have followed a corporate environmental policy focused on managing and reducing hazardous wastes and substances. Each year the company uses a combination of internal staff and external experts to audit all facilities (frequency varies according to location size) but all facilities receive at least one per year. Reports from all divisions are made to Canadian management yearly, but only one separate public environmental report has been published (in 1993). A second one is planned. Three employees have full-time environmental responsibility, and four committees run programs at larger processing facilities. Every location has an emergency response plan that provides information on equipment, emergency services, and appropriate public emergency authorities to be contacted. As part of crop management support, farmers receive instruction on fertilizer applications, including the quantities required by different crops.

Environmental Performance: In 1995, 20.1% of capital expenditures, or $6.2 million, was dedicated to expand three facilities: wastewater treatment at High River, Alberta, a warehouse used for storing 93 pesticides, and hazard monitoring equipment at grain operations. Cargill reports chemical releases and waste emissions to the National Pollutant Release Inventory. In 1999, its Clavet Saskatchewan plant reported an increase in air releases (71.43 tonnes compared with zero releases in 1998). The land release figures were inaccurate on the site that reports NPRI statistics (www.pollutionwatch.com), and were consequently removed. The High River site, with 1999 air releases (4,862 kilograms), land releases (3,726 kilograms) and water releases (167,474 kilograms) ranked in the 80-90 percentile for worst facilities in Canada in terms of major chemical releases or waste. Ammonia placed as the top-ranked release in terms of potential human health risk. At the High River beef rendering plant, paper, cardboard, cans, pallets, and food waste are recycled. Carbon dioxide emissions at the Saskferco Belle Plaine, Saskatchewan plant are recycled, and by 1997 no liquid effluents were being discharged, an achievement the company claimed as a first in the fertilizer industry. In 1999, Health Canada was investigating concerns that consumption of canola, one of Cargill's products, could lead to hypertension or strokes, but no results have yet been made available.

Genetically Modified Ingredients: Cargill's statement on biotechnology, issued in December 1999, maintains that Cargill will accept crops enhanced through modern biotechnology at its processing facilities. The company states that it will continue to accept and market genetically modified crops, conventionally bred crops, and speciality grains. Further, the company will work with farmers and customers to serve premium markets for identity-preserved grains and oilseeds, including niche markets for non-genetically modified crops. Cargill states that genetically modified crops are a powerful tool that may be used to raise living standards by creating distinctive value for farmers and feed and food customers, and the company will continue to support and promote genetically modified crops.

Community Responsibilities: For several years, Cargill's donations have exceeded its Imagine Campaign's pledge to give at least 1% of pre-tax profits to charity over a three year average. Usually the company gives in the 3% to 4% range, even when earnings dip, which places it as one of the higher charitable donors in this Guide. Cargill publishes its donation guidelines, though the Canadian office does not publish an itemized list of recipient groups and amounts, unlike its American parent. Employees help develop a corporate citizenship program, and a three-member donations committee sets charitable giving priorities, with some discretion for individual business units. Specific recipients include the Red Cross, the Terry Fox run, and Big Brothers, along with environmental groups, educational and arts groups. The company matches employee United Way donations with a $2 gift for every $1 donated. External scholarship programs include an Aboriginal business scholarship given to a student at Brandon University, Manitoba, and summer student employment through the University of Manitoba's Aboriginal business education program.

Expansion and Consolidation: Consolidation efforts during the 1990s saw the company buy and absorb the assets of retail fertilizer distributor Cyanamid Canada. Together with the Saskatchewan government, Cargill acquired 50% of a nitrogen fertilizer plant in Belle Plaine, Saskatchewan. It also built a beef processing plant in High River, Alberta (in 1989), before acquiring its Etobicoke, Ontario plant (in 1994). Cargill received government funding for over two decades, including $4 million to construct its Alberta beef processing plant (which in 1998 processed about 3,500 head of cattle per day.) During the same period, the company says that it invested just under $1 billion "in developing Canada's agricultural business." In June, 2001, Cargill announced that it would invest $50 million to build and operate a meat processing plant in Chambly, Québec.

www.cargillfoods.com

Cavendish Farms Ltd

Cavendish Farms, a dominant player in the frozen potato market, sells its products in Canada and abroad. It is the food subsidiary of diversified, privately-held Irving Ltd, the family empire that includes oil, pulp and paper, media, and ship building interests. Approximately 3-4% of Cavendish potatoes come from company farms, but most are sourced from independent farmers in Prince Edward Island, New Brunswick, and Maine. The company has two processing plants in New Annan, PEI.

Revenues: No information
Grocery Store Sales: 20%
Brands: Cavendish Farms
Corporate Status: Wholly-owned subsidiary of Canadian company.
Candor: The corporate spokesperson gave little response in 1998 and no response in 2001. Candor today is 12%.

Ethical Management and Consumer Relations: As a division of Irving, Cavendish Farms follows its parent company's code of ethics, which addresses internal activities, as well as relations and transactions with suppliers and customers. All staff sign this code, which is explained in an employee handbook. In the Maritimes, there is a long history of government subsidies to large family-owned businesses. In the early 1990s, Cavendish Farms and competitor McCain Foods each proposed major potato processing expansion projects. Both received government funds in nearby or adjacent locations, raising questions about duplication and political influence. In 1995, Cavendish invested $75 million in new production facilities and received a $25 million loan (at competitive interest rates) from the Prince Edward Island government. Cavendish Farms planned a second potato processing plant, but had to settle for a compromise when the PEI government decided to offer $10 million each to both Cavendish and McCain to build wastewater plants—and not the facilities each originally wanted. Cavendish Farms eventually built the wastewater plant, upgraded its original plant at New Annan, and then completed a second french fry plant across the road from the original facility.

2002 Employees Canada: No information   **1998 Employees Canada:** 800

Employee Relations: A significant part-time workforce augments Cavendish Farms' full-time staff. No strikes have occurred in the last ten years. In 1990, a union certification controversy arose when a local of the Canadian Auto Workers challenged the United Food and Commercial Workers for the right to represent a unit of workers at Cavendish Farms. The company refused to bargain until a union was chosen, and a collective agreement was eventually reached without a work stoppage. Workplace injuries have decreased over the past 10 years, a trend the company spokesperson attributes to the success of a health and safety committee. It trains employees on handling hazardous materials and addresses injuries associated with repetitive motion tasks, as well as maintaining an internal fire department. An on-site nurse provides rehabilitation therapy among other duties.

Progressive Staff: Employees can access counselling for substance abuse and retirement planning. Expenses for courses taken outside the company are fully reimbursed.

Sourcing and Trade: Cavendish Farms has no international operations and is not pledged to international protocols (such as the United Nations Global Compact, the Caux Principles, or the CERES Principles) that govern labour, living wage, or environmental performance standards with contracted suppliers.

Corporate Concentration: In 1993, Cavendish Farms wanted to increase the land it farmed by 6,000 acres in order to run a three-year crop rotation that used 4,000 acres each year. When the company requested government permission to farm a total of 12,000 acres of potatoes, the Prince Edward Island Federation of Agriculture and the National Farmers Union filed objections to the proposed expansion. At the time, large farms were entitled to no more than 3,000 acres. The opposition came in part from smaller, independent farmers concerned about the effects of vertically-integrated food companies that operate processing plants and corporate farms. The company's farmland allowance did not increase, and today, the company holds only 2,000 acres of land.

Environmental Management and Performance: An Environmental Management Plan is guided and implemented by three environmental committees, and the highest-ranking manager with environmental responsibility is an executive from the parent, J.D. Irving. In recent years, environmental expenditures include $16 million for a new wastewater treatment plant (no breakdown of company spending and government subsidy was provided) that included a third level of waste treatment and a 14-acre wetland beside the plant. This facility addressed problems associated with excessive emissions and nutrient loadings. Cavendish Farms reports chemical releases and transfers to the NPRI. Among Canadian industrial sites, the New Annan plant ranked in the 60-70 percentile in terms of major chemical releases or waste generation. Water releases declined in 1999 (55,280 kilograms of waste) compared with 1997 and 1998 levels. Ammonia was the top ranked pollutant release in terms of potential human health risks. Food waste is converted to animal feed, recycling programs collect paper and cardboard, and some of the company's products are packaged in recyclable containers. While the company noted that some environmental issues are addressed with its suppliers, no details were provided.

Genetically Modified Ingredients: No information

Community Responsibilities: Privately-held Cavendish Farms does not disclose donations figures. Management at Irving works with Cavendish plant committees to determine how charitable funds are allocated. The company extensively sponsors hospitals and healthcare facilities, community projects such as libraries, community baseball tournaments, and other sports events.

www.cavendishfarms.com

Church & Dwight Ltd / Ltee

The Toronto office of Church & Dwight Ltd markets baking soda products made by its parent company, Church & Dwight Company (based in Princeton, New Jersey), which holds 99% of the Canadian company. In 1846, Dr Austin Church invented baking soda as a leavening agent, and today, his family, along with the Dwight family, still holds a significant minority of shares in the company he started. Arm & Hammer is the company's flagship consumer brand, although Church & Dwight also sells bulk quantities of baking soda in industrial markets for use in fire extinguishers, toothpaste, cake mixes, carpet cleaners, sand blasting agents, treating drinking water, detergent, and other cleaning products. Consumer loyalty to its brand was so strong that the company sold its laundry detergent for many years without any advertising. The Canadian manufacturing operations, incorporated in Amherstburg, Ontario in 1937, were closed and converted to a distribution and quality control facility in 1994. In 2001, the company formed a joint venture with USA Detergents, Inc. to develop a laundry detergents partnership called ARMUS.

Revenues: No information
Grocery Store Sales: 66%
Brands: Arm & Hammer, Dental Care, So Clean, Wide Stick
Corporate Status: Wholly-owned by U.S. parent.
Candor: The Canadian unit has a 18% candor quotient.

Ethical Management and Consumer Relations: The company has a code of business practice, but employees do not have to sign it or take any reinforcement training. Formal policies address business gift exchange and product-testing issues.

2002 Employees Canada: 17   **1998 Employees Worldwide:** 950

1991 Employees Worldwide: 1,081

Employee Relations: The company no longer makes products here in Canada. Of 17 full-time Canadian employees in 1998, 14 worked at the Toronto office, and the other three in Amherstburg. Between 1991 and 1996, job cuts claimed 18 Canadian positions.

Equity and Family: In 2000, one of 12 board directors at the parent was a woman (no change from 1996), and zero of eight officers were women (compared with one of 16 in 1996). A formal equity policy guides employment at the parent and Canadian companies. No daycare referrals, flex scheduling, or extended maternity leave packages are available.

Progressive Staff: To enhance employee skills, the company refunds 100% of tuition for staff enrolled in work-related or degree program studies. Because of its small size, Canadian staff cannot adopt many of the parent's programs. While stock option plans are open to key managers and some directors, no other share opportunities are available in Canada. Profit sharing is available in the United States only.

Sourcing and Trade: The parent company owns plants in Venezuela and England. Approximately 95% of total global sales come from the U.S. and Canadian markets. Church and Dwight has never pledged to a code of international standards for labour or environmental conditions.

Environmental Management and Performance: Church and Dwight's environmental code emphasizes pollution prevention. Written and administered by the New Jersey head office, it ensures that internal energy audits assess each plant's performance. The parent employs a Director of Public Affairs and Environmental Management, but responsibility for the company's environmental record rests ultimately with the chairman, who serves as the board's environmental director. In the U.S., energy efficient light fixtures were installed at plants and offices, and new recovery systems reduce water discharges. Because it no longer manufactures product in Canada, Church and Dwight did not provide the National Pollutant Release Inventory with information on waste quantities. Company-wide goals are set for waste reduction, recycling, waste disposal, and production design changes. In North America, Church & Dwight recycles fine paper, cardboard, aluminum cans, bottles, plastic, and wood pallets. Packaging was redesigned in the 1990s, and between 1989 and 1992, the company introduced concentrated refill formats for certain products, and decreased chemical releases by 45%. The Amherstburg quality control center reuses 93% of its solid waste and recycles paper, plastic, and cardboard cartons. In 1992, Church & Dwight won the Council on Economic Priorities' Corporate Conscience Award for Environmental Stewardship (USA).

> **Animal testing:** According to company reports, all labs contracted for product testing must attempt to minimize reliance on animal testing through in-vitro screen tests, existing data on human use, ingredient assessment, and molecular modeling whenever possible. Church & Dwight contributes annually to the Johns Hopkins Centre for Advancement of Alternatives to Animal Testing.

Community Responsibilities: Through different multi-stakeholder partnerships, the American parent contributes to public education and training on environmental issues. In the 1990s, it funded a program on "water curriculum" for students, and a National Audubon Society T.V. special.

www.churchdwight.com

Clearly Canadian Beverage Corporation

Based in Vancouver, and founded in 1986, Clearly Canadian markets a range of natural carbonated and uncarbonated beverages made by other bottling companies from water extracted in Canada. Instead of producing its own product, the company contracts out to independent bottling co-packers in Canada and the U.S. This outsourcing strategy lets Clearly Canadian avoid investing capital in plants. Sales revenue exploded from $4 million in 1988 to $187 million in 1992, then dropped drastically to about $71.4 million in 1996. Canadian and American sales represent about 8% and 80% of total revenue, respectively. In 1999, Clearly Canadian transferred most of its operations to the United States.

2001 Sales Revenues: U.S.$23.3 million
Grocery Store Sales: 55%
Brands: Clearly Canadian Sparkling Flavoured Water, Reebok Fitness Water, Tre-Limone, Clearly Canadian Oxygen enhanced water
Corporate Status: Publicly traded, Canadian-based headquarters.
Candor: The corporate spokesperson gave an extensive response in 1998. Candor is 26%.

Ethical Management and Consumer Relations: While Clearly Canadian has no written code of ethics, a policies and procedures manual covers a number of topics such as equal opportunity, avoiding discrimination and harassment, interpersonal conduct, sexual harassment, workplace safety, conflict of interest, business gift exchange, and confidentiality. Training programs on some of these areas are also outlined. Clearly Canadian was one of the few beverage companies to report having an ombudsperson. However, this function is not independent of the organization, but forms part of the duties assigned to the vice president of legal affairs. A number of court cases have occurred since the 1990s. In July 2000, the British Columbia Securities Commission launched an investigation into allegations of illegal insider trading by Clearly Canadian Beverage Corporation's CEO, Douglas Mason. The case is still pending. An American class action suit against the company was settled in 1997 when a U.S. court approved an award amount of $2.5 million. Complications between the company and its insurer, Coronation Insurance, led to a dispute over the allocation of settlement and defense costs. In another case, Clearly Canadian lost a breach of contract suit to Blue Mountain Springs and was hit with $5.9 million in damages. The company appealed and subsequently settled all issues when it agreed to buy all of Blue Mountain's shares, thereby dissolving all outstanding litigation and appeals.

2002 Employees Canada: 26   **1991 Employees Worldwide:** 36

Employee Relations: Including offices in the U.S. and abroad, the company employs only a few dozen people. The total grew from 36 in 1991 to 76 employees in 1996 before dropping to 57 in 1998, including 51 Canadians. None belong to unions. The proportion of Canadians dropped following the transfer of key operations to the U.S. in 1999. The one unjust dismissal case over the last ten years was dismissed and the company awarded legal costs. Directors, officers and key employees can receive interest-free loans for the purchase of company shares. All employees can participate in a stock option plan—in which the company pays 100% of the stock value acquired—along with a 100%-funded profit sharing plan based upon a bonus structure. In the face of a $5.6 million net loss in 1994, the company's ten-member executive team was criticized for their high salaries, bonuses and perks. As part of a retirement plan deemed "controversial" in media articles, the company deposited $385,524 to the CEO's retirement account. The company spokesperson responded that the company pays a net after-tax funding premium, as required by the terms of the plan, which contains both a life insurance component and a retirement fund component. Consequently, the amount deposited to the account was derived from a contribution formula based on each executive's compensation level and the rate of return earned from deposits to the plan.

Equity and Family: In 2002, there are 12 female employees in total, including two managers. The company does not offer same sex couples benefits, but has an employment equity policy, along with minority and disabled hiring program that is monitored by a formal compensation committee of the board. Flexible scheduling and extended maternity leaves are available, along with retirement planning assistance.

Progressive Staff: As part of the company's health plan, employees can receive substance abuse counselling and annual flu vaccinations. Directors and officers are offered a fitness club subsidy. In 2001, the company spent $5,000 on training. Tuition and course expenses are fully reimbursed.

Sourcing and Trade: No information on human rights standards for co-packers or other contractors is provided. The company has never reported operating in developing nations, although suppliers may source fruits and flavourings from them.

Environmental Management and Performance: With no company-owned manufacturing plants, Clearly Canadian has no environmental code. It updates and distributes an operations manual with environmental standards to its co-packers. The spokesperson commented that " in many ways, the company is a third party to environmental policies." Internal auditors, guided by advice from outside consultants, conduct quarterly inspections at spring water well sites and bi-annual ones at bottling plants. The company reports office recycling programs. Its bottles and cans are all recyclable. The company says it participates and complies with container deposit regulations and programs, but did not indicate if 30% of its bottles were refillable, a threshold once required in Ontario.

Community Responsibilities: Clearly Canadian usually donates cash and products worth about $100,000 to a variety of charitable causes. Recipients are located in Vernon, British Columbia and Formosa, Ontario (where well sites operate), the lower mainland of B.C., and other locations in Canada and the United States. Specific recipients include the B.C. Children's Hospital ($50,000 over five years), a Girl Guide Camp in Vernon, B.C., women's shelters, and food banks that receive product donations. Water donations were distributed during natural disasters that hit B.C., Florida, Manitoba, and North Dakota.

Employees participated in a public education video on recycling that Clearly Canadian co-funded with Consumer's Gas.

www.clearly.ca

Clorox Company of Canada Limited

The Clorox Co. of Canada is a wholesale distributor of products made by its parent, The Clorox Company (USA), a publicly held international corporation. Clorox brands generate US$4.1 billion from annual sales in 94 countries. Its flagship product, Clorox liquid bleach, was first introduced to Americans in 1916. Today, more than 30 plants throughout the world employ 5,300 employees who manufacture a range of Clorox products. In Canada, two regional centres distribute Clorox products, while two newly-purchased manufacturing facilities, bought in 1999 and 2001, are located in the Greater Toronto Area. A Clorox-owned plant in Moose Jaw, Saskatchewan was closed in 1994.

Revenues: No information
Grocery Store Sales: No information
Brands: Armourall, Brita, Black Flag, Clorox Cleanup, Clorox Liquid Bleach, Hidden Valley, Impact, Jets, Kingsford, Kitchen Bouquet, Lestoil, Liquid Plumber, Pine Sol, Softscrub, SOS, Tilex
Corporate Status: Wholly-owned by U.S. parent company.
Candor: A spokesperson from the American office supplied many policy documents and reports, and offered responses to many of EthicScan's questions. Candor is 29%.

Ethical Management and Consumer Relations: A two-page *Ethics and Standards* statement defines proprietary information or trade secrets and identifies possible misapplications, along with conflicts of interest, insider trading, and inappropriate business gift exchange. During the first quarter of each year, corporate officers assign questionnaires to key managers to gauge employee compliance with its terms. Should alleged breaches of the code arise, employees are required to deal with legal counsel. The statement was last updated in 2001 as part of the Canadian President's annual update, review, and sign-off. A set of "Corporate Responsibility" policies address the company's obligations toward product safety, advertising, workplace health and safety, hiring practices, and social responsibility. As part of its advertising guidelines, Clorox avoids sponsoring television shows that display "gratuitous sex and violence," or "disparages ethnic, religious or political groups, distorts factual content, or glorifies drug and alcohol consumption." In August 1997, the company's QuickSilver auto cleaning product was connected to the death of a Canadian child. In response, the company recalled stock of the product, halted production, and set up a toll-free number for consumers.

2002 Employees Canada: 162   **1991 Employees Canada:** 84

Employee Relations: Unlike many companies profiled in this book, Clorox Canada's employment levels grew between 1991 and 1996, from 84 to 162 workers. The proportion of workers who belong to unions (10%) is the same in Canada and the U.S., with the Steelworkers representing most of the Canadian bargaining unit. No strikes occurred in the last ten years. The non-unionized steel wool-making facility was closed in 1994 when the

S.O.S. and Jet soap pad lines were consolidated in the U.S. Of the 54 workers laid off, one-third qualified for early retirement, and the rest received career counselling. In 1995, Clorox spent $49,000 ($700 per employee) on skills and knowledge development of its Canadian staff. Through a share ownership purchase plan, all full-time employees are reimbursed for transaction costs associated with purchasing company stock. Approximately 200 managers are eligible for stock options, and all non-unionized locations participate in the "Value Sharing" bonus, a program based on divisional performance.

Health and Safety: At Clorox's U.S. facilities, the "Lost Time Rate" (the working time employees miss after an accident) fell 48% between 1993 and 1994. Because eight American Clorox plants handle chlorine, a potentially dangerous chemical, the company set its safety and operating standards jointly with the federal Environmental Protection Agency.

Equity and Family: In Canada, two of seven managers and 63 of 162 employees are women. An equal opportunity policy states that Clorox does not consider a candidate's minority status when hiring. Instead, the company embraces "equality of opportunity in all aspects of recruitment, hiring, employment and advancement." This policy ensures protection against harassment, the terms for hiring people with disabilities, and guarantees protection for whistleblowers. In 1998, the U.S. parent had a program that sought to increase the number of Clorox-contracted businesses run by proprietors who are women or who identify as ethnic minorities. Employees responsible for purchasing must "actively seek and develop" these contracts. A Manager of Diversity, assisted by other human resources employees, designs and tracks the success of these programs. Excepting one plant in the U.S., all Clorox offices have barrier-free access for the disabled. Definitions and procedures for reporting incidents of sexual harassment are set out in a two-page policy, which a group of HR managers reviews each year.

Progressive Staff: Flex-scheduling options along with extended maternity leaves are available, though the latter must be taken without pay. The company began providing benefits for same sex couples in 2000. Assistance for substance abuse, career planning, and stop-smoking courses are offered at one of two sites in Canada through an Employee Assistance Plan. Training for repetitive stress injury, ergonomics, and wellness is offered. Up to 100% of total tuition expenses are reimbursed if the course is career related and successfully completed.

Sourcing and Trade: The company's 11,000 global employees manufacture products at more than 70 plants, and sell products in more than 80 countries worldwide. A one-page policy on standards of conduct for international management does not address sourcing, supply chain, and trading issues abroad. As a general practice, the company sources 100% of its inputs from Canada, the U.S., and Germany.

Environmental Management and Performance: Clorox Canada follows its parent's environmental code. Each year, an internal chlorine specialist works with divisional and plant engineers to conduct audits and ensure compliance with standards. Between 1994 and 1995, the last year for which data was reported, 12 environmental and 13 health-and-safety audits covered all company plants. No major compliance problems were discovered. Environmental management of product development, manufacturing, and packaging issues rests with a Vice-President, a Director, and three managers. A steering committee brings together representatives from key business units and departments. Limited information on environmental issues is reported in annual reports. Clorox has reported total environmental releases of 500 kilograms from its Moose Jaw, Saskatchewan site, down from 610 kilograms in 1998. The Moose Jaw facility ranks in the 10-20 percentile in terms of major chemical releases or waste generation for facilities in Canada. Clorox has taken a number of steps to reduce packaging and process waste. More than 27% of the glass, paper, and plastic used in Clorox packaging is derived from post-consumer recycled materials. The glass content for bottles of Hidden Valley salad dressing (one of the company's only food products) was reduced by 27% in the early 1990s while its recycled content increased to 25%. Re-designed display pallets used in warehouse club stores accommodate a greater number of bottles and reduce cardboard content in shipping boxes by 250,000 pounds per year. In the mid-1990s, recycled content for corrugated cardboard packaging averaged 35%, up from 30% in 1993. Between 1992 and 1994, the post-consumer recycled plastic content on three major products went from five million pounds to 16 million pounds. Clorox also works with its suppliers to increase recycled materials usage and to reduce packaging waste. A Canadian President of Clorox has sat on the board of CIPEC, an energy efficiency program, and has also served as chair of Corporations Supporting Recycling (CSR) and the Waste Diversion Organization (WDO) for resource conservation, waste reduction, commodity, and workplace recycling. Clorox won five environmental awards over the last ten years.

Animal Testing: "Very little" animal testing is conducted, the company reports, because most ingredient information is furnished by data banks which track chemical content. Financial support goes to a center for alternative testing at Johns Hopkins University, and the company says that its research staff assist industry and regulatory groups in the search for alternatives to animal testing.

Managing a Corporate Reputation: Clorox's name recognition is built on bleach products. Like other companies whose brands were built on products that come with potential or perceived threats, Clorox devised information campaigns in the 1990s to deal with these concerns. The company reports that chlorine is a raw ingredient in household bleach used in low concentrations as part of a sodium hypochlorite solution that accounts for 5.25% of total product content. Liquid bleach is an inorganic solution that breaks down quickly—primarily into salt and water—and that it does not build up in the environment. In the proper doses, chlorine is approved for disinfecting drinking water. The spokesperson indicated that the company does not sell its bleach product in Canada, therefore information related to bleach products and their testing relates to the American parent, Clorox USA.

Community Responsibilities: Between 1980 and 1995, Clorox donated a total of US$30.3 million, including money generated by its Foundation's endowment of US$4.5 million. The Foundation prefers to support innovative programs that it can help nurture during their developmental stages. Funds go to youth and public education (27%), community service programs (25%), employee gift campaigns (18%), and local civic causes (13%). In the mid-1990s, contributions ranging between US $2 and 3 million annually were distributed to over 600 agencies in communities where Clorox employees live and work. Paid staff members are seconded to not-for-profit organizations—in 1995, 650 employees volunteered over 65,000 hours at 605 agencies—and the company matches donations to charities and educational institutions. According to the spokesperson, Canadian operations are involved in their host communities. In the USA, Clorox donates bleach products on a regular basis to groups like the American Red Cross and other organizations working to clean and purify water supplies polluted after natural disasters. The company donates other products such as charcoal, insect repellent, and control bait systems to non-profit groups. It has contributed to six American education projects, including student clean-ups, conservation initiatives at Lake Merritt, and to the group, Science Education for Public Understanding. In 1993, the company received a Corporate Conscience Award for Community Involvement from the Council on Economic Priorities (now called the Center for Responsibility in Business).

www.clorox.com

Coca-Cola Bottling Company

Coca-Cola is so omnipresent that its logo allegedly is more recognizable worldwide than the Christian crucifix. First sold to Canadians in 1892, Coke began production here in 1905. The Coca-Cola Bottling Company (CCB), formerly Coca-Cola Beverages Ltd., operates in all ten Canadian provinces, producing, selling, and distributing carbonated beverages, fruit beverages and juices, still waters, isotonic beverages, and iced teas. CCB operates eight production facilities and approximately 60 sales, distribution, and other facilities. Acquired in 1997, CCB is the Canadian operating division of American parent, Coca-Cola Enterprises (CCE). CCE is traded on the New York Stock Exchange, with the Coca-Cola Company owning approximately 40% of its shares. Coca-Coca Ltd. (CCL) is a separate entity that is responsible for brand marketing and consumer promotions, and employs about 80 people in five offices across Canada.

> **2000 Revenues:** No information (CCB)
> **Grocery Store Sales:** No information
> **Brands:** A&W Root Beer, Barq's Cream Soda, Barq's Diet Root Beer, Barq's Root Beer, Coca-Cola Classic, Dasani water, Diet Coke, caffeine-free Diet Coke, Diet Sprite, Fresca, Five Alive beverages, Fruitopia fruit beverages, Minute Maid juices, Nestea iced teas, Planet Java Coffee beverages, POWERade sports drinks and Sprite
> **Corporate Status:** Wholly-owned by publicly-traded U.S. parent company.
> **Candor:** The company had a 58% candor quotient.

Ethical Management and Consumer Relations: Honour Roll. Coca-Cola Bottling Company's Ethics Code and Competition Act Compliance Policy explicitly prohibit illegal activities (such as bribes, illegal payments, and price-fixing) that arise in the food and beverage industry. The company's product-recall protocol includes toll-free consumer phone lines,

> **A Detailed Code of Ethics:** Coke expects employees to: avoid situations that could create conflicts of interest; comply with laws and regulations; not accept inappropriate gifts; not give gifts of over $25 (without approval); refuse bribes, influence payments or kickbacks; refuse illegal payments to government officials; not seek reimbursement for political donations; avoid insider trading; keep company information confidential; and stay off alcohol and drugs while at work. Transactions must be carried out according to explicit billing procedures, including those made to outside countries. Adherence to the code and compliance policy is monitored. Breaches or failures to report known breaches, are subject to disciplinary action. The code and compliance policy is translated into all languages spoken at Coke operations, and employees must sign-off on them. Formal employee input is gathered for the code's creation and evaluation. Staff and manager evaluations include an assurance that each person complies with the code of conduct.

and a consumer safety assurance system that is more rigorous than required by regulation. In June 2001, CCB's bottling operations were being audited for unpaid taxes related to transactions that took place between 1990 and 1997. The Canadian Customs and Revenue Agency (C.C.R.A) examined transfer pricing methods used by Coca-Cola in relation to the Canadian company's purchase of concentrate from a Puerto Rico-based subsidiary. By charging higher prices for the concentrate, the company in Puerto Rico experienced higher profits while the Canadian company would have faced lower taxable earnings. The case could involve up to $100 million in back taxes. In relation to this case, the 2001 spokesperson said the company was unable to comment on the actions of previous management, as the incidents occurred prior to current ownership.

2002 Employees Canada: 5,700   **1996 Employees Canada:** 4,400

Employee Relations: Following a July 2001 restructuring, 3% of CCB employees (170 of 5,700) were laid off, primarily in management and support departments. Prior to this cut, the company had not seen permanent layoffs in five years. In fact, employment at CCB had grown by 30%, much of it through the addition of 600 new sales, development, and management positions in 1997 and 1998. Between 1992 and 1996, total jobs fell 13% from 3,955 to 3,500. In 1995, 22 Windsor workers, with an average age of 48 years, negotiated a deal to save their jobs when they agreed to chop $3 from their hourly wage rates over three years. The company had planned to close the warehouse as part of reorganization, but these worker concessions helped save the facility. During the early 1990s, CCB closed eight of its 16 Canadian production facilities (three in Ontario), and cut its storage capacity from 68 warehouses to 29, to improve efficiency. When layoffs occur, CCB provides redeployment, retraining, job search assistance, and severance packages beyond the government minimum. The company manages 47 collective agreements, negotiated by three unions including the United Food and Commercial Workers (UFCW), covering 80% of its workforce. The company was one of few that reported two uncommon employment statistics: its outsourcing activity—less than 5% of production is contracted out—and employee turnover rate (7%), both of which are low for this industry. Over the past four years the company experienced four work stoppages, most recently in July 2001, when 100 UFCW workers at CCB's Weston production plant walked out, demanding job security, improvements in wages, benefits, and working conditions. A new collective agreement was ratified by August 2001. In 1995, a three-day strike over job security, pensions and wages involved 400 Toronto workers. Production at other Toronto plants was affected, and the union said some replacement workers crossed picket lines. The spokesperson noted that negotiations with the UFCW during this three-day strike were "always subject to good faith bargaining." The UFCW also tried to keep the company from moving 30 distribution jobs from Peterborough to Cobourg, Ontario. When the move to Cobourg did occur, a union lawyer was reported to have commented that many of the workers not offered jobs were senior people working at higher wage levels. At East York, Coke agreed to invest $1 million in the plant while the union conceded to an early retirement plan. A health and safety committee allows union and management to address issues jointly. Bottling facilities meet or exceed municipal requirements for water quality, and each plant maintains its own filtration equipment. All products meet the requirements of the Health Protection Branch and the Canadian Food Inspection Agency.

Equity and Family: Three of 10 senior managers and one of 13 board directors are women. Women hold approximately 51% of the jobs at head operations, and represent about 20% of the overall workforce (excluding trucking jobs). The company says it seeks qualified applicants for employment without regard to race, colour, religion, sex, sexual orientation, age, citizenship status, handicap, disability, or any other unlawful basis. It offers extended maternity leave and paternity leave, no money beyond provisions required by government regulations. Training reinforces an anti-harassment policy (covering gender, sexual orientation, race, and disability), and managers receive training on diversity issues. The code of conduct, which employees must sign, includes a commitment to diversity.

Progressive Staff: In early 2000, CCB introduced an Employee Assistance Program for all full-time employees. This confidential, third party provider, counselling and referral program addresses substance dependency, marital issues, financial advice, stress management, and smoking cessation. Employees provide feedback on internal practices through external verifiers who conduct interviews and surveys. In 2001, Coke spent approximately $1 million to train Canadian employees, the same level it spent in 1995. The company refunds all tuition costs according to pre-set guidelines. At some locations, employees with certain job descriptions can apply for flex-scheduling, work-at-home arrangements, job sharing, and compressed schedules. Hourly employees are guaranteed compensation for time worked in excess of 40 hours, while salaried employees obtain this protection through a supervisor's approval. Coca-Cola Bottling Company (including Canada) provides two types of investment plans for employees: an Employee Savings and Investment Plan (ESIP) and a Share Purchase Program (ESSP). Through the ESIP, employees with one year of service may purchase investments of up to 10% of their earnings (the company matches 50% up to a 7% employee contribution limit).

Sourcing and Trade: Whenever feasible, ingredients and packaging are sourced in Canada. The company supports local suppliers of equipment, vehicles, packaging, and ingredients. One ingredient is consistently sourced outside of Canada: the proprietary formula for its carbonated drink, available only through the Coca-Cola Company. The parent has operations in nearly 200 countries worldwide. Coca-Cola Enterprises (which owns 100% of CCB), operates in the United States, Canada, Britain, France, the Netherlands, Belgium, Monaco and Luxembourg. CCE has one of the largest American corporate stakes in the Chinese market, having invested $500 million in 16 bottling locations and seven facilities in mainland China.

Environmental Management: Environment, health, and safety policies are outlined in the corporate code of conduct and in standard operating procedures. Last updated in 1998, the code is backed up with employee training and sign-off. The policy mandates operating facilities in compliance with all environmental laws, regulations, and permits, including those governing the control, transportation, storage and disposal of regulated chemicals and substances (air emissions, waste water, solid waste, hazardous waste and storm water are included in "Regulated Materials"). In 1998, a new system for emergency preparedness set standard operating procedures for environmental spills and other incidents, including Special Points of Contact for each facility in the country. Together with CCB, CCL provides guidance, instruction, and an operating manual to CCB, and an Environment, Health, and Safety Policy at CCB provides training to employees. Some audits are carried out on a regular basis, although locations and timing details were not specified. Emission reduction targets are set as part of process development and product design procedures. Public environmental reports do not address or set targets beyond regulatory requirements, but they do report on progress to date. Two environmental reports go to the board twice a year. In Canada, ten personnel assume environmental responsibilities, including the president, vice-president of public affairs, general manager, and at least one staff member at each location, who spend more than half their time managing environmental matters. Between $1-2 million was spent on waste and energy initiatives in 1998.

Environmental Performance: According to the National Pollutant Release Inventory, Coca-Cola releases no major chemicals from any of its eight facilities (Calgary, Richmond, BC, Winnipeg, three Toronto sites, Trois-Rivières and Lachine, Québec). CCB's commitment to waste reduction and conservation methods includes adherence to Coca-Cola Company's corporate environmental system, Ekosystem. As a member of Corporations Supporting Recycling, it participates in every province's beverage container recycling program. In Ontario, CCB is one of the single largest corporate contributors to municipal recycling programs. Along with recycling paper, cans, bottles, and pallets, Coke reclaims materials from vending machines and applies them to other uses. Post-consumer plastic is ground into pellets that are used in the tool and die industry, metal is sent to scrap dealers, and refrigerant is recovered and re-used. Coca-Cola began using 10% recycled content in about one-third of its containers, and has engaged stakeholders on a variety of recycling issues.

Community Responsibilities: CCB is not pledged to the Imagine Campaign, which requires an average of 1% pre-tax earnings to be donated to charity. CCE contributed about $25 million in cash to charitable organizations (80% of total) and about $6 million in product donations (20%). Major 2000 donations went to the United Way, the Diabetes Research Foundation/Juvenile Diabetes Foundation of Canada, the Canadian Special Olympics, and many Canadian colleges and universities. Employees may give both paid and unpaid time donations to charitable causes, and the company loans its facilities to community agencies. Employee involvement in the community includes company-sponsored events such as the Juvenile Diabetes Foundation Walk for the Cure. CCB recognizes outstanding employee community service through a quarterly "Hall of Fame Award." CCB also provides training on community leadership to all local sales managers.

www.coca-cola.com

Colgate-Palmolive Canada Inc

The Colgate-Palmolive Company's Canadian subsidiary manufactures personal care and household goods at factories in Alberta, Ontario and New Brunswick. As one of the world's largest personal care product makers, Colgate sells US$9.4 billion worth of its goods annually in over 200 world markets. The company has augmented its product selection over the last 10 years, acquiring deodorant maker Mennen Co. and bleach maker Javex Company. In Canada, some private label manufacturing is done for household care products.

2000 Revenues: $200 million

Grocery Stores Sales: No information

Brands: ABC, Afta, Arctic Power, Ajax, Bio-Aid, Colgate, Fleecy, Glide, Irish Spring, Javex, Mennen, Palmolive, Skin Bracer, Speed Stick

Corporate Status: Wholly-owned by U.S. parent company.

Candor: The company answered 32% of questions.

Ethical Management and Consumer Relations: The parent company's *Code of Conduct Partnership Principles*, which is modified for Canadian operations, was last revised in 2000. Applicable to all subsidiaries, it requires an annual sign-off from Canadian directors, officers and other key employees who must ensure that all employees have reviewed the code at least once each year. Managers are mandated to create "a climate where employees can discuss legal and ethical issues freely." The code's most recent revision incorporated Colgate policies and practices that previously had not been formalized or written down. The *Principles* advise employees on issues like conflicts of interest, accepting gifts, trade secrets, and proprietary information. Suppliers are to be treated in a fair and uniform manner, and are selected based on price, quality, reliability, and integrity. Product advertising must not mislead or contain stereotypes, and should not be aired on programs the company deems excessively "sexual, violent, or antisocial." The company has a form of whistleblower protection, though no details were provided. The company's Business Practices Function audits compliance, trains employees, responds to questions about code guidelines, investigates reported violations, and monitors enforcement as well as legislative and regulatory changes that might affect the Code. This function periodically reports to senior management.

2002 Employees Canada: 500   **2000 Employees Worldwide:** 28,000

Employee Relations: Unionized workers at the Toronto and Edmonton plants represent approximately 20% of the total Canadian workforce. In 1995, the parent, Colgate-Palmolive Company, cut 3,000 employees (8.5% globally) at the managerial and factory levels. Total employment was slashed by a third (from 42,800 to 28,000) between 1984 and 1995. The Toronto area workforce lost 61 jobs in 1993 when Mennen and Javex plants were consolidated and reorganized, in addition to 260 cuts in 1991 and 1992. As policy, the company gives laid-off employees benefits, severance packages exceeding government requirements, and job-search assistance. In 1995, global training expenditures were $150 million. More than 16,000 workers participate in over 70 formal training programs around the world, and tuition costs are reimbursed fully.

Equity and Family: In Canada, one of four board directors and two of seven senior managers are women. The *Code of Conduct* states that employees are selected on the basis of their qualifications and without discrimination. A sexual harassment policy, supported by periodic training is part of the *Code of Conduct*. In the U.S., an affirmative action program has trained, educated employees, and offered promotion opportunities. In 1994, Colgate-Palmolive won recognition as "one of the best employers for working mothers" from *Working Women*. The same year, Colgate-Palmolive was listed in *The Best Companies for Minorities* (USA). In the early 1990s, in Canada, the Ontario Workers Compensation Tribunal awarded a black woman compensation benefits for the psychological effects she suffered following six years of racial and sexual harassment at a Colgate-Palmolive plant. It found that management did not intervene adequately to stop the persistently aggressive behaviour of the woman's co-workers. The company dropped its bid to appeal the ruling, and the compensation award was the first in Ontario to recognize the psychological effects of such harassment.

Progressive Staff: Innovative employee ideas are rewarded through the "You Can Make a Difference" program, offered in over 100 countries. Only executives and select senior managers benefit from a stock option plan. Staff support includes fitness club subsidies and stop-smoking programs. In North America, virtual meetings link over 100 locations via videoconference, allowing employees to listen and ask questions as senior managers review business results. Individual workers can set their own flexible schedules.

Sourcing and Trade: The parent company manufactures in more than 60 countries, including the Philippines, Mexico, India, and Vietnam, and holds distribution and production agreements in dozens of others, such as Russia and the Ukraine. In 2000, the parent company announced a new majority-owned joint venture with Sanxiao, the leading toothbrush maker in China. The company's Business Practices policy sets guidelines for procuring and selling internationally, and for acceptable labour and environmental standards. Colgate states that it "practices and seeks to work with business partners who promote" equal opportunity for all employees, a healthy workplace, a living wage, the opportunity to develop skills, freedom of association, and community and government involvement. No comments were made on standards, guarantees, or verification or what action management will take if they are not met. Grounds for terminating a business relationship with suppliers include: the exploitation of children, physical punishment, female abuse, involuntary servitude, or other abuse.

Environmental Management and Performance: A global Colgate-Palmolive Environmental Policy covers activities at all business units. If an affiliate operates in a country where legal regulations are less stringent than company standards, then the corporate policy takes precedence. The policy commits the company to continuously evaluate environmental impacts of products and production residues, to minimize environmental risk when products are reformulated, and to reduce product volumes through higher formula concentrations. The environmental effects of solid wastes and facility discharges to the air and water are reviewed periodically, but the company did not report who carries out these reviews, or how frequently they occur. A board steering committee reports on environmental matters twice a year. A Vice-President of worldwide issues is the most senior officer responsible for the environment. Volumes for NPRI substances were reported at three of its four sites. The volume of chemical releases and waste generated from the company's Edmonton plant (a total of 12 kilograms of environmental releases), along with the Moncton (five kilograms) and Toronto (25 kilograms) facilities, rank in the 0-10 percentile (low volume) of all facilities in Canada, while the Mississauga facility reported zero NPRI releases. Colgate-Palmolive Canada's toxic chemicals emissions volumes rank well below the industry average. Like other soap-making companies, Colgate-Palmolive introduced concentrated formula packages for various products in the early 1990s. When one product was converted from conventional plastic bottles to pouches, packaging contents fell by 80%. In the same period, the company began a "backhaul" program with vendors and customers, which reduced transportation volume, and consequently, fuel wastage, and costs.

Animal Testing: In 1999, Colgate-Palmolive declared a voluntary moratorium on all animal testing for Personal Care products designed for adults, and the ingredients used in those products. Excluded from this moratorium are products classified as drugs or pharmaceuticals, products subject to specific regulatory requirements, and products intended for oral application. The company states that it "will maintain the option of using animals for this category when we cannot find other appropriate means to insure the safety of our consumers and our people." No statistics are given on how many animals have been used for testing Colgate products or ingredients before or after the moratorium. No animal testing occurs in Canada, and all testing labs in the U.S. were closed in 1989. By the early 1990s, the company had donated more than $4 million to lab space and research for alternative testing methods, such as in vitro technology and the Choriallantoic Membrane Test (CAM), which uses the membrane of a fertilized chicken egg to predict eye irritation. When no acceptable alternative is available, and testing must be contracted out, the company states that only procedures that "do not cause pain or distress" are used, and anesthesia is administered when appropriate.

Genetically Modified Ingredients: No information

Community Responsibilities: In 1997, the last year charitable information was reported, Colgate-Palmolive Canada gave $90,000 (corporate and employee donations), exceeding the $80,000 given in 1996, and $77,000 in 1995. Although not a policy, the company attempts to exceed its previous year's donations level. Typically, funds go toward a scholarship fund for employees' children, athletic events and leagues, health and medical education, and local school support. In the mid-1990s, the United Way gave Colgate-Palmolive a Platinum Award, acknowledging both employee (a 97% participation rate) and company donations. Between 1996 and 1998, the company donated personal care products and bleach (for water purification) on three occasions to natural disaster victims in Manitoba, Québec, Ontario and New Brunswick. In 1995, the parent company won a major award for community involvement from the Council on Economic Priorities (USA).

www.colgate.com

ConAgra Grocery Products

ConAgra's corporate predecessor, Hunt Wesson, first sold products in Canada during the 1930s through a British Columbia food brokerage company known as Oppenheimer. After closing the Tilbury, Ontario plant in 1991, the company ended its manufacturing presence in Canada. Today, 96% of ConAgra products are imported and distributed by a national network of brokers who are managed from a sales, marketing, and logistics office in Don Mills, Ontario. The only products processed in Canada are a pasta sauce (packed in Québec) and some canned tomato products (in south-western Ontario). Hunt Wesson Inc. changed its name to ConAgra Foods Grocery Foods Group, and is now, along with four other groups (Frozen Foods Group, Dairy Foods Group, Snack Foods Group, and Refrigerated Foods Group) part of the ConAgra Foods Retail Products Company, a division of ConAgra Foods, Inc. Worldwide, the parent company, ConAgra of Omaha, Nebraska, sells US$274 billion of products every year.

Revenues: No information

Grocery Store Sales: No information

Brands: Chef Boyardee, Healthy Choice Pasta Sauce, Hunt's, Manwich, Orville Redenbacher, Pam Cooking Spray, Puritan, Snack Pack, VH Sauces

Corporate Status: Wholly-owned by U.S.-based parent company.

Candor: The company answered only 23% of questions.

Ethical Management and Consumer Relations: The parent company has a written code of ethics, its 21 page *Code of Conduct*, which covers topics such as diversity, harassment, workplace safety, drug and alcohol use, consumer relations, competition, confidential information, conflicts of interest, legal and environmental compliance, political activities, sourcing and trading, as well as reporting, investigation, and discipline for breaches of the code.

2002 Employees Canada: 333

Employee Relations: In 1998, 15 Canadian employees—nine in Toronto and six in Tilbury—worked on a salaried basis. That year, the parent, ConAgra, reported 82,169 staff, a drop of 1% from 83,123 in 1996. When the Canadian company closed the Tilbury plant in 1991, 57 jobs were lost. Support for employee development includes full tuition reimbursements for job-related courses, and training expenditures of $100 per year. Senior managers in Canada participate in an incentive plan as part of their compensation.

Equity and Family: In 1998, one of nine managers and seven of the 15 Canadian staff were women. At the parent company, two of 13 directors are women but only six of the 80 officers listed in the annual report are women. In 1998, two of 16 directors were women as were three senior managers.

Progressive Staff: The corporate spokesperson reported an open door management policy, but no details were provided on how this was guaranteed or supported.

Sourcing and Trade: The Canadian company apparently imports much of the products it sells here. The Canadian company has no foreign operations; the parent company is active in 32 countries worldwide. The parent's *Code of Conduct* includes statements on operating in foreign countries, but no specific information on sourcing from repressive regimes.

Environmental Management and Performance: With no manufacturing in Canada, ConAgra does not report any chemical releases and transfers to the National Pollutant Release Inventory. Beyond the recycling of office paper, cardboard, cans, and glass, the corporate spokesperson says that environmental policies do not really apply to operations in Canada.

Genetically Modified Ingredients: No current information is supplied despite the company's reliance on pasta, popcorn, grain, and related products. In 1999, the parent company announced a joint marketing agreement with Monsanto Company for ConAgra to accept corn that has been developed through the use of biotechnology from U.S. producers. ConAgra reported that it would separate or "identity preserve" genetically modified corn for sale in markets where GM corn has been approved for use or import.

Community Responsibilities: The parent company contributes 1% of pre-tax earnings to more than 300 non-profit groups in the USA. Its "Objectives and Results" policy includes a commitment to charitable donations. Typically, the company targets education, health, the arts, culture, and civic organizations. The parent company began an American initiative in 2000 called Feeding Children Better through which nearly 100 trucks have been donated to local food banks in the U.S., and over 60 Kids Cafes have been funded to help deal with child hunger. In the U.S. the parent company also awards grants to certain operations, whose employees choose a local environmental project or program to support. The children of employees can apply for post-secondary scholarships. Nature Conservancy, an environmental project in central Nebraska, received $262,500 from the company in the mid-1990s. In 1996, the ConAgra Foundation began matching employees' gifts to colleges and universities (a program open to Canadian employees). In the mid-1990s, two Canadian employees volunteered paid time to Meals on Wheels, while a senior executive was seconded on a part-time basis to the United Way in 1997.

www.conagrafoods.com

Cott Corporation

Toronto-based Cott Corporation is the world's largest supplier of premium retail branded soft drinks, and the fourth largest manufacturer of carbonated drinks. It operates research, beverage bottling, marketing, and customer service centers in 17 countries, including its core markets of Canada, the U.S., Mexico, and the U.K. The company had its start as a Pencer family-run soft drink supplier in the 1980s. In the early to mid-1990s, the company experienced astonishing growth with its licensed brand marketing strategy, with sales soaring from $40 million in 1990 to billions in 1996, and by 1999, the company had a customer base of 140 retailers. In 1999, Cott sold Destination Products International and The Watt Design Group. In 2001, it acquired a set of assets from the Royal Crown division of Cadbury Schweppes plc., including a concentrate research and manufacturing facility in the U.S. and the R.C. International business.

2000 Revenues: $1.5 billion
Grocery Store Sales: Supermarkets and mass merchandiser channels account for the bulk of the company's sales.
Brands: Allan, Appia, Benshaw, Blue Parrot, Can. D. Pop, Carignan, Carters, Carters Gold, Chateau, Chateau Dry, Christin, Cockatoo Waters, Cott, Cott Eau Naturelle, Cott Up, Denis, Desert Drinx, Destination Products, Diet Rite, Dr. Texas, Edge, Elite, Encore, English Royal, First Squeeze, Fizz Up, Fruit Mist, Hero, Hero Crush, Hero Jooce, Hero Lite, Its Clear, Its Cool ...Its Endless Summer, Its Cott To Be Good, Kik Kick, Lemon Blaster, Megasauras, Nectar Mousseux, Overdrive, Pirate, Pop Bottle, RC, Royal Charger, Slim Charm, Space Special, Sportsade, Stars & Stripes, Stone, Suncharm, Super Space, Tea Blaster, Torquay Summer In A Bottle, Texas Cola, Texas Red, Vercheres, Vess, Vintage, Whistle
Corporate Status: Canadian company.
Candor: The company provided little information. Candor is only 11%.

Ethical Management and Consumer Relations: The spokesperson mentioned the existence of codes of conduct and ethics training without providing details. This omission coincides with a number of high profile management controversies that involved ethical decision-making. Cott's growth was built in part on strong relationships with its suppliers and subsidiaries, but the company has experienced some problems within this network. In 1995, Cott was cited for breaching an agreement and failing to live up to a US$6.6 million obligation. The suit, filed by the former president and owner of Vess Beverages, alleged that Vess sold its equity to Cott on the condition that the former president would keep his position following the takeover. However, he alleged that Cott told him not to report to work, and denied him pay for his employment. The outcome of the case was not reported. In another case, Cott was accused in the U.S. media of "aggressive accounting" practices in 1994, when it allegedly failed to adequately expense certain costs and consequently inflated its stated profit. Cott denied these allegations, asserting that it maintained a positive cash position and relied on Canadian accounting practices that are more liberal than those used in the United States. In August 1992, Cadbury Beverages Inc. filed suit against Cott in the U.S. District Court for the Southern District of New York, alleging trademark infringement, unfair competition stemming from false designation of origin, and unfair competition. Cadbury sought a permanent injunction against Cott's use of the "Cott" name, along with restitution for lost profits, and unspecified damages. In April 1994, Cott petitioned for and received a summary judgement, but an appeals court reversed this dismissal. The company did not report the final outcome of this case.

Private Label and Retail Relationships: Cott's meteoric sales growth came at a time when private label strategies were transforming business relationships between grocery stores and manufacturers. The company's approach - supplying stores with drink products that advance their own brand - empowered retailers and made the big brands change how they did business. In the early 1990s, as grocery chains began marketing their private label brands, they often used what is known as a "shielding" marketing strategy. For example, Cott-produced pop would be displayed at key aisle locations with eye-catching signs and other material, enabling the store to create a strong presence for its brand. They also overshadowed lower sale prices offered by major soft drink brands. By 1995, the strategy was so effective that, according to then Cott CEO, Gerry Pencer, some major drink makers responded by offering millions of dollars to retail customers as a way of dissuading them from choosing private label products. To secure its position, Cott, like other grocery store suppliers, paid "pre-paid contract costs" or "cash allowances." With this practice, a common one in the grocery trade, advance payments are made to the retailer for guaranteed shelf space.

2001 Employees Canada: 700   **2001 Employees Worldwide**: 2,200

2002 Employees Worldwide: 2,600

Employee Relations: Worldwide, the company employed over 2,000 staff in 1999. Like most firms profiled in this book, Cott laid off employees during the 1990s. In 1997, 20 workers were cut from its former food division, Destination Products International Inc., while in 1995-96, 230 were downsized as part of a $25 million restructuring. As the company focused on Britain and North America, international expansion plans were stopped, offices closed, unprofitable customers abandoned, and weak product lines cut. Eighty per cent of the workforces in Canada, the U.S., and the U.K. belong to unions. In 1997, a Teamsters union spokesperson characterized labour-management dealings as "turmoil" and low trust. While the company has always contracted out some work for drivers, the union spokesperson said that the practice increased in Québec in 1996. Grievances, estimated at 50 per year at the Mississauga plant, were high, he added.

Equity and Family: In 2002, women hold approximately 35-40% of staff positions and two officers are women. Under the tenure of former president Heather Reisman, Cott was rated one of the best employers for women in 1994. At the time, a part-time employment equity officer tracked advancement, and women held 30% of full-time staff positions, and 15% of middle management jobs. No new information was reported in 2002. Cott has never set targets for women in management, nor ever reported an employment equity policy. Part of the company's reputation for advancing women in the mid-1990s came from its strategy to promote from within.

Progressive Staff: No formal flexible scheduling policy exists. Informal work arrangements allow office employees some discretion when structuring their hours. For example, in the mid-1990s, the company reported that one office supervisor worked from 4:45 am to 3:30 pm, while another worked from 5:00 am to 1:00 pm. Plant workers have less flexibility. The company provided no information on training or employee development. An employee share purchase plan allows any employee with three months of continuous work to contribute up to 3% of base salary towards the purchase of Cott shares on the open market, with the company matching two-thirds of the contribution. In the 1990s, incentives were offered for employees who met customer service, sales growth, and earnings goals. In 1999, Cott presented the first Gerald N. Pencer Award for Excellence in Innovation (named for the late CEO), recognizing employees who achieve profit and volume growth. Half of the $10,000 award comes in the form of Cott stock.

Environmental Management and Performance: The spokesperson reports the existence of environmental policies and the creation of an Environmental Management program to be launched in the fall of 2002. Between 1996 and 1999 no waste release data was submitted to NPRI from Cott Beverages' Scoudouc, New Brunswick facility or from its Calgary facility. In 1997, the company did report that 69% of its packaging weight is reused, 12.6% is recycled, and 18% is disposed. The company has reduced the weight of glass bottles and the number of pallets used, and now delivers bottles in reusable plastic cases or trays instead of disposable cardboard.

Community Responsibilities: No current information on community giving or investment was updated. A previous report indicated that the company's Corporate Contributions Program followed an "ad hoc" approach. In 1999, the proceeds from sales of a Cott branded-Thermos went to charity. A research center, The Gerry and Nancy Pencer Brain Tumour Centre, was set up in 1997 to improve care for people suffering from brain tumours. In the early 1990s, the company reported employee volunteer time donations, a scholarship fund for employees, and the sponsorship of sports teams, medical causes and the arts.

www.cott.com

Cuddy International Corporation

London, Ontario-based Cuddy International Corporation is Canada's largest poultry processor. The company breeds, hatches, grows, processes, and distributes food and poultry products as well as makes processed meats. The company was founded in 1950 by Mac Cuddy as a 100 acre turkey farm near Strathroy, Ontario. Cuddy operates several dozen farms, hatcheries, and processing plants around the world, including operations in Ontario (Strathroy, London, and Jarvis) and Québec (Couvoir).

> **2001 Revenues:** $350 million
> **Grocery Store Sales:** No information
> **Brands:** Cuddy Food Products, Cuddy Farms, Complete Cuisine Family (meal kits)
> **Corporate Status:** Canadian company.
> **Candor:** The company's 16% candor quotient is well below the sector average.

Ethical Management and Consumer Relations: No information was provided about whether or not the company has a responsible business practices code, a toll-free consumer number, or methods of handling consumer complaints. There was a serious family feud in 1995-97 over control of the business between the founder/chair and two of his sons.

2002 Employment Canada: No information

Employee Relations: In 1997, the company had 3,000 staff, including Canadian and U.S. operations. The United Food and Commercial Workers (UFCW) represents 1,000 Cuddy workers in south-western Ontario. In November 2001, Cuddy sold the plant which makes chicken items for major fast food chains to Winnipeg-based Cargill Ltd. One strike in 1995 involved 850 workers and 19,550 person days lost.

Equity and Family: No information is provided on the number of women, minorities, or aboriginal peoples working at the company.

Sourcing and Trade: The company has divested some assets, which at its height in 1998 had included operations in the United States, Scotland, France, and Italy. Principal customers in Canada include McDonalds Restaurants of Canada, Loblaw Companies, Great A&P, Master Choice, and President's Choice.

Environmental Management and Performance: Much of the company's early growth is attributed to Cuddy's experimentation with artificial light and other modifications in the poultry breeding and growing cycle. More than a million dollars was invested in re-engineering the workplace and implementing a massive and complex ergonomics program that sharply reduced repetitive strain injuries and other workplace health problems.

Community Responsibilities: No information on community donations, either cash or in-kind, is revealed.

www.cuddyfarms.com

Dare Foods Limited

In 1892, Charles Doerr began making cookies, crackers, and candy in Kitchener, Ontario. Today, his descendents sell Dare products baked or made in Ontario (Milton, Toronto, and Kitchener), Québec (St. Lambert, St. Martine, and Montreal) and the U.S. (South Carolina and Colorado). The company is still privately held and at least two family members are active in management. Dare recently acquired certain cookie, fine bread, and soup brands previously belonging to Culinar Inc. from Saputo Inc.

Revenues: $165 million
Grocery Store Sales: No information
Brands: Breaktime, Breton, Cabaret, Dare Cookies, Grissol, Juiced-Up Candies, Loneys, Simple Pleasures, Specialty Tin Tie Bags (Sun-Maid Raisin Oatmeal), Viau, Vivant, Whippet, Wisecracks
Corporate Status: Privately-held Canadian company.
Candor: Candor is 38%.

Ethical Management and Consumer Relations: The company has no written ethics code. No further information on ethical management policies and procedures was reported. Consumer protection policies include three toll-free consumer lines. In 1998, the corporate culture was described as "family-oriented."

2002 Employees Canada: 1,400 **1991 Employees Canada:** 800

Employee Relations: Dare employs an estimated 1,400 staff in Canada, and another 100 in the United States. Between 1991 and 1993, Dare's employment rose from 800 to 900 people. Six hundred work at the cookie and cracker plant in Kitchener, while another 300 are employed at candy plants in Milton and Toronto. In 1995, 516 workers belonged to the Bakery, Confectionery, and Tobacco Workers union. When layoffs hit the Hamilton plant (now divested) in 1991, 110 people lost their jobs. The 1998 union spokesperson said that the company relocated about a dozen of these workers to the Toronto plant. When job losses occur, employees are offered seniority recall rights, relocation where possible, and financial compensation. The company offers substance abuse counselling and 100% tuition reimbursement for workers taking job-related courses.

Equity and Family: A majority of Dare's food processing workers are female. There are no women in senior management or executive ranks but 28 of 99 managers and 42 of 111 "key contributors" are female. There have been no harassment cases since 1982. No information on the advancement of women, equity policies, or support programs at Dare was reported.

Progressive Staff: The union was not troubled by the company's moves in the 1990s to open non-unionized plants in the U.S. because management was forthright, the Kitchener facility was at capacity, and because there was no adverse impact on Canadian jobs. The union spokesperson says that management-labour relations are "good" and that there has been only one third stage grievance across both plants during the last three years. There is a full-time corporate safety co-ordinator and a safety committee at every facility. Performance-based profit-sharing exists, but for managers only. Dare Foods offers a 100% tuition reimbursement to workers who take skills upgrading courses.

Sourcing and Trade: Foreign sourcing and production has increased over the last decade. In 1993 Dare Foods had a 20% share of Mexico's imported cookies and crackers market through an alliance formed with a Mexican distributor. The company has two operations in the United States. No policies governing foreign trade or sourcing were reported.

Environment-Friendly Products: In the early 1990s, Dare conceived a product called Rain Forest cookies that used Brazil nuts and cashews purchased from operations run by aboriginal communities. This sourcing relationship was marketed as a means of preserving forests, because the nut crops create an economic value for trees, and theoretically prevented their removal. From this product's earnings, Dare donated a cash percentage to Cultural Survival, a non-profit organization that helps indigenous groups build additional processing capacity without threatening the rain forest's existence. The effectiveness of this well-intentioned initiative has not been proven, in part due to the limited mass of land that the forests occupy and, in part, because of the absence of an independent audit.

Environmental Management and Performance: No information on environmental policies, procedures, or staff was reported. At the Milton plant, where great quantities of sugar and starch are used, waste effluents contain high bio-chemical oxygen demand levels. In the early 1990s, a pilot program began studying ways the company might be able to recover concentrated sugar solutions from its wastewater. Possible market applications for the by-products included animal feed supplements. No updated information on this initiative is provided. Few bakery companies, including Dare Foods, provide information to the National Pollutant Release Inventory on chemical releases and transfers from their sites.

Community Responsibilities: Little information is disclosed on community engagement or charitable donations. The Dare family makes separate donations through a Dare Family Trust to recipients like the Kitchener-Waterloo Community Foundation and the Grand River Hospital. Dare Foods was a supporter of the Canadian cycling team at the 2000 Sydney Olympics, as well as a contributor to Cash For Kids, and a Canadian Food For Children program.

www.darefoodsinc.com

Dial of Canada

Dial of Canada distributes products made by its American parent, The Dial Corporation. These include cleansers, polishes, and detergents. All communications with the company are conducted through a "Canadian Sales Department" at the head office in Scottsdale, Arizona. The company's name, structure, and activities have changed over the last decade. Prior to 1991, it was known as the Greyhound Dial Corporation. In September 1996, it was split into separate publicly traded entities, Dial and Viad. Dial Corporation put itself up for sale, as of August 4, 2001.

> **2000 Revenues:** $1.6 billion (parent)
> **Grocery Store Sales:** No information
> **Brands:** Armour, Borateem, Borax, Custom Cleaner, Dial, Fels Naptha, Liquid Dial, Lunch Buckets, Pure & Natural, Purex, Renuzit, Sarah Michaels, Spirit, Tone
> **Corporate Status:** Wholly-owned subsidiary of U.S.-based parent company.
> **Candor:** No information was provided. Candor is 18%.

Ethical Management and Consumer Relations: The company distributes its code of conduct to executives and managers, but not to other levels of employees. No corporate policies were reported governing the negotiation of retail shelf space or business gifts. According to company reports in 1996, the parent was engaged in various major lawsuits over issues ranging from alleged fraud, negligence, misrepresentation, mismanagement, excessive compensation, and improper investments.

2002 Employees Canada: No information

Employee Relations: In Canada, Dial has very few staff, none of them in manufacturing. After major product lines including Purex liquid bleach were phased out, six global plants closed worldwide in 1995, laying off 700 workers. Between 1991 and 1995, the parent company's global workforce grew slightly from 29,042 to 31,356 workers. Officers, directors, and key employees are eligible for stock option plans and a management incentive plan.

Equity and Family: The parent company has placed two women on a board of nine directors, but none in senior management. The situation has not changed much in ten years: in 1996, one woman worked in senior management. In 1991, one woman sat on a board of 11, and two of 17 were in senior management.

Progressive Staff: Dial conducts electronic meetings enabling employees to exchange comments simultaneously and anonymously via personal computers. A Dial subsidiary, Dobbs International Services, runs a program to improve the reading and writing skills of its own employees.

Sourcing and Trade: The parent company operates offices in five countries, manufacturing plants in four countries (Guatemala, Mexico, Argentina, and the United States), and distribution centers in 40 others. No policies regarding sourcing, supply chain, or trading practices were reported.

Environmental Management and Performance: No information on environmental policies or procedures is released. The parent, Dial Corp., has employed an environmental officer since 1990. In the early 1990s, the parent's environmental research and development budget was directed toward pollution reduction, packaging enhancements, and employee education. In-house animal testing ceased in 1985 and sub-contracting to outside test laboratories ended soon after. Concerns have been raised by environmental groups about the toxicity of compounds derived from the decomposition of nonlyphenol ethoxylate, an ingredient found in Dial's detergent products. These compounds may damage the reproductive health of aquatic animals exposed to them, though Dial is not aware of any studies conclusively demonstrating a link between the compound and toxicity in animals or human beings. However, the company concedes that new studies supporting this claim may emerge. Since government agencies in North America and Europe are considering regulation of this chemical, Dial has reformulated its detergents in order to eliminate it long-term in future products. In addition, the U.S. Food and Drug Administration is currently considering standards that would limit or even preclude soap manufacturers from putting certain antibacterial ingredients in their soap products. This move would hinder the marketing advantage of Dial's antibacterial soap, because Triclosan, the active ingredient in Liquid Dial, is one of the FDA's concerns. The use and effects of antibacterial agents have been the focus of media attention, yet the company declined comment on this controversy.

Community Responsibilities: Dial's philanthropic efforts focus on civic organizations (particularly those that help the economically disadvantaged), cultural, and sports groups. Committees of employees, located at manufacturing facilities and at Dial's corporate headquarters, make local funding decisions. Dial, which aims to help communities in which its employees live, has sponsored the United Way and Habitat for Humanity in Atlanta and Phoenix. Employees join this latter effort by working with homeowners and children to provide home ownership for the working poor.

www.dialcorp.com

Dover Industries Limited

Dover Industries of Burlington, Ontario has its corporate roots in two south-western Ontario firms—flour miller, S.J. Cherry & Sons, and grain dealer, T.H. Taylor Company Ltd—as well as a Hamilton, Ontario company, Robinson Cone, which made ice cream cones and packaging. The current company, incorporated in 1940 in Hamilton, mills flour and makes paper products, ice cream cones, mixes, and packaging. Today, Dover processes flour at two mills in Halifax, Nova Scotia and Cambridge, Ontario, makes containers in Toronto, cones in Burlington, and packaging in Brampton and Burlington. Other divisions include Howell packaging, Bondware, and Robinson Cone. A single shareholder owns 50.4% of the company. In 1994, the company divested its assets in Taylor grain, which processed soft wheat, corn and soybeans in south-western Ontario.

> **2000 Revenues:** $135 million
> **Grocery Store Sales:** 10%
> **Brands:** Dover, Hi-Fibre, Robinson Cones, Swans Down
> **Corporate Status:** Majority-owned Canadian company.
> **Candor:** The company has a 29% candor quotient.

Ethical Management and Consumer Relations: Dover's code of ethics was written in 1992 and includes a section on exchange of business gifts. Dover was one of the few companies profiled here to say it supports its code with some type of ombudsperson. Like those other companies, this function is run internally by an internal manager who assumes the job part-time. In other non-food sector companies, the ombudsperson is more often an outsider.

2002 Employees Canada: 530

Employee Relations: In 1998, 75% (400) of all Dover employees belonged to unions, including the United Food and Commercial Workers, the Retail, Wholesale and Department Store Union, the United Steelworkers, and the Graphic Communications International Union. No layoffs were reported when the company sold Taylor grain in 1994. The workforce was reduced by almost 10% between 1991 and 1996, after 45 jobs were cut in Burlington. A union representative said in 1998 that no union de-certification or unjust dismissal cases had occurred over the previous ten years. The company spokesperson said Dover hires its workforce from local communities.

Equity and Family: At Dover, women comprise 37% of the workforce, seven of 49 managers, two of ten senior managers, and one of 11 directors. The company attempts to improve their conditions through employment equity and anti-sexual harassment policies. A Dover employee charged the company with permitting harassment based on sexual orientation (Bartlett v. Dover Corporation). The British Columbia Human Rights Tribunal has not reported a final decision in the case.

Progressive Staff: Employees who take educational or skill-enhancing courses outside the company can have costs wholly reimbursed. Substance abuse counselling is available to employees through an Employee Assistance Plan, and flexible scheduling programs are also offered. Dover offers an incentive plan to all manufacturing employees working at the supervisory level or higher and to clerical workers at one office.

Sourcing and Trade: Dover Industries has no international operations, and reports no policies on ethical procurement or trade issues.

Environmental Management and Performance: Since 1994, all Dover operations are subject to a common environmental code and annual audit system. A number of process improvements have been recommended and implemented. No full-time officer is assigned environmental responsibilities, but five staff handle partial duties. According to the National Pollutant Release Inventory, no major chemical releases or waste substances were emitted by Dover Flour Mills' Cambridge, Ontario plant between 1995 and 1999. The company reports workplace recycling programs for paper, cardboard, cans, glass, and food waste.

Genetically Modified Ingredients: No information

Community Responsibilities: Community support takes the form of charitable donations to sports teams, student work programs, and food donation drives. Through payroll deductions, Dover employees have the chance to donate to the United Way.

www.dovergrp.com

E.D. Smith & Sons Ltd.

E.D. Smith makes jams, sauces, pie fillings, blended fruit, and sauce products from a 175 acre farm and a food processing plant at Winona, Ontario, the heart of the Niagara fruit belt. It also produces sauces under the E.D. Smith, HP, and Lea & Perrins labels. Other private label products include jam and jelly packing for supermarkets and other large retailers. Ownership has stayed in the Smith family, and today the great-grandsons of founder E.D. Smith own and run the company. Early on, the Smiths considered wine making, but the founder's wife objected to alcohol on moral grounds, so the family turned to fruit and vegetable products. The family house from the 1850s still stands in the middle of its facilities. Today, E.D. Smith does not have any farm operations and it procures produce from local growers during the fall harvest. The company was put up for sale in 2000-01, but has yet to secure a buyer.

2000 Revenues: $150 million
Grocery Store Sales: At least 90%
Brands: E.D. Smith, EDS, Habitant, HP Sauce, Lea & Perrins, Lite n' Fruity
Corporate Status: Privately-held Canadian company.
Candor: The president stated that he would be unable to give any information, as the company was being sold, but "next time around" the company will par-

Ethical Management and Consumer Relations: Although no details were provided about a formal code of ethics, the company has individual policies that address topics like exchange of business gifts. New employees are trained on a set of corporate values, but not on ethical decision-making in a corporate environment. Supervisors and management participate in internal "vote group" sessions that evaluate all policies and procedures. Employees can make anonymous submissions to an internal Ombudsperson (handled on a rotating and part-time basis by top executives) or through the corporate newsletter. A reply is guaranteed in both cases. The company has been given an award for Allergen Safety by the Anaphalaxis Foundation of Canada.

2002 Employees Canada: 380   **1998 Employees Canada:** 333

Employee Relations: Staff levels at E.D. Smith have increased by 14% over five years. In the late 1980s and early 1990s, employment was cut in half (from 425 to 200) when technological changes and automation reduced staff requirements for fruit cooking. This downsizing also reflected a move to a non-seasonal production schedule, requiring fewer temporary workers. The company's only American plant, a Mississippi fruit sauce and product maker, was sold, with the new owner keeping 85% of the workforce. To those let go, E.D. Smith gave severance benefits and counselling. A full-time safety officer works with the health and safety committee to provide training to managers and workers, and ensures that safety audits are conducted on a monthly basis.

Equity and Family: No information on advancement of women was reported. An anti-sexual harassment code is backed up with training.

Progressive Staff: Subsidies for employee safety and skills training are available in one of three forms: on-site training, classroom training at a corporate center, or off-site work-related courses. Some funding is available for non-professional studies. Through internal feedback mechanisms, employees can comment on company direction and policy. In the late 1990s, E. D. Smith was recognized one of Canada's 50 Best Managed Private Companies (as rated by Arthur Andersen Consulting, the Canadian Imperial Bank of Commerce, and the *National Post*), a nomination based partially on staff policies. Since 1993, when the company transformed its workplace improvement and suggestion program to a "profit incentive plan," permanent employees have had initiatives and performance rewarded.

Sourcing and Trade: In recent years, the company has increased its imports of raw materials from outside of Ontario in part because of fluctuations in supply from local tomato growers. Produce comes from Manitoba and Québec. In order to supplement fresh ingredients throughout the year, the company also sources raspberries and blueberries from B.C. Dates come from Australia, Asia, and Eastern Europe, strawberries from Mexico, and a small amount of produce from Chile. E.D. Smith markets products in the Far East, Australia, Europe, the Middle East, and the Caribbean. No policy incorporating labour or environmental standards exists on procurement of ingredients from foreign countries.

Environmental Management and Performance: While no employee has full-time responsibility for environmental management, a quality control manager does this part-time. No formal committees steer environmental initiatives. An American sanitation institute is hired to audit operations as an external verifier. The company works with its suppliers to reduce packaging. No environmental performance reports are released publicly.

Community Responsibilities: No donations policy exists, although the company tends to donate to communities where it operates. E.D. Smith supports local sports and family activities, events in the Niagara Region like the Winona Peach Festival, and national organizations like the Canadian Diabetes Association. Other sponsorships go to the foundation of the Canadian Association of Family Enterprises, Tim Horton's children's camps, and the Parkinson Foundation.

www.edsmith.com

Effem Foods Ltd.

While Effem Foods is best known for its chocolate bars, the parent company, founded in Chicago in 1911 by Forrest Mars, also pioneered canned meat for dogs as well as a nutrient-enriching process for converted rice. The Canadian company, founded in Montreal in 1948, operates out of Bolton, Ontario and is privately held by Mars International. The company built a pet food facility in Bolton in 1986, followed by a confectionery products plant in Newmarket in 1988. The parent company is the largest confectionery business in the world. McLean, Virginia-based Mars International also manufactures snack foods, rice, pet care products, vending machines for beverages and automated payment systems. Internationally, Mars has plants in the U.K., Portugal, Japan, and New Zealand, along with 50 other separate businesses in over thirty countries.

Revenues: No information

Grocery Store Sales: No information

Brands: Bounty, Cesar Food for Dogs, Cooking Sauces, Dove Caramel, Fast & Fancy Rice, Kal Kan Foods for Cats, Mars Bar, Maltesers, M&M's Plain & Peanut Chocolate Candies, Pedigree, Sheba, Skittles Candies, Snickers Bar, Starburst Fruit Chews, Stuff'n Such stuffing, 3 Musketeers, Twix, Uncle Ben's Rice and Sauces, Waltham Formula Life Stage Diets for Dogs and Cats, Waltham Veterinary Diets for Dogs & Cats, Whiskas

Corporate Status: Wholly-owned subsidiary of privately-held U.S. parent.

Candor: In the U.S. and Canada, company policy forbids plant tours and, except for advertising, little information is ever made public. Because executives typically decline interviews, and because a core group of about 30 managers run all Mars International operations, it is not surprising that Effem has a 10% candor quotient.

Ethical Management and Consumer Relations: In 1981, the Mars family defined the company goals and culture as "Five Principles of Mars" (quality, efficiency, responsibility, mutualism, and freedom) and disseminated them to employees. The company believes these principles address such concepts as profit, freedom, stakeholder relations, and the egalitarian spirit, which as company policy and practice, are supposed to transcend barriers of age, gender, race, or religious conviction. The two Mars brothers who operate the global company (Forrest Jr. and John) live modestly, disdain perks and fancy clothes, and try to translate these personal values into a no-frills company. An advertising controversy arose in the late 1990s, when a U.S. group, the Action & Information on Sugars and the Health Education Authority, criticized a promotion for Milky Way. Because the ad described Milky Way as "the sweet you can eat between meals without ruining your appetite," the groups said it breached a guideline of the Independent Television Commission that banned any advertisement encouraging children to eat frequently. Although the complaint was not upheld, Mars was warned by the ITC that it had to clarify its message in a way that did not endorse eating between meals.

2002 Employees Worldwide: 30,000   **1990 Employees Worldwide:** 26,000

Employee Relations: Conditions at Mars offices around the world are standardized. All employees receive the same benefits, pension, holidays, and sick pay. Each must clock times, eat in a common dining room, and eschew press interviews. No one occupies a private office. While many plants worldwide operate on a 24-hour basis, the Canadian spokesperson did not confirm such a schedule here. Employees receive personal performance bonuses as a share of company profit, and these can amount to the equivalent of three weeks compensation.

Equity and Family: Effem reports formal employment equity policies, as well as same sex couples benefits. Programs for adoption and maternity leave extensions exceed government-set minimums.

Progressive Staff: Employees can receive assistance for alcohol or drug abuse and retirement counselling. The company operates without multiple management layers, and managers do not have personal secretaries.

Sourcing and Trade: Although the parent company owns no plants in any developing nations, it does source ingredients like cocoa there. In developing economies that rely on these crops, notably West Africa, cocoa and sugar are typically grown by peasant farmers whose livelihoods are often precarious, or on plantations where crops are harvested by low paid labourers. Effem reports no social responsibility standards in its international sourcing for sugar, cocoa, and nuts.

Environmental Management and Performance: In the early 1990s, the company reported an environmental policy but provided neither copy nor description. In Canada, a corporate committee implements environmental policy, which includes the recycling of paper, glass, aluminum cans, and office service supplies. Food waste and meat by-products are recycled into pet food. More details were available on operations in the U.K., where the code emphasizes energy efficiency, conservation strategies, and the monitored use of CFCs. In Canada, all vehicle engines are converted to accept unleaded gas, and effluent discharges are treated in order to remove pollutants before being returned to local water systems. Effem Foods did not provide the National Pollutant Release Inventory with information on its chemical releases and transfers.

Genetically Modified Ingredients: No information

Community Responsibilities: Most corporate giving occurs at the divisional, not national level. Mars prefers programs where the contribution goes directly to recipient groups, so donations focus on hospitals, schools, and groups in locales where employees work. Non-cash gifts of property, computers, and equipment went to selected organizations in Hackettstown, New Jersey in the early 1990s.

www.mars.com

Energizer Canada Inc.

Founded in 1909 in Toronto, Energizer Canada is part of a global company that sells millions of Energizer and Eveready batteries every year. It supplies almost 40% of the domestic battery market, serving as a distribution center for Energizer Holdings, Inc. (USA). This parent company sells to over 140 countries, and has 22 production plants in 15 countries. Since November 1997, when Energizer Canada stopped manufacturing here, it has packaged batteries from Walkerton, Ontario. The company was a subsidiary of Ralston Purina of St. Louis, Missouri until being divested in 1999.

> **2000 Revenues:** US$163.1 billion (global parent)
> **Grocery Store Sales:** 35%
> **Brands:** Encore, Energizer, Eveready
> **Corporate Status:** Wholly-owned by the U.S.-based parent company.
> **Candor:** The company has a 12% candor quotient. Limited information came during fact verification in 1998 and 2002.

Ethical Management and Consumer Relations: Energizer's *Business Practices and Standards of Conduct* policy was written by its former parent, Ralston Purina. It requires no annual training or sign-off from employees.

2002 Employees Canada: No information **2001 Employees worldwide:** 10,480

Employee Relations: When production ceased at the Walkerton plant in 1997, 56 staff were laid off. The company set up an outplacement program that helped almost all employees—many were technicians and engineers—find new jobs within seven months.

Equity and Family: A daycare facility is available to Canadian employees.

Progressive Staff: Through a comprehensive Employee Assistance Program, former parent Ralston Purina provided its employees, their dependents, as well as retirees with parental and eldercare assistance, counselling for financial matters, substance abuse, and stress. It isn't known whether these policies continued post-divestment. Management formally solicits employee suggestions through the "General Methods Improvement Program," and publishes an employee newsletter. Energizer Holdings Inc. offers an employee share ownership plan, but no information on possible gainsharing at Energizer Canada was reported.

Environmental Management and Performance: There is little information on Energizer's environmental management systems, waste reduction, or recycling initiatives at its distribution facility. Former parent, Ralston Purina set a company-wide environmental code that Energizer has followed, but no indication of any changes after the divestment was given. According to the parent company's 2000 annual report, Energizer is identified by the U.S. Environmental Protection Agency as a "Potentially Responsible Party" (PRP) under the

Comprehensive Environmental Response, Compensation, and Liability Act, and may be obliged to participate in the clean up of nine federally designated "Superfund Sites." According to the company, Eveready's batteries are packaged in shrink-wrap, rather than blister packs, which saves 70% in packaging materials.

Post-Consumer Waste from Batteries: Energizer says it became the first company to sell mercury-free batteries when it introduced a zinc-chloride battery called Encore in 1990. Although batteries are said to be 99.9% mercury-free, they still contain other pollutants, like lead, cadmium, and zinc. When batteries become post-consumer waste, their mineral contents pose environmental concerns. Open storage disposal can lead to leakage, while incineration may result in possible toxic emissions or groundwater contamination. Energizer's spokesperson said that all other toxic substances exist in miniscule amounts, causing no threat when disposed through household garbage. No secondary market exists for materials recovered from batteries. To deal with nickel-cadmium rechargeable batteries, the company participates in the Canadian Household Battery Association's "Charge Up to Recycle" program, which sends batteries to a facility in Pittsburgh.

Community Responsibilities: No information was provided on charitable giving, support of community-based causes, employee voluntarism, or stakeholder engagement.

www.energizer.com

Gay Lea Foods Co-operative Limited

Gay Lea Foods was established as the United Dairy and Poultry Co-operative in 1958. Today, it sells a range of milk products to the retail, food service, and industrial sectors. Based in Weston, Ontario, the co-operative operates four Ontario plants—Teeswater, Guelph, North York, and Weston. With the acquisition of Longlife of Canada Ltd in 1989, Gay Lea expanded its fluid milk and cream operations. Gay Lea also acquired the Uniondale Cheese Factory at Lakeside, Ontario in 1992. When the co-operative stopped making cheese and yogurt in the late 1990s, it closed a few Ontario operations - plants in Uniondale and Baden, a dairy bar in Guelph, all three of which were preceded by the closure of a cheese cutting operation in Woodstock. The four main facilities were expanded and refurbished. The Teeswater plant is reputed to be the oldest operating creamery in Ontario. All Gay Lea shares belong to 4,200 members and employees, so farmers earn a return on their investment and have a voice in the milk business. As a co-operative, the company helps farmer-owners exchange information about production.

2001 Revenues: $220 million (approximately)
Grocery Store Sales: No information
Brands: Gay Lea, Nordica
Corporate Status: This business is a member-owned Canadian co-operative.
Candor: Honour Roll. The spokesperson was helpful and extremely prompt throughout the research and draft review stages. Gay Lea's candor is 75%.

Ethical Management and Consumer Relations: No code of responsible business practices guides employee decision-making, and no ethics advisor or training are available. The company's Vision 2000 corporate planning exercise produced guidelines for sales representatives who negotiate product placement in retail stores.

2002 Employees Canada: 400   **1991 Employees Canada:** 430

Employee Relations: Honour Roll. Employment levels have remained relatively stable at Gay Lea for the past decade. Due to seasonal and other fluctuations, staff ranged between 440 and 418 between 1988 and 1996 and between 400 and 425 employees since 1998. After the Uniondale and Baden plants closed in 1998, only the Guelph plant had unionized staff. A wage dispute put 43 Guelph workers on the picket line for nine days in 1995, causing a loss of 250 worker days. The company has a good safety reputation—averaging five to six lost time accidents per year, and only four in 2001—and the Ontario Dairy Council has given Gay Lea several health and safety awards over the last ten years. Annual training expenditures typically are about $50,000 (or $150 per employee).

Equity and Family: In 2001, one of six senior managers is a woman (compared with zero of five in 1998), although none sit on the board (unchanged over three years). In 1998, women represented approximately 14% of the total workforce, and 5% of middle managers.

An anti-sexual harassment policy is supported by periodic training workshops on a range of harassment issues. Individual employees can negotiate extended maternity leaves, and informal policies grant paid days off for childcare and eldercare.

Progressive Staff: Gay Lea gathers employee suggestions through idea suggestion boxes, rewards employee incentives through a bonus structure based on both company profits and employee performance, and distributes a member newsletter (*The Gazette*) and an internal newsletter (*The Informer*), both quarterly. An Employee Assistance Plan refers staff to free, confidential family, financial, and substance abuse counselling upon request. Although no formal flextime policy is reported, the company uses summer work hours, allowing employees in most departments to work half-days on Fridays.

Sourcing and Trade: The company discloses the percentage of materials sourced in Canada. All sales occur domestically. As a co-operative, Gay Lea sources milk only from member farmers, and sourcing is directed by the Milk Marketing Board and quotas.

Environmental Management and Performance: Gay Lea has no formal environmental code. As of April 2002, the company has developed an environmental policy, incorporated environmental training in the company's orientation training package, and trained all staff in the policy. One Health Safety Supervisor, a position created in 2001, is responsible for health, safety, and environment. The company carries out joint health and safety audits of operations on a monthly basis, during which an environmental non-compliance section is covered, but no separate internal environmental audit has been developed or carried out. On average, Gay Lea earmarks $250,000 annually for waste reductions and equipment replacement. Capital investments target on-going waste and effluent reduction projects. For example, effluent discharges were cut at the Weston cultured products plant in 1995, and rinse water recovery and recycling systems enhanced removal of cheese particles from wastewater. Gay Lea facilities did not report NPRI data between 1994 and 1999. Company-wide, recycling of paper, cardboard, wood pallets and food waste as well as disposal reduction programs have cut annual non-perishable refuse and perishable waste. Because the co-op maintains its own vehicle fleet, energy conservation is monitored. The Guelph plant in particular, reports high reuse and recycling achievements. In the early 1990s, the Ontario Ministry of the Environment ordered the Teeswater plant to raise the height of a stack after complaints arose from the surrounding community. The plant also had food processing effluents that exceeded provincial standards for suspended solids, BOD, and ammonia nitrogen. Gay Lea contracted external consultants to assess its waste treatment system, and developed a successful amelioration plan.

Community Responsibilities: Current figures for charitable contributions are not supplied. Historically, Gay Lea has given a great deal of product, some cash, employee time, and facilities usage to community groups.

www.gaylea.com

General Mills Canada Inc.

General Mills was best known for its Betty Crocker packaged and baked products, and for its cereals, but has expanded its presence to include Pillsbury Refrigerated Dough Products and Green Giant products through the acquisition of Pillsbury in 2001. Wholly owned by General Mills Inc., the Canadian company's last plant (in Etobicoke, Ontario) was closed in November 1997. Since the Pillsbury acquisition, the company has a renewed manufacturing presence in Canada, with plants in Midland, Ontario, and in Winnipeg, Manitoba. General Mills had been the third largest cereal maker in Canada, controlling 18% of the breakfast market. In 2002, the spokesperson stated that the company had the second-largest stake in the breakfast market, though a market share figure was not reported. Its Cheerios brand, introduced in 1954, remains the second most recognizable cereal in Canada. Before acquiring Pillsbury, the parent company expanded through joint ventures with PepsiCo and Nestlé. The company predicts revenues in Canada of $700 million in fiscal 2003, approximately doubling the pre-acquisition, 2001 revenues of $350 million.

> **2000 Revenues:** US $6.7 billion (parent); $500 million Canada
> **Grocery Store Sales:** 95%
> **Brands:** Betty Crocker, Bowl Appetit, Bugles, Cheerios, Chex, Chips, Cinnamon Toast Crunch, Count Chocula, Dinner Kits, Dunkaroos, Fibre One, Fruit by the Foot, Fruit Roll-ups, Green Giant Canned & Frozen Vegetable Products, Golden Grahams, Gushers, Hamburger Helper, Lucky Charms, Nature Valley Granola, Oatmeal Crisp, Old El Paso Salsa, Pillsbury Pizza Pops and Mini Pizzas, Pillsbury Toaster Strudel, Pillsbury Refrigerated Dough Products, Pop Secret, Reese's Peanut Butter Puffs, Sodalicious, Trix, Tuna Helper
> **Corporate Status:** Wholly-owned by U.S.-based company.
> **Candor:** The company has a 49% candor quotient.

Ethical Management and Consumer Relations: The company's 14-page ethics code which covers topics like conflict of interest, protection of company resources, and conduct within and outside of the company, requires an annual sign-off by all employees. At the parent company, a Public Responsibility Committee of the board provides guidance for CSR issues. The company's consumer safety assurance process—built on a comprehensive product recall system, toll-free consumer phone line, and advertising guidelines—exceed government standards. In the U.S., a *Fortune* survey of 8,000 senior executives, directors, and financial analysts ranked General Mills first in the food industry, based on four financial criteria and four reputation criteria which were "of interest to socially responsible investors."

2002 Employees Canada: 650   **1996 Employees Canada:** 350

Employee Relations: Canadian employment has dropped over the last five years, following the closure of an Etobicoke plant, though the parent company's global operations had grown slightly (from 10,000 people in 1998). With the acquisition of Pillsbury in November

2001, the company nearly doubled in size from 220 to 650 employees in Canada, and from 11,000 to 19,000 worldwide. When the Etobicoke operation shut down, half of the employees were able to retire with enhanced severance packages. Other affected workers received "generous packages" and a full out-placement service, which offered job search assistance over a nine-week period. A joint health and safety committee solicits "team involvement" to solve problems in the workplace. Employees at all levels receive regular training, tuition reimbursements (up to 100% of costs for courses outside the company), and the power to help create training programs. Turnover at General Mills was 4% in 2000 and dropped to 3.5% in 2001, which is low for this industry. Salaried employees can take advantage of an individual RRSP contribution plan in which the company matches 50% of the employee's contribution. The company pays out up to another 50% variable cash incentive at year-end, based on a formula derived from the attainment of individual objectives and the Canadian division's performance. Due to the acquisition of Pillsbury, the company currently supports two separate pension plans, but the spokesperson stated that these would be harmonized as of January 2003. The parent company's employee share ownership plan covers salaried and non-unionized workers, and includes a company contribution that matches a portion of employee contributions.

Equity and Family: Honour Roll: General Mills' record for advancing women and diverse groups is one of the best in the entire EthicScan database. In Canada, the board retains three women among its five directors, up from two in 1998, while senior management employs a woman president and two other female officers. Approximately 35% (33 of 91) of all managers are women, down from nearly 50% (26 of 56) the year before, due to the merger with Pillsbury. A program from the parent company, "Women in Leadership: the Power to Build the Future," enables senior leaders to enhance diversity in the workforce by combining employee networks and making strong recommendations. Since 1991, General Mills Canada's employment equity policy has tried to address gender and racial imbalances among staff with a program that monitors data on employee composition. It reports progress to the board of directors. In the U.S., the company has a corporate diversity officer, a Supplier Diversity program, and an objective that more than two-thirds of newly hired employees are women or representatives of racial minorities. Advancement results are reported publicly. In 2001, Catalyst, a U.S.-based group that promotes equity by recognizing corporate efforts to promote women gave "Women in Leadership" one of its awards. Employees participate in formal mentoring through advancement programs, such as the Black Champions network, which strives to increase the representation of African Americans. In Canada, employees are protected by an anti-harassment policy (covering gender, race, sexual orientation, and disability). Although there is no back-up training, employees are required to sign the policy at the time of hire. Workers in same-sex relationships are eligible for all health benefits. Extended maternity, paternity, and adoption leaves are available, along with daycare and eldercare referrals, and paid days off for family needs.

Progressive Staff: Honour Roll. Counselling referrals for substance abuse are administered through an EAP, and retirement planning seminars are extended to spouses. An on-site fitness facility is available, and the company offers a stop-smoking program and drug coverage as part of health benefits. Three to five times each year an employee newsletter, *SweetTalker*, is published. Flexible scheduling, telecommuting and job-sharing options are available, but the spokesperson did not specify how many employees take advantage of these programs.

Sourcing and Trade: Although General Mills Inc. has operations in 30 to 40 countries worldwide, and joint ventures in Europe with Pepsi and worldwide with Nestlé, no information was provided on policies guiding foreign operations, or on sourcing for Canadian manufacturing operations.

Environmental Management and Performance: General Mills' Environmental Policy applies to all subsidiaries, including the newly acquired Canadian facilities and the Etobicoke plant, prior to its closure. The company has stringent technical, environmental, and quality requirements for co-packers. Internal staff carry out environmental audits, every 12 to 24 months, and audits results are reported internally. At the parent company, waste management has become a profit center, and reduction programs have a target of zero waste shipments to landfill sites.

Community Responsibilities: The Canadian company favours donations to four sectors: social services, health and hospitals, education, and cultural groups. In 2001, the company gave a total of $500,000, including approximately $200,000 worth of in-kind donations. The company's 2001 United Way contributions amounted to $146,000, of which over $80,000 came from employees. In the U.S., the parent gave approximately US$15 million in the same year. In 1997, the company gave a total of $150,000, including $100,000 (half from employees) to the United Way. Although no pledge is made to the Imagine Campaign, the company donated a flat percentage of pre-tax profits to its host communities. General Mills plays a self-described "leadership role" within the food sector to encourage more companies and employees to become involved with "giving campaigns." Donations go through the parent's General Mills Foundation (created in 1954) and by the end of the 1990s, total grants donated were worth $242 million. Applications and guidelines are clearly provided on the company's website. Employee volunteers sit on Community Partnership Councils, which review funding applications and requests for volunteers in 22 communities throughout Canada and the United States. The parent company is one of the few to publish an annual Corporate Citizenship Report, detailing charitable giving, community involvement, its "Challenge U" scholarship program, its "Boxtops for Education" program, and product donations.

www.generalmills.com

George Weston Limited

Toronto-based George Weston Limited is one of the largest integrated food processing and distribution businesses in North America, owning the continent's second largest baked goods producer, and Canada's largest food retailer. It operates through two distinct segments: Weston Food Processing (fresh and frozen bakeries, biscuits, and specialty food products), and Loblaw Companies Limited. Weston Bakeries has 14 bakeries in Canada including eight in Ontario, and one in each of Vancouver, Calgary, Regina, Winnipeg, Montreal, and St. John's, Newfoundland. Founded in 1882 by George Weston, the current company's majority share-holder (61%) and chairman, Galen Weston, is the grandson of the founder. Over the last decade, George Weston divested its interests in forest products, E.B. Eddy (1998), salmon products (1998), and chocolate products (1988). A number of other units were acquired—including Bestfoods Baking (2001), Provigo Inc., Agora Atlantic Foods (1999), and Signature Brands Limited (1998)—helping the company increase its revenues by about 50%.

2000 Revenues: $22.3 billion

Grocery Store Sales: No information

Brands: Arnie's Bagelicious, Atlantic Save Easy, Atlantic Superstore, Brunswick, Casa Mendoza, Connaisseur, Connors, Country Bakeshop, Country Harvest, Dietrich's, D'Italiano, Entenmann's, Extra Foods, Fortinos, Heritage Salmon, Interbake Foods, Loblaws, Loeb, Lucky Dollar Foods, Maier's, Maplehurst, Neilson, No frills, No name, Ovenbaked, Pepe's Mexican Foods, Petrofsky, Port Clyde, President's Choice, Provigo, Ready Bake, San Francisco, Signature Brands, Stroehmann, Thomas' English Muffins, Too Good To Be True, Valu-mart, Weston, Wonder, Your Independent Grocer, Zehrs

Corporate Status: Majority Canadian-owned, publicly traded.

Candor: The company has a candor quotient of 40%.

Ethical Management and Consumer Relations: All employees sign an eight-page *Code of Business Conduct* at least once every three years. It is translated into languages spoken in communities of operation and contains a human rights provision. Comprehensive in scope, the Code addresses adherence to law, appropriation of company assets, misuse of confidential information, conflicts of interest, outside business activities of employees, gifts to and from customers or suppliers, illegal payments to public officials, and political and charitable involvements. To support the Code, the company strikes Business Conduct Committees at each major subsidiary and division, and members include the relevant Presidents and Chief Financial Officers. Employees can seek guidance from the Committee, which deals with issues confidentially and without bias. Toll free consumer numbers also support each division. A $531 million suit brought against two Weston subsidiaries and 71 other companies in Alaska in 1995 alleged violations of anti-trust laws. The case was dismissed but is being appealed.

2001 Employees Worldwide: 126,000 (including retail and manufacturing)

Employee Relations: The company spokesperson said that employment levels have increased over the last five years, but provided no figures. Collective bargaining agreements, covering 82,000 of the company's 113,000 employees (73%), are negotiated by a number of unions (including the UFCW Union, United Fishermen and Allied Workers, the Bakery, Confectionery, and Tobacco Workers, and Retail, Wholesale Canada, and the Teamsters). In 2000, a three-day walkout by UFCW staff at Zehrs in 24 Southern Ontario centers ended when the company said it would create 300 new full-time jobs over six years. Three other strikes hit the company in the early and mid 1990s. In 1995, a strike at National Grocers (Peterborough, Hamilton, and Kitchener) put 164 staff out for 1,260 worker days. In 1993, 127 employees walked off the job at a Vancouver bakery owned by George Weston Ltd over management calls for forced overtime and hiring more part-time staff. About two months into the strike, the plant was closed, causing 145 layoffs. In 1992, a Toronto strike involved 1,324 workers. Recent workplace health and safety statistics were not reported, but one fatality of a bakery worker was reported in Toronto in August 2001. No details were given.

> **The Changing Structure of Work:** In Canada, Weston stopped delivering fresh bakery products with its own company-operated system and began contracting to independent distributors. In the U.S., consolidation eliminated many bread delivery routes. In its food retail operations, it has downgraded most full-time employees to part-time status, shed permanent workers, and hired more temporary staff. In 1991, as Weston Bakeries in Québec strove to become the most technologically advanced bakery in North America, technological advancement reduced staff from 350 lower-skilled workers to 100 more highly-skilled workers.

Equity and Family: Two women sit on a 12 person Board of Directors (a slight improvement from 1992, when one of 15 were women), but no other information on gender advancement was reported. The company's *Code of Business Conduct*, which is signed by employees, includes reference to workplace harassment, and covers gender, sexuality, race, and religion.

Progressive Staff: George Weston Limited offers flexible scheduling, fitness club subsidies, and stop-smoking programs on a divisional basis. In 2000, the Zehrs retail division extended its drug plan coverage to the families of part-time workers. In the late 1980s, when management at Zehrs realized that part-time and night-shift workers were being passed over for promotions, management introduced a training program to help workers update technical, administrative, and customer service skills, enabling greater career advancement. Subsidiary Weston Bakeries has offered an in-house literacy course in Québec since 1991, when it discovered that many senior workers could not read or write well enough to operate new high-tech machinery. Internal communications programs include employee newsletters at each division. George Weston Limited runs a stock option program though no details were given. The B.C. Packers subsidiary offers a profit-sharing program for key employees.

Sourcing and Trade: In 1998, Weston made 42% of its food processing sales in Canada, and exported 58% to the U.S. or other countries. After divesting its American retail business in 1995, the company's U.S. interests were limited to six food-processing operations (in Virginia, Delaware, Indiana, Massachusetts, Pennsylvania, and Maine). Weston is the largest private-label cookie maker in the U.S., producing most of America's Girl Scout cookies. In 2001, the majority of production contracts for President's Choice and No Name products were held with Canadian companies, though no policy ensures these relationships. Despite the existence of aquaculture operations in Canada and Chile, the company has no code to monitor conditions or their effects on other species. Neither is it pledged to international codes like the United Nations Global Compact, the Caux Principles, or the Global Trading Initiative that deal with ethical sourcing and trading.

Environmental Management and Performance: A four-page booklet, *Environmental Principles,* and a three-page *Resource, Environment, and Waste Management Policy,* applies to all Weston, Loblaw, and Provigo companies. Internal personnel conduct environmental audits, assisted by external consultants. Four full-time George Weston Limited employees assume environmental duties, including a Director, Environmental Affairs. Most units have a senior environmental person on staff. Regular reports from Operating Group Presidents detail environmental practices throughout their group and are filed with the Environmental Health and Safety Committee of the Board. No major capital environmental expenditures for waste reduction, energy conservation, or energy efficiency were reported. George Weston did not provide the National Pollutant Release Inventory with information on chemical releases and transfers from any of its Canadian operations.

Community Responsibilities: George Weston Limited did not reveal charitable contribution figures in 2000, but the spokesperson said that the company is committed to contributing at least 1% of annual pre-tax profits, cash and in-kind, to charitable organizations in Canada. It also promotes employee voluntarism. Corporate donations come from operating divisions, Loblaw Companies Limited, George Weston Limited, and the Garfield Weston Foundation. In 2000, support emphasized medical research, education, conservation and community projects. Specifically, the company gave money to the Canadian Olympic Foundation, the Salvation Army, local food banks, the Girl Guides of Canada, the Collingwood Horticultural Society, Canadian Outward Bound Wilderness School, the Alberta Birds of Prey Foundation, and the Banff Centre for the Arts. Weston joined the Canadian Merit Scholarship Foundation in 1998 to assist university students who demonstrate leadership and commitment to their communities. In 2000, 24 Garfield Weston Merit Scholarships were awarded to students at colleges and universities.

www.weston.ca

Gerber Canada

Gerber first sold strained baby food in Canada in 1933, five years after its launch in the United States. Dan Gerber created the Gerber Products Company using baby food recipes invented at his father's canning company. The company's first Canadian plant was built in Niagara Falls in 1948. Today, Gerber is the top selling baby food in America. Although Gerber Canada distributes baby food, baby care products and apparel, most sales come from food. Its single Niagara Falls manufacturing plant closed in 1989, reducing operations to a 20-person sales office in Toronto. Gerber Products Co. is now a wholly owned subsidiary of Novartis, the pharmaceutical, agri-business and nutrition company that formed after two Swiss companies (Sandoz and Ciba-Geigy) unified their corporate structures through mergers. Gerber Canada is a division of the Canadian subsidiary of Novartis. In the early 1990s, Gerber (USA) shed trucking, toy and furniture activities in order to focus on its core businesses.

2000 Revenues: No information
Grocery Store Sales: No information
Brands: Gerber, Novartis
Corporate Status: Wholly-owned subsidiary of Swiss parent company.
Candor: Gerber provided answers to 18% of the questions posed.

Ethical Management and Consumer Relations: Gerber Canada uses the ethics policy of Novartis, which includes sections on procurement and exchange of business gifts. Due to the public's sensitivity toward safety issues and infant food, Gerber has developed a safety assurance process that exceeds government regulation. In the area of consumer information, Gerber claims it was the first company in Canada to have a "Best Before" or optimal date printed on baby food, a practice that is now standard. One defective product case occurred in the 1990s, when almost one million pacifiers were recalled following reports alleging that four had broken into pieces, creating a hazard for babies.

2002 Employment Canada: 10

Employee Relations: The company thinned its Canadian staff from 20 to 10 between 1997 and 2001. Employment at the American parent has declined over the last ten years, from 12,015 (1991) to 11,000 (1996). After production moved to a larger, more efficient U.S. factory, Gerber Canada shut down its Niagara Falls plant, laying off 120 Niagara Falls workers and 20 Toronto workers.

Equity and Family: In 2001, one of three senior managers in Canada was a woman. This proportion has not really changed since 1998, when three of 11 managers and senior managers were women, though it does represent a small improvement over one of ten managers in 1991. Formal career and succession planning programs help employees develop professionally. The company does not offer daycare referral or on-site facilities, but an anti-sexual harassment policy is supported with training.

Progressive Staff: Gerber has an employee newsletter, an open-door management policy, and scholarship programs for employees and their children.

Sourcing and Trade: The company says that it controls its own supply of bananas, and that a corporate agricultural department controls other bulk purchases. No other information on ethical supply chain sourcing was given.

Environmental Management and Performance: Gerber recycles fine paper, cardboard, and aluminum cans. The company says it supports recycling in Ontario, but does not say how. Formal audits of company-owned and contracted farms are integrated into the parent company's environmental management system, and waste reduction initiatives exist, though no details were provided. Packaging innovation introduced a family-sized recyclable plastic container for pure juices. Environmental demands are made of suppliers and compliance is monitored. The parent company goes to great lengths to control procurement, ensuring that there is no measure of residual pesticides in its food. Crops must be rotated so that exposure to insects and disease can be avoided with minimal use of pesticides. Formal audits of company-owned and contracted farms are integrated into an environmental management system.

Genetically Modified Ingredients: No information

Community Responsibilities: No charitable donation statistics were reported. Gerber Canada has the discretion to support local causes through its own budget. It contributes 150% of all staff donations directed at educational institutions. A gift-matching program is run through the Gerber Foundation. Gerber played a key support role in a very poignant story from the early 1990s. When called upon by a young man with severe food allergies, the company went to great lengths to accommodate his highly specific nutritional needs. A doctor discovered that the only food he could eat was Gerber meat-based formula, a product that was discontinued long ago. Without this food, the young man would have died, according to his doctor. Upon learning of his situation, the company's research division devoted extra time and space towards producing batches of this food especially for him. He lived until 1995.

www.gerber.com

Gillette Canada Inc.

Founded in 1906, Gillette Canada is a wholly-owned marketing subsidiary of its American parent, The Gillette Company, which has annual revenues of $9.3 billion. With subsidiaries that include Braun Canada and Duracell Canada Inc., Gillette distributes products such as blades and razors, toiletries, toothbrushes, and batteries - through offices in British Columbia, Alberta, Ontario, and Québec. In 1999, the head office moved from Montreal to Mississauga, and no manufacturing facilities are left in Canada.

2001 Revenues: $250 million (estimate)
Grocery Store Sales: 31%
Brands: Braun, Daisy, Dry Idea, Duracell, Foamy, Gillette, Mach3, Mach3 Turbo, Oral B, Right Guard, Sensor Excel, Soft & Dry, Venus for Women
Corporate Status: Wholly-owned subsidiary of U.S.-based parent company.
Candor: The Gillette spokesperson in Boston was helpful with EthicScan's draft profiles. The candor quotient is 73%.

Ethical Management and Consumer Relations: Gillette has a company-wide code of ethics, which is reinforced by an annual employee sign-off and regular ethics training. Specific policies govern business gift exchange and negotiating product placement in retail stores. Executive performance evaluations include criteria beyond financial and market goals, but the spokesperson provided no details. Consumer safety assurance processes include a toll-free phone line and advertising guidelines. The Duracell operation was accused by its competitor, Eveready, of breaching the Trademark Act when it compared its product to an Eveready product in a 1995 advertisement. Subsequently, Duracell was disallowed use of Eveready's trademark image in its commercials.

2002 Employees Canada: 296   **1997 Employees Canada:** 200

Employee Relations: Half of Gillette's Canadian employees work in sales offices across the country. All are salaried and non-unionized. The Gillette and Duracell operations have undergone major organizational changes over the last few years. Last year, Canadian employment fell almost 13%. Between 1997 and 1999, Gillette cut 1,700 jobs worldwide after acquiring Duracell, although Canadian totals increased. A 6% decline in staff occurred between 1995 and 1997 following the 1995 closure of a Montreal Distribution center. Duracell's Mississauga plant closed in 1997, affecting 110 workers, who all received career adjustment assistance from an action center. Canadian operations changed drastically between the 1980s and the mid-1990s as Gillette closed plants in the Montreal and Toronto areas. Downsized employees received outplacement counselling, job search assistance and severance packages that exceed the government minimum. Globally, the parent company's employment figures declined (from 40,000 to 35,000) between 1997 and 2001.

Equity and Family: Five of 41 managers and one of 12 senior managers are women. The company's Equal Employment Opportunity Policy states that Gillette does not consider race and gender when hiring, basing decisions only on merit. There is a corporate advisory committee on diversity issues and corporate-wide target goals for advancement. Performance is measured and management is responsible for progress. Harassment protection is part of the company's overall disciplinary code, and is not addressed separately. A number of work-life balance programs were introduced in the 1990s. The "Work and Family" program permits unpaid leaves (of up to 12 weeks) for family care needs. Employees can also structure their work hours using: staggered hours, a half-hour flex arrival schedule, an extended workweek, or reduced hours. No childcare referral or facilities are offered, but paternal and adoption leaves are.

> **Health and Safety:** All international operating units employ an environmental health and safety specialist. The Gillette Medical Evaluation Laboratories has an Occupational Hygiene Department that directs internal audits in order to evaluate safety and environmental management systems. One workplace fatality occurred in Mexico in January 1999, at the parent company's Naucalli Manufacturing Center. In a 2000 report, the company stated that it "thoroughly investigated the accident and subsequently implemented changes in certain processes and procedures." It shared the results of this investigation with its other facilities.

Progressive Staff: Health and employee support is strong at Gillette. Counselling services address career, retirement, and financial needs; a health care specialist is contracted for employees to consult on general health advice and referrals; and stop-smoking seminars and partial fitness club subsidies are offered. Gillette's corporate newsletter, *The Pinnacle*, is published quarterly. Training support includes a 100% tuition reimbursement for courses that employees successfully complete. An employee share ownership plan includes a contribution from the company through retirement savings plans matching contributions, but only executives receive stock options. Before the takeover, all Duracell employees were eligible for stock purchases through "The Duracell Shares" program, and all were able to convert their stock to Gillette stock after the takeover.

Sourcing and Trade: The parent company has operations in 15 countries (down from 24 in 1998), including four manufacturing facilities in China and one in Russia. Amnesty International has considered all three countries repressive regimes at some point over the last few years. Gillette is one of the few covered in this book to report a policy governing supply and procurement from repressive regimes, but the spokesperson provided no details.

Environmental Management: Environmental policy and support has a long-standing tradition at Gillette. The parent's environmental code (under review in 2001) is supported by an Environmental Management System and Corporate Environmental Affairs department (introduced in 1974). The code sets principles, standards, and targets, tracks progress to date, and mandates a separate public Environmental Health and Safety (EH&S) Report. Internal reporting procedures were formalized in the 1980s. Duracell had an environmental code that applied to the Mississauga plant before it was dismantled, but the spokesperson did not indicate how or if this code would be reconciled with the Gillette policies. Leading the EH&S function, a Vice President of Corporate Product Integrity works with the Senior Operating Officer at each business unit to ensure compliance with the policies and procedures. A senior management review board, the Committee on Health, Environment, and Safety, creates policies, and reviews procedures and compliance, ensuring regular audits of all business. Conservation measures and energy-efficient designs are built into all new and renovated facilities. The 2000 EH&S report states that management "is investigating emissions trading, fuel switching and other means, in addition to ongoing energy conservation."

Environmental Performance: A worldwide Pollution Prevention Program set emission reduction targets at 50% by 1997 (with 1990 as the base year). The company said it achieved that target by 1992, and hit 76% by 2000. These targets were also successfully applied to the newly-acquired Duracell operations. Water consumption is said to be on the decline relative to per unit production, with annual savings of 250 million gallons of water since 1995. All ozone-depleting chemicals were eliminated from Gillette products worldwide in 1994, the company reports. Gillette products contain no major greenhouse gas since the company uses recovered CO_2 or nitrous oxide. All CFCs, perfluorocarbons, halons, and methyl chloroform have been phased out. In 1998, the company said that alternatives were being investigated to replace the Volatile Organic Compound ingredients in its toiletries, hair spray, and underarm products, but no update was given. The parent company set a target of zero wastes or emissions, but has not set a deadline for this goal. In 2002, Gillette's greenhouse gas emissions are primarily CO_2. The company reports waste output for operations and power purchases. Emissions increased 9% between 1998 and 1999, due to increases in energy consumption. With no manufacturing facilities in Canada, Gillette does not report to the National Pollutant Release Inventory. Seven of the parent company's American facilities filed Toxic Release Inventory (TRI) reports under U.S. federal regulations. In Canada, workplace recycling programs collect fine paper, cardboard, cans, wood pallets, and packaging materials at offices and warehouses, and the company is considering a recycle/reuse program that could

Battery Waste and Disposal: Although Duracell encourages customers to return their spent batteries, it maintains no public recycling process. The spokesperson said that none of the materials in battery products require special disposal treatment. Secondary markets do not exist for materials recovered from batteries. Duracell no longer carries mercury cell batteries and its manufacturing manager reported no other byproducts from manufacturing processes. Off-site recycling efforts at U.S. plants dramatically cut TRI- listed chemicals requiring off-site treatment or disposal between 1997 and 1999. Before production was shut down in Canada, waste was diverted to more than one site—thereby avoiding heavy concentrations of toxins—and many shipments went to the United States. Where possible, some materials were directed to re-use and recycle programs, and dust collectors trapped some residual hazardous materials from the air.

recover slightly damaged products. Recycled content accounts for 29% of all Gillette packaging worldwide, up from 7% in 1991. For example, all PaperMate pen blister cards, packs and shipping cartons are made from recycled materials. Duracell tries to use recycled fiber in its packaging. Worldwide, the parent company reported 13 notices of violation over the past two years, including three wastewater effluent violations in 1998 and seven in 1999, along with two hazardous waste management deficiencies in 1998 and one in 1999. Fines for these infractions, none of which occurred in Canada, totaled just over US$5,000.

Animal Testing: In the 1990s, Gillette products were boycotted by the activist group, People for the Ethical Treatment of Animals (PETA). The group questioned the validity of "cruelty-free" claims printed on Gillette's and competitors' labels, along with general statements about the extent of animal testing. In November 1996, the Gillette Company announced that no lab animals were used to test personal care and consumer products or any of their ingredients, and that no animals were used for safety or research testing of cosmetics for three consecutive years. Based on this information, PETA ended its campaign against Gillette. The company said that PETA's actions did not affect its decisions on animal testing and that it will always comply with government regulations requiring animal tests for any new chemical or ingredient. Gillette has invested millions into the development of alternative tests, supporting the Centre for Alternatives to Animal Testing at Johns Hopkins University, the American Humane Society, and many other grant programs, university research projects, and trade association activities. Gillette says that it cooperates with animal interest groups and, in every annual report published since 1990, has disclosed the number of laboratory animals used and the tests performed on them.

Community Responsibilities: Internationally, Gillette donates 1% of pre-tax earnings to charity. In Canada, the company gave approximately $150,000 to charities in 2000, up from product and cash donations of $79,600 in 1995, but less than the $251,800 given in 1994. In 1997, Duracell's President received an award from the United Way for continued support during a difficult year for the company. Local "Employee Advisory Groups" make decisions on how to direct corporate giving. Generally, social and health groups receive priority. Personal care kits containing Gillette products, Duracell batteries, and Oral B toothbrushes have been sent to Canadian communities suffering from natural disasters (Saguenay-Lac St. Jean, Québec flood of 1996, Manitoba flood of 1997, and the Québec ice storm of 1998). Used computers are given to social agencies and schools located in low income areas.

www.gillette.com

Glaxo SmithKline
Consumer Health Care Canada

This consumer healthcare company makes over-the-counter medicines, nutritional drinks, and oral care products. While antecedent companies of this newly-merged business once manufactured in Ontario, today it has only a sales, marketing, distribution, and administrative presence in Canada. GSK's Canadian history begins with the Toronto distributor, Harold F. Ritchie & Company Ltd, which began by selling ENO Fruit Salts to Canadians in 1907. By 1989, it had grown into a truly global company, when SmithKline Beckman (U.S.) merged with the Beecham Group (U.K.). In 2000, Glaxo-Wellcome and SmithKline Beecham merged to form Glaxo SmithKline, creating one of the world's largest pharmaceutical companies. Block Drug was added to Glaxo SmithKline's Consumer Health Care business in 2001. Worldwide, more than 42,000 employees run 107 production plants in 40 countries, another 40,000 work in sales and marketing, while approximately 16,000 people conduct research.

> **Revenues:** No information
> **Grocery Store Sales:** Approximately 35%
> **Brands:** Aquafresh, Baby's Own Soap, Beano, Contac, Flex Toothbrushes, Gaviscon, Geritol, Oxy, Polident, Poli-grip, Sensodyne Toothpaste, Spectro Jel, Tums
> **Corporate Status:** Wholly-owned subsidiary of British parent company.
> **Candor:** Through detailed responses to EthicScan's draft profiles and phone interviews, SmithKline Beecham answered more than 80% of our questions in 1998. Today its candor is 14%.

Ethical Management and Consumer Relations: The company follows its global parent's code of conduct. The spokesperson stated that before the recent merger, both companies had similar policies in place, and these policies continue to apply in all areas. Other ethics policies address business gift exchange, harassment, and fostering a tolerant workplace environment.

2002 Employees Canada: 190 (CHC only, 1,800 for GSK Canada total)

Employee Relations: Glaxo SmithKline currently employs over 100,000 people around the world. In 2000, more than 50,000 people worked for the parent company, down from 62,800 in 1991 (though an accurate sense of change is difficult given the company's merger history). Among Canadian employees, 190 work in the consumer and health care divisions. No Canadian, and few global, employees belong to unions. When the Weston, Ontario factory closed in 1993, 146 workers (who made Tums, Aquafresh, Oxy, and ENO) were laid off, leaving 100 in sales, marketing, and administration jobs.

Equity and Family: At the parent company, four of eight senior managers and two of 15 directors are women, reflecting an increase from zero of 13 senior managers and two of 16 directors in 1998. No other information on equity or advancement policies was reported. In the mid-1990s, the Job Accommodation Network listed SmithKline Beecham as a company with a strong record for accommodating and hiring people with disabilities.

Progressive Staff: Work-life policies for Canadian employees include flexible scheduling and employee assistance plans. GSK's employee assistance plan includes counselling for individuals, couples, and families, as well as workplace stress. Also included in the EAP is health information, child and elder care, legal and financial counselling, crisis counselling, work at home options, and a year-round compressed work week.

Sourcing and Trade: Despite parent company operations in 35 countries, no policy addresses international employment or supply chain standards. The 2002 spokesperson stated that employment standards policies exist within local businesses. Glaxo SmithKline operates a large manufacturing facility in Mississauga, Ontario through its Pharma division. The company began investing $40 million into basic and clinical pharmaceutical research in 1992, the year the federal government extended patent protection for Canadian brand name drug manufacturers.

Environmental Management: In 1998 SmithKline Beecham reported a set of "results-oriented Environmental Standards" as part of its environmental code. These mandate the improvement of environmental performance on an on-going basis, and each facility must plan how it will comply with worldwide standards, which are set to be more stringent than legally required minimum standards set in countries of operation. An audit program conducted by an internal/external team assesses environment and safety performance at production and lab facilities around the world, and helps each location identify priorities. Each site receives an audit once every three years. At SmithKline Beecham's U.K. office in 1998, a Vice-President of Environment and Safety received assistance from Site Environmental Co-ordinators. The Environment and Safety Department was accountable for technical and legal compliance. Personnel with various job descriptions have environmental goals specified in their job descriptions and objectives, and managers identified concerns particular to their fields. Canadian operations are guided by these objectives and subject to regular assessments. Each site provides data for an annual questionnaire administered by the Corporate Environmental and Safety Standards committee.

Environmental Performance: The SmithKline Beecham Environmental Standards required impact assessments on all new packaging designs. In the 1990s, the company encouraged environmental improvement through package redesign with an internal performance award that was established in 1995. The Aquafresh Flex toothbrush package eliminated 70% of the material used in its box in North America when it replaced rigid polystyrene with a lightweight pack. Globally, conservation efforts reduced waste at SmithKline Beecham labs and consumer healthcare plants, respectively, by 17% and 24% between 1992 and 1996. Externally, SmithKline Beecham won a variety of environmental awards for CFC reductions, energy efficiency, solvent and air emission reduction, and waste minimization.

Genetically Modified Ingredients: No information

Animal Testing: The spokesperson for the Consumer Health Care division was unable to confirm or deny whether animal tests are performed in Canada. The parent company reports that it meets the demands of regulatory bodies concerned about any new ingredient that lacks an established safety record. Testing is carried out once a comprehensive internal review determines that the ingredient will produce positive health benefits. The company says that it participates in the development of alternatives to animal testing, and ensures the animals are cared for beyond regulatory requirements. The parent company has also published a lengthy statement on animal testing on its website, which outlines policies, some of the species of animals used in testing, and the purposes for testing on those species.

Community Responsibilities: Through the 1990s, SmithKline Beecham Canada Inc. was pledged to the Imagine Campaign Company and Glaxo SmithKline has continued with this pledge. Through United Way campaigns, the company matches donations of employees. It also donates used laptop computers to community organizations, including the Arthritis Society, the Heart and Stroke Foundation, and the Canadian Mental Health Association. In the U.S., SmithKline Beecham was selected a winner of *Business Ethics Magazine's* 1998 Award for Philanthropic Excellence. In 1995 and 1996, SmithKline Beecham won the Mayor's Award given by the Town of Oakville for charitable contributions. Other funding goes to local hospitals, health groups, arts groups, community sports events, and marathons.

Access to Drugs: An international controversy erupted in the 1990s over inaccessibility to expensive, life-saving drugs in developing nations. Lobbying was led by groups like Doctors Without Borders, activist shareholders, and international development advocates who forecast elimination of a whole generation of people. In May 2000, Glaxo SmithKline agreed to supply three HIV/AIDS medicines at cost (price reductions reportedly were 90%) to people in 63 nations deemed "Least Developed Countries" by the UN. Similar arrangements were made for drugs that treat malaria, diarrhea, and worms through NGOs, UN agencies, and employers in Africa. No conclusive, independent evidence indicates that drug supplies have increased.

www.gsk.com

Goudas Food Products

Goudas Food Products and Investments Ltd. sells almost 600 food products under the Mr. Goudas label, and another 600 products through a retail network in Ontario and overseas. This Concord, Ontario-based company was founded in Toronto by Peter Goudas in 1971. These products include ginger beer, lentil soup, black beans, lichee fruit, tomato sauce, rice pudding, peaches, 20 kinds of basmati rice, and chick peas.

2001 Revenues: No information
Grocery Store Sales: No information
Brands: Billy Bee Honey, Horlinks drinks, Montini coffee, Mr. Goudas, Nestle Baby food
Corporate Status: Privately-held Canadian company.
Candor: The company has a 11% candor quotient. It is one of only two in this Guide that deliberately has no website.

Ethical Management and Consumer Relations: No mention is made of an ethics code or guidelines for dealing with customers, suppliers, regulators, or other stakeholders. The company keeps a rabbi on call to certify kosher foods, and a Muslim expert to advise on halal rules. Goudas Food Products is looking into ways to emboss cans so that the blind can tell them apart.

2002 Employees Canada: No information

Employee Relations: No information is provided about the location, employment levels, or working conditions in food processing plants that are owned by or supply Goudas Foods.

Equity and Family: No mention is made of employment of disadvantaged groups. Local people are hired to prepare and taste test the company's various ethnic foods.

Progressive Staff: In order to guarantee product quality and consistency, Goudas has a stake in every factory which supplies its products.

Sourcing and Trade: The company has operations in 13 countries. Beans are grown in Peru and Australia, peaches in Greece, bamboo shoots in Thailand, and rice in India. Mr. Goudas Foods is not voluntarily pledged to international sourcing policies like the Global Trading Initiative or the United Nations Global Compact.

Environmental Management and Performance: No mention is made of environmental management systems, audits, or recycling.

Community Responsibilities: Current figures for donation of cash, in-kind products, or staff voluntarism are not available.

No website

Heinz Canada

Most famous for the ketchup it has made in Leamington, Ontario since 1909, Toronto-based H.J. Heinz Canada produces and distributes food for service and retail markets. As a wholly-owned subsidiary of American-based H.J. Heinz Company, the Canadian company's consumer products include soups, beans, infant foods, pet food, and frozen foods. It operates another plant in Wheatley, Ontario. After acquiring two Borden Foods Corp. divisions, the company added dry bouillon and soup, along with a line of pasta sauce, to its product mix (bouillon and soup is in the U.S. market, pasta sauce in all of North America). The Pittsburgh-based parent sells more than 4,000 different products in 200 countries.

> **Annual Revenues:** Greater than US$4 billion
>
> **Grocery Store Sales:** No information
>
> **Brands:** 9-Lives, Catelli, Chef Francisco, Classico, Heinz, Ken-L-Ration, Kibbles 'n Bits, Medi-Cal, Omstead, Ore-Ida, Pablum, Pounce, StarKist, Techni-Cal
>
> **Corporate Status:** Wholly-owned subsidiary of American parent company.
>
> **Candor:** Responses were returned returned promptly and extensive information provided. Heinz has a 62% candor quotient.

Ethical Management and Consumer Relations: Although there is no corporate code of ethics, a variety of individual policies and procedures, circulated to all employees through a company handbook, address ethical issues. They are supported with some training. Heinz has three toll free consumer lines, one of which is specifically for baby food products.

2002 Employees Canada: 2,000   **1996 Employees Canada:** 2,000

Employee Relations: Honour Roll. About two-thirds of the Canadian workforce is unionized. Major layoffs occurred between 1992 and 1994 when the Leamington workforce was downsized from 1,400 to 800. Instead of shutting down the plant—an option the company considered—the workers saved their jobs by conceding pay and benefits cuts, and the pay concessions were subsequently lifted in 1997. The plant changed product lines and increased production for the U.S. market, turning around Leamington's prospects. A union spokesperson noted that relations with management are typically "good." Heinz was one of few companies to report two particular pieces of data: the amount of production contracted out (2%), and the enforcement of a maximum workweek (48 hours). Of the 50 grievances filed annually, approximately four require going to third party arbitration. In a single year (1999-2000), workplace injuries were cut dramatically (from 58 to 32). Through a joint safety committee, the company provides health and safety training and ergonomic workplace assessments. The costs of tuition and books for courses taken outside the company are reimbursed 100%. In 1997, the last year data were reported, Heinz spent between $400,000 and $500,000 to train 2,000 employees. The company offers shares at 15% below market price to employees through a payroll deduction of up to 15% and has a stock investment plan for executives. Key salaried and operating employees receive profit-based bonuses that range between 12% and 20% of their income, based on projected targets. Hourly workers have productivity bonuses based on similar targets.

Equity and Family: Four of 21 Board directors are women. In 1998, when the Canadian executive committee had one woman among 11 members, other women held 17% of executive positions, 30% of management, and 43% of general workforce jobs. Currently Heinz's executive team is made up of 8 members, of whom one is a woman. Heinz's employment equity plan includes a policy that sets targets for hiring, provided candidates are found in eligible pools. Sexual harassment procedures are covered within the general corporate guidelines. When women take maternity leaves, benefits are extended with a top-up of salary beyond the government minimum. Employee Assistance Programs include alcohol and drug abuse counselling, retirement and financial planning seminars, and computer purchase assistance plans. In Canada, one employee newsletter (*Eye on Heinz*) is published quarterly, a second newsletter *(Around Heinz)* is published twice a year, regular employee attitude surveys provide anonymous suggestions from staff, and breakfast meetings expose the CEO to employees at the Toronto location and to managers across the country at least once each quarter, and regular employee meetings with the CEO occur in Leamington as well.

Sourcing and Trade: The parent company operates in 200 countries. The spokesperson said that no inputs or ingredients come from repressive regimes and indicated that the company guarantees a range of protections against abuses (such as the use of child labour, exploitation of women, forced labour, low health and safety standards, excessive disciplinary practices, unpaid extended work hours, and wage exploitation). However, no formal policy was cited or provided. Heinz has produced private label brands for baked beans, soup, tomato juice, pet food, mustard, relish, and pasta.

Environmental Management and Performance: Heinz Canada applies its parent's environmental code. Internal and external auditors inspect company facilities separately but no details on these audits were provided. Although no one occupies a full-time environmental affairs position, management and union representatives address environmental issues. An environmental committee at Leamington handles specific issues (such as solid waste reduction), and liaises with the municipality on wastewater issues. At the industry level, the company participates in national packaging protocols through its trade association, although no specific reductions were reported. Fine paper is recycled, along with cardboard, pop cans, bottles, and shrink-wrap, and food waste products go to farmers who use it for feed and fertilizer. Scrap wood from pallets is distributed to employees and members of the community. Heinz Canada has no chemical farm practice standards. From its own co-generation facility, Heinz maximizes the efficiency of the gas it consumes and sells unused power to Ontario Hydro. Plastic is recycled internally, meaning that the company does not tax the local municipal recycling program. The parent company was the only food producer in the U.S. to recommend that its fruit and vegetable growers avoid 12 fertilizer chemicals that the Environmental Protection Agency began reviewing in the 1990s. According to media reports, it was the first time that a food processor provided growers with a list warning about a legal investigation into chemicals. In Canada, Heinz has not provide the National Pollutant Release Inventory with information on any releases or transfers.

Genetically Modified Ingredients: As of 2000, the company's policy is not to knowingly procure Genetically Modified Ingredients. In addition, the spokesperson states that Heinz's lines of baby food have been analyzed for GM content and any GM ingredients were removed.

Community Responsibilities: Heinz Canada did not update its philanthropic information in 2001. In the 1990s, it sponsored athletic teams, nutritional research, children's causes, the Variety Club and UNICEF. 2001 United Way contributions amounted to over $106,000, with $77,659 being raised in the Greater Toronto Area. As a longtime supporter of the Children's Miracle Network, Heinz Canada ran a program that collected baby food labels, donating six cents to local children's hospitals and foundations for every label returned, which has amounted to $2.2 million given to 11 Children's Hospital Foundations since 1991. During recent emergencies, such as the Winnipeg flood of 1997 and the Québec ice storm of 1998, donations of animal, baby, and other food products (worth between $100,00 to $150,000) were given to people needing relief.

www.heinz.com

Hershey Canada Inc.

While Milton Hershey incorporated his candy company in 1894, Hershey Foods did not expand into Canada until 1963, when a chocolate plant opened in Smiths Falls, Ontario. The Canadian subsidiary is held by Hershey Foods Corp., the parent company which operates 17 plants in the United States, two in Germany, two in Italy, one in Mexico, along with joint ventures in Japan and South Korea. In addition to the Smiths Falls location, the Canadian company has plants in Dartmouth, Nova Scotia, and Montreal, Québec. Since 1991, Canadian, Mexican, and American facilities have used an integrated North American production strategy to satisfy continent-wide chocolate demand. Recent plant divestitures include Amherst, Nova Scotia, Sherbrooke, Québec, and Hamilton, Ontario.

Annual Revenues: Greater than US$4 billion
Grocery Store Sales: No information
Brands: Amazin' Fruit, Bridge Mixture, Brown Cow, Chipits, Eat-More, Glossettes, Goodies, Nibs, Moundy, Oh Henry, Ovation, Pot of Gold, Reese Crunchy Peanut Butter Cups, Reese's Pieces, SKOR, Special Crisp, Super Twizzlers, Top Scotch
Corporate Status: Wholly-owned subsidiary of American parent company.
Candor: Responses were returned promptly and extensive information provided. Hershey has a 25% candor quotient.

Ethical Management and Consumer Relations: Hershey Canada, which has no formal code of ethics, follows the parent company's *Corporate Philosophy Statement.* This document sets standards for conduct, care for employees, and business gift exchange. An *Ethical Business Practices Committee* oversees a hotline for staff and customers in both Canada and the United States. Until 1970, Hershey did no advertising. Today, it devotes 4.3% of total sales to media sponsorship, and another 10.9% to other types of promotion. Over the last decade, the company has faced a few advertising controversies. In 1994, a group called Kids Against Junk Food alleged that an ad for Gummy Bears misled audiences by suggesting that the candy contained greater amounts of fruit ingredients than it did. In 1995, Hershey settled a dispute with the rock group R.E.M. over a radio promotion that mentioned the band's name to promote its Kit Kat chocolate bar. The band had neither approved the ad nor endorsed Kit Kat. In 1992, a television ad attempted humour when it depicted a sour-faced Asian man eating some other (non-Hershey) candy—suggesting he was humourless—and the effect of the ad, as alleged by some offended viewers, was damaging to that ethnic minority.

2002 Employees Canada: No information   **1997 Employees Canada:** 1,470

Employee Relations: Hershey Canada's workforce grew slightly in the 1990s, although the number of plants shrank from six to three. In 1998, the majority of employees (62%) belonged to one of four unions representing workers at Smiths Falls and Dartmouth operations. The company fully reimburses tuition and book expenses for outside courses. In the early 1990s, production jobs shifted locations when operations were streamlined, moving the Planters peanut and Lifesavers lines from Toronto to Smiths Falls. All 119 unionized workers were offered the chance to relocate with a $5,000 moving allowance. The last time Hershey reported workplace injuries statistics to EthicScan, incidents had declined to 86 in 1995 from 157 in 1994.

Equity and Family: In 1996, women comprised 58% of total staff, 27% of managers, 18% of senior managers, and zero of three board directors. Hershey Canada has formal equity programs that address workplace issues facing women, minorities, disabled people, and aboriginal peoples. Hershey Canada supplements employees' UIC maternity benefits to a maximum of 55% of regular earnings for eight weeks. Equity policies have a long tradition at Hershey's parent company. In 1989, an equal opportunity monitoring program, launched in the U.S. in 1970, evolved into a "workplace diversity program" focusing on hiring women and minority workers and promoting them to managerial positions. Hershey Canada introduced a "Valuing Diversity" workshop in 1996.

Progressive Staff: Workplace programs include open door management policies, a reward program, incentives for cost saving suggestions, and an employee newsletter (the *Hershey Hotline*, released 12 times a year). Children of Hershey employees can apply for post-secondary scholarships.

Sourcing and Trade: An informal sourcing policy urges managers to contract with suppliers from communities where Hershey operates, if they are competitive. Internationally, the parent company has operations in seven countries. Hershey Canada sources cocoa from Brazil and the Ivory Coast of Africa, countries that supply two-thirds of the world's cocoa and have a history of labour abuses and low prices paid to small producers. Although the company mentioned policies that guide investment and contractual decisions involving countries with repressive conditions, no details were offered. No formal policies exist that guarantee worker or environmental protection governing the procurement of key confectionery ingredients like sugar, nuts, and cocoa.

Environmental Management and Performance: Hershey Canada wrote its first environmental policy in 1996. Subsequently, it has implemented other management systems and audits regimes. No single staff member has full-time environmental duties in Canada, but four people and two committees share responsibilities. Money is spent to replace equipment, improve energy efficiency, reformat packaging processes, increase energy efficiency, and recycle manufactured by-products. Hershey does not provide the National Pollutant Release Inventory with information on its chemical releases and transfers. It reports quantities of materials (cardboard, aluminum cans, glass bottles, wood pallets, and packaging material) recycled in the workplace. Early environmental initiatives include the parent's construction of a wastewater treatment plant in the 1920s. More recently, it worked with farmers to decrease the use of phosphate-based fertilizer along the Susquehanna River.

Genetically Modified Ingredients: No information

Community Responsibilities: In Canada and the U.S., Hershey has a long-standing reputation for giving generously to communities where it operates. During the 1990s, the parent contributed US$2.5 million to US$8.1 million annually. At its highest level, this giving represented 2.2% of pre-tax profits. Hershey Canada encourages volunteerism, matches employee donations, and loans of facilities to community groups. Children's causes tend to dominate sponsorship, including groups like the Childrens' Miracle Network. In 1909, company founder, Milton Hershey, began a long period of progressive and philanthropic programs when he built a school for orphaned boys near his company's first factory. Later, homes were built for rent or sale to Hershey workers, and by the time of his death in 1945, an entire social infrastructure had been erected around the chocolate factory. His planned town had a community center, a library, theatres, a museum, a hotel, and golf courses.

www.hersheys.com

High Liner Foods Incorporated

High Liner Foods Incorporated, founded as W.C. Smith & Co. in 1899, is one of Canada's largest seafood producers. With 44.3% of the frozen packaged seafood market, it is also the country's seventh largest frozen food company. Two plants in Nova Scotia and Newfoundland make and market four national brands, while a plant in New Hampshire processes seafood for U.S. consumers. American markets now account for 30% of revenues. Known as National Sea Products until 1999, the company has diversified its product lines into pasta. 51% of Lunenburg, Nova Scotia-based High Liner's equity is held by firms controlled by the Jodrey (Scotia Investments Limited) and Sobey (Empire Company) families.

> **Annual Revenues:** Greater than $300 million
> **Grocery Store Sales:** 63%
> **Brands:** Captain's Chicken, Fisher Boy, Gina Italian Village, High Liner, Light Tonight
> **Corporate Status:** Majority controlled Canadian company, traded on the TSX.
> **Candor:** Honour Roll. Initially, the company was reluctant to participate in 2001, but eventually gave information for most questions. Candor is 84%.

Ethical Management and Consumer Relations: High Liner Foods has a written ethics code, backed by a comprehensive support system. Although no training is provided, employees sign-off on the code, and compliance is part of employee and manager evaluations. The code provides whistleblower protection, guidelines for exchange of business gifts, and terms for negotiating the placement of products in retail stores. High Liner's consumer safety process assurance system—a toll-free consumer phone line, product recall system, and guidelines for advertising—surpasses regulation.

2002 Employees Canada: 1,300 **1996 Employees Canada:** 1,241

Employee Relations: Including American workers, High Liner employs 1,411 people. Job totals increased by 4.75% over the last five years. Seventy-six per cent of Canadian workers belong to unions. The Canadian Auto Worker's and the Fishermen Union Allied Workers in Newfoundland represent almost all hourly workers and trawler crews. Downsizing and restructuring dramatically transformed the company throughout the 1990s. In the mid-1990s, 118 jobs were cut in Lunenburg and Arnold's Cove. Between 1992 and 1994, the 700 people laid off included processing workers, management, supervisory and clerical staff, and offshore personnel. In 1992, two processing plants—one in Nova Scotia and one in Cape Breton—were closed permanently. At the time, the company declined a $3 million assistance offer from the Newfoundland government: help if the (then) National Sea Products would keep the groundfish plant running until the facility could be converted to a shrimp processing operation. Between 1987 and 1992, media reports said that 2,200 jobs were eliminated. When layoffs occur, the company reports redeployment and retraining support, along with severance packages beyond government minimum standards. Two strikes took place in the

1990s: an 11 day walkout of 650 workers at the Lunenburg plant in 1995, and a 1992 stoppage in Halifax over the allocation of overtime. The latter strike, led by the CAW, was ruled illegal. According to media reports, labour relations have a bitter history, and at one time, the corporate culture was reputed to encourage authoritarian attitudes among supervisors. The company stated that in recent years labour-management cooperation has improved, in part due to Total Quality Management and "Good Ideas" plans implemented in the 1990s. More than 50% of staff work beyond a 40-hour week. The company would not discuss over-time or extra compensation policies. Internationally, joint health and safety committees have implemented ergonomic workplace assessments. A tragedy struck in 1993, when a company-owned scallop dragger sank after icing up, killing three men. According to a company report, the 30-year-old boat flooded with water after a forward hatch compartment was left open.

Equity and Family: Women occupy 25% of senior management ranks, up from 10% in 1996. They also hold 12.5% of management positions (down from 20% in 1996) and 50% of total workforce jobs, but no board directorships. No equity policies were reported. Paid days off are given for any cultural or religious holiday, and same-sex couples benefits exist. Family support programs include extended maternity leave, paternity leave, and adoption leave.

Progressive Staff: Flexible scheduling and telecommuting plans are used by less than 1% of employees. Through an EAP, workers can access counselling for drug abuse, along with retirement planning assistance. Communications programs include a newsletter (*The High Liner*), bi-annual crew briefings from the company President, and formal employee feedback surveys. Employee development and education are encouraged through tuition refunds for course work (greater than 75% of costs), and scholarships for the children of employees.

Sourcing and Trade: Honour Roll. Along with its direct investment and operations in the United States, High Liner procures "a significant quantity" of fish and other inputs from sources in Russia, China, the United Kingdom, and Norway. It is one of few companies to report a supply chain code guaranteeing no involvement with suppliers who use forced labour. This code is applied to contractors and licensees and contains standards prohibiting child labour, exploitation of women, unsafe workplace conditions, excessive disciplinary practices, and attempts to thwart collective bargaining. When asked about independent verification of this code, rectification procedures, employee recourse, and public reporting, the company said that these areas were "not applicable" without saying why. High Liner Foods produces a "substantial amount" of private label products in North America.

Environmental Management and Performance: High Liner Foods' written environmental code sets principles, standards, and targets. Managers report progress internally (four times each year) and externally (through a section in the annual report). External teams do not audit performance on this code. An employee committee supports a Manager of Engineering and Maintenance and environmental officers are present at each business unit. A Board committee reviews compliance, assesses potential risks, and monitors company attempts to rectify problems. Although the spokesperson stated that the company has made "several" capital investments for waste management and energy efficiency in recent years, no examples were cited. Along with reducing materials used in packaging, the company demands that suppliers reduce their packaging where possible, and it monitors compliance. Paper, packaging materials, and food wastes are all recycled or composted (no quantities reported), and fish waste is sold as animal feed. In the early 1990s, some fishermen complained that companies, including the former National Sea Products, were dumping tonnes of dead fish from trawlers. The problem came from increased competition to catch the most valuable species. If a ship brought in fish that were too small, or belonged to the wrong species, some fishermen would dump them to make room for more profitable catch that met the terms of their licenses. High Liner states it cooperated with the Federal Government to alleviate this problem, and initiated an effort that was "instrumental in getting a no-dumping provision" inserted into federal regulations. The 2002 spokesperson stated that this story was "old news."

Fish Stock Depletion: In the early 1990s, a crisis hit Canada's ocean fisheries when Atlantic groundfish stock became severely depleted and fishermen's quotas were cut. Company catches fell by a staggering 92% between 1988 and 1995, forcing the streamlining of operations, the sale of trawlers and plants, and plant conversions. Over the course of eight years (from 1987 to 1993) the company made no profits. In 1993, management adopted a foreign fish procurement strategy, and today 90% of raw inputs come from sources around the globe, allowing High Liner to operate with only five company-owned offshore scallop vessels and five wetfish stern trawlers. With this strategy, the company has generally been profitable since 1993, but at major cost to Atlantic fishery jobs.

Genetically Modified Ingredients: No information

Community Responsibilities: High Liner's charitable giving fell from $43,935 (1999) to $24,052 (2000), likely due to a dip in profitability. The spokesperson stated that charitable giving for 2002 was projected to be $43,000. The company's donations policy, approved by the Board, directs at least 50% of contributions to communities with High Liner plants, and 80% of donations are cash. Typically the company targets medical services, education, and youth recreation. A five-member committee helps with decisions and administration of donations. High Liner reported paid time for employee volunteerism in 1997 but not in 2001.

www.highlinerfoods.com

Hostess Frito-Lay Co.

One of the largest players in the salty-snack food business, Hostess Frito-Lay sells approximately 30 million kilograms of potato chips and other snacks each year. PepsiCo Food International has owned the company since 1992, four years after predecessor companies, Hostess and Frito-Lay, merged. The brands and operations of Miss Vickies, which once controlled 1% of the chip market, were acquired in the mid-1990s. Hostess Frito-Lay operates two plants in Ontario and a head office in Mississauga, Ontario. In 2001, parent Pepsi Co. acquired Quaker Oats Company, and subsequent restructuring may have an impact on Hostess Frito-Lay.

2000 Revenues Canada: $828 million

Grocery Store Sales: No information

Brands: Cheetos, Doritos, Frito-Lay, Hostess, Miss Vickies, Rold Gold, Ruffles, Sunchips, Tostitos

Corporate Status: Wholly-owned by U.S.-based parent company.

Candor: The spokesperson was cooperative at all stages. Candor is 36%.

Ethical Management and Consumer Relations: Hostess follows the 12-page code of conduct of PepsiCo, written in the late 1970s, and last updated in 2001. Available in both English and French, it is modified for Canadian operations. It receives an employee sign-off, and includes guidelines for exchange of business gifts. Consumer assurance procedures include a toll-free consumer phone line listed on Hostess products. Charges of anti-competitive practices were raised against Hostess Frito-Lay in the early 1990s, prompting an investigation by federal authorities. A competitor, Old Dutch, alleged that Hostess Frito-Lay had attempted to prevent consumers from trying its product, which was entering the Ontario market after decades of success in the west. Old Dutch accused Hostess Frito-Lay of two things: buying out entire stocks of Old Dutch chips, and enticing variety and grocery store owners to avoid stocking products. A regulatory spokesperson told EthicScan that the Department of Consumer and Corporate Affairs looked at the evidence as a potential civil case in 1991. Its investigation found that there was "some basis for the allegations," but described the extent of Hostess Frito-Lay's questionable activity as "limited." The company guaranteed that such actions would not occur in the future, and on that basis, the government closed its case.

2001 Employees Canada: No information

Employee Relations: In 1998, union spokespeople reported that 39% of the workforce at the Cambridge plant (465 people) belonged to the United Steelworkers of America, and more than 400 London workers were members of the Retail Wholesale Employees, until the plant was subsequently decertified in March 2000. Upon acquiring Miss Vickies in the mid-1990s, Hostess Frito-Lay absorbed its 40 employees in Ontario, Québec, and British Columbia. Ontario regulatory reports recorded 78 permanent layoffs between 1992 and 1993.

Subsequently, the SunChips line at the Cambridge, Ontario facility expanded, adding 60 jobs in 1993. Over the last five years, strikes shut down the Cambridge plant's manufacturing division in February 2000, and the Thunder Bay sales division in 1999. A 1998 union representative described union-management relations at the Cambridge plant as "poor." (No union comment was made in 2001.) Grievances were a concern, and the union spokesperson described the grievance of one worker who had sustained an injury in the company parking lot, but was not allowed to return to the plant. After grieving the case, the union prevailed and the employee resumed work. A 1998 company spokesperson described the union perspective quoted above as "one person's opinion."

> **Workplace Health and Safety:**
> 2000 injuries: 4.8 per 200,000 exposure hours
> 1999 injuries: 11.5 per 200,000 hours
> Hostess Frito-Lay was one of the few companies to report workplace injuries, noting a dramatic improvement over the last few years. Earlier in the 1990s, health and safety performance was poor. According to the 1998 union spokesperson, the repetitive strain injury rate was about 20 per month. In 1995, the Cambridge plant reported 369 injuries of various kinds. The turnaround came in part from actions of joint committees at each site, and ergonomic assessments of workstations conducted by external consultants.

Equity and Family: No data was provided on women in management or senior management ranks. Two of PepsiCo's 13 board directors are women. Hostess has offered same sex couples benefits since provincial legislation permitted them, and an advisory committee on diversity issues works out of the Frito-Lay North America office. All distribution centers, manufacturing sites, and head office locations have disabled access. No statistics on the percentage of people working according to flexible and telecommuting schedules were provided, though the spokesperson said that accommodation is made on an individual basis. Family support for employees comes through a six-month maternity leave top-up, paternal, and adoption leave (no terms mentioned).

Progressive Staff: A company EAP provides staff counselling for alcohol and drug abuse. In 2001, a fitness facility opened at the company's new head office. Communications programs include at least five newsletters at different locations across the country. Through the PepsiCo Foundation, the parent company offers scholarships for children of Hostess Frito-Lay employees. Tuition and book expenses are refunded 100%. The 2001 company spokesperson described an ESOP, called "Sharepower," in which stock options are granted to employees. Eligible earnings are generally based on an employee's basic salary, plus any commissions, overtime, and most bonuses earned in the previous year. PepsiCo also makes stock options available to all full-time employees after one calendar year of employment.

Sourcing and Trade: No information

Environmental Management and Performance: Hostess Frito-Lay follows the environmental code and policies of Frito-Lay North America and conducts internal environmental audits. Only the parent company reports environmental information publicly, through the PepsiCo annual report. There is one full-time environment officer along with a "Green Team Environmental Committee," comprised of managers and technicians at each plant. Conservation teams at each plant work with a National Conservation Team, but no details were provided. The spokesperson stated that the company recycles cardboard, packaging material inserts, glass, and pop cans. Unpackaged waste products go to another company that converts them to cattle feed. Cardboard boxes are reused, "saving millions of boxes" and thousands of pounds of cardboard. Although the company said it has an energy resource conservation, waste reduction, and commodity recycling, no details were given. The company has not been assessed any environmental, health and safety penalties or convictions.

Genetically Modified Ingredients: The spokesperson says the company's "zero tolerance" policy means that GM ingredients "do not enter our facilities." She did not specify how Hostess Frito-Lay guarantees that the potato, oil and other ingredients it sources are completely GMO free. (Again, this information may change following corporate restructuring related to the parent's acquisition of Quaker Foods).

Community Responsibilities: No donations figures or charitable activities were reported. Prior to recent corporate restructuring, the company spokesperson said that Hostess may become involved with the Imagine Campaign and other charitable activities in 2002. The company is working with the Conference Board of Canada and the Canadian Centre for Business in the Community, a not-for-profit group that supports private sector and charitable relationships. Future donations will be organized through the PepsiCo Foundation, and information published in the PepsiCo *Annual Report*. Past sponsorships have gone to Hockey for the Homeless (the president of this organization is a VP Sales in Ontario), Big Brothers/Big Sisters, the Apple Blossom Festival Children's Parade in Kentville, Nova Scotia, and Creative Encounter with Science in Guelph, Ontario. Hostess Frito-Lay has supported scholarships programs in Hamilton, Ontario and Lethbridge, Alberta.

www.fritolay.com

Humpty Dumpty Snack Foods Inc.

Founded in Cambridge, Ontario in 1987 by a former executive of Hostess, Small Fry Snack Foods quickly grew into a hundred million dollars in sales, snack foods company. In 1994, it completed an uncommon acquisition when it bought Humpty Dumpty, a large competitor. This purchase was followed by the acquisition of Murphy's Potato Chips in 1996, and Small Fry's first public offering of shares in June of 1997. Today the company has four plants in Prince Edward Island, Québec, New Brunswick, and Ontario. In 2000, Small Fry completely acquired the corporate name of Humpty Dumpty after purchasing all trademarks, distribution system, and assets in the U.S. market. In 2000, the operating company (Small Fry Snack Foods) amalgamated with the parent company and became known as Humpty Dumpty Snack Foods Inc.

> **Revenues:** $169 million
> **Grocery Store Sales:** 34%
> **Brands:** Humpty Dumpty Chips, Humpty Dumpty Snacks, Jack's Snacks, Maine Coast Kettle Chips
> **Corporate Status:** Wholly-owned subsidiary of Canadian company.
> **Candor:** Fewer than a third of EthicScan's questions were answered. Candor is 28%.

Ethical Management and Consumer Relations: Although no formal written code of ethics was reported, Humpty Dumpty does have a policy to guide salespeople negotiating product placement on retail shelves. Its consumer assurance process exceeds regulation, and includes a toll-free consumer phone line, product recall system, and advertising guidelines.

2002 Employees: 983   **2001 Employees:** 907

1999 Employees: 789

Employee Relations: Excepting 50 American employees, all staff work in Canada. Small Fry's workforce grew modestly in recent years with acquisition of new U.S. distribution rights. Approximately 43% of workers belong to the Retail Wholesale Union, the Milk and Bread Drivers, or the Teamsters. About 200 jobs were lost during the restructuring that followed the 1994 absorption of Humpty Dumpty. Another 175 workers were cut with the closure of Murphy's Potato Chips plant in Kitchener in 1996, though 40 jobs were added in Toronto, when product lines were transferred. Laid off employees received eight weeks paid notice, plus severance allowances based on years of service. Employment action centers placed all but three or four workers into other full-time jobs, according to the company spokesperson. In July 2001, employees at the Lachine, Québec plant (represented by the Bakery, Confectionery, and Tobacco Workers International Union) went on strike for a new collective agreement. The strike was settled within two weeks. On average, about 25 grievances are filed annually, the spokesperson noted, with approximately 1% requiring formal third stage arbitration. Grievances are quite cyclical, depending on the season, with noticeable spikes occurring around collective agreement negotiations.

Equity and Family: Two of 11 senior managers are women, but there are no women on the seven-member board of directors. The spokesperson reported that the company follows provincial equity legislation at each operating facility, has passed provincial monitoring in Ontario in 2002, and had updated policy to achieve compliance with new Québec legislation. Harassment protection (gender, sexual orientation, race, and disability) is covered by company policy and reinforced with training. The spokesperson reported two human rights cases from the 1990s involving racial issues, neither of which resulted in convictions. Humpty Dumpty does not provide further home-work balance or family support programs, though the spokesperson commented that the company does comply with local regulations for all labour standards.

Progressive Staff: Humpty Dumpty refunds 100% of the cost of courses, and 50% of the cost of books. No other programs were mentioned.

Sourcing and Trade: A procurement code was developed in conjunction with provincial and federal agriculture ministries. When purchasing ingredients, the company insists that potato growers and suppliers of oil and other supplies meet the standards of this code.

Environmental Management and Performance: No formal environmental policy exists. A chemical engineer has part-time environmental responsibilities, supported by a staff committee that works to improve packaging usage, sanitation, and recycling. During the 1990s, energy and resource conservation programs were created, along with waste reduction and perishable goods disposal programs. Workplace recycling programs were reported for cardboard, office paper, and wood pallets, and any useable waste from food processing is sent to local farmers for animal feed. Between 1990 and 1997, the company reduced excess packaging materials by about 20%. Humpty Dumpty did not provide the National Pollutant Release Inventory with information on its chemical releases and transfers, but the spokesperson said it has no major pollution problems.

Genetically Modified Ingredients: As a member of the Food and Consumer Products Manufacturers of Canada (FCPMC), the company follows the industry group's policy on GMOs, which is to use only genetically modified ingredients that have been approved by Health Canada.

Community Responsibilities: No current donations information is provided. Typically, Humpty Dumpty sponsors local activities wherever it operates, donating about $100,000 in product and cash each year, although a spokesperson stated that there is no specific mechanism in place to track the dollar amount of donations. The company was an official supplier to the Canadian Olympic team during the 1996 summer games.

www.humptydumpty.com

Imperial Tobacco Canada Ltd

With over 60 different brands of tobacco products, Imperial Tobacco Canada Limited controls about 70% of Canada's domestic cigarette market. Incorporated in Montreal in 1912, Imperial is now a wholly owned indirect subsidiary of B.A.T. plc. Currently, the company has two cigarette-making plants, one in Montreal and the other in Guelph, Ontario, along with four tobacco processing plants in Aylmer, Ontario. The outstanding shares of Imperial Tobacco's former corporate parent, Imasco Ltd (50% was owned by Canadian individuals and institutional investors, 42% was held by B.A.T. Industries of the United Kingdom) were bought by B.A.T. Canada in February 2000. The two companies were amalgamated under the name of Imperial Tobacco Canada Limited.

Revenues: No information
Grocery Store Sales: 18% of revenues in 1996
Brands: Avanti, Cameo, du Maurier, Matinee, Peter Jackson, Player's
Corporate Status: Wholly-owned subsidiary of U.K.-based parent company.
Candor: Honour Roll. The 2001 spokesperson provided a great deal of information during several phone interviews. Candor is 81%.

Ethical Management and Consumer Relations: Imperial's twelve point *Code of Ethics* include employees' responsibility to maintain free competition, truth in communications, proper terms of business gift exchange, fair supplier relationships, and respect for confidential or insider information. The Code receives a sign-off from senior officers once a year. In the early 1990s, Canadian-made cigarette brands were being smuggled from the U.S. and sold here illicitly at cheap prices because no taxes were charged. Allegations circulated in the media that Canadian companies intentionally supported this contraband market by exporting large shipments to the U.S., knowing full well that these products would make it back to Canada through black market rings. Imperial successfully refuted the allegations with reports and records that its exports dropped by 30% during the period in question, from four billion cigarettes in 1991 to 2.8 billion in 1992.

2002 Employees Canada: 1,900   **1991 Employees Canada:** 2,404

Employee Relations: Honour Roll. During the 1990s, Imperial's total workforce fell steadily, by about 20% between 1991 and 1997, before dipping another 9% between 1997 and 2000. Seasonable employment totals vary from year to year. Generally, 119 full-time and 413 seasonal people work in Aylmer (compared with 83 full-time and 435 seasonal in 1997), 569 are in Guelph (670 in 1997), and another 956 at Montreal (997 in 1997). Three employees work outside Canada, at ITL USA. Employment levels have dropped largely because technological advancements made jobs redundant. Investments have achieved higher productivity rates and lower costs. By 1999, all outsourced tobacco product production could be produced by a fully-automated $28.5 million plant run by six employees on two shifts. All leaf tobacco processing was consolidated at the Aylmer plant, Canada's only tobacco processing facility to produce both domestic and export goods. Imperial handles layoffs by cutting staff gradually, voluntarily working with unions to create generous severance pay packages, and encouraging early retirement. In Guelph, Aylmer, and Montreal, 59% of all workers belong to union locals, organized mainly by the Bakery, Confectionery, Tobacco Workers, and Grain Millers International. The labour spokesperson described turnover as "very low." Injuries have fallen steadily during the 1990s, from 135 in 1992 to 60 in 1999, and down to 49 in 2000. The spokesperson attributed these results to increased automation, since robots complete work previously done by people. Training expenditures of $2,370 per employee represent over 20 paid hours per employee per year, and course reimbursements go as high as 100% of tuition and book costs. All non-unionized employees can receive up to 5% of their annual salary as a bonus, based on the company's market share and other factors. Only executives are eligible for the company's share ownership or stock option plans.

Equity and Family: Women hold three of 45 board directorships, 49 of 275 (18%) of senior management jobs, and 34% total workforce jobs. An anti-sexual harassment policy includes guidelines for employees and supervisors. No formal employment equity program is in place, but the company claims that it meets or exceeds all federal and provincial legislation requirements. Since 1996, Imperial has offered a same sex staff benefits package, but guaranteed no paid days off for cultural and religious observances. Such decisions are left to the discretion of individual managers. Disabled people can access the majority but not all of Imperial's buildings. Parental leaves of 34 weeks are available to all employees, but only non-union staff at Montreal can use a daycare service that is partially funded. Office employees can arrange for flexible times schedules around the "core hours" between 9:30 to 3:30, and all employees are compensated for time worked beyond a 40 hour week, either in pay or in extra time off.

Progressive Staff: Imperial Tobacco encourages sports activities among employees by providing funding and time for employees to organize teams and events. A gymnasium will be available at the new Montreal head office by the end of 2001, and employees have organized a weight watchers program. The company communicates internally through newsletters, and e-mail notices which reach more than half of company employees. Open door management is part of corporate philosophy. Imperial's staff policies have consistently ranked it as one of Canada's 100 Best Companies to Work For by the Globe and Mail's *Report on Business* magazine.

Environmental Management and Performance: Imperial's company-wide environmental code is supported by comprehensive facilities' audits conducted by external personnel every two years. Internal progress reports are filed each year with Corporate Risk Management and the Board of Directors. Along with a Senior Advisor in Risk, one employee takes on a 30% time environmental portfolio. The spokesperson said the company was "not yet at the stage" where life cycle environmental systems and emission reduction targets are part of process development. No formal waste reduction program exists, but one is being considered. Each year, 45% of process waste is recycled, including cans, glass, pallets, tobacco dust, and paper products. As a participant in the Voluntary Challenge Registry, an initiative of the federal government to promote the reduction of greenhouse gas emissions, Imperial Tobacco won a "Silver Award" for its reduction efforts. The company is a member of several provincial environmental associations in Québec and Ontario, and environmental sponsorships include a $75,000 annual payment to Collecte sélective Québec, a nonprofit organization that promotes blue box recycling programs across Québec. The company recently worked with the Catfish Creek Conservation Authority to plant 10,000 white pine trees and increase local forest area coverage from 14% to 28%.

Genetically Modified Ingredients: The company responded to questions on GM issues, noting that currently, no tobacco grown in Canada uses genetically modified inputs. Since the federal government has not yet defined the term "genetically modified," Imperial Tobacco does not yet have a policy in this area.

Sourcing and Trade: Although no policy obliges the company to do so, approximately 70% to 95% of Imperial's raw materials are sourced in Canada, including 98% of tobacco inputs. All products are sold in Canada, excepting 1% sold in duty-free shops at borders. Most equipment comes from Europe, and since no cigarette paper manufacturers operate in Canada, all of its paper supplies are sourced abroad. With no foreign sourcing code of its own, Imperial generally follows BAT's regulations for managing labour issues abroad.

Community Responsibilities: Honour Roll. Imperial Tobacco donated almost $6 million in 2000, and it will honor another $2.5 million of commitments made by former parent, Imasco, until the end of 2003. The Imperial Employees Charity Fund raised $95,630 in 2000, and $91,080 in 1999. Donations are administered under Imperial Tobacco's name, and policies managed by a donations manager, executives from Public Affairs, upper management, and one support staff. Individual business units provide input into the larger corporate decisions and each receives a modest budget that permits them to support local organizations. Imperial helps national and local charities, particularly ones located in communities of operation. Since 2000, the company focus has been on health care (particularly on care for the aged), post-secondary education, and support for the arts. Since its inception, the company's du Maurier program has provided $40 million in capital grants to more than 350 arts groups. The company spokesperson noted that charitable activities are never associated with "non-adults" and do not contribute towards promoting Imperial Tobacco or its products, a point hotly criticized by the anti-smoking lobby.

Tobacco Sponsorship: Anti-smoking advocates have scrutinized the role of tobacco sponsorship in the arts and sport, raising concerns that attaching cigarette logos to cultural events promotes smoking. Tobacco companies respond that these sponsorships merely redistribute brand sales among existing smokers. Federal legislation has banned advertising on radio and television, and forced tobacco companies to pull out of all sponsorship activities by October 2003. The company cannot, by law, give any in-kind donations. Any employee donation that is $25 or greater is matched by the company, provided no legal exclusions apply.

When Imperial decided to sell its cigar business, a factory in Joliette, Québec was slated for closure. Management met with community groups and the city's mayor and council to strike a plan that would minimize the closing's impact on the community. Imperial offered to sell the plant to the city for a token amount, because, according to the spokesperson, its desire was to "not leave an empty building." Ultimately, another company bought the plant.

www.imperial-tobacco.com

Johnson & Johnson Inc.

With sales of US$29.1 billion, Johnson & Johnson (USA) calls itself the world's largest healthcare products maker. The Montreal-based wholly-owned consumer products subsidiary sells baby care, feminine and oral hygiene products in Canada. Its sole Canadian consumer plant in Montreal produces feminine hygiene and some baby products in Québec. A Johnson & Johnson Medical Devices division has a manufacturing plant in Peterborough, Ontario. Janssen Inc. of Canada, is another wholly owned operating subsidiary of the American parent.

> **2000 Revenues Canada:** Approximately $300 million
> **Grocery Store Sales:** No information
> **Brands:** Band-Aid, Carefree, Compeede foot care, KY jelly, OB, Purpose, Reach toothbrush, Shields condoms, Shower to Shower, Stay-free, Stimudent
> **Corporate Status:** Wholly-owned by U.S. parent company.
> **Candor:** The spokesperson did not return phone calls or faxes. Johnson & Johnson provided responses to 13% of EthicScan's questions.

Ethical Management and Consumer Relations: Johnson & Johnson incorporates many components from its parent's code of ethics, which is embedded in the company "Credo" that was first written during the Depression of the 1930s. Beginning with doctors, nurses, patients, and parents, the "Credo" lists a hierarchy of those to whom the company is accountable, putting employees and communities ahead of suppliers and distributors. The last group cited is shareholders. This "Credo" was modified once in the 1970s and again in 1989, when environmental commitments were added. The parent company's relationship with the CSR community in the U.S. has grown through its association with the not-for-profit group, Business for Social Responsibility, an organization that provides resources to companies who wish to address their corporate social responsibility.

> **Ethics Policies and Consumer Crisis:** In 1982, the parent company was hit with arguably the most serious product tampering attack in US history. Someone maliciously spiked its flagship product, Tylenol, with cyanide, killing and harming a number of consumers. Johnson & Johnson's response (pulling potentially poisoned products from shelves and innovating new package seals that soon became the industry's responsible standard) was so fast and effective, that it restored consumer confidence. The "Credo", the foundation for the company's consumer assurance process, is generally credited for bolstering the company's crisis management plan. Over subsequent decades, the company's market share and reputation were both enhanced by its policies and actions.

2002 Employees Canada: No information   **2000 Employees Worldwide:** 98,500

Employee Relations: No employee information was reported in 2002, but in 1998 the company employed 800 Canadians. In 1997, Johnson & Johnson Medical Products (distinct from the consumer products business) eliminated 200 jobs when it moved production to the U.S., Juarez, Mexico and Neuchatel, Switzerland. Structural changes at the Medical Products division began in 1992 and 1993, when five hospital supply companies were consolidated into one division, resulting in layoffs for 78 Peterborough staff.

Equity and Family: No statistics were provided on advancement of women nor equity policies. Johnson & Johnson is one of 80 businesses in the world to endorse standardized policies of workplace principles for treating people with AIDS . In the U.S., the parent company subsidizes off-site daycare, provides an on-site center, and operates a sick bay for the children of workers who might otherwise miss work to take care of their kids. On-site classes are offered for parenting skills, nutrition, toddler health, and stress management. In Canada, the company offers paid time-off for emergency family care, unpaid time-off for care of sick dependents, and adoption leaves. The parent company has received public recognition for its support of women, and has been named a top employer by the Women's Business Enterprise National Council (a lifestyle magazine for people with disabilities), *Working Mother* magazine, and *Fortune Magazine's* list of "100 Best Companies to Work For."

Progressive Staff: No information is provided on employee assistance, internal communications, gainsharing, or workplace wellness initiatives in Canada.

Sourcing and Trade: The American parent operates companies in 51 countries, including China (where independent labour unions are illegal). No policies on international management or foreign sourcing were reported. The Chinese operation, Xian-Janssen Pharmaceutical, was rated by Fortune China as one of the 10 most admired global companies operating in Asia, based on product quality, corporate citizenship, community outreach, support for education, charitable contributions, and environmental stewardship. No information about the operation's labour practices was listed.

Environmental Management: An "Environmental Responsibility Cycle" identifies nine stages of product responsibility, from product development to consumer disposal. At each stage, the company strives to make the effects of its products environmentally neutral. Through the environmental stewardship standards contained in the parent's *Worldwide Practices Manual,* foreign divisions follow environmental benchmarks, even if the country of operation has standards that are less stringent than those found in North America. Periodic environmental assessments ensure that third-party auditors evaluate the company's 200 facilities. Training for product and packaging development is extended to 2,000 people working in research, operations, and marketing. Environmental standards and objectives are measured as part of managers' performance. Since 1993, the parent company has published public environmental, health, and safety reports, and the most recent ones incorporate the Global Reporting Initiative (GRI) guidelines for content and organization. (The GRI was established in 1997 by the Coalition for Environmentally Responsible Economies (CERES) and the UN as a way to standardize global CSR reporting.) Taskforce committees at Johnson & Johnson convene managers from North America, Europe, and Africa to set and oversee the implementation of policies affecting legal compliance, public affairs, environment, health, and safety. Ultimately, the parent company's Vice-Chairman is responsible for corporate environmental policy.

Environmental Performance: The American company eliminated more than 5.5 million pounds of packaging from 32 products (between 1988 and 2000), and increased its recycling by 83% (from 1991 to 2000). Over the last decade, the parent company reduced its use of energy by 23.1% (just short of a 25% goal), packaging by 27% (goal of 25%), office paper by 50%, water by 79%, toxic chemicals by 95%, hazardous waste by 19%, solid waste by 77%, and wastewater disposal by 88%. Between 1989 and 1994, Johnson & Johnson operations in more than 120 countries removed CFCs from all manufacturing processes. In Canada, Johnson & Johnson does not report to the National Pollutant Release Inventory on its chemical releases and transfers. The parent company is part of the Dow Jones Sustainability Index, which lists global companies that demonstrate a commitment to sustainability.

Genetically Modified Ingredients: No information

Animal Testing: None is conducted in Canada. The parent company's policy states that in order to maintain product safety, some testing is mandatory. Guidelines establish the conditions under which animals are to be tested, along with a corporate commitment to replace, reduce, and refine animal testing. Over the last decade, Johnson & Johnson has spent more than $10 million on different non-animal tests, including *in-vitro* testing.

Community Responsibilities: In Canada Johnson & Johnson's annual donations average $50,000. In 2000, the parent, and all its international companies, gave more than $200 million in cash gifts and product donations, representing 3.3% of pre-tax profit worldwide. In-kind donations represent 72% of these donations, with cash (25% American and 3% international) representing the rest. In Canada, an employee fund directs $30,000 to ten different organizations (including the United Way, the Canadian Cancer Foundation, and the Québec Heart and Stroke Foundation). Johnson & Johnson's parent has donated products worth tens of millions of dollars to organizations concerned with maternal and child health care support (such as UNICEF's worldwide child survival program, and the Environmental & Occupational Health Sciences Institute at Rutgers University). It also supports education, community organizations, the arts, and environmental groups, and is involved with many conservation organizations (including the Global Environmental Management Initiative, the US National Audubon Society, the Nature Conservatory, the World Business Council for Sustainable Development, the World Wildlife Fund).

www.jnj.com

JTI Macdonald

Founded as RJR Macdonald Inc. in 1858 in Montreal, JTI Macdonald is Canada's third largest tobacco producer, with a 15% domestic market share. Operations include a Montreal cigarette-making plant, sales offices scattered across the country, and a head office in Toronto. A processing operation in Tillsonburg, Ontario was sold in 1996. The majority of the company's products are made from Virginia flue-cured tobaccos grown in southwestern Ontario. When former parent, RJR Nabisco sold its non-U.S. operations in May 1999, the Canadian company was acquired by Japan Tobacco Inc., and its name changed accordingly.

Revenues: No information
Grocery Store Sales: No information
Brands: Export A, Red Camel, Tempo, Tueros, Vantage
Corporate Status: Wholly-owned subsidiary of Japan-based parent company.
Candor: The corporate spokesperson gave some response to EthicScan's research. Candor is 26%.

Ethical Management and Consumer Relations: JTI Macdonald has a written code of ethics that addresses the negotiation of product placement on store shelves and the exchange of gifts with retailers and suppliers. In Japan, the parent company has voluntarily halted product advertising on television and radio because it is working to create self-regulation advertising standards. The Canadian federal government launched a $1 billion suit against Canada's major cigarette makers in an attempt to recoup lost cigarette tax money. In 2000, a decision in a New York district court ruled that Canada's case was based on a flawed argument, and it was then thrown out as a breach of U.S. law. The law states that U.S. courts are not responsible for enforcing foreign tax matters. The only place to settle the case now will be in Canadian courts. By 2002, the Canadian government was no closer to succeeding.

2002 Employees Canada: 550   **1991 Employees Canada:** 790

Employee Relations: In 2001, 45% of Canadian employees were unionized. Between 1991 and 1997, unionized jobs in Canada dropped 79%, from 520 to 290, while salaried positions increased 21%, from 270 to 326. The Bakery, Confectionery and Tobacco Workers union represents production site employees in Montreal. No strikes have occurred in the last ten years. No worldwide employment figures were provided. Between 1998 and 2001 annual employee training expenditures increased from $250,000 to $300,000. No gainsharing plans exist for employees.

Equity and Family: No information on the advancement of women in management was provided. In 1996, women comprised 38% of the general workforce, 30% of management (compared with 12% in 1991), and two of six executive committee members. The company offers same sex couples benefits, but has no policy on sexual harassment.

Progressive Staff: Three types of confidential counselling services are available through an Employee Assistance Plan. An electronic employee newsletter is produced every six weeks and posted for all employees through the company Intranet. Employee incentive rewards are evaluated based on the achievement of personal objectives set each year. Employees can be reimbursed for up to 100% of tuition costs spent on courses offered outside the company. Flexible scheduling is available to employees, though the spokesperson did not indicate whether or not this program was extended to production workers.

Sourcing and Trade: For its Canadian operations, the company attempts to source domestically, but no formal policy enforces this priority. JTI Macdonald has no policy or code related to procurement from countries operating under repressive regimes, and no information was reported on international supply chain operations.

Environmental Management and Performance: The parent company's Global Environment Committee formulates the JT Global Environment Charter and the JT Environmental Action Plan, but details on these frameworks or application for Canadian operations were not provided. No separate environmental or sustainability report is published publicly. An unspecified number of employees have part-time environmental responsibility for recycling programs. Internally-generated commodities—paper, cans, glass, packaging—are covered, while manufacturing by-products, such as tobacco and filters, are managed through waste reduction initiatives at the plant level. The company manages the environmental performance of its own vehicles.

Tobacco Promotion and Youth: In the 1990s, a public interest organization called INFACT led a boycott of what was then RJ Reynolds. The group claimed that the company-created heavily-promoted cartoon character, Joe Camel, encourages under-age youths to smoke. The campaign was based on a series of 1991 articles in the *Journal of the American Medical Association*, which argued that Joe Camel was as recognizable to children as Mickey Mouse. Furthermore, the article suggested that the campaign was more successful with children than with adults, and that Camels were the brand of choice among young people who smoked. The company has consistently contested these allegations. In the 1980s, RJR launched a Canadian poster campaign in transit shelters for its Tempo cigarettes, targeting young smokers. After public response criticizing the ad's appeal to youth, the corporate spokesperson stated that the campaign was intended for 18-to-24-year-olds. Another poster used in the late 1990s as part of RJR's sponsorship of Canadian Music Week, was also criticized in the media for allegedly appealing to young smokers. In a separate case, the Canadian Cancer Society, concerned about the proximity that a billboard (advertising a company brand) had to a school, filed a complaint against RJR Macdonald in 1996, charging non-compliance with the tobacco industry's advertising code. (According to Canadian regulations tobacco ads cannot be placed within 200 metres of an elementary school.) The company stated that it "gave precise and strict instructions about the 200 metre limit to the agency responsible for billboard placement," and when it discovered the violation of the Code, it began a review of "every single billboard and poster placement to ensure compliance" with the limit.

Community Responsibilities: No information on Canadian charitable or corporate citizenship activities was reported. In Japan, the parent company supports classical music through the Affinis Arts Foundation, and it has also established the JT Bio-history Research Hall for the study of life sciences.

www.jti.com

Kellogg Canada Inc.

The founder of Kellogg Co., self-described as the world's leading producer of ready-to-eat cereals, invented Corn Flakes in 1906 as a vegetarian health food for patients convalescing at a Michigan sanatorium. Founded in 1914, Toronto-based Kellogg Canada Inc. was its first plant outside of the United States. Today its one factory in London, Ontario supplies all of the Canadian market with 63% of its capacity, using the rest to make products for export, mostly to the United States. The parent company manufactures cereal at 26 plants in 17 countries, and sells products in more than 150 countries. Over the last decade and a half, Kellogg Co. has restructured its interests, divesting its Shirriff division (puddings, pies, and potatoes), as well as its fruit spreads, dessert toppings, and caramel spread business. The W.K. Kellogg Foundation, one of America's largest foundations, holds 34% of the parent company's shares.

> **2000 Revenues Canada:** $550 million
> **Grocery Store Sales:** No information
> **Brands:** All-Bran, Almond & Raisin Muslix, Apple Crisp Muslix, Bran Buds with Psyllium, Bran Flakes, Corn Flakes, Corn Pops, Crispix, Cruncheroos, Eggo Waffles, Froot Loops, Frosted Flakes, Honey-Nut Corn Flakes, Just Right, Kellogg's Nutri-Grain Cereal Bars, Kellogg's Pop Tarts, Mini-Wheats, Raisin Bran, Rice Krispies, Special K, Vector
> **Corporate Status:** Wholly-owned subsidiary of publicly-traded U.S.-based parent company.
> **Candor:** Kellogg's participation was exemplary in 1998, providing 97% of the data requested. Candor is 70%.

Ethical Management and Consumer Relations: Honour Roll. Kellogg's code of conduct, written in 1960 and updated on an ongoing basis, contains a human rights provision. It is signed by employees, translated into the languages spoken in countries of operation, with compliance as part of employee and manager evaluations. A separate policy addresses giving and receiving of gifts with suppliers and customers. As early as 1981, the Kellogg Company adopted "Social Responsibility" as part of its organizational goals, and later (in 1986 and 1992) incorporated "five shared values" including "Integrity and Ethics and Social Responsibility." The parent company's board includes a social responsibility committee, and the VP of Corporate Affairs at the Michigan head office acts as Chief Ethics Officer. The spokesperson said that the company conducts an independent social or ethics audit, but no details were provided. Kellogg's consumer safety process assurance includes a toll-free consumer phone line, and a product recall system that exceeds government regulation. Kellogg's advertising budget typically represents 5% to 10% of its revenues. The company has adopted advertising guidelines and is a member of the group Concerned Children's Advertisers.

2002 Employees Canada: 950   **1991 Employees Canada:** 1,291

Employee Relations: The Canadian workforce has dropped steadily by over 25% in the last decade. Substantial cuts accompanied a parent company restructuring (14,511 staff in

1997, down from 17,239 in 1990), though it now employs 19,000. A Toronto office closed, and the Shirriff and Farm House pudding and frozen pie plants were sold. Other production lines were moved to Kellogg's $300 million high-tech plant in London, while the Eggo waffle business was transferred to the United States. While Canadian jobs have fallen slightly over the last five years (41 in Toronto and 16 in London), the parent's totals have increased by about 25%. Approximately 60% of Canadian workers belong to unions, including the American Federation of Grain Millers. The company offers redeployment, retraining, career transition assistance, and severance packages beyond the government minimum for downsized workers (who can receive the equivalent of three months to two years of salary). On one occasion 540 London employees went on a two-week strike over the issue of pensions. A 1997 union spokesperson (American Federation of Grain Millers) described labour relations as "going very well" at the London location, although he mentioned periodic problems with the company's efforts to contract out. The annual employee turnover rate was reported at 9%, which is average to high for this sector. All employee levels receive some form of training and opportunity to help design programs. In 2000 the company spent $1,500 per employee to upgrade skills (equal to about 1% of total payroll), more than double what was spent ($700) in 1997. The company takes advantage of "in-house training opportunities" where possible, and tuition is fully refunded upon successful completion of coursework. All employees can buy shares using a payroll deduction plan.

Health and Safety:
2000 Injuries: 4 per 200,000 hours
1999 Injuries: 5 per 200,000 hours
Lost-time accident frequency rates have not improved over the last five years. The company recorded its best performance in 1995 (3.6 per 200,000 down from 3.96 in 1990). Safety conditions in London improved in the early 1990s, when lost-time accidents and lost work days criteria justified an internal award, the Kellogg Company Safety Excellence Award, each year between 1992 and 1996.

Equity and Family: The proportion of women in senior management has increased from 8% in 1991 to two of eight in 2001 (25%). Women hold 12 of 32 (38%) management positions, but zero of five on the executive committee. In the overall workforce, women were 33% in 1997, up slightly from 31% in 1991. Formal policies address workplace diversity and the hiring of minorities, disabled and aboriginal peoples. An anti-harassment policy (covering gender, sexual orientation, race, and disability), which is reviewed annually, supports diversity training. Kellogg Canada is in the process of establishing an advisory committee on diversity issues.

Progressive Staff: Honour Roll. Retirement planning, eldercare, and substance abuse counselling are available through EAP referral programs. Fitness subsidies are open to all employees, while an on-site gym is open only to management at head office and the London plant. Internal communication includes a newsletter, *Kellogg News of Canada* (published four times per year), and supervisors who conduct semi-annual performance reviews. Kellogg was one of the few companies to report statistics on flexible work arrangements: between 5-10 %

of employees work on flexible schedules, while another 10-15% take advantage of telecommuting programs.

Sourcing and Trade: Although Kellogg operates in 20 countries, no policy guides international sourcing, trade, or foreign procurement. Since the mid-1990s, plant sites include India, Guangzhou, China, and Latvia. The company says it makes every effort to develop partnerships with local suppliers. Kellogg makes no private label goods for any other company, an unusual practice in the cereal industry.

Environmental Management and Performance: Kellogg Canada supports its environmental code with employee sign-off and training. Every year a team of internal and external staff at the London plant audits packaging and production processes, solid waste disposal, wastewater discharge, and air emissions. An environmental report is filed with the board of directors at the parent each year. In 1996, a steering committee organized four sub-committees to address individual areas of environmental concern. Kellogg Canada does not report to the National Pollutant Release Inventory with information on its chemical releases and transfers. Kellogg has reduced packaging, and placed environmental demands on packaging requirements of suppliers, who are monitored for compliance. The company supports provincial recycling programs. In 1996 it reported recycled quantities of paper, cardboard, cans, glass, wood pallets, and plastic, along with reuse and recycle programs for other metals and waste oil. Similar details were not provided in 2001. Excess food and reusable wastes are sent to food banks and reclamation centers. In the mid-1990s, the company spent $500,000 to increase its volume of recoverable solid materials. By the mid-1990s, the company had removed its last remaining underground diesel fuel storage tank and destroyed all stored PCBs. In 1997, wastewater effluent was reduced significantly (by over 60%). In 1996, recognition of waste sent to landfill improvements came with a Recycling Council of Ontario "Bronze Award."

Genetically Modified Ingredients: GMO controversy hit the company in March 2000 when Greenpeace planned demonstrations in 35 cities across Canada to protest the presence of genetically modified ingredients in Frosted Flakes and Special K. Because Canada's oversight system does not separate genetically modified corn from traditional corn, both products are likely to contain genetically modified ingredients. The 2001 Kellogg Canada spokesperson said the company buys ingredients for its products on the open market, and that, since biotechnology-produced grains have been approved by Health Canada, "all Canadian manufacturers are using these ingredients in the same proportion that they occur in the national supply." Until the Canadian General Standards Board (CGSB) develops and implements a labelling standard, neither the presence nor absence of GMO ingredients can be listed. Kellogg Canada supports the CGSB's approach to labelling foods, which will set an "understandable, informative, verifiable" standard, which is "not false and not misleading." The spokesperson from the parent company's headquarters added that the company would always respond to consumer preferences. Should U.S. standards come to match those in Europe, the Canadian plant's entire export potential could be compromised.

Community Responsibilities: No donations statistics were provided in 2000. Kellogg Canada traditionally gives 1% of its pre-tax profits, and is pledged to maintain this level. Typically it splits donations between cash and gifts-in-kind. Employee donations to educational causes and institutions are matched through payroll deductions, group events, and individual gifts. The company focuses on nutrition and children. Along with funding a scholarship for the Boys and Girls Clubs of Canada, the Kellogg Hope Fund gives money to the Hospital for Sick Children in Toronto, Kids Help Phone line, the Canadian Foundation for AIDS Research, the Children's Wish Foundation, and Invest in Kids. The company has partnered with major health charities, include the Canadian Cancer Society, Canadian Diabetes Association, Health Canada, Heart and Stroke Foundation, and the Department of Nutritional Sciences at the University of Toronto. It also sponsors scientific research at several Canadian institutions studying the effect of fibre and diet on various diseases. Between 1996 and 1999, Ontario breakfast programs were funded up to $100,000 each year. Donations go to major food banks as well as flood relief efforts like those in Saguenay, Lac St. Jean, and Winnipeg.

www.kelloggs.ca

Kraft Canada Inc.

Kraft Canada Inc. was created after the 1989 merger of General Foods and Kraft Ltd. Today, it is a subsidiary of Kraft Foods North America, a subsidiary of Kraft Foods Inc. of Northfield, Illinois. Until June 2001, when Kraft Foods Inc. became a publicly-traded company, it was a subsidiary of Philip Morris Companies Inc. Philip Morris (now in the process of changing its name to Altria Group, Inc.), which still holds the largest portion of Kraft Food's shares, is one of the world's largest tobacco companies. In December 2000, Philip Morris completed its acquisition of Nabisco Holdings. Nabisco's brands have subsequently been integrated into the Kraft Foods business worldwide. As a diversified foods products company, Kraft Canada operates five plants in Québec, 14 in Ontario, and one in British Columbia. After divesting Hostess Frito-Lay in 1992, Kraft Ltd acquired Nabob Foods, along with Nabisco's ready-to-eat breakfast line (including cereal brands like Shredded Wheat and Shreddies) in 1993. The Canadian company has a strong position in the domestic cheese market, accounting for approximately 30% of all cheese sold (by volume). Through brands like Maxwell House, Nabob, and Sanka, it also controls roughly 35% of the Canadian coffee market.

> **2000 Revenues:** $2.2 billion
> **Grocery Store Sales:** Over 95%
> **Brands:** Aylmer, Baker's Chocolate, Bull's Eye, Cheez Whiz, Cracker Barrel, Crystal Light, Cool Whip, Delissio, Del Monte, Dream Whip, Handi-Snacks, Jell-O, Kool-Aid, Kraft Cheese, Kraft Dinner, Lunchables, Maxwell House Cafe, Maxwell House, Milka, Milk-Bone, Minute Rice, Miracle Whip, Nabisco cookies and crackers, Nabob, Philadelphia Cream Cheese, Post cereals, Sanka, Shake n Bake, Shredded Wheat, Shreddies, Stove Top, Tang, Toblerone, Velveeta
> **Corporate Status:** Wholly-owned subsidiary of publicly-traded U.S. parent company.
> **Candor:** Kraft provided responses to 39% of EthicScan's questions.

Ethical Management and Consumer Relations: Kraft Canada's Business *Conduct Policy* was written by former parent Philip Morris and is updated annually. This code is read and signed by every corporate department on a quarterly basis. It covers the exchange of business gifts, is translated into all languages spoken in countries of operation, and supported by mandatory ethics training. A North American operations handbook covers the negotiation of shelf space. Each operating unit has an in-house lawyer who also serves as an ethics officer and is responsible for policy issues and compliance.

2002 Employees Canada: 7,300 **1997 Employees Canada:** 4,000

Employee Relations: The acquisition of Nabisco has resulted in the large increase of Kraft full-time employees between 1997 and 2002. Upon completing the acquisition of Nabisco in December 2000, Kraft Foods Inc. employed 114,000 workers globally. In March, 2002, Kraft Foods Inc. announced that approximately 7,500 jobs would be cut by the end of the year due to the acquisition. As of March 2002, the company had already cut 3,200 former Nabisco workers, and closed 16 plants. Approximately 30% of the Canadian workforce belong to one of six different unions including the United Food and Commercial Workers; Canadian Cereal Workers; Bakery, Confections, Tobacco, and Grain Millers; International Association of Machinists and Aerospace Workers; Canadian Auto Workers; or International Union of Operating Engineers. Whenever downsizing, Kraft retrains, relocates, and reassigns whenever possible. According to a union spokesperson, labour-management relations were "reasonably good," grievances negligible, and workers involved in decision-making. Outsourcing is a union concern, and a joint committee was struck to monitor off-site production. In 1992, Kraft General Foods was fined $3,500 in British Columbia for failing to have an industrial first aid certificate.

Equity and Family: The sole woman among Kraft Canada's four officers is the company President. 22% of senior managers, 35% of managers, and 53% of the general workforce are also women. At the parent, three of nine Directors are women. An employment equity policy is in place, as is one dealing with sexual harassment. Daycare referrals, extended maternity leave, a teen line which gives support to parents who have teenagers, a Family Leave program and a wellness plan comprise Kraft's family support program.

Progressive Staff: To promote employee health, Kraft offers on-site fitness facilities at two Toronto locations, as well as weight loss and nutrition counselling classes. An EAP provides counselling for substance abuse, mental health, personal and emotional issues, retirement planning, eldercare, child care, work related and career issues, and financial planning. In 2000, Kraft spent approximately $6 million training all its employees. Tuition costs are refunded for work-related courses. Through its parent, Kraft offers incentive schemes and stock option plans for senior managers, directors, and some middle managers.

Sourcing and Trade: Kraft Canada has recently instituted a North American sourcing policy, and the company states that at least 70% of inputs are purchased domestically, although no formal policy targets this level. Ninety-eight per cent of sales come from Canada. The parent company operates in 140 countries, including China, where joint ventures in Beijing include manufacture of canned coffee, chewing gum, and powdered beverages.

Genetically Modified Ingredients: No policy on genetically modified foods was reported. In 2000, Kraft's American parent recalled millions of packages of taco shells sold in retail stores under the Taco Bell brand, after tests showed that some of the shells contained a strain of corn whose genetically modified composition was approved only for animal feed, not for human consumption. Aventis CropScience produced the corn, Starlink, and now must pay between $100 million and $1 billion in compensation to farmers in the United States. Aventis subsequently cancelled its license to sell Starlink. U.S. officials said in March that there was little risk to human health from consumption of Starlink. Kraft's spokesperson did not comment on this case.

Environmental Management and Performance: Honour Roll. In 1997, Kraft Canada customized an environmental policy (last updated in 2000) developed by Philip Morris and Kraft North America. Every 18 to 24 months, an internal staff team audits facilities nationwide. Kraft's environmental management system builds on the principles and standards laid out in the policy, sets performance targets, and reports progress. At the parent company, quarterly environmental reports go to the board of directors, annual progress reports are released publicly, and an environmental section is included in its annual report. One full-time environmental director, who reports to both the Canadian President and to Kraft Foods North America, is supported by part-time managers at each site and by an Environmental Steering Team. In the late 1990s, Kraft's environmental operating expenditures ($3 million) exceeded capital expenditures ($2.1 million). Some of this money was used to develop audit protocols and to decommission a waste disposal site. Kraft also partnered with the Township of South Storemont, Ontario (near the Ingleside plant), to upgrade the municipal sewage system so that the company could discharge directly to the sanitary sewer. No releases from any of Kraft Canada's six facilities were reported to the NPRI in 1999, though three Ontario facilities (Ingleside, Williamstown, and Toronto) all reported releases for at least one year prior to 1999. Cobourg, Ontario, Mont-Royal, Québec, and LaSalle, Québec have never reported NPRI releases. Kraft's spokesperson commented that reports submitted to the NPRI consistently demonstrate no toxic emissions. Workplace recycling programs collect fine paper, cardboard, wood pallets, plastic, and food waste. All plants have energy conservation programs, while all plants work to reduce waste by donating excess products to food banks, and by converting other wastes to animal feed. Waste reduction initiatives at subsidiary Nabob Coffee of Burnaby, British Columbia were recognized with "Role Model" and "Inspiration" awards from the Greater Vancouver Regional District.

Community Responsibilities: In 2000, donations levels were $2 million (in cash and products), largely unchanged since 1997. Kraft focuses its giving on hunger, education, community support, and literacy, although it also supports the United Way through local campaigns at operations and headquarters, and educational initiatives such as the Prime Minister's Award for Teaching Excellence. The company supports literacy through the Mr. Christie's Book Awards, and the Mr. Christie's Smart Cookie Award. Application guidelines are published on the company's website, and a gift matching program supports institutions selected by workers. Kraft Canada donates around 1.5 million pounds of products annually to the Canadian Association of Food Banks in addition to funding programs and research related to hunger awareness. The company encourages employee voluntarism through an annual half-day of participation at local food banks, during which employees are bussed from headquarter locations to food banks to sort and pack food. In recognition of its contributions to food banks ($1 million to Toronto's Daily Bread Food Bank in 1999, for example), Kraft won Canadian Association of Food Banks' Awards for responsible corporate citizenship in 2001, 1999, and 1997. Along with product and cash donations, Kraft established a national "anti-stigma" campaign intended to help improve the image of disadvantaged people. In the past, the company has also sponsored the World Wildlife Fund in Canada.

www.kraftcanada.com

Lantic Sugar Limited /
Rogers Sugar Income Trust

In 1992, BC Sugar bought Lantic Sugar (founded in Montreal in 1915), quadrupling its sugar operations and extending its markets across the country. In 1997, Onex Corp. acquired BC Sugar (75% ownership share) along with Balaclava Enterprises (25% owner share), while Rogers Sugar Income Trust was spun off into a publicly-traded company. Although the two entities remain legally separate, Lantic holds a contract to manage Rogers' operations, and together, they represent the largest sugar refinery in Canada and the fourth largest in North America. The combined companies now sell Canadians about 60% of our sugar. Lantic has two sugar cane operations in British Columbia and Québec, and another in New York State, while Rogers owns a beet operation in Alberta. The combined companies have refineries in Montreal and Vancouver. About three quarters of sales come from industrial purchasers, with grocery and other retail outlets sharing the remaining 25%. In 2000, Lantic closed its Saint John, New Brunswick facility and expanded its Montreal plant.

> **2000 Revenues:** $251 million
> **Grocery Store Sales:** 25%
> **Brands:** Lantic, Rogers
> **Corporate Status:** Canadian owned, partly publicly traded.
> **Candor:** Lantic chose not to participate, feeling that its previous participation in 1998 took "a lot of work for scanty results." Its candor quotient is 18%.

Ethical Management and Consumer Relations: No information on codes of conduct, whistleblower protection, training, complaint, recourse, or consumer safety policies was provided. Lantic Sugar reported a code of ethics in EthicScan's 1992 consumer guide.

2002 Employees Canada: No information   **1998 Employees Canada:** 1,269

Employee Relations: Attrition and increased automation have reduced the number of refineries, sugar cane operations, and refinery workers. Six unions represent about 71% of the remaining workers, with locals in six provinces. In 1996, Lantic asked its employees for concessions in order to protect 525 jobs at the Montreal and New Brunswick refineries. The Vancouver workforce was cut 15% over 18 months between 1995 and 1996, following cuts of 15% over nine months in 1993. Following a month-long lockout at Fort Gary, Manitoba, a return to work deal stipulated that no strike or lockout would occur for at least nine years. A strike at Lantic's Saint John, New Brunswick refinery in the early 1990s kept 230 workers on the picket line for four days. Workplace injuries declined dramatically in the mid-1990s (from 101 in 1993 to 46 in 1995), as a result of an Accident Prevention Policy. The 1998 company spokesperson said that the company's accident claim costs are 50% better than those of other companies in the same compensation subclass. Three internal safety awards are presented each year.

Equity and Family: No board directors at either Rogers or Lantic are women. In 1998, 16% of Lantic's staff and 2% of its management were women (down from 22% of staff and 4% of management in 1992). This is substantially lower than most companies in this book. No information on employment equity was provided, but Rogers offers a same-sex benefits package.

Progressive Staff: In 1995, $600,000 was spent on employee training. The company covers all job-related tuition expenses. For non-work-related courses, 50% of costs are covered. Referrals including financial and psychological counselling, are made at all sites. Lantic provides five annual $1,000 scholarships for the children of staff. When Lantic introduced a flexible work schedule at its Saint John refinery in the mid-1990s, productivity went up and costs went down. Flextime is also offered at Rogers. The Montreal refinery uses semi-autonomous teams and work area "ownership" concepts, eliminating the need for middle and night shift supervision. A share ownership plan subsidizes stock purchases up to the equivalent of 5% of annual base salary. Through a profit sharing program, approximately 4% to 5% of annual earnings are shared with employees.

Environmental Management and Performance: A written environmental code was drafted for all divisions in 1992 (and updated in 1996), though details are not provided. Internal reports are submitted quarterly to the board. A full-time Director of Environmental Management is assisted by four staff environmental committees. Lantic Sugar Ltd. reported no toxic chemical releases to the NPRI at its Saint John, New Brunswick, or Montreal facilities between 1994 and 2001. Paper, cardboard, wood pallets, and packaging materials are all recycled, and efforts are made to refine any spilled product to ensure that very little raw materials are wasted.

Sourcing and Trading: Competition in this sector has decreased to the point that two firms control the market in Canada.

Community Responsibilities: No information on community responsibilities was provided in 2001. In 1995, $268,000 in corporate and employee contributions went toward various causes, including the United Way, a program for bone marrow testing, and operation of the Lantic sugar museum, which attracts nearly 6,000 visitors each year. Political contributions from Lantic and related companies are significant, and at times include both cash and organizational assistance with fundraising.

www.rogerssugar.com

Lassonde Industries Inc./Lassonde Inc.

Founded in 1918 in Rougemont, Québec, Lassonde is the largest juice supplier in Québec and the Maritime provinces. It bottles apple juice, packages vegetable and fruit juices, and licenses its processes and packaging technologies to other companies. Aristide Lassonde started Lassonde et Fils Inc as a canning enterprise, but switched to juice production in the late 1950s. Today, 80% of sales come from fruit juices and drinks, 5% from canned goods, and 25% from refrigerated products. The Lassonde and Barrie families run this third generation family-directed company and own 80% of its equity. Over the last few years, it has acquired Mar-Brite Foods, as well as the apple juice and beverage businesses of both Cobi Foods and Greatvalley Juices of Nova Scotia. Along with a Ruthven, Ontario facility, Lassonde owns two sprawling, high-tech cannery/processing plants in Rougemont, Québec and Kentville, Nova Scotia. Foreign production include interests in China.

> **2000 Revenues:** $236 million
> **Grocery Store Sales:** 94%
> **Brands:** Bright, Lassonde, Martin, Olinda
> **Corporate Status:** Canadian company.
> **Candor:** Most of the profile was completed and the spokesperson was very cooperative. The union liaison contact was very prompt with his replies. Candor quotient is 52%.

Ethical Management and Consumer Relations: Lassonde's eight-page *Code of Ethics* applies to all subsidiaries and divisions. It covers issues related to social responsibility, confidential information, interest conflicts, stock trading, information privacy, as well as profitability and community engagement. Any employee who witnesses a breach of the Code principles must advise the Ethics Committee accordingly. This committee, which consists of two executives and one external member, reports to the Board of Directors.

2002 Employees Canada: 600   **1991 Employees Canada:** 500

Employee Relations: Approximately 400 additional employees work outside of Canada. About 60% of Lassonde's Canadian workers belong to locals at two unions: Syndicat des travailleurs et des travailleuses de a' Lassonde (CSN), and Syndicat des salaries de a' Lassonde (CSN). In Rougemont, two locals each represent 120 to 130 workers, up from 95 to 100 workers in 1997. Smaller bargaining units of Lassonde workers are managed by Union des routiers, brasseries, liqueurs doucés et ouvriers de diverses industries, Local 1999 (Teamsters), the Bakery, Confectionery, and Tobacco Workers and Grain Millers International Union, Local 446 and the United Food and Commercial Workers International Union Local 175. In 1992, a seven-week strike at Rougemont affected 82 workers, for a loss of 3,120 person work days. Of the 50 grievances reported annually, none have reached arbitration stage in the last five years.

Equity and Family: Women represent one of 22 senior managers, down from two of 12 in 1996. None sit on the board of directors. An employment equity program supports women, but no components cover visible minorities, aboriginal peoples, or the disabled. The company's Ethics Committee reviews Lassonde's anti-harassment policy, and employees receive training during orientation sessions.

Progressive Staff: An Employee Assistance Plan covers substance abuse and psychological counselling, retirement planning, and referral services for seniors and children with special needs. A company newsletter is published five or six times each year. Employee performance is evaluated using a corporate system (introduced in 1991) that includes written reviews and rewards for cost saving ideas. Tuition costs for work-related training is refunded 100%. No employees work beyond 40 hours per week, the spokesperson reported, and overtime is paid when extra shifts are needed. Only top managers qualify for the company's stock option plan.

Sourcing and Trade: As the only Québec company to make apple juice from fresh apples, Lassonde buys 35,000 to 50,000 tonnes of apples every year, or about 75% of Québec's entire crop. It dedicates approximately 5% of its production capacity to private-label manufacturing for foreign companies who engage Lassonde under long-term contracts. Between 10 and 12 foreign countries import Lassonde products, including China, the Caribbean, Mexico, and Europe. Lassonde operates plants in three countries, including one in China, a regime classified by Amnesty International as repressive. With a 61% holding in one Chinese joint venture, and 50% in another, Lassonde produces juice for the Chinese market. No formal labour rights policies guide foreign relations or activities, but the spokesperson noted that the Chinese subsidiary follows "good practices." He did not specify what they were. In the 1990s, Lassonde bought 5% of Tipco Foods, a Thai company that makes pineapple concentrates, for $1.5 million, but then sold this stake by 2001. Lassonde's license for Clarifruit, its fruit clarifying process, was traded to different business interests in developing countries in exchange for juice supplies.

Environmental Management and Performance: Lassonde's environmental code was updated in 2000. Environmental reports are filed with the Executive Committee, but no public sustainability report has ever been issued. No employee has full-time environmental duties, although the vice-president of Engineering and two other staff share such responsibilities. A staff environmental committee, set up in the late 1980s, was disbanded in the 1990s. In 1995, the company worked with two levels of government to install a $3 million wastewater treatment system that rectified a persistent water quality problem in the Rougemont plant's apple-pressing area. Environmental expenditures of $500,000 went toward other wastewater treatment facilities, equipment upgrades, and fuel retrofits, allowing the Québec plant to switch from oil to natural gas. The company says that it has greenhouse gas emission problems, but reports no plans for reductions. At one time Lassonde produced its own packaging materials, but now sources them externally. Although the company gave no data on material recycling or reuse, it did report the existence of internal recycling programs.

Genetically Modified Ingredients: No information

Community Responsibilities: In 2000, Lassonde gave $90,000 to charitable activities, up from $80,000 in 1997. The company typically splits donations between cash and products. Its primary recipients include Tel-Jeunes, a hotline for troubled youths, and Centraide, Québec's United Way campaign. Sports teams receive support in communities where the company operates.

www.lassonde.com

McCain Foods Limited

When the parents of Wallace and Harrison McCain started a Maritime seed potato exporting company in 1914, they founded a family business that decades later would become a global french fry and frozen foods empire. From the family headquarters in Florenceville, New Brunswick, the company now sells more frozen fries than any other company in Canada, Britain, Western Europe, and Australia. It also sells juice, meats, cheese, frozen vegetables and other frozen prepared foods. To support these plants, there are food production facilities located in New Brunswick, Prince Edward Island, Ontario, Manitoba, and Alberta. There are fertilizer mixing plants in New Brunswick and Prince Edward Island. The company's supplier for seed potatoes is McCain Produce Inc. McCain has subsidiaries in: Québec; Grand Falls, NB; Coaldale, AB; Toronto, ON; and Mississauga, ON. There are several plants worldwide. During the mid-1990s, an expansion drive increased the plants in Florenceville, New Brunswick, Portage la Prairie, Manitoba, and Borden-Carleton, Prince Edward Island. In 1993 and 1994, internal disputes between the families of the two principal second generation brothers led to the removal of Wallace from his position as co-CEO by the board of the family holding company. That branch of the family went on to take over and refashion Maple Leaf Foods.

2001 Revenues: $5.3 billion worldwide
Grocery Store Sales: No information
Brands: Ellios (Canada), Gusto, McCain, Napoli, Niagara, Old South, Picnic, Valley Farms
Corporate Status: Privately-held Canadian company.
Candor: For a privately-held enterprise, McCain supplied a fair level of information, proving answers to 36% of the questions posed.

Ethical Management and Consumer Relations: In 1997, the corporate spokesperson said that the company was considering its first code of ethics. By 2002, the company said it was in the process of developing a code that would require an employee signoff, and that would be translated into the languages spoken in countries where McCain operates.

2002 Employees Canada: 5,000   **1997 Employees Worldwide:** 12,500

Employee Relations: Four Canadian factories are unionized: a juice plant and a pizza plant in Toronto, and two operations of the Québec subsidiary (Charcuterie). In 2001, the UFCW represented employees at the Toronto juice plant, excluding lab workers. A union spokesperson reported no strikes over the last decade and no outsourcing contracts, adding that grievances are settled in the plant before any arbitration is necessary. A joint union-management committee deals with health and safety issues, and the company promotes safe driving in transport and leasing with the McCain Transport Safety Awards (based on driver records, accumulated miles, and lengths of service). Tuition refunds are 100% reimbursed for any academic course an employee takes and passes. Annual scholarships for the children of employees have been awarded since 1974, and in 2001, each of these winners received $15,750 over four years.

Equity and Family: Official statistics on the advancement of women within the McCain Group of companies were not reported, although one female family member sits on the "family" board of the McCain Group. None sit on the "operating" board at McCain Foods Ltd. No formal equity hiring or promotion policy exists. Traditionally, management has been male-dominated. The Human Resources Development Canada (HRDC) 1999 Report for employment equity ranked McCain's subsidiary, Day and Ross Inc., as superior for aboriginal peoples, poor for women and members of visible minorities, and very poor for persons with disabilities (based on a sample of 1,523 employees). The spokesperson noted that, while there is "certainly multicultural representation," such data are not tracked. A sexual harassment policy exists, but only supervisors receive training on it. Daycare assistance is offered at some local sites, and the company says it is improving access.

Progressive Staff: The company provides a fitness facility at the head office, and intra-company athletic events at various operations. *The Star*, McCain's multi-lingual publication, is in its 28th year of quarterly publishing, and "Bright Ideas" is an employee suggestion reward program. Flexible scheduling is subject to each manager's discretion, but is not available throughout the group.

Corporate Concentration: McCain's dominance in the potato market (it buys half of Canada's annual crop) has drawn attention from agricultural critics who suggest that the company exercises too much power over farmers. According to newspaper reports, McCain sets demanding prices and rigid production schedules for supplier farmers. The McCain spokesperson noted that the company owns one potato farm in Florenceville, P.E.I., which produces about 7% of McCain's potatoes, the rest are procured from farms in different parts of Canada. He explained that the company buys most of its potatoes from farmers who are pre-contracted (terms are set before planting in April), and approximately 20% to 40% of potatoes are bought from farmers who are not pre-contracted. Some additional purchases occur on the open market, and final prices and quantities for these transactions depend on the company's requirements for a given year. Potato delivery does not begin until August, but prices vary according to the time of harvest and crop quality, and contracts spell out all variable elements that might affect final terms. McCain negotiates prices with the associations that represent farmers on a regional basis (the New Brunswick Potato Agency, the Keystone Vegetable Growers of Manitoba, the Prince Edward Island Potato Processing Council) while individual farmers decide quantities they can supply.

Sourcing and Trade: It is said that citizens of the country where McCain operates often feel that the company is indigenous, rather than Canadian. International subsidiaries and operations include more than 55 frozen food and potato processing plants on six continents. The company has international operations in more than 60 countries, but no written policy addresses labour conditions abroad.

Environmental Management: In February 2001, McCain implemented a new environmental policy and program that requires performance audits certified by an independent verifier. Reports prepared by local operating companies are audited by corporate engineers and distributed internally. A new support system for this code is in development. Once in place, it will roll out a reporting system based on principles, standards, targets, and progress to date. Personnel with full-time environmental responsibilities include one administrative employee, and one engineer, who report to a vice president with part-time environmental duties. The board of directors has an environmental committee. Recent investments are directed at new eco-efficient equipment, and toward packaging reductions. The UFCW spokesperson reported an incentive program that encourages employees to improve waste and environmental processes.

Environmental Performance: McCain Foods (Canada) reports major chemical and waste releases for its three Canadian sites to the National Pollutant Release Inventory (NPRI). In 1999, McCain's Florenceville, New Brunswick facility ranked in the 80-90 percentile for all companies reporting (15,000 kilograms released to air, and 131,000 kilograms to water). This facility's air releases have been steady since 1997, while water releases have risen since 1997 and 1998, though they remain significantly lower than the 1996 level. Its top ranked pollutant for potential risk to human health is ammonia. Grand Falls, New Brunswick ranked in the 70-80 percentile of all reporting companies (84,700 kilograms to water in 1999, down substantially from 226,535 kilograms in 1998). No information on the top ranked NPRI pollutant was available for this facility. Borden-Carleton, Prince Edward Island also placed in the 70-80 percentile in 1999 (128, 970 kilograms to water, down slightly from 131,500 kilograms in 1998), and again, no information was available on specific pollutants with potential human health risks. Recycling of paper, cardboard, metal, wood pallets, batteries, and polystyrene is practised. Packaging volumes are reduced through the use of lighter and recycled material, and a new loading/packaging system saves 8% of the plastic used in french fry packages by shrinking the bag size. A three-year crop rotation of potatoes, grain, and alfalfa reduces soil degradation. At one time McCain planted 60,000 seedlings each year to replace trees used for paper in packaging, but that program, along with one that sent cauliflower and broccoli trimmings to local cattle farmers, has been discontinued. The company donates to many environmental groups, including the World Wildlife Fund. In partnership with the Young Naturalist Foundation of Toronto, McCain's helped to distribute a 64-page *Green Ideas Book* to teachers at registered pre-schools across Canada.

Genetically Modified Ingredients: No information

Community Responsibilities: The company is a participant in the Imagine Campaign, and as such donates 1% of pre-tax earnings each year. The spokesperson noted that community support is the "primary thrust" of the McCain Foundation. Donations during the 1990s were to a mix of different community groups, including New Brunswick food banks, hospital capital programs, museums, as well as the Winnipeg Ballet, the Alliance for a Drug Free Canada, and various literacy groups. Small bursaries are donated to agricultural students in Portage la Prairie, Manitoba, and community college students in Woodstock, New Brunswick. Other donations are made to universities, including Acadia, Moncton, and Dalhousie, in some cases targeting students working on graduate dietician degrees.

www.mccain.com

McCormick Canada

McCormick Canada makes spices, seasonings, flavourings, and specialty foods (decorations, food colouring, soup mixes, and garnishes), and sells most of its products in Canada. Based in London, Ontario, this Canadian subsidiary company is wholly-owned by McCormick & Co. (USA), the largest seasoning and flavoring company in the world. With two main divisions—Strange (the industrial food business) and Club House (the retail and food service division)—McCormick Canada operates plants in Alberta and Ontario. The Canadian company's roots extend back to Gorman & Dyson, which began in 1883 making coffee, turpentine, liquid ammonia and sewing machine oil before moving into spices, extracts, and baking powder. Today, these lines survive in the Club House Foods division.

Annual Revenues: $100 to $200 million
Grocery Store Sales: 55%
Brands: Cake Mate, Club House, Gilroy Farms, Golden Dipt, Hy's, McCormick, Produce Partners, Sierra, Spice Cargo, Spice Classics
Corporate Status: Wholly-owned subsidiary of U.S.-based parent company.
Candor: The spokesperson was somewhat helpful with EthicScan's surveys. The company has a 43% candor quotient.

Ethical Management and Consumer Relations: Every year McCormick staff sign the company's ethics code, last revised in 1989. All salaried staff must also sign a Purchasing and Business Ethics Statement. To help instill the company's values, every new employee receives a copy of Charles McCormick's book, *The Power of People.* One core value states, "we believe in doing business ethically and honestly."

2002 Employees Canada: 480   **1996 Employees Canada:** 450

Employee Relations: The parent company's global employment levels have grown, from 7,600 in 1990 to 9,000 in 2001. It cut 540 positions in 1994 through job eliminations, retirement, and plant closings. To address layoffs, the company offers early retirement, retraining, and advance notice of technological change. Less than 5% of McCormick Canada's production is contracted out. In 2000, four days were lost due to accidents, down dramatically from 15 in 1999. Training expenditures totaled $150,000 (or $295 per employee) in 2001. Pay incentives include profit sharing and a share ownership plan that offers all employees a purchase price guarantee. During the Great Depression of the 1930s, when Charles McCormick took over McCormick & Co. from his father, he immediately boosted wages, reduced weekly work hours, and initiated participative management programs that still exist today.

Equity and Family: Women's progress has not changed dramatically over the last five years. In 2001, one of 11 Canadian directors was a woman, up from none of four directors in 1997. Women also comprise 18% of senior management, 43% of management, and 45% of the workforce. Procedures prohibiting discrimination in hiring and promotion are supported by a formal anti-harassment policy and reinforced with training. An employment equity program was reported, though no details were given. Extended maternity leaves, and paid days off for child and eldercare are available, but daycare services or referrals are not. Flexible work schedules can be negotiated.

Progressive Staff: Career, retirement, and substance abuse counselling are available to all employees. McCormick's health promotion program includes some staff fitness activities, company sports teams, and smoking cessation assistance. *Seasonal Thymes*, an employee newspaper, is published twice a year, and other company information is given to employees at quarterly meetings. McCormick empowers employees through a participative management program established in 1932. Individuals and teams are recognized for cost-saving ideas. External verifiers conduct formal feedback sessions, the spokesperson reported, without specifying any details. The parent company was listed in both the 1993 and 1998 editions of *The One Hundred Best Companies to Work For in America*. A corporate education program immediately reimburses 100% of tuition for all work-specific courses, while "general upgrade" is paid back 50% up front, and 50% when the course is successfully completed. Children of employees are eligible for a corporate-run scholarship program that is held for four years of school.

Sourcing and Trade: A "small" percentage of ingredients and input materials is found in Canada, but the majority are sourced from Asia and Latin America. Internationally, the parent has operations in India, Indonesia, China, Mexico, Singapore, Thailand, and El Salvador, among other countries. No nutritional, labour, or human rights requirements screen supplies from international brokers. However, the company says that it does not knowingly source from any company breaching labour standards, and it ensures that none of its joint-venture partners use slave labour. No procedures exist to verify or screen international brokers or suppliers for pesticide use or environmental management. The company says that it does not knowingly source from any company breaching environmental standards.

Environmental Management and Performance: McCormick's environmental code, written in 1991 and updated in 1995, applies to all facilities. Internal and external personnel complete audits each year, and the board receives a report on results and developments. Along with two staff committees that handle environmental matters, three employees assume part-time environmental responsibilities, the most senior of whom is a director of engineering and facilities management. The company spent $25,000 on an effluent analysis study in 1995. Other expenditures are dedicated to equipment replacement, energy efficiency, and reformatted packaging. McCormick does not provide the National Pollutant Release Inventory with information on its chemical releases and transfers. In the mid-1990s, the company provided data on quantities of paper, cardboard, cans, glass, and food waste recycled. Conservation programs reduce the energy consumed by lighting and motors, and perishable goods are reused or recycled as compost. The parent company's packaging division began producing recycled plastic containers in 1992.

Genetically Modified Ingredients: No information

Community Responsibilities: Although the company does not report corporate charitable donations, it says it achieves the Imagine Campaign's charitable gift goal of a minimum of 1% of pre-tax profit. In the mid-1990s employees gave approximately $30,000 each year. Funds go to the Junior Achievement mentoring and sponsorship program, as well as to Theatre London. McCormick Canada has one of the best-developed and longest-standing employee volunteer programs of any company covered in this guide. Once day a year, 90% of staff work voluntarily on a designated Saturday and donate the value of one day's wages to a charity of their choice. The company then matches the value of each gift with funds directed to one local charity selected by each operation. Since these "charity days" began in the late 1960s, cumulative donations from the company and employees have exceeded $1 million. Other community support includes the loan of facilities, equipment donations, plus paid and unpaid time for voluntarism. Volunteer activity is publicized in the company newsletter.

www.mccormick.com

Maple Leaf Foods Inc.

Toronto-based Maple Leaf Foods Inc. operates the largest marketing and global trading company in Canada, and is one of the country's largest diversified food processing companies. Formerly known as Canada Packers, the company was transformed by a series of mergers, followed by a 1995 takeover worth $1.1 billion that put corporate control into the hands of the Ontario Teachers Pension Plan Board (39.9%) and McCain Capital. Following the bitter family split at McCain Foods, one of the two McCain brothers took over management of Canada Packers. With three primary segments (Meat Products Group, Bakery Products, and Agribusiness), Maple Leaf Foods processes meat, poultry, and some frozen foods. It also mills bakery ingredients inside and outside of Canada and distributes fresh and prepared meats, bakery, seafood, and other consumer food products. The company owns and operates two hog slaughtering and processing plants, one small beef slaughtering plant, and numerous sales and distribution facilities. Well-known subsidiaries include Maple Leaf Consumer Foods, Maple Leaf Pork, Maple Leaf Poultry, Maple Leaf Foods International (meat), Canada Bread and Maple Leaf Bakery USA as well as other agribusiness interests. In early 2001, Maple Leaf acquired Schneider's Manitoba fresh pork operations, after selling Country Style Food Services Inc. and buying some assets of Burns Foods.

Annual Revenues: $4.7 billion
Grocery Store Sales: No information
Brands: Canada Bread, Dempsters, Landmark Feeds, Maple Leaf, Maple Leaf Prime Naturally, Maple Leaf Medallion, Mega-Bites, Olivieri, Shur-Grain, Top Dogs
Corporate Status: Privately held Canadian company.
Candor: A good deal of information was provided by a public relations consulting firm representing Maple Leaf. Candor quotient is 51%.

Ethical Management and Consumer Relations: Honour Roll. Maple Leaf Foods has a written code of ethics (updated in 2000) that is distributed company-wide, signed by employees, and supported by training. The code deals with a range of various issues, including conflicts of interest, bribes, or kickbacks, the selection of suppliers, and business gifts. Compliance with the code is part of employee and manager evaluations, and employees help to create it and assess its effectiveness. A "Leadership Edge Plan" also helps guide employees through six core "values": acting with integrity; treating people with respect; accounting for results; sharing; trusting; and admitting mistakes. Consumer assurance mechanisms include toll-free numbers for all Maple Leaf companies. In July 2001, a *National Post* article reported that inspectors from the Canadian Food Inspection Agency (CFIA) regularly receive discounted products from many of the plants they regulate. At Maple Leaf, a discount on fresh chicken that is commonly offered to employees once a week is also extended to CFIA inspectors. A spokesperson from CFIA was quoted as saying that the organization has "never had any problems or cause for concern" and that the practice is long-standing. A spokesperson for the Minister of Agriculture and Agri-Food stated that the Minister was not aware of this practice and would review it.

2002 Employees Canada: 14,500   **1995 Employees Canada:** 10,500

Employee Relations: Worldwide, Maple Leaf Foods employed 14,500 people in 2002. Although the company's staff has grown since 1995, consolidation has eliminated about 1,900 Maple Leaf jobs since the mid-1990s (1,000 in Ontario and 600 in Alberta). Approximately 50% of current employees work in meat products, 35% in bakery products, and 15% in agribusiness. About 70% belong to unions (UFCW, BCT, RWDSW, Teamsters, CEP, UFWA, CSN, and URAWU). Maple Leaf Consumer Foods completed an expansion of a bacon facility in North Battleford, Saskatchewan, adding 100 new positions. In 1999, Maple Leaf Pork opened a state-of-the-art processing facility in Brandon, Manitoba, and another in Calgary, while expanding its Burlington plant with a second shift. Rothsay was slated to expand its Winnipeg plant and increase capacity by 50% with nine new jobs. When the Winnipeg pork plant was slated for closure in 1999 an agreement ratified by 70% of employees gave a buyout package to 865 hourly employees. Each received a minimum of $5,000, plus a top-up based on the number of years of service. Between 1993 and 1998, Maple Leaf faced five unjust dismissal cases, whose outcomes were not reported. No health and safety statistics were provided in 2001, but the company spokesperson stated that, "Health and Safety has shown consistent improvement since 1997." In 1996, Maple Leaf Foods was fined $80,000 when the company pleaded guilty to three 1994 safety violations at its Brantford plant, after a meat blender amputated a worker's arm. Subsidiary Olivieri Foods Limited was fined $3,000 in 1995 for repeat violations of industrial health and safety regulations related to removal of safeguards around machinery.

Unrest and Restructuring: Corporate attempts to renegotiate wages and consolidate operations have been accompanied by work stoppages at Ontario, Saskatchewan, and Alberta facilities in 1997 and 1998. Lockouts over wages affected 180 workers in the Saskatchewan plant, 260 in Hamilton, and 356 in Walkerton, Ontario. Another strike put 900 Burlington workers out on picket lines. During this period some production was outsourced to a Québec factory, co-owned by Schneider Corp. In Burlington, employees voted to accept a deal that rolled back wages and benefits by $6 to $9 an hour, and offered one-time buyout packages of between $10,000 to $33,000 to compensate for the wage cutback. While management argued that wage cutting was necessary to increase competitiveness, a study commissioned by Maple Leaf Foods itself found that wages were only one of five factors affecting competitiveness. The other factors included size of plants, operational design and technology, average size of carcasses fed into meat operations, and the number of shifts, as well as the quality of the end product. In 1997, the company closed its Edmonton plant, following a strike vote by employees, in which 809 workers walked out for ten days over wages. At the time, some Ontario teachers questioned their Pension Board over its ownership of Maple Leaf Foods shares, citing reports that management was attempting to decertify unions, and that the company threatened to close the Edmonton plant should workers vote to strike. This plant was closed permanently and replaced by a facility in Brandon that opened later, employing 1,150 people.

Equity and Family: Maple Leaf's record for advancing women lags the average for companies covered in this book. One of 13 board members is a woman, and women hold only 16 of 100 senior management positions, a proportional boost from four of 50 in 1996. Women hold about 20% of management positions, up from 15% in 1996. No 2001 information was reported on women in the general workforce, but in 1996, they held 30% of these jobs. Six of ten divisions in Canada have an employment equity program and anti-harassment policy (addressing issues affecting women, visible minorities, disabled people, and aboriginal people). This policy receives a sign-off, annual review, and training. Maple Leaf offers family support through extended maternity, paternity, and adoption leaves. All ten divisions offer day-care referral (up from two of seven in 1996), and flexible days off for family reasons. The Ontario Human Rights Commission's (OHRC) 1999-2000 *Annual Report* lists the racial harassment case of Marica Robertson v. OHRC and Maple Leaf Foods under its Board of Inquiry's Court of Appeal. No outcome was reported.

Progressive Staff: Some training is provided for all employees (though specific figures are not tracked), formal employee input goes into training, and expenses for external tuition and books are fully reimbursed. An employee share purchase program exists, along with a "stock option for annual bonus" program for senior managers, based in part on performance. Most divisions provide employee assistance programs that offer counselling services for drug and alcohol use, stop-smoking programs, and retirement planning. Referrals are available for eldercare and children with special needs. Newsletters, suggestion programs, and incentive rewards are run at most divisions.

Sourcing and Trade: Maple Leaf Foods has operations in Canada, the U.S., Europe, and Asia. Through its International Food Trading division, the company exports many different North American food products to over 60 countries, and imports from 20 countries. Maple Leaf's prepared meats group sources its beef and pork as commodities on the open market, either through suppliers or through brokers in Canada or the United States. Maple Leaf Mills purchases its flour from Canada and the northern U.S. Maple Leaf does not own any fishing vessels, but relies instead on independent west coast fishermen. Foreign interests include meat operations in Japan, Hong Kong, and other Pacific Rim countries. Despite this international activity, no policies guiding business practices in foreign regimes were reported. Maple Leaf makes a range of private label products, including President's Choice hams, Miracle bologna, Swiss Chalet wings, IGA sausages, and Sobey buns.

Environmental Management and Performance: Maple Leaf's environmental code guides all business units and subsidiaries. The company reports that it complies with existing environmental legislation, and is in compliance and workplace safety. Independent audits are conducted, and the results reported to an Environment, Health, and Safety Committee of the Board on a quarterly basis. A Director is the highest-ranking officer with full-time environmental responsibilities. The company strives to improve its use of packaging materials, and works with suppliers to develop more recycled content packaging. No major chemical or waste releases were reported to the NPRI from Maple Leaf Foods' Brandon plant or Maple Leaf Consumer Foods' Winnipeg facility. The one location that reported any releases—the Maryborough Township, Ontario Rothsay plant (a Maple Leaf Foods subsidiary)—ranked in the 60 to 70 percentile of all plants releasing chemicals or water pollutants in 1999. Releases to air were down compared with results from 1996 to 1998, while land releases were up, and it was the first time that water releases were reported. Ammonia was ranked as the top release in terms of potential human health risks. The Rothsay subsidiary also recycles animal and poultry by-products into commercial tallow and protein products (such as soaps, cosmetics, paints, rubber, animal feed, pet food, and fertilizers). Waste is collected from slaughterhouses, food processors, restaurants and institutional consumers.

Genetically Modified Organisms: No information

Community Responsibilities: Maple Leaf Foods is pledged to the Imagine Campaign because it commits at least 1% of pre-tax profits over a three year average to charity. A donations committee meets four times a year and tends to support national organizations in the areas of education, the arts, women's shelters, food and nutritional research, health, and social services. Food donations are given to community groups where Maple Leaf operates, and the company supports time off for employee involvement in community causes. To assist residents in need during natural disasters, employees donated time in Québec (1996 flood) and Manitoba (1997 flood) by helping prepare sandbags and inspecting food facilities to ensure that food preparation processes were safe.

www.mlfi.com

Maple Lodge Farms Ltd.

Since its founding in 1956, Maple Lodge Farms has become the largest chicken processor in Canada. Today, it operates one plant in Ontario and a related plant (Nadeau Poultry Farms Ltd) in New Brunswick. For the retail market, Maple Lodge prepares and sells freshly processed chicken and deli chicken products. For fast food contracts (such as Swiss Chalet and KFC), it processes value-added chicken products and flavoured wings. Each year, 2.5 million kilograms of Maple Lodge poultry products are distributed across Canada. Ownership is private, with all shares in the hands of the May family.

> **Annual Revenues:** Greater than $250 million
> **Grocery Store Sales:** No information
> **Brands:** Chicken Bacon, Chicklinks, Granny Mae, Maple Lodge
> **Corporate Status:** Privately-held Canadian company.
> **Candor:** Maple Lodge provided only a fraction of the information requested. Today, including union interviews, its candor quotient is 20%.

Ethical Management and Consumer Relations: No corporate code of ethics, toll free consumer line, or related management practices exist. A policy on business gift exchange is distributed to employees.

2002 Employees Canada: No information   **1998 Employees Canada:** 1,400

Employee Relations: Of an estimated 1,400 total staff, about 1,220 plant, maintenance, and clerical workers in Ontario and New Brunswick are unionized. Workplace management planning is centralized. Each quarter, a joint meeting between two shareholders from the May family, two union representatives, and two management representatives discuss company issues like collective agreements. Layoffs hit a small (but unspecified) number of truck drivers in the mid-1990s. Some workers were re-assigned jobs within the company, while those let go received outplacement services. The last reported strike, November 1992, received negative coverage in the media. At that time, a one-week walkout over wages put 1,000 Brampton workers on the picket line. While the company claimed that violence erupted on the picket line causing injuries, neither the union nor local police confirmed this report. The company stated that an injunction was obtained to limit picketing activity, which quelled "violence and disorder on the picket line." A 1997 UFCW spokesperson who represents shippers, drivers, production employees, garage workers, and janitors, noted that discipline problems account for many of the 400 grievances that reach third-party arbitration each year. She noted that plant management is quick to respond to any discipline breaches. Although the union's relationship with the company's human resources department was described as "good," overall relations with the company were called "poor" by the union but "good" by Human Resources staff. Health and safety is a major concern, suggested the 1997 union spokesperson, since accidents happen on a daily basis and problems do not receive sufficient attention. For example, while repetitive strain injuries are common, the union representative alleges that the company made little effort to accommodate affected workers. By way of contrast, the corporate spokesperson said that temporary light duties are assigned to such workers until they recover.

Equity and Family: Six women occupy director positions on the company board, all of whom are either wives or daughters of the founding family. A large percentage is of the company's Ontario workforce is comprised of recent immigrants. Workers come from diverse backgrounds—an estimated 26 languages are spoken on shop floors. Although 40% to 60% of these people are women, the 1997 union spokesperson commented that the more skilled jobs on the plant floor tend to go to men. The company disagreed, commenting: "there is no discrimination between women and men with respect to skilled jobs." The union spokesperson said that, generally, women occupy "Levels One and Two" (unskilled and semi-skilled category) jobs. She pointed out that in 1997 only one woman worked in transport preparation, while no women work in shipping. The corporate spokesperson states that jobs in these categories are allocated to both men and women, depending on the physical demands of the job. To address gender issues, the company reported a pay equity program and an in-house job evaluation program (no details were given). No comprehensive employment equity, same sex benefits, or anti-harassment support were mentioned. Maple Lodge provides maternity leave extensions only when medical complications demand them.

Progressive Staff: No details on training programs or expenditures were provided, but tuition and book expenses for work-related courses are reimbursed.

Sourcing and Trade: The company reported no international operations. No other information was provided on sourcing practices, ethical trade policies, or humane poultry raising requirements.

Environmental Management and Performance: Few details on environmental policy or support systems were reported. Generally, the company's response to environmental management is driven by government regulation. Pesticide and antibiotics monitoring is the responsibility of a provincial producer board (The Chicken Farmers of Ontario), and company standards do not surpass those set by the government. In 1997, Maple Lodge shifted to a Hazard Analysis Critical Control Point Program audit for inspection purposes, and adopted a modern system that would comply with forthcoming standards to be enforced by the Canadian Food Inspection Agency. Inspections, which come from both government and industry personnel, are subject to a strict audit protocol for concerns like microorganisms (like salmonella). The company reports that it is allowed to sell chickens domestically because of approvals from the Animals Branch of Agriculture Canada. For export products, the plant is approved by the U.S. Department of Agriculture. A waste treatment plant manager acts as a full-time environmental affairs officer, and a staff environmental, health, and safety committee sits at the Brampton facility. Maple Lodge did not provide the National Pollutant Release Inventory with information on its chemical releases and transfers. The company has a full set of workplace recycling programs and special technological processes for protein recovery. In the late 1990s, air quality at the Ontario plant was improved after a new filtration system was introduced into the rooms where chickens are hung and processed. This change led to a decline in neighborhood complaints and formal provincial recognition of the company's efforts. At Maple Lodge, waste by-products such as feathers, beaks, and feet are ground up for use in pet foods. Some waste is composted.

Genetically Modified Ingredients: No information. Chickens are bred and raised under intense husbandry conditions including artificial light and continuous feeding.

Community Responsibilities: No community giving or engagement was reported in 2001. A Maple Lodge Farms Foundation was created in 1997 to co-ordinate charitable donations. Through the collective agreement, the union organizes gift-matching drives for causes such as the Leukemia Research Fund. The company also runs a fundraising program for school groups and other organizations in the communities where it operates. Local sports and hospitals in the Brampton area also receive money, as do universities. Co-op students are hired at the head office for work in finance and business planning.

www.maplelodgefarms.com

Melitta Canada Inc.

In 1908, founder Melitta Bentz patented a perforated brass pot that she designed to brew coffee through a "drip" method, using a fitted paper filter. By 1912, her company was making its own filter papers to fit the pots. Today, Melitta Canada is a separate sales and marketing unit of the German parent company, Melitta Unternehmensgruppe Bentz KG. Reporting to the North American division based in Clearwater, Florida, the Canadian business receives its coffee products from a roasting and packaging plant in Cherry Hill, New Jersey, along with a contracted facility just outside of Toronto, Ontario. Melitta accounts for about 30% of Canada's coffee filter market, and Canadian sales represent 17% of Melitta's North American business. Grocery products are sold through a national network of brokers, and Melitta sells small appliances and houseware products through a direct sales force.

2000 Revenues Canada: $21 million
Grocery Store Sales: 85%
Brands: Melitta
Corporate Status: Wholly-owned German-based company.
Candor: In 2000, the company provided some information, but less than in 1998. Melitta has a 31% candor quotient.

Ethical Management and Consumer Relations: All subsidiaries adopt the parent company's code of ethics (written in 1985, updated in May 2001), which guides in-store payments for stocking allowances and product placement on retail shelves. The value of business gifts are limited to nominal amounts, usually less than $25. No other information on ethical management and guidance was reported. Approximately 12% of Melitta's product costs go toward advertising.

2002 Employees Canada: 12 (10 full-time, 2 contract)

1991 Employees Canada: 50

Employee Relations: Canadian staff has grown from ten in 1996, but declined dramatically compared with 50 a decade ago. These staff, who work in marketing and distribution, represent a small proportion of the worldwide total. None of Melitta's North American operations are unionized. Globally, the company shrunk from 7,324 employees in 1991 to 4,588 in 1996 as restructuring and technological advances rendered jobs redundant. A filter paper production facility moved from Rexdale, Ontario to Clearwater, Florida in April 1991, eliminating 50 hourly jobs. The company reported that it paid all laid off workers severance packages that exceeded Ontario government regulations. Coffeemaker production is now outsourced to sub-contractors. The 2001 spokesperson had no figures on employee training, stating that "it depends on how many employees take advantage" of the available funds. In 1995, Melitta Canada spent a total of $5,604 ($560 per worker) to train staff. All tuition and book expenses are refunded (up from only 50% in 1997). As a privately-held company, Melitta has no opportunities for employee stock ownership, but does offer a "Melitta Merit Program." In North America, it matches a savings program dollar for dollar up to a maximum of 6% of an employee's annual salary. A Management by Objectives system offers performance bonuses based on corporate earnings and mutually set goals and objectives.

Equity and Family: One woman sits on the four-person Canadian executive committee. One quarter of management and approximately half of the entire Canadian workforce are women. A formal employment equity program addresses issues faced by women, minorities, the disabled, and aboriginal peoples. It is complemented by an anti-harassment policy. The spokesperson stated that, generally, the company had no problems managing diversity in Canada.

Progressive Staff: Melitta is one of the few companies to report any kind of comprehensive "Participative Management Policy," though no details were given. Fitness subsidies and stop-smoking programs are available. *Kaffee Klatch*, the corporate newsletter, is issued quarterly.

Sourcing and Trade: The parent company operates in seven countries, including a Chinese factory that makes domestic appliances and small coffee machines for the catering trade. The company does not own any coffee plantations. No policies govern company sourcing and trading practices. All products sold by Melitta Canada are sourced from sister companies, with the exception of coffee. Filter paper comes from American sources and is produced in Clearwater, Florida. In the mid-1990s, coffeemakers were produced in a maquiladora region in Mexico, but the company reports that it no longer engages this supplier. When Melitta had operations in Mexico, it stated that dedicated staff were kept on site to monitor quality control and provide technical assistance, and that the company directly monitored labour conditions to ensure a productive and safe work environment. No independent monitors were engaged. Melitta Canada reports that its operations are audited by Deloitte & Touche, but the scope of audits is not mentioned.

Environmental Management and Performance: The company's environmental policy applies to all subsidiaries. In the early 1990s part of this policy was printed on packages of Melitta's filter papers. No environmental audits are required in Canada, but internal personnel at U.S. operations consult with external experts as required. Environmental affairs are managed part-time by a Vice-President of Corporate Manufacturing. All operational personnel share responsibility for environmental management. No environmental expenditures were reported in 2001, but in 1995 (the last year statistics were reported) the North American company spent $80,000 to improve air quality in the thermal after-burner at its coffee roasting plant in Cherry Hill, New Jersey. With no manufacturing in Canada, Melitta does not report to the National Pollutant Release Inventory. In the mid-1990s, the U.S. company stopped using chlorine to bleach its filter papers white, choosing instead a natural brown filter. The company would not confirm whether or not this policy still applies today. Prior to 1991, Canadian pulp was used to make Melitta filters, and the company contributed to a fund set up by the Canadian Forestry Association, which planted two trees for every one cut. In areas harvested for Melitta filters—a product that requires virgin paper to meet filtration specifications—seven trees are planted for each one used. The Melitta Group has strict specifications for filters, so suppliers must adhere to stringent requirements affecting pulp and the use of chlorine bleach. Air quality standards that apply to coffee roasting are stringently followed, and scrap from filter processing is recycled.

Genetically Modified Ingredients: No information. The spokesperson stated that, since it buys from agents and not directly from suppliers, Melitta cannot enforce policies on pesticide usage.

Community Responsibilities: No information on philanthrophy is reported. In 1994 and 1995, Melitta Canada donated 1.8% of pre-tax profits ($9,700 and $8,900), combining cash (50%) and product donations. It also offers student work programs and organizes corporate athletic programs. In the mid-1990s, Melitta sponsored Wildcare, a Toronto organization, Cash for Kids, an event that helps children with Crohn's disease and colitis, and events at a local hospital.

www.melitta.com

Nestlé Canada Inc.

Nestlé Canada produces and sells food and nutritional products made at eight plants in Canada. Its brands cover a wide range of categories: beverages, milk products, dietetics, chocolate, confectionery, ice cream, prepared dishes, and cooking aids. Its parent company, Nestlé SA of Switzerland, has operations around the world, including others in Canada such as Alcon, L'Oreal, Nestlé Purina Pet Care, and Perrier, employing 225,000 people at 489 factories on six continents. In June 1999, Nestlé Canada sold its Laura Secord interest, including 175 Canadian retail stores (1,600 employees) to Archibald Candy Corp. of Chicago. Major acquisitions include the 1997 purchase of the frozen products division of Ault Foods Ltd. for $221 million. With this deal, Nestlé acquired an ice cream and frozen novelty plant in London, Ontario, several warehouses and distribution centres, various Ault trademarks (Meadowgold, J. Higby's and Famous), plus the license rights to other brands (Sealtest Parlour and Haagen-Dazs).

> **Annual Revenue:** $1.6 billion
> **Grocery Store Sales:** No information
> **Brands:** Aero, After Eight, Carnation, Coffee Crisp, Coffee-Mate, Crosse and Blackwell, Crunch, Good Host, Goodstart, Perrier, Haagen-Dazs, Kit Kat, Lean Cuisine, L'oreal, Nescafe, Nestea, NeQuik, Pastaria, Powerbar, Smarties, Stouffers, Tasters' Choice
> **Corporate Status:** Wholly-owned by Swiss-based parent company.
> **Candor:** Nestlé provided answers to 29% of EthicScan's questions.

Ethical Management and Consumer Relations: *Nestlé Corporate Business Principles*, the firm's code of ethics, guides employees on issues like national legislation, international recommendations, infant health and nutrition, human rights, child labour, business partners, conflicts of interest, competition, and environmental protection. It was last updated in 2002, receives an annual sign-off and is posted on the company's intranet. Compliance with the Code is monitored by 200 internal auditors in Nestlé's markets as well as a team of 25 corporate monitors who report to the international Head of Auditing. Nestlé has a strong set of consumer assurance mechanisms. Each year, about 100,000 customers call its toll-free number, usually with questions about ingredients, product recipes, distribution, and nutrition. Working with the top allergy associations in Canada, the company regularly publishes information about ingredient changes that may affect consumers with allergies. Nestlé's Scientific and Regulatory Affairs has publicly stated that the company supports detailed food labels, saying that Canadians should have a choice in the forms by which they take their nutrients. When Nestlé announced that it would cease producing chocolate bars in a nut-free facility, and that five of its popular products would not carry the same safety guarantee for people with nut allergies, thousands of consumers wrote and telephoned to complain, and Nestlé reversed its decision. A product recall case arose in March 2000 when Nestlé Canada recalled specific dates and codes of its 385-ml cans of infant formula, Goodstart Liquid Concentrate, because temperature fluctuations in the final stage of canning may have affected the sterility of the contents. Using 19 Canadian daily newspapers, the company published the information consumers needed to verify whether or not their cans should be returned for a refund, and provided a consumer hotline. Like its competitors, there is no independent ethics audit.

Infant Formula: For the last two decades, multinational infant formula makers have been sharply criticized for their marketing practices, primarily in developing nations. At the center of the controversy is compliance with an International Code of Marketing of Breast Milk Substitutes written by the World Health Organization (WHO) and UNICEF (a branch of the United Nations), which is supposed to guide all companies. According to this Code, the promotion of formula should occur only through the medical system, so that mothers can get the advice of doctors. It is treated as a guideline for creating legislation in developing nations, but has never been legislated in Canada. Nestlé SA sells formula through 74 offices throughout the world, and though it holds almost 30% of the world market for formula, the entire infant foods category accounts for less than 6% of worldwide business. In 1999, the International Baby Food Action Network (IBFAN), a non-governmental organization that monitors international formula marketing, released, *Breaking the Rules, Stretching the Rules, 1998.* This report details how 15 infant-formula companies, including Nestlé, violated the WHO/UNICEF code. Products were said to have been promoted directly to the public in health care facilities, and free supplies were allegedly distributed in many developing and industrialized nations. Specifically, alleged breaches of the code include: inappropriate use of posters, calendars, and other displays (Nestlé has distributed educational posters dealing with pregnancy, child birth, infant feeding, or care in a number of countries); improper and misleading use of images (in 1997, a Nestlé diary with a book mark advertising Lactogen Gold was given to health workers in Indonesia); and ill-conceived sponsorships (Nestlé funded travel for health professionals in Colombia, Brazil, and Mexico and gave doctors fellowships and awards in Argentina). Further, Nestlé has been accused of neglecting to translate publicity materials and product instructions into local languages where products are sold. Advocacy groups have charged that babies in developing countries have died as a result of this negligence. Accusations of this kind are not new. In Canada, during the 1990s, two advocacy groups - the Taskforce on the Churches and Corporate Responsibility and a group called INFACT - approached Nestlé Canada with concerns about the way its Carnation product was promoted.

The corporate spokesperson said that Nestlé provides health professionals with educational materials and samples that are distributed to mothers who cannot or choose not to breast-feed. The company says that where countries have not adopted their own standards, Nestlé voluntary applies the WHO Code in its entirety. The company also internally audits adherence to the Code, and any negative findings are reported directly to the CEO. Nestlé further stated that in 2000, four cases resulted in disciplinary measures being taken against the managers found to be violating company instructions. Nestlé responded to IBFAN's

Infant Formula (continued): report, stating that it investigated all the allegations and discovered that only three had any foundation, and that these had already been remedied. In 1997 (prior to the 1999 IBFAN report), a company spokesperson supplied EthicScan with a comment: "Nestlé participated in bringing the issue of infant formul marketing in developing countries to the World Health Organization twenty years ago, and the company agreed in advance to abide by the Code, which is a recommendation to governments. The company has followed both the letter and the spirit of the Code in developing countries. Nestlé favours strong national codes giving practical effect to the principles and aims of the WHO Code, which are supported by independent, transparent monitoring mechanisms....Canada, which is not considered a developing country, has not enacted the Code into law."

2002 Employees Canada: 3,500   **1991 Employees Canada:** 5,000

Employee Relations: Employment in Canada has dropped massively (30%) over the last decade, in part due to the divestment of Laura Secord, which employed many retail workers. Seven unions (including the Teamsters, National Automobile, Aerospace and Agricultural Implement Workers Union of Canada, and the CAW) represent 55% of Canadian workforce. In the early 1992, layoffs hit the Trenton frozen food plant, which in the latter part of the decade turned around its performance dramatically after reopening with a foodservice focus. Chocolate operations were also transferred from Toronto to Britain, and displaced workers received severance and benefit packages as well as relocation counselling. When the Mississauga plant closed, those let go received advance notice of the layoff, severance pay, job search counselling, and extended benefits beyond the plant's closing date. A strike occurred in April 1997, when more than 300 workers at the then newly acquired Nestlé Canada Inc. ice cream plant in London, Ontario walked out over a proposed five-year wage freeze for some workers, and over the use of more part-time staff. In 1996, a three-day strike over pay increases hit the Toronto Confectionery plant. The company spokesperson stated that Nestlé is very proud of the state of its relationship with employees and their union representatives.

Equity and Family: Women hold 40% of total jobs, 29% of management positions and 24% of senior manager jobs. The company has a Canadian Advisory Board made up of three women and six men. Nestlé has an employment equity policy, a sexual harassment policy, and same sex couples benefits. Family support includes income supplements, daycare referral services and parental leaves that extend for as long as one year. Flexible scheduling and alternative work arrangements have been available for more than 20 years, longer than most companies profiled by EthicScan. Nestlé was the only company to report on-site breast-milk expression rooms for mothers who wish to continue breast-feeding once they have returned to work.

Progressive Staff: Nestlé invests heavily in training (no 2001 statistics were reported, but in 1996 it spent more than $3 million), giving each employee a minimum of 40 hours of training per year, including one on one coaching, field visits, on the job training, and classroom sessions. The company fully reimburses expenses by employees who take educational or skills improvement courses. Formulas for employee bonuses are based on the achievement of corporate and divisional targets, paying out amounts that are approximately 4% of an employee's total remuneration. Nestlé's "goals" and training motivate employees to work in teams for continuous process improvement. The company formally rewards employees through the Nestlé Recognition Program, and since 1994 has given over 2000 awards to individuals and teams. The company employs numerous employee communications methods including a quarterly newsletter, a company intranet, and regular visits by the CEO to all facilities. Employee Assistance Programs, including 24 hour referral services, are available to all employees and their families.

Sourcing and Trade: Nestlé Canada's Export Division exports products to countries around the world including the Middle East, Mexico, the U.S., Hong Kong, and Australia. It sells evaporated milk to the Caribbean and Africa. Nestlé's Chesterville, Ontario plant makes Nescafé products for Canada and the United States. Nestlé SA and subsidiaries manufacture food and other products in 77 countries, including repressive regimes such as China. In 1997, Nestlé Canada reported that its policy on child labour states that Nestlé companies will not provide employment to children before they have completed compulsory education. Nestlé is one of the only companies profiled in this book to indicate that it abides by the principles of the International Labour Organization convention concerning the minimum age for employment. The company also subscribes to the UN Global Compact. Nestlé reported that, in 2000, it audited more than 1000 of its over 3000 suppliers and that when instances of non-compliance were found, corrective measures were required to be taken if the business relationship was to continue. The company comments: "As an international company, Nestlé is active in dozens of countries with widely divergent systems. [The company] believes it is inappropriate to become involved in political issues, regardless of our own opinions and preference." Nestlé says that it provides employment and training for local people, purchases both raw materials and supplies locally, and creates wealth which contributes to the well-being of the community in which it operates. For example, the children of employees with jobs at a Nestlé facility may be able to stay in school longer, thus improving their future prospects.

Coffee Sourcing: As a major coffee processor, Nestlé must deal with concerns over the environmental impacts of coffee beans (planting and harvesting methods can degrade soil) and trade relations (wages, working conditions) with farmers in developing countries. To negotiate favourable prices and terms of sale, companies often deal directly with the governments of coffee growing countries, not farmers. In many cases, this control has come at the expense of conditions faced by landless workers and independent growers. Although no companies profiled in this book gave details about where they source their coffee, nor independent verifications of practices and conditions, Nestlé did respond to some of these concerns. It reports environmental policies that aim to preserve and improve soil productivity, protect water resources, minimize the use of agrochemicals, and reduce energy usage. Since 1986, Nestlé subsidiaries have purchased coffee for local production requirements, and in 1997, direct purchases from growers accounted for approximately 15% of requirements (the other 85% is sourced on the international market). The company reports that it works extensively with coffee farmers to raise the income they receive. In co-operation with governments, coffee research institutes, and other agencies, Nestlé says that it has established a set of 250 different coffee varieties for plant-improvement programs. Technical support for improved cultivation methods and post-harvest treatment of coffee is provided to growers, and the company states that it pays a premium for its purchases.

Environmental Management and Performance: In Canada, Nestlé follows the parent company's environmental policy, a six-point document that mandates compliance with regulations and desirable relations with associations, suppliers, and other stakeholders. Comprehensive environmental audits are scheduled every year at all operations (and conducted by a team of internal and external auditors). An internal environmental progress report is issued to senior management, while annual plans are filed to the parent's headquarters in Switzerland. Two employees in the Canadian company have full-time environmental responsibilities, each factory has an environment officer who reports directly to the site manager, and other committees are formed as required. In the mid-1990s, the company expanded waste holding lagoons in Chesterville, Ontario to accommodate higher production levels, and new ovens were built at the Toronto factory to cut energy consumption. From 1995 to 1996, Nestlé spent $7.7 million on pollution improvements, and $4.8 million in operating expenditures. Nestlé Canada is one of the only companies profiled to have signed the Voluntary Challenge Registry with the Federal Government, setting a plan to cut greenhouse gas emissions (with a target of 1% reduction per year of energy used per unit of production). Nestlé did not provide the National Pollutant Release Inventory with information on its chemical releases and transfers. Energy and Resource Conservation Programs are in place at all factories, and Canadian plants have full workplace recycling programs (for cardboard, wood, metal, glass, paper, cans, plastics, and food waste). Food wastes go to farmers to be used for animal feed, spent coffee grounds are burned to generate steam, and frying oils and starches are re-refined or reclaimed for the manufacture of adhesives. Suppliers participate in packaging changes, pallet recycling, and the elimination of inks containing heavy metals. At food-service coffee factories, catalytic after-burners are installed to recycle gases given off during roasting for energy. All nine of Nestlé's Canadian factories are both ISO 14001 and internally certified. In 2000, all nine factories won plaques as "Industrial Energy Innovators" from CIPEC and the Ministry of Natural Resources, Canada.

Animal Testing: The parent company, Nestlé SA, uses animal testing only to fulfill regulations governing product safety and fundamental research. For more than 20 years, it has dedicated millions of dollars toward developing alternative methods to animal testing.

Community Responsibilities: As one of the first 100 companies ever designated an Imagine Caring Company, Nestlé has consistently donated more than 1% of pre-tax profits to charity. Products are donated to food banks across the country (through the Canadian Association of Food Banks, which distributes donations nationally based on need). Company facilities are loaned, employee volunteer time is donated, and student work programs are offered. The company is committed to supporting charities in communities of operation and helping youth development. It is a founding sponsor of the Kids Help Phone line and has recently entered into a partnership with Family Services Canada. An annual golf tournament raises $250,000 per year for the Kids Help Phone. Nestlé was a founding member of ParticipACTION, and has also given money, volunteer time, or in-kind contributions to the University of Guelph, the Canadian Children's Foundation, National Institute of Nutrition, Multiple Sclerosis, and many other charitable causes.

www.nestle.com

Ocean Fisheries Ltd.

Ocean Fisheries was founded in 1962. Today this Vancouver-based company operates three processing plants and an office in British Columbia. The Safarik family holds all company stock privately. Approximately 50% of its business comes from Canada, with the rest derived from sales in more than 20 other countries (including the U.S., Japan, Australia, New Zealand, the U.K., and other European countries). In addition to being a market leader in the food service business, Ocean Fisheries accounts for around 17% of Canada's retail canned salmon, tuna, and other seafood markets (approximately half of all revenue).

> **2001 Revenues:** Approximately $100 million
> **Grocery Store Sales:** 50%
> **Brands:** North Pacific, Ocean's, SandwichMate, SnacKit
> **Corporate Status:** Privately-held Canadian company.
> **Candor:** Ocean Fisheries provided answers to 44% of EthicScan's questions.

Ethical Management and Consumer Relations: Ocean Fisheries has no written code of ethics, training, ethics ombudsperson, or advisor. The spokesperson stated that the company does have a book prepared by an outside consultant that deals with personnel, crisis handling, and interpersonal relationship issues. Only nominal business gifts (examples include T-shirts and golf balls) are considered acceptable gifts. As a policy, the company responds to all consumer queries within 24 hours through an e-mail system called "Talk to Us," and follows up on each complaint with a letter. The company spokesperson reports that the Canadian Food Inspection Agency (CFIA), the European Food Safety Inspection System (EFSIS), and major U.K. retailers monitor compliance with rigid standards of food processing, employee relations, sustainability issues, and fair hiring, and that the company continually gets a high rating. The company is rated QMP and QMPI by the CFIA, as well as holding an EFSIS Certificate of Inspection, the highest level of compliance awarded. The company has a strong Quality Assurance program which performs internal audits of operations and is audited at least annually by the CFIA and EFSIS. Additionally, all the plants that the company buys import goods from must be EFSIS approved. Approximately 1% of Ocean Fisheries product costs go toward advertising, including in-store demos.

2002 Employees Canada: 500

Employee Relations: The company's employment totals have been relatively stable over the last couple of years. In 1998, it employed 95 full-time staff—down 24% from the 125 employees in 1991. Typically, the company relies on a seasonal staff contingent of 1,500 workers during the peak period between March and August. All Prince Rupert employees are members of the United Fishermen and Allied Workers, representing 10% of the company's total employees. Ocean Fisheries reported that 5% of its production is contracted out. The company has never closed a plant, although it sold its U.S. operation in May 1992. One province-wide fisheries strike (not aimed specifically against Ocean Fisheries), shut down the industry for 11 days in July 1992, putting 2,000 fishery personnel and 1,000 food processing workers on the picket line. No other strikes have occurred.

Equity and Family: Precise figures for the number of women in the company were not reported. Due to the seasonal nature of its operation, this number varies. Typically, five to six women occupy management jobs, while 30 to 35 work in other positions, including technical staff and supervisors. Management does not track data on visible minorities in management or in the workforce. The numbers of native fishermen and Asian plant workers are high, reflecting the composition of the surrounding communities. Minority, disabled, and aboriginal hiring programs exist. Ocean Fisheries also reports an anti-harassment policy, covering sexual and racial issues. Although no training or sign-off was reported, the policy is reviewed annually, and all employees have a copy of the policy manual which includes information on steps to take if an employee wants to lodge a complaint. The spokesperson said that the company has no harassment or human rights cases or convictions. Family support initiatives include maternity leave extensions (one month beyond the five-month minimum) and paternity leave opportunities. Same sex couples benefits are not offered, and employees cannot take paid days off for cultural and religious observances.

Progressive Staff: Expenses for course tuition and books are reimbursed 100%, and the company grants time off for work-related courses (such as information technology, business, technical training, food processing, or Masters of Business Administration). Performance-based profit sharing is available to all full-time salaried staff, with a bonus program that rewards worker incentives. An Employee Assistance Plan provides counselling for substance abuse referrals, financial planning, marital problems and retirement planning. Non-management employees who work beyond a 40-hour week are guaranteed compensation. The company has an open door management policy, and the spokesperson stated that all employees have access to the President.

Sourcing and Trade: Honour Roll. Ocean Fisheries has no U.S. or foreign operations. Approximately 70% of inputs and ingredients for products processed in Canada are sourced in Canada, and the spokesperson said preference goes to Canadian suppliers. This policy does not apply to imports of finished products. To source herring, groundfish, and salmon, the company relies on its own vessels but contracts out about 40% of salmon shipments from independent fishermen. The company's tuna comes from Thailand, Malaysia, and the Philippines. Strict guidelines cover labour standards at its plants and contracted operations, the spokesperson noted, leading the company to buy only from a select number of approved plants listed by the Federal Department of Agriculture. No underage or forced labour is used according to the company, and the spokesperson stated that its operations and the plants they buy from are approved by EFSIS and audited by the companies on a QA system, both of which include inspection of compliance with labour standards.

Environmental Management and Performance: The company's environmental policy is updated on an on-going basis. Audits are conducted by a combination of internal and external personnel, including the B.C. government. The spokesperson explained that formal reports to the board of directors do not occur because the board is composed mainly of the company's owners. The company is run by a management committee composed of the President and the Vice Presidents of finance, marketing, operating systems, and the fleet. Supporting a Vice-President of operating systems (with part-time responsibilities for environmental matters) are plant managers who track environmental issues and handle municipal relations at each of the company's three plants. Ten different managers handle other aspects of environmental responsibilities. The spokesperson stated that the B.C. government audits the company's environmental performance. Conservation programs reduce water and fuel usage, and improve waste disposal, spill containment, and water purity. Ocean Fisheries gave no information to the National Pollutant Release Inventory regarding plant chemical releases and transfers. Workplace recycling programs exist for paper, cardboard, and wood pallets, and ten tons of metal and 200 gallons of waste oil are recycled annually. All solid by-products are used for fishmeal, food, or animal feed, and a system of filters screens liquid waste before its discharge. Ocean Fisheries states that its fishing practices were the first to be approved by Earth Island Institute (EII), which in 1998 confirmed that the company's "policies [did] meet the EII dolphin-safe criteria and results of their monitoring program." Although aquaculture is well developed in Canada (the whole industry earns $600 million per year from the sale of farmed fish and shellfish) Ocean Fisheries is not involved in aquaculture and uses only wild fish stocks. The spokesperson further stated that the company is concerned with recent changes in provincial regulations regarding aquaculture, and that it is interested in preserving the health of wild fish stocks in British Columbia and Alaska.

Genetically Modified Ingredients: The spokesperson stated that the company uses only wild fish stocks, and thus does not support GMOs.

> **Transgenic Fish:** Ocean Fisheries reports that it sources fish from wild stocks only. However, the entire industry will face increasing pressure to consider the potential applications of modern gene technology. What likely will be the first genetically modified creature on our dinner tables? Experts say salmon. Carrying genes from two other fish species, these salmon fish will grow at two to three times the rate of ordinary species, creating a great incentive for the fish industry to exploit them. Because hatcheries will likely sell to commercial fish farmers, GMO critics worry that these fish could escape and become a threat to naturally occurring salmon. The David Suzuki Foundation has spoken out about potential risks to human health and natural environments posed by GM fish, specifically, their impact on wild fish stocks. Farmed fish often find their way out of fish-farm pens and into rivers and oceans. Breeders claim that all transgenic fish raised for the marketplace are sterilized females that are incapable of reproduction, but critics say these techniques are not foolproof. Proponents also point out natural selection weaknesses of the transgenic species, saying that they have poorer swimming abilities and are more vulnerable to diseases, thereby reducing the likelihood that they will overcome natural species.

Community Responsibilities: The company gave $20,000 to charity in 1999, 2000, and again in 2001. Such levels are down from 1997, when $35,000 was donated to general causes, along with $10,000 set aside for amateur sports, plus $5,000 from employees. The spokesperson did not indicate what percentage of pre-tax profits its philanthropic giving represents, but stated that the drop in giving is linked to the drop in profitability of the company and the fishing industry in general in the last two years. Ocean Fisheries makes cash donations to Simon Fraser University and the University of British Columbia, as well as matches employee gifts. Paid time off supports employee voluntarism. Up to 1,500 cartons of food are donated to food banks, representing the largest single donation of food from any company in British Columbia's lower mainland. Locally, the company gives to sports teams, community centers, the B.C. Children's Hospital in Vancouver, the United Way, and the Air Canada Whistler Ski Cup.

www.oceanfish.com

Old Dutch Food Limited

Old Dutch Food Limited, which claims to have invented the salt and vinegar potato chip, began in Minneapolis in the 1930s, before expanding to Winnipeg in 1954. Owned by the Aanensen family since 1951, it now sells more salty snacks in Canada than it does in the USA. It has plants in Ardrie, Winnipeg and Calgary and a head office in St. Paul, Minnesota. The company is an anomaly in the marketing-intensive snack industry, because it spends relatively little on advertising. Old Dutch innovated a marketing practice, now common in the chip business, whereby independent travelling representatives fill empty store shelves instead of waiting for orders to be placed.

2000 Revenues: $170 million
Grocery Store Sales: No information
Brands: Dutch Crunch, Old Dutch, Rave
Corporate Status: Privately owned by Aanensen family, who are also shareholders in the U.S. company.
Candor: The company has a 46% candor quotient, which is high for a privately held company.

Ethical Management and Consumer Relations: With no ethics code, advisor, or recourse programs for employees, the company deals with questions related to business gift-giving, competition and other sales practices on an informal basis. A policy on privacy of employee records exists. A toll-free phone line and product recall systems are in place, but no details on incidents or usage were supplied.

2002 Employees Canada: 750   **1991 Employees Canada:** 625

Employee Relations: Employment in the U.S. has been relatively stable (450 in 2001 compared with 425 in 1991). These employment totals do not include road salesmen, who buy their own trucks, supply stores, and purchase product from the company at a discount. Approximately half of the workers at the Winnipeg and Calgary plants are represented by the UFCW. The percentage of unionized workers is 75%, up from 50% in 1996. In 1996, the company closed its Mississauga office, laying off about two dozen staff (the spokesperson says that some of these were probably independent staff, not employees). Downsized employees received retraining, relocation, and early retirement options. The company has a policy of giving advance notice of technological changes. In 1997, the union spokesperson reported no unjust dismissal cases or work stoppages over the last 10 years. Relations with management were described as "good." Because no on-site manager works in the plant, communications can be a problem when staff issues arise. The union spokesperson says that the company, which employs many immigrants, has a low turnover rate among its staff. No health and safety or injury statistics were reported. Up to 75% of tuition and book expenses are refunded if the course is directly related to employment and pre-approved by the company.

Equity and Family: Old Dutch is rare in that its board has a female majority: two of three directors are women. Two of ten senior managers are female. The union spokesperson estimates that the general workforce is 50% to 70% women. No formal program addresses advancement of women, minorities, aboriginal peoples, or the disabled. A sexual harassment policy is advertised through a widely distributed poster that gives information on appropriate places for workers to file complaints. No signoff is required, and no training given. Maternity leave benefits do not extend beyond what is required by law. The company reports no human rights cases or convictions.

Progressive Staff: Referral counselling for employees with substance abuse and psychological problems is available at all sites. Employees who work more than 40 hours a week are guaranteed appropriate compensation, but no details exist about how many employees typically put in overtime.

Sourcing and Trade: Old Dutch sales represent over half of the total Manitoba, Saskatchewan and Alberta markets, and about 40% of British Columbia. Private label production occupies 5% of total sales. Some international sales come from Hong Kong and Japan. The company spokesperson stated that Old Dutch no longer sells to China as this was an interim agreement until the Chinese purchaser could build its own plant. Four large Mennonite potato farms near Winkler, Manitoba supply most Old Dutch potatoes for the Winnipeg plant; two of these are the largest potato growers in Canada. The Alberta plant sources from Alberta farmers. A portion of the Canadian product is exported to the United States. Management ensures the company does not source from repressive regimes, but the spokesperson gave no details.

Environmental Management and Performance: Old Dutch has no written environmental code, nor audits of its environmental performance. No full-time environmental officer or staff committee exists, and Old Dutch Foods Ltd. reported no NPRI releases for its Calgary facility in 1999 or 2000. Recycling programs are in place at all plants, and include paper and waste product recycling. The company works with suppliers to minimize waste in the delivery of inputs and ingredients. For example, the firm that makes Old Dutch's packaging film reduced the gauge of foil wrapper, saving an undisclosed amount of film. The company manages a substantial truck fleet in order to meet the delivery schedule required for its product; potato chips have a shelf life of about six weeks, so product supplies need constant replenishing. Old Dutch works with farmers to support sustainable farming and reduce, for example, the use of herbicides and pesticides. Most farmers in Canada and the United States are said to be receptive. This "sustainable practice" does not extend to organic farming at present, which is said to be cost-prohibitive.

Genetically Modified Ingredients: The company's position on genetically modified foods is on hold, pending federal guidelines and definitions.

Community Responsibilities: The Aanansen family donates to charitable organizations both privately and through the company. Products and cash go to a range of local causes, including schools and hospitals. The company allows time off for staff voluntarism. Old Dutch Foods also loans its facilities to community groups.

No website

Parmalat Canada

Parmalat Canada is a dairy and bakery food processor created in 1997, when its Italian-based parent, Parmalat Finanzioria SpA bought Ault Foods Ltd and Beatrice Foods and merged the two. Its parent is a world-leading food company, processing and marketing milk and dairy products, fruit juices, tomato-based products, and bakery goods. Its subsidiaries span over 30 countries. In Canada, Parmalat's plants (in Alberta, Manitoba, Ontario, and Québec) make cheese, tablespreads, fluid milk and beverages, along with cultured and bakery goods. It serves regional and national markets through the foodservice, deli, and retail grocery store channels. In 1998, the company acquired Astro, a yogurt and cultured products brand.

2001 Revenues: Approximately $2 billion
Grocery Store Sales: No information
Brands: Astro, Balderson, Beatrice, Black Diamond, Colonial cookies, Lactantia, Parkay, Windsor wafers
Corporate Status: Wholly-owned subsidiary of Italy-based parent company.
Candor: The company spokesperson was very prompt at the draft one stage. The candor quotient is 50%.

Ethical Management and Consumer Relations: Canada-specific corporate values and guiding principles were defined and launched in winter, 2000. They are in the process of being integrated with a corporate code of conduct, and are available in both English and French. Compliance with Parmalat's code of conduct is part of employees' and managers' formal performance reviews. Whistleblower protection is under review, and guidelines for exchange of business gifts are in development. In 2001, the company negotiated with Coca-Cola Co. over use of the slogan "Life Tastes Good," which Coke launched as a Canadian ad campaign in April 2001. Parmalat began a campaign for its Lactantia milk in September 2000 with the same slogan, although it registered the slogan in March. The companies agreed that Parmalat would allow Coca-Cola Co. to use the slogan on its Coca-Cola brand.

2002 Employees Canada: 5,000 **1998 Employees Canada:** 4,600

Employee Relations: Slightly more than half of Parmalat's employees belong to one of 10 different unions (CSN, CSD, Canadian Marine Officers Union, CUSCW (TUAC), CAW, Teamsters, Operating Engineers, UFCW, United Steelworkers of America, and CEP). Prior to the Parmalat acquisition, both Ault and Beatrice had downsized and divested operations, so no major layoffs occurred during the merger. When layoffs do occur, the company guarantees outplacement services. In 2001, the company announced that it planned to close its Kingston, Ontario plant by February 2002, resulting in a loss of 47 jobs. In 1997, 250 former Ault employees whose operations had been spun-off prior to the merger filed a class action lawsuit, alleging that Ault management denied them bonuses and vacation pay. A judge ordered Ault to pay $6,000 in legal costs associated with the suit because of intimidation tactics. Although Parmalat inherited this suit, its spokesperson said that the alleged actions were aimed at previous management.

Equity and Family: No information on the advancement of women was reported. The company has an "equal opportunity" approach to career advancement, making decisions based on qualifications and competency. Reviews or audits of Parmalat's anti-harassment policy are conducted on an *ad hoc* basis as required. Some locations have received training on the policy. In the event of an alleged human rights complaint, the spokesperson says that an internal investigation would take place, and its results would remain private and confidential. According to the company spokesperson, staff composition reflects the ethnic composition within host communities. The company is consolidating employee information into one common technology platform that will track these data. Same sex couples are eligible for benefits through the salaried benefit plan. There is no formal policy for paid days off for cultural and religious observances. While access to all buildings is not currently available, some improvements are underway, despite there being no formal accommodation policy.

Progressive Staff: In spring 2001, Parmalat spent approximately $1 million to train all salaried employees on teamwork and continuous process improvement. Employee feedback helps shape the content of training programs. The company pays all tuition and book costs for any job or career related course. With the creation of Parmalat in 1997, existing gain-sharing plans for plant employees were maintained, while a separate new plan was introduced for management. No stock options are available in Canada, but all salaried employees are eligible for a management incentive based on corporate financial performance and individual achievement.

Sourcing and Trade: The parent company has operations in over 30 countries, including China, but no formal policy guiding human rights or environmental standards. In Canada, dairy companies like Parmalat have long complained about rules imposed by provincial milk marketing boards. These regulations require domestically sold milk to be sold with protections, to ensure they command a higher price than exported milk. As a result, Canadian-based dairy processors must source their milk at a fixed cost, but sharply lower their profit margins in order to sell competitively in the retail market.

Environmental Management and Performance: Reporting and accountability procedures at Ault and Beatrice were revised and consolidated when Parmalat drafted its environmental policy in the late 1990s. Hygienic requirements for producing milk mandate regular inspections of each dairy's product line. The spokesperson makes no distinctions between hygiene inspections and broader environmental audits and said that both occur. Strict environmental evaluation procedures are part of any new site acquisition. The spokesperson stated that Parmalat has commenced environmental training, appointing champions within the company. The company reported NPRI releases from one of its five facilities. Its Winchester, Ontario plant placed in the 80-90 percentile of all major chemical and waste generators (209,200 kilograms released to water in 1999, exceeding 1997 and 1998 figures). No information was given for potential human health risks of the top ranked NPRI pollutant. The Brampton, Kitchener, Etobicoke, and Montreal facilities report no NPRI releases. In the 1990s, at least three fines worth a total of $95,000 were paid by Beatrice's Malcolm Food Specialties site, and by Ault's Aylmer and St. George Ontario locations.

Genetically Modified Ingredients: No policy was discussed.

Health and Safety:
2000 Injuries: 611
1999 Injuries: 602
The corporate spokesperson noted that injury cases include medical aids, lost time incidents, and situations involving modified work arrangements. Certified joint health and safety committees oversee all locations. The company conducts ergonomic workplace assessments as needed, and internal personnel train employees on health and safety issues and on working in confined spaces and on heavy equipment, such as forklifts.

Community Responsibilities: In the late 1990s, Parmalat donated 0.5% of its pre-tax profit to charity, which represented $300,000 and $400,000, excluding the monetary value of in-kind donations and other product sponsorships. No figures for staff donations were available. Written guidelines direct a donations committee, which meets four times each year. Input on decisions is solicited from individual business units, which have no formal distribution authority. Corporate priorities focus on helping children and the elderly. Recipients include the Kids Help Foundation, hospitals, the United Way, the Salvation Army, educational institutions, and food banks. The company matches employee gifts to the United Way, though no other gift-matching program was mentioned.

www.parmalat.com

Pepsi Bottling Group (Canada), Co.

Founded in Montreal in 1934, Pepsi operated as Pepsi-Cola Canada Beverages ("PCCB") until 1999. In February 1999, the company divided bottling operations from its drink concentrate business, creating Pepsi Bottling Group Canada. Today, two separate companies exist in Canada: The Pepsi Bottling Group, Co. ("PBG Canada") and Pepsi-Cola Canada Limited ("PCCL"). In the early 1990s, PCCB began acquiring franchise bottlers, and by 1999 was distributing 85% of system sales through a company-owned bottling network. The American parent company, PepsiCo, owns approximately 40% of PBG and 100% of PCCL. PCCL has three operating divisions: Pepsi-Cola Canada (the beverage concentrate company), Hostess Frito-Lay, and Tropicana Canada. Pepsi-Cola products are sold through PBG Canada and 18 franchise bottlers, who operate 13 bottling plants and 34 distribution facilities. When PepsiCo restructured its holdings in 1997, it spun off its $10 billion fast-food operations (Pizza Hut, Taco Bell, KFC) into Tricon Global Restaurants. PepsiCo recently acquired Quaker Oats, including its Gatorade brand. Soda pop revenues (approximately $1 billion) come from concentrate sales to restaurants and concessions (30%), and from bottled products (70%).

2001 Revenues (PBG): No information
Grocery Store Sales: No information
Brands: Aquafina, Brisk Iced Tea, Caffeine-free Diet Pepsi, Diet Pepsi, Diet 7-Up, Dr. Pepper, Lipton Brisk Lemonade, Lipton's Iced Teas, Mountain Dew, Mountain Dew Code Red, Mug Root Beer, Pepsi, Pepsi Blue, Pepsi Twist, 7-Up, 7-Up Tropcial Splash, Sobe, Starbucks Bottled, Tropicana, Wild Cherry Pepsi
Corporate Status: Majority owned by US parent company.
Candor: In 2001, answers supplied by public relations firm, resulted in a 47% candor quotient.

Ethical Management and Consumer Relations: Pepsi's 12-page ethics code (written in the late 1970s, updated in 2001) applies worldwide to all Pepsi subsidiaries and receives a sign-off from management. Neither PBG nor PCCL has separate codes modified for Canadian operations. The code outlines Pepsi's global relations and its expectations for employee conduct when dealing with customers and suppliers on matters like gifts and payments, safety and environmental protection, political and community activities, conflicts of interest, and insider trading. All Pepsi companies reinforce the code by requiring employees to read it and take training. A "Right Side Up" program, developed by management and employees, works to strengthen corporate culture and sustain "common values" during transitions that accompany franchise acquisitions. Employee units must "enroll" in the program, hold annual meetings, and publish a regular newsletter and health survey. Like its competitors, it does not issue an independent social audit.

2002 Employees Canada: 3,552 (PCCL & PCB)

1991 Employees Canada: 1,600

Employee Relations: As Pepsi acquired operations throughout the 1990s, direct staff figures increased steadily (2,750 in 1996), although 3,000 jobs were lost, mostly from layoffs at franchise bottlers. Global job figures for the parent company have dropped (313,145 in 1996 to 125,000 in 2000) as operations were rationalized and restaurant chains divested. PCCL has 60 employees in Canada this year. Approximately 66% of workers belong to unions. A 1997 strike over wages and benefits put 490 Québec employees on the picket line for 20 days, affecting half of Pepsi's Québec operations. In the mid-1990s, a union spokesperson said that relations were generally "excellent" at the Mississauga plant and "unbelievably good" at the Orillia plant. No health and safety statistics were reported in 2001. PCCB's accident severity rate dropped between 1995 (83.7 lost days for 1 million raw cases of pop sold) and 1996 (58.4 days). After a Calgary PCCB worker died when he became trapped in a palletizer in 1995, a team of employees and managers investigated the accident. The corporate spokesperson said that the worker had been properly trained and that the company determined a list of "issues for resolution," along with an appropriate "action plan." The company has joint health and safety committees, a part-time safety co-ordinator at the management level of each facility, and a full-time safety manager at the corporate office.

Equity and Family: Honour Roll. Women represent 17% of PBG managers, and just over 14% of its senior managers, which is below average for companies in this book. At PCCL, there are 13 women out of 20 managers (65%), two women among six senior managers (33%), and two of 13 board directors (15%), all of which are high compared with other companies. Within its employment equity policy and plan, PCCB puts forth no quota system for hiring, but its operating program (workplace accommodation and community assessment) ensures that hiring reflects local demographics. At PCNA (Pepsi Cola North America), an advisory committee informs management on diversity issues, and gender guidelines influence Board nominations. A 'women-in-sales' career placement training exists, along with internal women's and minority support groups. PCNA assigns executives to diversity portfolios—one of the only companies profiled in this book to do so—and they are required to complete multi-year strategic plans for diversity. Annual employee reviews deal with diversity as part of other programs ("Act with Integrity," "Create a Positive Work Environment," and "Align and Motivate Teams"). An annual organizational health survey incorporates diversity questions, for which senior managers are held accountable. There have been no human rights cases at PCCL or PBG. An anti-harassment policy (PCNA and PBG) covers gender, race, sexual orientation, and disability issues. It is reviewed annually, supported with training, and receives an employee sign-off. PCNA and PBG also grant same sex benefits and paid days off for cultural and religious holidays. Family support programs include daycare referral at all PBG sites, and maternity and paternity leave benefits are topped up or may be extended. Paid days off for child and eldercare need to be worked out with the manager.

Progressive Staff: Honour Roll. At PBG, flexible scheduling is offered, and compensation for working over 40 hours is guaranteed. Nationally, PBG trains workers on workplace safety and ergonomics. Stop-smoking programs are offered, and on-site fitness facilities exist at many locations. Substance abuse, family counselling, child and eldercare support are offered at PBG and PCNA. The company distributes a variety of newsletters on topics ranging from employee benefits to health issues. Employee development is extensive, including full tuition refunds, and scholarships for employees and their children. Formal employee feedback is gathered through surveys. A "Sharepower" program allows employees to buy stock worth a maximum of value of 10% of their annual pay. Some managers participate in an incentive-driven profit sharing program.

Sourcing and Trade: PBG procures 99% of its supplies in Canada. No information was provided on foreign sourcing codes or human rights protections at PBG, PCNA, or PepsiCo. This lack of information coincides with a major public relations crisis faced by parent PepsiCo. in the mid-1990s, when allegations arose over human rights abuses in Myanmar (Burma). In 1994, the Shan Human Rights Foundation reported that forced labour was used in Burma to dig a canal to supply water to a Pepsi plant. Although Pepsi did not directly control the construction site, it suffered negative media attention when 600 of 60,000 forced labourers died in March 1994. The country's ruling dictatorship granted Pepsi a virtual monopoly over other pop makers. PepsiCo. began disentangling itself from the situation by selling its 40% interest in Pepsi Burma, while attempting to maintain a franchise agreement in which Pepsi-Cola Products Myanmar would continue to bottle and market Pepsi and 7-Up. Nobel Laureate Aung San Suu Kyi was quoted in the media, "As far as [those concerned with human rights] are concerned, Pepsi has not divested from Burma." PepsiCo eventually did leave Burma and ended its franchise agreements in January 1997. All production and distribution of Pepsi products in Burma finally ceased in May 31, 1997.

Environmental Management and Performance: Honour Roll for Environmental Performance. Despite corporate restructuring between 1992 and 1999, PCCB continues to follow its own one-page environmental policy. It coordinated environmental management with safety practices and instituted other manufacturing and warehouse initiatives. The company offers extensive environment training through a manual. Comprehensive audits (teams of internal and external personnel) examine packaging lines every two years, along with waste management, energy usage, and other systems every year. At PBG, monthly environmental reports are filed with the Canadian executive team, and performance results are reported internally, against internal standards and targets. At PCNA, one full-time employee, a vice-president (Environment and Government) handles environmental affairs and is supported by part-time environmental coordinators at each plant. In 2001, the spokesperson stated, "Pepsi is committed to minimizing the impact of our business on the environment with methods that are socially responsible, scientifically-based and economically sound. We encourage conservation, recycling and energy use programs that promote clean air and water and reduce landfill waste." Reduction programs from the mid-1990s set targets at zero waste and effluent emissions for 2000. In the early 1990s, the company replaced CFC refrigerants used in its vending and cooling equipment, and began using certified maintenance personnel to recover and recycle all refrigerants whenever vending equipment was inspected or refurbished. According to the National Pollutant Release Inventory, PBG released no major chemicals or waste from its Calgary, Delta B.C., Winnipeg, Mississauga, or Moncton sites between 1996 and 1999. The St-Laurent, Québec site reported 900 kilograms of land releases in 1997 but nothing since. Statistics for workplace recycling programs were provided for paper, cardboard, cans, glass, polystyrene, polypropylene, pallets, food, and other processing waste.

Animal Testing: PepsiCo has contracted out all animal testing needed to verify the safety of Pepsi ingredients. According to the spokesperson, "through inter-industry associations, PepsiCo may sponsor studies to demonstrate the safety of ingredients used in its food. In all cases, the testing is governed by federal regulations which specify the study procedures and define appropriate test subjects. All studies are conducted in accordance with good laboratory practices and regulations. The food industry continues to take all feasible steps to minimize the number of studies requiring animal subjects in safety testing and to use alternative testing whenever possible."

Genetically Modified Ingredients: The spokesperson said that no GM ingredients are used in PBG's soft drink manufacturing process, but did not say how the company verifies this statement.

Community Responsibilities: In 2000 PCNA donated $15.7 million, but no current statistics on PBG's community or charitable giving are provided. Corporate and employee donations go through a Pepsi Foundation, established with a $1 million endowment by Pepsi Cola Canada and ten of its affiliated bottlers. In Canada Pepsi companies have supported the United Way, (Mississauga, Montreal, Winnipeg, and Vancouver), its member agencies, and some sporting events. Local philanthropic giving is encouraged at production and distribution facilities. In particular, the Foundation funds organizations that have a mandate to educate teens on the realities of drug and alcohol usage. For example, a 40-minute, multi-screen high school assembly program has been produced each year since 1989 and shown to over four million junior and senior high school students. The company also offers a gift-matching program, and college and university co-op programs. It competes actively with Coca Cola in product placement in schools and recreation facilities.

www.pbg.com

Playtex Limited (Canada)

Playtex Limited, a wholly owned subsidiary of Playtex Inc. (USA), had its start in Canada in 1953 as a maker of bandages and tampons at a plant in Arnprior, Ontario. Today, this factory remains the company's sole operation in Canada. In 1997, Playtex Inc. began buying lines of over-the-counter health and beauty aids, adding $250 million to its revenues and reducing its commercial reliance on tampons.

1998 Revenues: $37.7 million
Grocery Store Sales: No information
Brands: Banana Boat, Cherubs, Playtex, Woolite
Corporate Status: Wholly-owned subsidiary of U.S. based parent company.
Candor: Playtex has a 23% candor quotient.

Ethical Management and Consumer Relations: Playtex's ethics code includes a policy on the exchange of business gifts and training for employees. The company was involved in a tragic consumer safety story that brought extensive litigation: the deaths of women who suffered toxic shock syndrome (TSS) as a result of using super absorbent tampons. Beginning in the 1980s, Playtex faced hundreds of allegations for its role in making and distributing a product eventually deemed unsafe. By 1996, Playtex had faced nine court cases related to its handling of TSS, in which four of the plaintiffs prevailed, with three winning compensatory and punitive damages. The company removed its super-absorbent tampon product from all markets, and stopped making any products containing polyacrylate, the chemical substance that contributes to TSS. Warnings about toxic shock syndrome now appear multiple times on a package of tampons.

2002 Employees Canada: 170   **1991 Employees Canada:** 200

Employee Relations: Between 1991 and 2002, Playtex's employee totals fell from 200 to 171. No Arnprior plant workers are unionized. No health and safety statistics were reported.

Equity and Family: In 1998, two of ten senior managers were women, and one sat on a board of nine directors. In both the workforce and management ranks, women comprise 51% of all employees. While no formal written policies governing employment equity, hiring, or advancement have ever been reported, the 1997 spokesperson commented that "we practice all." Some training supports the company's sexual harassment policy, and Playtex was one of the first companies EthicScan surveyed to offer a same-sex couples policy. Family support programs include a maternity leave beyond the government-mandated minimum, a flexible scheduling policy, and scholarships for employees' children.

Progressive Staff: Through an EAP, substance abuse counselling is offered. A newsletter, *Playtex Spirit*, is published four times per year. A full tuition refund is offered for external courses. Directors and other key employees can participate in a stock option plan, while salaried workers are eligible for profit sharing.

Sourcing and Trade: Although Playtex sources half of its supplies from outside Canada, no international sourcing policy for ingredients exists. The parent company has operations in Canada and the U.S.

Environmental Management and Performance: The Canadian company has no environmental policy, audit program, or system for tracking and reporting environmental progress. No employee works full-time on environmental responsibilities, and no committee monitors environmental impacts. Playtex gave no information to the National Pollutant Release Inventory on its chemical releases and transfers. Workplace recycling (paper, cardboard, and wood pallets), energy conservation, and waste reduction initiatives were started in the early 1990s, but no details on progress were reported. Playtex also has policies governing animal testing, but would not publicly release them to EthicScan.

Community Responsibilities: No information on donations is reported. The 1998 company spokesperson said that Playtex donates money to food banks, health causes, and local sports teams. It also offers student work programs and pays employees for time donated at non-profit organizations.

www.playtexproductsinc.com

Private Label Brand

Canada's national or trans-regional grocery retail chains - Loblaw Companies Limited, Sobeys Incorporated, Great Atlantic & Pacific Company of Canada, and Canada Safeway - and to a lesser extent, regional chains like Metro Inc. and Overwaitea, have grocery products prepared under contract for them. Separate departments conduct the private label business for each of Canada's major grocery retail chains. Usually run by senior level vice presidents, these offices focus on marketing strategy, product development, packaging design, and supplier negotiation with large food companies contracted to make the products. Loblaw's private label business - Loblaw Brands Limited - is a $2 billion a year business run as a division in the company. The Agora Food unit at the Oshawa Group (now part of Sobeys Incorporated) handles private label product development and marketing. With over 4,000 private label product units, Sobeys dominates grocery sales in eastern Canada, while Safeway is present in Ontario and all four western provinces. Metro and Provigo are dominant players in the Québec market.

Ethical Management and Consumer Relations: Private label divisions tend to follow the internal management policies and practices of their retail divisions, including guidelines for shelf placement. Provigo's code of ethics, distributed to staff and suppliers, deals with relations between suppliers and retailers. The 1998 spokesperson said it receives a sign-off from those who read it, but gave no other details. Loblaw Brands mentioned that it exercises some discretion over the placement of products on store shelves, but gave no details on how this fits in the retail company's overall policies, or how it affects relations with suppliers.

Employee Relations: Most companies employ two or three dozen people in sales, marketing, and support staff positions. Loblaw Brands is bigger, with approximately 150 employees. Unions are basically absent from these offices, excepting one employee (United Food and Commercial Workers) union at Loblaw Brands, and another at Metro (the CSN union).

Sourcing and Trade: Private label products include a wide range of canned goods, perishable raw materials, and processed or packaged goods whose ingredients are literally sourced globally. No company reported a comprehensive system for tracing ingredients through supplier chains, or a specific method for screening out processors operating where oppressive labour practices may exist. None rely on independent verifiers or auditors of suppliers' systems. In 1998, most brands relied on the general reputations and informal assurances from the brokers they contracted. Four companies reported some limited screening of direct foreign suppliers, though no human rights or environmental details were given. Safeway said it monitored sourcing issues as a component of its quality management program, while Metro-Richelieu (now called Metro) sometimes checked brokers' operating licenses, quality, and reputations. The Loblaw Brands spokesperson indicated that some ingredient sources were subject to inspections for labour and environmental practices. Sobeys noted that before it engages any foreign producer, company representatives visit plants and ensure that performance meets Canadian standards.

Environmental Management and Performance: In 1998 Loblaw Brands said it exercised some influence over its supplier's environmental practices, but no details were provided. At Agora Retail Brands (Oshawa Group), the private label operation has its own environmental standards and goals, and it focuses on packaging design reductions, recyclability, and thin-walling packaging materials. It demands supplier action on environmental issues such as pesticide usage—they must meet regulatory compliance—as well as a commitment "to meet all applicable local production and labour laws." Provigo's suppliers must abide by the company's ten-part environmental policy, which sets standards for compliance, the consumption of resources, and recycling. Suppliers must follow guidelines for handling materials such as oil, and when controlling air emissions, liquid waste, and residual material. Sobeys chooses suppliers based on their management integrity, which includes issues such as pesticide compliance. The standards followed for packaging are set by industry, and the company ensures that these are met. Canada Safeway said its private label packages are subject to environmental reductions or improvements. Environmental demands are made of its suppliers' packaging or production, and performance is monitored.

Community Responsibilities: As a separate division, Loblaw Brands has some discretion over its charitable gifts. Unlike its parent which has retail operations only in Canada, it sells 5,000 President's Choice and no name product items in Canada, the United States, Barbados, Bermuda, the Bahamas, Cayman Islands, Colombia, China (Hong Kong), Israel, Jamaica, and Trinidad. Metro's private label department also has some autonomy for giving. Prior to its acquisition by Sobeys, each division and regional operation at Agora reported that it had a budget for donations and contributes to the Oshawa Group philanthropic target of more than 1% of pre-tax profits (thereby exceeding the standards set by the Imagine Campaign). Agora's cash support is divided among community charities and organizations (70%), health (20%), and culture and education (10%). Food is donated on a regular basis, and additional food and funding has helped thousands of workers and residents living in communities devastated by natural disasters. Consistent with Sobeys philanthropic strategy, its "Our Best" products are donated to food banks and charitable events, but no separate autonomy is given to the private label department.

Brands:
Canada Safeway: Cragmont, Lucerne, Town House
Great Atlantic and Pacific Company of Canada: Equality, Selection
Loblaw Companies Limited: Club Pack, no-frills, no-name, PC Organics, President's Choice, Pride of Arabia, Too Good To Be True
Metro Inc: Merit Selection, Super C
Oshawa Foods: Our Compliments, Smart Choice
Sobeys Incorporated: Agora, Boni Choix, Our Best

Procter & Gamble Inc.

Toronto-based Procter & Gamble Inc. of Canada is the wholly owned subsidiary of consumer products giant Procter & Gamble Company (USA), which operates in 70 countries, marketing more than 300 personal care, food, household, and laundry products to nearly five billion consumers in 140 countries. The Toronto operations were founded in 1915, and today, the corporate head office and the Iams company are in Toronto. There are manufacturing plants in Belleville and Brockville, Ontario, sales offices in Calgary, Montreal, and Halifax, and a distribution warehouse in Hamilton.

2000 Revenues: $1.9 billion
Grocery Store Sales: 100% (retail products, excluding pharmaceutical and commercial brands)
Brands: Always, Bounce, Bounty, Camay, Cascade, Charmin, Cheer, Clairol, Cover Girl, Crest, Dawn, Dryel, Downy, Febreeze, Folgers, Gain, Head & Shoulders, Iams, Inner Science, Ivory, Max Factor, Metamucil, Mr. Clean, Noxzema, Nyquil, Olay Bar, Old Spice, Oil of Olay, Pampers, Pantene, Pepto Bismol, Pert, Physique, Pringles, Puffs, Pantene Pro-V, Safeguard, Scope, Secret, Swiffer, Tampax, Tide, Vidal Sassoon, Vicks, Zest
Corporate Status: Wholly-owned subsidiary of U.S.-based parent company.
Candor: The company spokesperson was very helpful throughout the entire research process in 2001. Its candor quotient is 57%.

Ethical Management and Consumer Relations: The parent company's ethics code is not modified for the Canadian company, though it was updated in 2001. Employees must sign-off at the time of hire and take reinforcement training. A business gift exchange policy states that gratuities are "generally not acceptable." In the late 1990s, P&G's cough syrup, Formula 44D, was accidentally distributed with an incorrect label. The company responded by publicizing a toll-free number and a procedure for returning bottles. P&G Canada operates a regular 1-800 number staffed by eight Toronto workers who answer 600 to 700 calls a day from customers with questions or concerns about products. This call center also gathers data on how consumers use products.

2002 Employees Canada: 2,000   **1999 Employees Canada:** 3,100

Employee Relations: Worldwide, P&G employs 102,000 people. Canadian staff levels fell following the sale of the Weston, Ontario manufacturing plant in the 1990s. Employment dropped 20% in 2000 in Canada. Redeployment and retraining are typically provided, along with severance packages that exceed the government minimum. No Canadian employees are unionized, and no strikes or lockouts have shut operations over the last decade. The corporate spokesperson declined to furnish any health and safety statistics.

Equity and Family: At P&G, 43% of managers are women, as are 28% of senior managers. Managers' performance evaluations include ratings on effective managing of diverse employee groups. Campus recruitment drives highlight the advancement of women in non-traditional fields. An anti-harassment policy, which employees must sign at the time of hire, covers workplace interactions between men and women, and attitudes toward sexual orientation, race, and disability. Employees receive training on anti-harassment and ethics policies, and on accommodating the disabled. Fifteen weeks of maternity leave benefits are topped up to 95% of an employees base salary.

Progressive Staff: Honour Roll. P&G was a pioneer in offering comprehensive benefits to employees. On-site fitness facilities are available at the head office, and the company subsidizes fitness club memberships for employees. Counselling referrals are made for employees dealing with substance abuse. Should an employee be transferred, job-search services assist uprooted spouses. Depending on the nature of educational courses taken, employees are reimbursed on a scale that covers job-related training up to 100%. All internal communications are conducted over the company Intranet, which features an employee suggestion program, the "My Idea" page. Every other week, ten employees are selected for a "Breakfast with the President." A scholarship is available for children of employees. Profit sharing is treated as a retirement benefit, and the company offers stock options for deserving employee ideas. P&G was rated 11th Best Company to Work For in 2001, according to a survey conducted by Hewitt & Associates and published in *Report on Business Magazine.* The ranking is based on career opportunities, benefits, pay, training, company perks, and employee satisfaction.

Sourcing and Trade: Only a fraction of the company's products are made in Canada. With plants in 40 countries, the parent company applies its sourcing code to all of its global facilities. If P&G suppliers and contractors violate the code's principles, the company says it will end the business relationship. The spokesperson said this section is "not applicable" to Canadian operations, but no details were supplied.

Environmental Management: P&G Canada follows its parent's environmental quality policy, which commits operations to: set waste reduction priorities; comply with law and regulation; disclose the environmental impacts of P&G products and packaging; and train employees on environmental dimensions of their daily activities. In Canada, an Associate Director of Environment works with two full-time environmental employees. The U.S. parent has a V.P. and an environmental committee of the board. In 1999, the parent company

Genetically Modified Ingredients: P&G's spokesperson commented, "when carefully regulated and responsibly used, GM ingredients are safe and can be an important part of the world food supply." Labelling is necessary only when the presence of GMOs makes a "significant change" in the nutritional content or safety of the food. The company supports voluntary labelling as long as it meets "clear, stringent, and enforceable criteria." P&G labels its foods according to local laws and regulations. In countries, where consumers express a strong aversion to GMO foods, even when legislation permits their use, P&G will strive to provide them with GMO-free products, "as far as is technically feasible," the spokesperson said.

issued its first sustainability report. The *2000 Sustainability Report* outlines corporate changes made after a review of Global Reporting Initiative (GRI) guidelines (a set of global social responsibility standards), as well as feedback from report users, and other stakeholders.

Environmental Performance: The Brockville plant reported 100 kilograms of air releases to the NPRI in 1999, placing it in a low 0-10 percentile of major chemical or waste emitters in Canada. No information was available on the top ranked NPRI pollutant in terms of potential human health risks. The parent company reports quantities of materials recycled in the workplace in its sustainability report. P&G's Belleville site partnered with two other companies in a scrap recycling effort, saving $944,492 and increasing revenues by $114,468. Quantities recycled were not listed. The company's "environment friendly" product claims do not list an independent third party verifier who substantiates the claim. Globally, P&G has had 48 violations, and paid $US 13,400 in total fines for the last five years.

Animal Testing: P&G reported a reduction in the numbers of animal tests conducted, and the number of animals used, without providing details. Alternative tests are conducted where possible, and no testing is done in Canada. Since 1984, total animal usage for the company's worldwide research has decreased 52% in personal care product development, and 90% in household product development. Like many other consumer companies, P&G has contributed to the Johns Hopkins Centre for Advancement of Alternatives to Animal Testing as part of its total $24 million spending on the development of alternative tests. A corporate award, given to P&G by The Humane Society of the United States, recognized the company's efforts to advance alternatives to animal testing. P&G's *2000 Sustainability Report* notes that its employee, Dr. Stitzel, "is the first representative of any company to be recognized with this award."

Community Responsibilities: P&G's 2001 donations—$2,000,000 to charitable organisations and $1,300,000 in-kind donations—are greater than levels given in 1997 ($1,164,592). P&G supports health, social service, education, and cultural organizations, and favours charities operating in areas where employees live and work. A 2000 gift of $1.2 million to the United Way, from the company and employees, made P&G the largest consumer goods sponsor of the United Way in Canada. Other donations are allocated to universities, social service organizations, and hospitals, including a $1 million, 5-year gift to the Belleville General Hospital for a new maternity and child care centre ("The P&G Family Center"). Non-saleable products are donated through the Canadian Association of Food Banks to member food banks across Canada. Cosmetics and facial tissue are donated to "Look Good... Feel Better," an organization that helps women cope with "the appearance-related side effects of living with cancer." In 1996, P&G was named Goodwill Canada's Community Partner of the Year in recognition of the involvement of P&G employees in training programs for Goodwill clients. P&G states that it works with non-governmental organizations to understand their concerns.

www.pg.com/canada

Quality Meat Packers Limited

Toronto-based Quality Meat Packers was founded in 1931. It is a large meat packer and marketer with one plant in Toronto and another in Brampton, Ontario. As a privately owned company with little public profile, almost no public information on its activities exists.

> **2000 Revenues:** No information
> **Grocery Store Sales:** No information
> **Brands:** Country Manor, Town Club
> **Corporate Status:** Privately held.
> **Candor:** The 2001 spokesperson answered many questions, sometimes without explanatory details, resulting in a 73% candor quotient.

Ethical Management and Consumer Relations: No code of ethics, training, or other support programs were reported. The company has a toll-free phone line for consumers, a product recall system, a consumer safety process assurance that exceeds regulation, and advertising guidelines. No details on any of these procedures were provided. No cases or convictions for false advertising, product recall or safety, Competition Act violations, or bribes have arisen against Quality Meat Packers.

2001 Employees Canada: 620   **1996 Employees Canada:** 900

Employee Relations: Staff levels have declined substantially over the last few years, as the workforce declined 27% over one year (850 workers in 2000), and 31% since 1996 (900 employees). The spokesperson said that no layoffs had occurred over the last five years, which suggests that some operations were divested, but this possibility was not confirmed and no other explanation or details were mentioned. Twenty employees were laid off (location unspecified) in the early 1990s, and they received severance packages that surpassed the legislated minimum. The vast majority of staff (88%) belong to organized bargaining units, although no union names were mentioned. Half of Quality Meat's employees work beyond a 40 hour week, and they are guaranteed compensation for extra hours worked. On average, 80 grievances are filed annually, with eight reaching the arbitration stage, which is higher than other companies profiled. Over one year, reported injuries fell from 45 (in 1999) to 30 (in 2000), and the company reports joint health and safety committees, and ergonomic workplace assessments for workstations. No training expenditures or gainsharing programs were reported. Quality Meat Packers has twice been convicted of unjust dismissals, although no details were given.

Equity and Family: Quality Meat Packers does not rate highly for advancement of women. None sit on the two-person board or in senior management, and 21 of 72 (29%) managers are women. Family support policies are scant—as no extended maternity leave, daycare services, adoption leave, or paid days off for child or eldercare are offered—placing the company well below most companies profiled. Assistance for eldercare and services for children with special needs can be recommended through the company's EAP (along with substance abuse counselling and help with retirement planning), but the only other family support policy offered is paternity leave. An anti-harassment policy covers sexual issues, race, sexual orientation and disability, and although no training supports the policy, employees are required to sign-off on it. Health support includes a stop-smoking program, workplace wellness seminars, and drug coverage as part of health benefits. More than 75% of the costs for courses taken outside the company are refunded.

Sourcing and Trade: No details on Canadian or foreign sourcing, or international procurement codes were reported. The company did indicate that it has some kind of sourcing standard that applies to all operations, contractors, and licensees, and that it requires independent audits, surprise visits, and employee recourse, but no qualitative comments elaborated what terms were included. Given that the company is in the meat business—which has rigorous sanitary regulations covering all areas of sourcing—it is not surprising that management attends to these issues.

Environmental Management and Performance: Despite the fact that it handles meat, Quality Meat Packers reports no formal environmental code or audits. Four full-time employees manage environmental matters, supported by a staff environment, health & safety committee. The spokesperson stated that environmental support and expenditures related to waste management and energy conservation were "not applicable." No regular filings with information on the company's chemical releases and transfers are made to the National Pollutant Release Inventory, and no recycling programs for products, by-products, or workplace activities were reported. The spokesperson did report that no environmental violations or convictions had occurred, and indicated that the company has products with attributes that may be deemed and verified as "environment friendly" (no details were mentioned). Reductions and environmental improvements to packages have been implemented, and environmental demands of suppliers are monitored, but no explanations were given.

Community Responsibilities: The company spokesperson reports that Quality Meats pledges its commitment to the Imagine Campaign to donate at least 1% of pre-tax profits annually, yet the company name did not appear on the Imagine Campaign list of Caring Companies as of July 1, 2001. The company spokesperson said that Quality Meats sponsors health, athletics, and environmental organizations and initiatives, but again, no details were provided.

www.westrow.ca

Redpath Sugars

Redpath Sugars, one of Canada's remaining two major sugar refiners, supplies both consumer and industrial markets. John Redpath began refining raw sugar in Montreal in 1854 for the Upper and Lower Canadian markets. Today, the company operates as a wholly owned subsidiary of Tate & Lyle plc of the U.K., a global sugar, cereal sweetener, and starch-processing group. From its Toronto refinery, Redpath's sugar products are distributed through offices in Québec and Ontario. It is the largest Canadian exporter of sugar-content products to the United States. After a series of acquisitions and consolidations in the 1990s, the sugar sector was left as an oligopoly of Redpath Sugars and Lantic/Rogers, which together control over 90% of the sugar produced in Canada.

Annual Revenues Canada: Greater than $300 million
Grocery Store Sales: No information
Brands: Redpath
Corporate Status: Wholly-owned subsidiary of U.K.-based parent company.
Candor: Redpath provided responses to 22% of EthicScan's questions.

Ethical Management and Consumer Relations: Redpath has never reported a written code of ethics or related support policies, except for a Conflict of Interest policy since 1978. A major concern in the sugar industry is monopolistic control and attendant lack of price competition. For decades, the sector has been criticized by consumer and industry groups such as the Canadian Sugar Users Coalition (CSUC), which represents large food and confectionery companies who worry about the effects of limited competition. In 2000, the CEO of a small Canadian upstart company, Richdale Sugar, filed a complaint with Canada's Competition Bureau claiming that Redpath was practicing "conscious parallelism" and was using exclusivity and tied selling arrangements to influence grocery retailers. In its submission to the Competition Bureau, Richdale claims to have suffered a number of "abuses" including the loss of a contract that could have attracted the mainstream market to its product. The bureau never launched an investigation. Redpath makes no comment on such issues.

2002 Employees Canada: No information   **1998 Employees Canada:** 415

Employee Relations: In 1998, 347 of Redpath's 415 Canadian employees worked at its Toronto refinery. No employment total updates were reported in 2002. Fifty-five percent of these refinery employees belong to the Chemical Energy & Allied Workers, the Teamsters, or the International Operating Engineers unions. No strikes or lockouts have occurred during the last ten years. No workplace injuries statistics are reported. A Joint Health and Safety Committee holds safety meetings every month, and the refinery passed audits conducted by the Workers' Compensation Board in the mid-1990s. Skills development and education are encouraged through 100% tuition refunds for employees who complete approved work-related courses. All employees are eligible to participate in an optional Stock Purchase Plan through which the company will match employee contributions up to a maximum 6% of an employee's annual salary.

Equity and Family: At the Toronto office, women constitute no senior managers, but 27% of managers (about average for the companies profiled in this book). Women represent 38% of office staff and 14% of hourly workforce employees. No formal hiring or promotion targets or programs exist, and the spokesperson said that all personnel are hired based on qualifications only. An anti-harassment policy deals only with sexual issues, and it is not supported with training. On an individual basis, flexible scheduling can be arranged with managers. The only health support mentioned was an on-site fitness facility at the head office. Employee communications are conducted through a newsletter (four times each year), and feedback sessions with the company President (twice each year).

Sourcing and Trade: Redpath purchases raw sugar from the Caribbean, Australia, South and Central America, and Africa. It reports no guidelines for Canadian or international sourcing. The company stopped sourcing in Cuba in the mid-1990s, in part because industrial customers in the U.S. demanded non-Cuban sugar, as U.S.-Cuban tensions were intensified by the passage of the Helms-Burton trade agreement (which entrenches trade blocks between the two countries). Compliance with such U.S. extraterritorial laws in Canada is contrary to Canadian law.

Consolidation and Competition: In Canada, government support has kept sugar one of the last remaining tariff-protected industries. In response, CSUC companies (like Weston, Cadbury, Culinar, Effem, and Ault) complain about high prices that result from limited sugar competition. When these companies import sugar from the U.S. and Europe, trade protections guarantee a minimum price for Canadian producers, leading to higher prices for confectionery makers, who argue that these costs are passed on to the consumer. In November 2000, the Canadian International Trade Tribunal (CITT) reaffirmed the five-year imposition of a 44% duty on sugar from the U.S. and 64% on sugar from Europe. The duties were imposed and extended for five years, after the Canadian Sugar Institute (a lobby association representing Redpath and Lantic/Rogers) complained in 1995 that American and European companies were dumping government-subsidized sugar into Canada. The Tribunal ruled that no evidence was produced to prove that duties increased consumer prices. Since 1995, Canada's anti-dumping orders continue to limit the import of refined sugar, effectively removing American refiners and leaving the entire Canadian market with no meaningful competition. In 1995, when Canada imposed duties on sugar imports, Redpath signed three-year contracts with major food producers at deep discounts, exercising the kind of power that has increased resistance from the CSUC.

Environmental Management and Performance: Redpath Sugar's environmental code applies to all subsidiaries. Audits require a team of internal and external personnel. A staff environment committee works with a manager who has half-time environmental responsibilities. Environmental operating and capital expenditures, including the monitoring and testing of equipment, totaled about $40,000 in 1997. Redpath Sugars reports chemical releases and transfers to the National Pollutant Release Inventory. In 1999, the Toronto facility recorded its highest levels of toxic air releases (17,475 kilograms of primarily hydrochloric acid), ranking it in the 40-50 percentile in terms of total chemical releases or waste generation in Canada. Resource conservation programs work to reduce water and power consumption, and a waste audit reduction program addresses packaging issues. The spokesperson reported quantities of materials recycled for paper, wood pallets, and calcium carbonate, a substance used in sugar.

Community Responsibilities: No information for recent charitable donations is reported, and the company is not committed to the Imagine Campaign. In 1997, Redpath pledged $66,000 in cash, and in 1994 and 1995, the company divided $75,000 among 20 or 30 groups, including the United Way, the Heart Fund, and local food banks.

www.onex.com

Robin Hood Multifoods Inc.

The company now known as Robin Hood first came to Canada in 1909 when the Minnesota-based American parent (then known as the International Milling Company) bought a small flour mill in Moose Jaw, Saskatchewan. After expanding through strategic acquisitions during the 1980s and 1990s, all of Robin Hood Multifoods interests were bought by International Multifoods. The company became one of two units in the North America Foods segment of International Multifoods Inc. Serving both consumer and industrial markets, Robin Hood makes and sells mixes, oats, grain, and flour products through retail stores, along with whole-sale lines for industrial food producers and users. Robin Hood's condiments, flour, and bakery products are made at seven plants: four in Ontario, two in Québec, and one in Saskatchewan. In 2001, the company announced plans to acquire the Pillsbury desserts and special products businesses, along with the U.S. Robin Hood brand. A deal is expected to close in fiscal 2002.

> **Revenue:** No information
> **Grocery Store Sales:** No information
> **Brands:** Bick's, Gattuso, Golden Temple, Habitant pickles, Hungry Jack, Martha White, Old Mill, Pillsbury, Red River, Robin Hood
> **Corporate Status:** Wholly-owned subsidiary of U.S.-based parent company.
> **Candor:** The company has a 26% candor quotient.

Ethical Management and Consumer Relations: The parent company wrote and distributes Robin Hood's code of ethics, which all employees are expected to sign. While the code has no provision for the negotiation of retail shelf space, it does cover conflicts of interest and business gifts. In 1993, packages of Robin Hood Low Fat Oatmeal Muffin Mix were recalled, and a toll-free number publicized, when the company realized that small amounts of unidentified nut powder were found in the product. At issue were consumers with nut allergies. In another case in the 1990s, an Ontario court deemed the ads for Robin Hood's frozen piecrusts "false and misleading," because they made claims directly against rival brands, Tenderflake and Gainsborough. The judge ruled that the ads hurt the reputation of the two Maple Leaf Foods products by diminishing consumer good will for the company. A company spokesperson said that the ads intended to communicate legitimate product differences, but the company eventually revised its campaign.

2002 Employees Canada: No information   **1996 Employees Canada:** 1,437

Employee Relations: Close to half of Robin Hood's Canadian employees (47%) belong to one of five unions. This number dropped following the sale of the frozen bakery products division in 1998. In the last five years, one round of layoffs has occurred in Scarborough, where redeployment opportunities along with severance packages beyond the government minimum were offered. The last reported strike put Port Colborne workers on the picket line for five months in 1991, after 16 jobs were cut due to technology changes. While a union report claimed 130 workers were involved, a company spokesperson said only 100 took part.

Equity and Family: Nothing was reported on the advancement of women in Canada for Robin Hood. Within the Robin Hood Multifoods Inc. unit of the North America Foods segment, one of ten officers is a woman. An employment equity policy has existed since 1991, and anti-harassment protection covers sexual issues, sexual orientation, race, and disability. However, neither policy receives training or an annual sign-off. According to the equity ratings for federal contractors compiled by Human Resources Development Canada (HRDC) in 1999, Robin Hood Multifoods ranked "good" for women, aboriginal peoples and members of visible minorities, and "very poor" for persons with disabilities. In 1996, the company earned (according to a different set of HRDC measures) grades of CA for its employment of women, CA for Aboriginal people, BC for those with disabilities, and AB for visible minorities with AA being the highest grade.

Progressive Staff: According to the corporate spokesperson, 20% of employees work according to flexible schedules. The company has an employee assistance plan, but provided no details. It also sponsors separate scholarships for employees and their children. Along with an employee share ownership plan, Robin Hood Canada offers all salaried staff a stock incentive plan, and a voluntary employee savings plan.

Sourcing and Trade: No international operations, standards, or policies guiding international sourcing, labour, or trade practices were reported.

Environmental Management and Performance: Robin Hood has an environmental management code, but the spokesperson offered no details to describe it. Comprehensive audits occur at some operations, but their frequency and personnel were not reported. A Vice-President of engineering has part-time environmental responsibilities, and oversees environmental committees at each plant. The company has reduced the volume of material it uses in its packaging, though no information has been provided since the early 1990s. Robin Hood does not report information on chemical releases to the National Pollutant Release Inventory.

Genetically Modified Ingredients: The company provided no information about management of GMOs in the company's flour, mixes, or condiments products.

Community Responsibilities: No current information on community giving is reported. Historically, the company has loaned corporate facilities to community groups, paid for the volunteer time of its staff, and matched gifts to educational institutions. Funding recipients have included the United Way, local sports, health, and cultural groups.

www.robinhood.ca

Rothmans Inc.

Toronto-based Rothmans Inc. is Canada's only publicly traded company involved exclusively in the manufacture and distribution of tobacco products. Rothmans Inc. is a widely held holding company that owns 60% of Rothmans, Benson & Hedges Inc. (RBH), its tobacco products manufacturer and distributor. (Philip Morris owns the other 40%.) Rothmans Inc. was established in Montreal in 1954, but the parent company's history stretches back to London, England, where Louis Rothman began making tobacco products in 1890, more than a decade after Richard Benson and William Hedges began in 1873 (Benson & Hedges came to Canada in 1906). Today, RBH operates cigarette-manufacturing plants in Brampton, Ontario and Québec City along with sales offices in every province except Prince Edward Island and New Brunswick. RBH currently holds about 22% of the domestic cigarette market. In 2000, Rothmans International divested its holdings of Rothmans Inc., leaving it as the holding company for the operations of RBH. This review deals with both Rothmans Inc. and RBH.

2000 Revenue: $533.2 million

Grocery Store Sales: No information

Brands: Accord, Belmont, Belvedere, Benson & Hedges, Canadian Classics, Craven A, Dunhill, Mark Ten, Rothmans, Superoll fine cut, Viscount

Corporate Status: Majority held, publicly traded Canadian company.

Candor: Less than a quarter of questions were answered. The candor quotient is 24%, the lowest of the three tobacco companies reviewed in this guide.

Ethical Management and Consumer Relations: No information is reported on ethics codes, reinforcement, or training. This lack of information is notable, given the many ethical issues that surround the production, sale, marketing, and consumption of tobacco products. At least four cases related to inappropriate marketing, misrepresentation, and health costs were reported in the media between 2000 and 2001. In January 2000, a claim that cigarette companies have failed to sell fire-safe cigarettes was launched against RBH and other tobacco companies. Allegedly, a defective product caused a fire that resulted in injury and possible death of a plaintiff, and a motion to certify the claim as class action was tabled. If granted, the class action could affect an undetermined number of people. A March 2000 lawsuit was launched against multiple tobacco companies, in an attempt to recover approximately $40 billion for alleged misrepresentations regarding the dangers of tobacco products. In May 2000, the company was fined for numerous by-law infractions at its Don Mills office, including employees smoking at their workstations. In 2001, the company participated in the tobacco industry's constitutional challenge of the federal Tobacco Act, including a direct attack on the province of British Columbia's attempt to recover health care costs related to tobacco products. Rothmans and the other tobacco makers claim that federal legislation places "unwarranted, unnecessary and unconstitutional restrictions on the manufacture and sale of its products." In February 1995, a class action suit was launched against Rothmans and its two competitors over the adverse health effects of tobacco. The suit—which seeks punitive and exemplary damages worth more than $3 million—is Canada's first attempt at a tobacco class action suit. It alleges that tobacco companies knowingly addicted millions of Canadians to nicotine. Rothmans states that it is defending itself against these charges and assumes no liability. Another suit, launched in May 1997 by an Ontario individual, seeks damages of $1 million over the claim that Rothmans hid evidence that cigarettes cause cancer and are addictive. The company denies the allegations and is defending itself through the courts.

> **Tobacco Marketing Practices:** Rothmans has faced numerous challenges from anti-smoking groups over marketing and health issues. The advocacy group, Physicians for a Smoke-Free Canada, prompted a 1995 Health Canada investigation into the charge that a 16-year-old individual (minimum age for the purchase of cigarettes is 19) received a free carton of cigarettes through a Rothmans, Benson & Hedges mail order program conducted in conjunction with a consumer questionnaire. Promotions to underage consumers constitute a breach of the Tobacco Products Control Act. The 1998 corporate spokesperson said that at no time did any 16-year-old receive any product, explaining that the case arose because a teenager lied about his age on a form. Before he received the product, his mother intervened and confiscated the package. The company said that it did not breach the Tobacco Products Control Act and contested the allegations in court where, according to the corporate spokesperson, the presiding judge commented that the firm carried out all due diligence under the law, and was not marketing to youth. The 1998 spokesperson reported that RBH sponsors programs such as Operation ID and School Zone that encourage retailers to ask customers for proof of age, in an effort to deny access of tobacco to underage consumers.

2002 Employees (RBH): 750

Employee Relations: For 15 years, Rothmans has been steadily reducing staff (from 2,400 in 1986 to 750 today) in an effort to cut costs. At RBH, 414 employees are salaried and 337 are hourly. The most recent layoffs came in June 2001, when RBH eliminated 65 positions from its Québec City plant: voluntary retirements accounted for 58 of the 65 lost positions. Throughout the late 1980s and early 1990s, some laid off workers were relocated while others were given early retirement or job-search assistance. Generally, management-labour relations are good, a 1998 union spokesperson said, adding that the company had not attempted to outsource any of its inputs or contracts. The union spokesperson said that no strikes have occurred in Canada over the last decade. Health and safety issues are dealt with through a joint committee, and workplace safety audits are part of compliance efforts.

Equity and Family: In 2001, one of nine directors was a woman, along with two of 14 executives and officers. Placement at other levels was not reported. No policies or programs for equity or advancement of women and minorities are mentioned.

Progressive Staff: Employee performance is evaluated through a "360 Degree Feedback Program." To communicate information about benefits, pension plans, and other employee matters, management relies on a company-wide intranet. Rothmans' "Vision Plus Program" is designed to reward business ideas that increase productivity and efficiency. According to the union, the company offers no regular share ownership, stock, or profit sharing programs for employees.

Sourcing and Trade: No information was provided on domestic sourcing of tobacco, filters, tallow, or flavour enhancements. Rothmans declined to report on international operations, sales or management policies.

Environmental Management and Performance: An environmental code is supported by annual environmental audits, though details were not given. No information on environmental staff is provided, and no environmental committee of the board exists. To modernize its facilities, minimize environmental impacts, and replace equipment, the company spent $7 million in 1996. Environmental challenges at the operational level include package waste and energy consumption (especially in tobacco curing), along with storage and transportation issues. No specific data indicates how the company deals with these issues. Rothmans did not provide the National Pollutant Release Inventory with information on its chemical releases and transfers.

Genetically Modified Ingredients: No information is provided on corporate specifications on tobacco, filter, paper, or chemical suppliers.

Community Responsibilities: No details on charitable giving or community responsibilities are reported. Rothmans is well known for sponsorship of an annual fireworks event that bears its name. Historically, the company has spent $5 million on the "Symphony of Fire" each year. It has also attached its name to the Canadian Grand Prix and the Rothmans International Film Festival. Federal legislation prohibits tobacco companies from continuing branded sponsorship of sporting and cultural events, because the government accepts that there is a connection between tobacco sponsorship and the promotion of smoking. In 1998, the Rothman spokesperson said the company would prefer to continue sponsoring these programs, stating that it believes sponsorships do not initiate smoking among people. However, in November 2000, the company announced it would no longer put on the Symphony of Fire, nor would it sponsor a major film festival due to the regulatory restrictions. The company reports that some of the funds previously used in cultural and entertainment sponsorship will be re-directed towards marketing initiatives aimed at increasing market share. For many years, RBH contributed to the Canadian Rehabilitation Council for the Disabled, along with Foster Parents Plan, the Canadian Mental Health Association, the Opera de Montreal, the Winnipeg Art Gallery and the Centre Stage Company in Toronto. In total the firm supports about 150 organizations annually.

www.rothmansinc.com

Saputo Inc.

Saputo Inc. manufactures a range of dairy and grocery products, snack cakes, cookies, fine breads, and soups, in Canada and the United States. The St Leonard, Québec-based company, formerly known as Saputo Group Inc., is now Canada's largest (and North America's fifth largest) dairy processor. Saputo is the country's largest cheese maker accounting for 34% of the cheese production in Canada (fourth largest in the U.S.(7% of US market), and our largest snack cake manufacturer. Giuseppe Saputo founded his company in 1954 as a specialty cheese producer for the Italian community in Montreal. The firm has grown through a steady stream of acquisitions, including Stella Foods in 1997, Culinar in 1999, Cayer-JCB Group, and Dairyworld in 2000. In July 2001, Dare Foods purchased Saputo's cookie, fine bread, and soup production interests. Saputo re-organized itself into four main divisions: cheese (Canada), cheese (U.S.), bakery, and milk (Dairyworld). Saputo has 36 plants in Canada, and 16 in the USA. Two shareholders—Gestion Jolina Inc. (40%), and Placement Italcan Inc. (10.4%)—control the company. The Saputo family, previously the company's major shareholder, still holds an interest, and Lino Saputo, the founder's son, serves as CEO.

2000 Revenue: $2.2 billion

Grocery Store Sales: No information

Brands: Ah Caramel!, Armstrong, Baxter, Caron and Cayer, Dairyland, Dragone, Frigo, Granny's, Hop & Go, Jos. Louis, Li'l Cravings, May West, Passion Flakie, Saputo, Stella, Vachon

Corporate Status: Majority held, publicly traded, Canadian company.

Candor: The company has a 24% candor quotient. Usually publicly-traded companies have higher transparency than privately-held companies.

Ethical Management and Consumer Relations: Saputo Inc. does not have a formal ethics code or any supporting programs. Little information on consumer policies or company practices is available. The company spokesperson stated that they are not a "policy kind of company" but that "just because it's not written doesn't mean these types of things are not getting done."

2002 Employees: 7,200 (1,700 in U.S.)   **2002 Employees Canada:** 5,500

Employee Relations: Following its sizeable acquisitions, Saputo's employment levels grew almost 30% in one year (from 5,250 in 2000). No information was reported on layoffs that might accompany its various related sector acquisitions. Saputo closed one Dairyworld plant in 2002 in Bashaw, Alberta, which affected 88 employees. Of 35 available transfers, 20 were accepted. In addition to honouring the collective agreement layoff package, workers who stayed until the plant closed got an extra few weeks pay. In April 2002, Saputo announced the closure of a tart-making plant in Aurora, Ontario, and the loss of 94 jobs in total in the bakery division, by the end of September 2002.

Equity and Family: Saputo has appointed two women to its eight-person board, but has none among its seven senior managers. Few of the jobs at the company's milk, cheese, cake, and food processing plants lend themselves to family-friendly flex-work schedules.

Progressive Staff: Saputo has an Employee Share Ownership Plan, through which employees can purchase up to 2.5% of their salary maximum of ($2500) in shares. The company contributes an additional 25% of the employee's contribution at the end of the fiscal year, provided that the employee has kept their shares until that time. No other policies were mentioned.

Sourcing and Trade: No information on procurement networks, standards about legal compliance, or any related trading, animal husbandry, or wage policies were reported.

Environmental Management and Performance: Cheese plants and dairies throughout North America typically generate waste such as food, solvents, wood, and waste water, but no information on Saputo's environmental or waste management was provided. No written policy exists, but the company spokesperson mentioned that recuperation of whey, the largest byproduct of the cheese-making process, was necessary for any cheese producer. According to the National Pollutant Release Inventory, Saputo reported no chemical or waste releases from its Mont Laurier, St-Hyacinthe or St-Leonard, Québec sites in 1999. A major fire hit the company's Lena, Wisconsin ricotta cheese factory in 1996, but no other information was reported.

Animals and Genetically Modified Ingredients: Cattle are bred, and fed antibiotics, to increase milk supply. Saputo provides no public information on the company's flour, pastry, soup product, or other ingredients.

Community Responsibilities: Although it is publicly traded, Saputo does not divulge donations information. No community investment guidelines or public reports are published. The spokesperson stated that Saputo would be introducing a corporate citizenship report in the next annual report, which is to outline donations to universities, charities created, and other giving.

www.saputo.com

Sara Lee Corporation of Canada Ltd.

Sara Lee came to Canada in 1963, more than two decades after its parent started in Chicago in 1939. Today the Canadian company operates ten plants as a wholly owned subsidiary of Sara Lee Corporation (USA). Although best known for its frozen cakes, the company operates in a variety of sectors (packaged meats and bakery, coffee and grocery, household, personal care, baby care, shoe care, insecticides, hosiery, and knit products). Globally, the parent's sales approach $20 billion. Food products are sold through retail and wholesale foodservice channels. Sara Lee has become one of America's largest sock makers, and tobacco products make up slightly less than 2% of total sales. About 40% of the parent company's sales, and 45% of its operating income come from international operations.

Annual Revenues: Approximately $250 million
Grocery Store Sales: No information
Brands: Cameo, Daisyfresh, Dici, Donna Karen hosiery, Endust, Hanes Her Way, Hillshire Farm, Irish Mead, Jimmy Dean, Kiwi, Lauentis, L'Eggs, Liz Claiborne, Sara Lee, Superior, Tana, Ty-d-bowl, Wonderbra
Corporate Status: 100% owned by US-based parent company
Candor: The 1998 corporate spokesperson in Chicago gave a fair amount of information. Today's candor quotient in 2002, however, is only 13%.

Ethical Management and Consumer Relations: Sara Lee Canada follows its parent's code of ethics (revised in 1997), as part of the company's "Global Values" program. Employees sign off on it at the time of hire, or whenever it is revised. A *Global Operating Principles* brochure outlines sections on respect for diversity, ethical practices, the environment, and community. In Canada, a vice president is assigned partial "Public Responsibility" duties, and the parent company's board of directors includes an "Employee and Public Responsibility" Committee. During the 1990s, marketing typically accounted for approximately 8% of revenue. In 2001, Sara Lee Corp. pleaded guilty to one count (U.S. federal misdemeanor) of producing and distributing adulterated hot dogs and deli meats that were linked to more than a dozen deaths. Along with a fine of US$200,000, the company agreed to pay a US$1.2 million civil settlement to the government for the meat it sold to the U.S. Department of Defense, and a $3 million contribution to a food safety research fund at Michigan State University. A lawyer for the company said the company recalled all affected meat in an effort to be a good corporate citizen, and the prosecuting attorney said there was no evidence the company knew the meat was contaminated.

2002 Employees Canada: No information   **1998 Employees Canada:** 1,800

Employee Relations: In 1997, Sara Lee Canada employed 1,800 manufacturing, marketing, and distribution staff, including 1,300 workers at subsidiary, Canadelle Inc. At the time, about 70% of the company's Montreal, Toronto, and Brampton staff belonged to the Retail, Wholesale, Bakery, and Confectionery Workers. Between 1995 and 1996, the parent company reduced its workforce from 149,100 to 135,300 employees as 42 manufacturing and distribution facilities were closed worldwide. Between 1990 and 1993, several "inefficient plants" in Canada were shut down, affecting between 250 and 300 jobs.

Equity and Family: No data are supplied on employment of disadvantaged groups or work/home balance initiatives at any of the company's ten plants. Women account for two of the parent company's 18 directors, six of 40 senior managers, 43% of managers, and 58% of the entire workforce. No extended maternity leave is offered, but daycare assistance is. "Diversity 2000," a series of a two-and-a-half day diversity conferences for 300 executives, was instituted in the 1990s.

Progressive Staff: Employee development initiatives include training and mentoring programs. Since 1989, the parent company has contributed funds worth 15% of stock market valuation toward employee share purchases, and executives are eligible for a stock option plan. In Canada, the company provides a scholarship program for the children of employees. No other progressive staff policies were mentioned.

Sourcing and Trade: In the mid-1990s, aside from its plants, Sara Lee owned stores in Mexico, South Africa, the Philippines, and Indonesia. Today, manufacturing units operate in the Caribbean and the maquiladora zone of Mexico. Little information on foreign sourcing, standards, or supply chain management are reported. The parent company entered China in 1996, following the completion of a joint venture with a hosiery marketer (Vocal). No formal code incorporating policies dealing with workers rights, fair wages, or responsible supervision has been written. The 1997 spokesperson noted that the company would not knowingly employ people under the age of 16 years. A *Global Operating Principles* brochure states: "Sara Lee will not knowingly use suppliers of either raw materials or finished products that have been produced by prison, or forced labour." The company did not update this information in 2002.

Environmental Management and Performance: In Canada Sara Lee relies on its parent company's environmental code and monitoring program to check compliance with environmental laws. In 1996, Sara Lee Corporation distributed an eight-page report, *Our Environmental Commitment* including Supplier Selection Guidelines that state: "Sara Lee expects suppliers to promptly develop and implement plans and programs to correct any non-compliant practices." A 1996 environmental report mentioned an education program for American manufacturing operation managers (though the company employed no full-time environmental officer at the time). Environmental expenditures of $4,000 each year in the early 1990s were directed at product and packaging reformulation. Sara Lee did not provide the National Pollutant Release Inventory with information on its Canadian chemical releases and transfers. In the U.S., an initiative from local workforces created a recycling program for paper, manufactured by-products, and packaging materials. Other changes include the recycling of garment ink containers, and the elimination of a polystyrene "egg" package for hosiery. To reduce its use of natural resources, the Canadian company continually examines its methods of operation and product packaging. In 1996, Sara Lee Corporation was assessed a fine of US$2.46 million for violations of the American Environmental Protection Act . The company contested this judgment.

Community Responsibilities: No information is reported on community giving in Canada. The parent has pledged to donate 2% of its domestic pre-tax earnings. Traditionally, the parent company sponsors programs for the economically disadvantaged, child and spousal abuse, illiteracy, and the homeless. Through the Sara Lee Foundation, about 30% of the parent company's total giving goes to the arts, 30% to the disadvantaged, and other significant contributions to women's organizations. Along with cash, donations take the form of in-kind support of products and goods, employee voluntarism, and executive service on boards of community service organizations. A Community Service Leadership Award is given to senior employees who donate their time to charitable organizations. A $25,000 award goes to the organization where an executive contributes service. The Foundation's Matching Grants Program sponsors cultural, health, environmental, and conservation groups.

www.saralee.com

Schneider Foods

Schneider Corporation of Kitchener, Ontario is one of Canada's largest producers of premium quality food products. Founded in 1890 by John Metz Schneider, who began making pork sausage in his home, the company sells branded and private label products in retail and foodservice markets throughout Canada, the U.S., Japan, and other countries. Among its more than 1,000 products, Schneider specializes in ham, sausage, wieners, bacon, luncheon meats, specialty meats, and bakery goods. The company operates in Kitchener, Ayr, St. Marys, Guelph, Hanover, Toronto, and Port Perry, Ontario; Winnipeg, Manitoba; Surrey, British Columbia; and St. Anselme, Québec. A number of joint ventures extend its interests to Québec, Duluth, Minnesota, Saskatoon, and Toronto. For over 100 years, the company was controlled by the Schneider family, who held 72% of company' stock and were active in management. In 1998, Smithfield Canada Inc. bought 60% of the corporate shares. In January 2001, Maple Leaf Foods bought two of Schneider's Winnipeg hog plants, and Schneider in turn bought Maple Leaf Foods' interest in National Meats Inc. Schneider Foods divested its fresh pork operations in Winnipeg, Manitoba, in an effort to change the company's business mix in favour of more value-added prepared and convenience food items.

Annual Sales: Greater than $1.25 billion

Grocery Store Sales: 82%

Brands: 1890 Heritage, Cappola, Fat Free, Fleetwood, Grill'ems, Hot Stuffs, Hot Reds, Hot Stuffs, Juicy Jumbos, Lifestyle, Lunchmate, Mainstreet Deli, Mini-Sizzlers, Oktoberfest, Olde Fashioned, Pepperettes, Red Hots, Schneiders, Steakettes

Corporate Status: Wholly-owned subsidiary of Smithfield, its U.S.-based parent company.

Candor: The corporate spokesperson provided detailed written and phone responses. Candor quotient is 74 %.

Ethical Management and Consumer Relations: Honour Roll. Schneider Corporation has a four-page *Code of Ethics and Standards of Conduct*, introduced in 1974. The code addresses the exchange of business gifts, privacy of employee records, and human rights. Managers and salaried employees review and sign it during annual performance evaluations. Once a year, the CEO informs the committee of any events that might relate to the code, and responsibility for its administration rests with the Board's audit committee. The code is translated into the languages local to countries of operation. Schneider's Recall Manual describes the procedures to be followed in the event of a product recall. The Canadian Food Inspection Agency audits its recall procedures yearly as part of a certification process. Twice a year, a mock recall exercise is conducted at each location to ensure products can be identified, located and returned. Since 1970, the company has experienced three product or safety recalls, but none has resulted in a conviction.

2002 Employees Canada: 3,524   **1991 Employees Canada:** 3,369

Employee Relations: Employment declined in 2001 due to the sale of the company's pork assets. In Ontario, the Schneider Employees' Association represents 1,790 employees, and the company deals with the CAW, the Teamsters, IBEW, CWA/TNG, a Quebec union, and CSN/FC. The UFCW represents 10% to 12% of the Winnipeg workers. Prior to the ownership change in 1998, dramatic layoffs resulted from a company refocus and improved efficiency effort. Management pointed to problems with high labour costs, inflexible union contract language, and outdated, inefficient processes. When the company closed part of a meat packing plant in Kitchener in 1997, an action center gave training and counselling services to the 150 downsized workers. One hundred others took early retirement. At its pork processing plant the same year, 400 workers were affected when 300 jobs were cut and 100 were reassigned to a different facility. These changes came when Schneider stopped killing pigs and started buying slaughtered animals on the open market. On average, 200 grievances are filed (approximately five reach arbitration) annually. As well, a relatively high number of unjust dismissal cases are initiated each year (3-5 on average), but since 1996 no decisions have gone against the company. Three convictions occurred between 1991 and 1996. Lost time injuries declined from 238 in 1999 to 220 in 2000. In 1992, Schneider was fined $60,000 after a Kitchener employee's arm was caught in a conveyor belt and broken in several places. The judgment found the company negligent for failing to install a guard over the sprocket area, and neglecting to ensure that a conveyor had received an appropriate cleaning.

Equity and Family: In 2001, there were 84 women among the company's 318 managers (25%), two in 23 senior manager ranks (9%), and two among six corporate officers. There are two female VPs and no women on the five-member board. Compared with 1998, these results represent a slight improvement in management (16%) and senior management (7%), but a drop at the board level (17%). Two human rights cases filed against the company ended in the company's favour, without findings of culpability or liability. A new "managing diversity" program deals with equity issues. An anti-harassment policy is supported with training but no annual review or sign-off. Diversity protections (sexual orientation, race and disability) are covered in the *Standards of Conduct* policy and in the *Corporate Values Statement.* Three "Family Responsibility Days" are available to employees each year for child or eldercare emergencies, but the time must be made up.

Progressive Staff: Honour Roll. The company offers employee assistance counselling services (such as on-site Alcoholics Anonymous and stop-smoking sessions), a "Health, Wealth and Wise" program, sports teams, and fitness facilities at some, but not all, locations. Approximately 5% of Schneider employees work on some type of flexible schedule. Tuition refunds between 50 and 100% are made to all employees, and two annual scholarships are awarded to children of employees. Approximately $575,000 was spent on external training for employees in 2000, and the company will compensate employees up to 100%, based on relevance of the training to the job. Individual locations have the discretion to institute incentive pay plans.

Using The Best Ideas: Since 1964, Schneider management has solicited worker feedback through a suggestion program that rewards the best ideas. A snapshot of the program's results between 1984 and 1996, reveals a remarkable success: it attracted more than 81,500 suggestions, giving the company an estimated cumulative savings worth $40.1 million. Program awards totalled $4.2 million. An external verifier conducts a separate formal feedback process.

Sourcing and Trade: Honour Roll. The company does not pledge to International Labour Standards; rather it has established its own. Worker protection policies are included in *Standards of Conduct* employment criteria, and these standards are applied to contractors and licensees as per government regulation. Parent company Smithfied is active in seven countries (USA, Canada, France, Poland, Brazil, Mexico, and the Czech Republic). Raw ingredients for meat and poultry use in Canada come from the U.S., New Zealand, and Australia. Schneider Foods buys materials only through federally regulated plants, and foreign purchases are controlled through government agencies. Schneider has no other policies that guard against sourcing from companies that use slave or child labour, and no explanation was given on how different governments guarantee against exploitative labour.

Environmental Management and Performance: Environmental Performance Honour Roll. Schneider's environmental policy includes employee training, but requires no sign-off. Independent consultants audit all of Schneider's operating facilities. A Manager of Environmental Affairs reports performance results to the board three times each year, and the company has both a separate public environment, health, and safety report, along with an environment section in its annual report. Two full-time employees are responsible for environmental management, and duties include: integrating reduce-reuse-recycle principles into daily business practice; participating in government and industry initiatives; and regular reporting to the board. In 2001, the company was planning a project to reduce energy consumption, and that year conducted a CIPEC energy efficiency audit of the key production facilities. In 2002 there are five key projects with projected energy consumption reduction goals of 10%. Past efficiency enhancement projects have addressed water consumption, sewage abatement, solid waste reduction, and air emissions. Recovery and recycling efforts led Schneider to establish a waste management department, which has improved water conservation and reduced internal paper usage by 40%. A continuous improvement program has diverted 50% of the office and processing waste at the Kitchener plant, and a process improvement initiative sent an extra 550 metric tons of packaging to recycling depots. In 2000, the Ayr poultry plant was fined $34,000 for exceeding wastewater limits. Schneider does not report chemical releases or waste generation to the NPRI, but the company is a signator to the Canadian Industry Program for Energy Conservation (CIPEC). Environmental awards from the Kitchener-Waterloo Chamber of Commerce, and the Ontario Ministry of Environment and Energy, have acknowledged reductions of biochemical oxygen, suspended solids, fat, oil, and grease wastes. Neither the company nor its competitors publicly and voluntarily releases the results of inspection of its operations.

Community Responsibilities: Honour Roll. Schneider Corporation is pledged to the Imagine Campaign and for the last five years has given beyond the program's minimum 1% pre-tax earnings benchmark. Company policy dictates that a minimum of 1% and a maximum of 2% will go to charity (in 2001 donations totalled $264,000, up from $150,000 in 1999). Each year, the donations committee—made up of the CEO, the chief financial officer, and a VP—presents an itemized list of recipients and amounts to the board. Gifts focus on civic groups, health, arts, and education, and in 1999 over 50 organizations received support. The company supports United Way campaigns in five cities.

www.schneiders.com

S.C. Johnson and Son Ltd

S.C. Johnson & Son, a consumer products division of its American parent, S.C. Johnson, has operated its one Canadian manufacturing operation in Brantford, Ontario since 1920. After its last major expansion in the 1990s, the Brantford factory increased its exports to 92% of all production, supplying demand in the U.S. and other international markets. Output rose from three million to 16 million cases per year over a decade. The parent company operates factories in 46 countries and distribution centers at 110 locations around the world, with over 50% of sales coming from outside the United States. Originally founded as a producer of parquet flooring, the Racine, Wisconsin-based parent company quickly developed products to maintain wood floors. It remains privately owned and run by a Chairman who descends from founder, Samuel C. Johnson. In 1997, the company bought the product lines of DowBrand and integrated them into its portfolio of consumer and household products.

Annual Revenue: $4.2 billion U.S. for the global parent
Grocery Store Sales: 60%
Brands: Armstrong, Drano, Edge, Future, Glade, Mr. Muscle, Pledge, Raid, Shout, Toilet Duck, Twinkle, Vanish, Windex
Corporate Status: Wholly-owned subsidiary of privately-held U.S.-based parent company.
Candor: This privately-held company responded extensively to EthicScan's questions, answering just under half of the questions. Candor is 48 %.

Ethical Management and Consumer Relations: A corporate ethics code, *This We Believe,* includes guidelines on relations with suppliers and consumers, advertising, and dealing with bribery and inappropriate exchanges. The code was last updated in 2001.

2002 Employees Canada: 450   **1992 Employees Canada:** 245

Consumer Safety and Labels: S.C. Johnson faces consumer controversy over its responsibility for listing ingredients on insecticide products. In the early 1990s, the company was following the law when it listed only "active ingredients" which kill insects. These chemicals typically account for only 1% or 2% of the product. Any "non-active" ingredient classified "proprietary" need not appear on product labels. But scientific reports indicate that some supposedly "inert" chemicals are still officially listed as toxic by the Canadian Environmental Protection Act. Canadian government regulators assume that consumers are sufficiently protected, because labels instruct users to avoid fumes and wash hands following product usage. However, consumer choice and public health advocates argue that the effects of unlabelled ingredients should be more explicitly stated. The company is being urged to adopt a standard higher than mere compliance.

Employee Relations: The global parent employs 9,500 employees. Canadian employees aren't unionized. Part-time Canadian workers are hired to handle seasonal product demands, and company policies guarantee redeployment and retraining in the event of downsizing. All full-time staff at S.C. Johnson & Son are eligible for a performance-based profit sharing program.

Equity and Family: Honour Roll. An advisory committee oversees diversity issues management, and the spokesperson reported anti-harassment policies related to gender, sexual orientation, race, and disability. Training supports these policies, along with an annual review, though no explanatory details were provided. The company also provides same sex couples benefits. S.C. Johnson offers an industry-leading six weeks of paid maternity leave and 11 weeks of benefits top-up with further unpaid leave of up to one year, exceeding federal and provincial minimums. Employees can take up to five paid days off for child/elder care each year.

Progressive Staff: Honour Roll. The parent company has a reputation for providing excellent employee benefits, and is regularly listed as "one of the best companies to work for" in *Fortune Magazine's* annual survey, and the Canadian company has also made *Report on Business Magazine's* list of "50 Best Companies to Work For." S.C. Johnson Canada owns an eight-cabin resort on Lake Joseph in Ontario, where employees can vacation for a nominal fee. Fitness facilities at the head office are available to all staff, as well as a personal trainer, nurse, massage therapist, and chiropractor. A scholarship program is open to children of employees.

Sourcing and Trade: Although the parent company has operations in 69 countries worldwide, no foreign sourcing code or any other voluntary international standards were mentioned.

Environmental Management and Performance: The parent company's worldwide *Corporate Environmental Policy* was last updated in 2001, and its environmental performance is audited by external and internal teams and is certified by ISO 14001. The spokesperson said that emission targets are included in the design of products, and that a life cycle approach was incorporated into its environmental systems. In Canada, S.C. Johnson does not report to the National Pollutant Release Inventory regarding chemical releases and transfers. By 1995, air, water, and solid waste emissions were cut by 50% at manufacturing facilities worldwide, and 90% of the paper, cardboard, plastic, glass, and steel materials at factories and offices were being recycled. The Brantford plant recycles steel from aerosol cans, allowing a 75% reduction in energy needed to manufacture new cans. In 1999, S.C. Johnson Canada installed a $2 million biofilter to reduce fragrance emissions. At some S.C. Johnson factories, heat is reclaimed through devices that re-circulate air around different areas of the plant. Through memberships in municipal recycling organizations in Québec, Nova Scotia, and Ontario, S.C. Johnson contributes to local recycling programs. In Canada, the company funded tree-planting and education programs at the Apps Mill Nature Centre, and during the early 1990s, won awards for contributions to recycling, package redesign, and tree planting.

Community Responsibilities: Honour Roll. Although not pledged to the Imagine Campaign, S.C. Johnson Canada donates the equivalent of 3% of its pre-tax earnings, exceeding Imagine's 1% minimum voluntary requirement. In 2001, $590,000 went to a local community centre along with $400,000 to a regional cancer centre. A committee that draws from all levels of plant and office employees makes charitable decisions. Major gifts in 1998 included an $80,000 cash donation to the United Way (employee donations are matched by the company), and a $250,000 dialysis machine for a Brantford hospital. Additionally, S.C. Johnson Canada supports a nearby daycare centre through charitable donations.

www.scjohnsonwax.com

Scotsburn Co-operative Services Ltd

Maritimes-based Scotsburn Co-operative makes ice cream, fruit drinks, orange juice, milk, and dairy products. It also manufactures and distributes feed for livestock and fuel for home and farm use. Operations began in 1900 with a federal Department of Agriculture initiative that brought together farmers in Scotsburn, Nova Scotia who wanted to start a butter cream-ery. Subsequent growth added an egg and poultry grading station, and a credit union, before several smaller dairies were amalgamated with these operations into a single co-op. Today, Scotsburn is still owned entirely by farmer members who use common services (marketing support for milk or cream, the purchase of farm supplies) and control decision-making. All sales come from Canada. Operations include five processing plants in Nova Scotia, three fluid milk plants in Newfoundland, and one jointly-owned ice cream and novelty plant in St. John, New Brunswick. A small American operation makes sour cream ingredients and orange juice concentrate.

> **Annual Sales:** Approximately $200 million
> **Grocery Store Sales:** 50%
> **Brands:** Scotsburn
> **Corporate Status:** Member owned Canadian co-operative.
> **Candor:** An 18% candor quotient is down from an Honour Roll in EthicScan's last guide. Candor is 18%.

Ethical Management and Consumer Relations: Although Scotsburn has no formal ethics code, a one-page conduct policy clearly spells out the co-op's expectations of employ-ees. Specific policies establish terms for negotiating the placement of products on store shelves and the exchange of business gifts.

2002 Employees Canada: 595   **1991 Employees Canada:** 595

Employee Relations: Scotsburn's employee totals have remained stable since 1997, but grew when the company acquired Newfoundland's Brookfield Ice Cream (1995). Four unions represent 60% of staff (369 workers) at ten locations, most of whom work in pro-cessing, production, packaging dairy products, transporting, distributing, and selling. While some seasonal layoffs occur every year, a formal severance policy assists employees who are permanently laid off by offering retraining, relocation, and advance notice for tech-nological changes.

Equity and Family: In 1997, women comprised 22% of all managers, 5% of senior man-agers, one of nine board directors, and 15% of the general workforce. Such numbers lag behind other companies in this guide. The company's advancement of women actually declined between 1991 and 1997 (10% fewer women in the workforce and 15% fewer in sen-ior management), although management figures increased by 12% over that period. An employment equity policy was introduced in 1992, along with an anti-sexual harassment pol-icy, but no training reinforces either. Family support policies include a maternity leave exten-sion from five months to 34 weeks, and an adoption leave program.

Progressive Staff: Any employee who takes a job-related course can have his or her expenses reimbursed, and a bursary program helps children of employees pursue post-secondary education. Profit sharing exists for all employees, and contributions vary depending on yearly results. Through an EAP, confidential staff counselling is offered for substance abuse at all sites, along with seminars for retirement and financial planning. A newsletter, *Dairy Diary*, is published three times a year.

Sourcing and Trade: Operating with a buy-local policy, Scotsburn procures more than 90% of inputs from Canadian suppliers. Co-operative governance and sourcing principles are practiced. Private label manufacturing comprises 5% to 10% of the company's business, mostly in the ice cream category.

Environmental Management and Performance: A corporate environmental code guides all subsidiaries, and comprehensive internal audits take place every year. Annual branch audits ensure compliance with regulations governing emergency spills, petroleum storage, used oil, ozone-related emissions, and dangerous substances. Results are compared with historical data on solid waste, water consumption, plant effluents, CFCs, fuel consumption, packaging and paper. An Environmental Advisory Committee ensures that all operations comply with appropriate legislation. In 1997, five staff shared environmental responsibilities, including the publication of environmental manuals for all locations. Training seminars reinforce the manual's contents, and ensure a workable fit within day-to-day operations. Reports to the board are made each quarter, and an environment section is printed in the company's annual report. Scotsburn did not provide the National Pollutant Release Inventory with information on its chemical releases and transfers. By limiting truck speed to 90 kilometres per hour, the company conserves vehicle fuel, and a mechanism automatically shuts down engines that idle for longer than three minutes. Over the past few years, two trucking routes were eliminated and others combined to reduce the total number of destinations on sourcing trips. Between 1992 and 1996, minor milk and petroleum spills occurred but no fines or prosecutions were reported. Other conservation projects include reducing electricity and water usage, recycling packaging materials, and diverting wastes to animal feed wherever possible.

Genetically Modified Ingredients: No information on organic, antibiotics, or GM contents in milk, ice cream, eggs, juices, or other products is disclosed.

Community Responsibilities: The co-op does not reveal details on donation figures or community involvement. In the mid-1990s, Scotsburn donated in the $35,000 to $49,000 range (company and employee contributions), down from $100,000 in 1990. Contributions are equally divided between cash and in-kind product donations. Employees receive paid time-off to volunteer, and internal "clubs" raise funds for charities chosen by local staff. Refrigerated vehicles are loaned for community events, and gift-matching programs support universities and hospitals. Local sponsorships include hockey, softball, the Kidney Foundation, the Children's Wish Foundation, UNICEF Masquerade for Children, a Kids Help Phone line, and the theatre group, Festival Antigonish.

www.brookfield-dairies.

Scott Paper Limited

Scott Paper Ltd. was founded in 1923 in New Westminster, British Columbia. Today, the company operates three mills in Québec and one in BC, as well as one plant in Alberta. In 1995, the Scott Paper Co. (USA), the Canadian company's former parent, was taken over by Kimberly-Clark, which consequently assumed control of the Canadian entity. In 1997, Kruger Inc. purchased Scott Paper Ltd., after Kimberly-Clark divested its stake. Approximately 96% of the company's production is sold in Canadian markets.

> **Annual Revenues:** No information
> **Grocery Store Sales:** No information
> **Brands:** Babies Only, Capri, Cashmere, Cottage, Cottonelle, Duvet, Premium, Purex, Scotties, ScotTowels, Soft & Pure, Thrifty, Viva, WhiteSwan
> **Corporate Status:** Wholly-owned by privately-held Canadian company.
> **Candor:** The company's candor quotient is 47%.

Ethical Management and Consumer Relations: No information on ethical management polices were reported. Scott Paper has two toll-free consumer phone lines and a contact form is available on the company's website. Consumers could call collect, under previous management. No competition, consumer safety, or false advertising cases or convictions have been reported.

2002 Employees Canada: 1,921   **1996 Employees Canada:** 1,914

Employee Relations: All employees work in Canada, and employment has been stable over the last five years. The majority (77%) of Scott's Canadian workers are members of the CSN, the CEP, or the OTEU Union. According to the company spokesperson, no work stoppages have occurred at Scott Paper for a decade. The spokesperson described the turnover rate as minimal. Workplace injuries increased by about 25% between 1999 and 2000 (from 14 to 19), but this level is dramatically lower than incidents in the early 1990s. Between 1992 and 1994, workplace injuries fell from 108 to 55 per year, earning the company a 1996 award from the Canadian Occupational Safety and Health Association for safety innovation.

Equity and Family: Zero of seven directors and one of 16 senior managers are women. In 1998, the company spokesperson estimated that since 1991, women have consistently held 11% of general management positions and 16% of workforce jobs. Equity policy has changed little since 1992. The company has a general anti-harassment policy that covers gender, sexual orientation, race and disability. Scott was one of first companies to offer its employees a same-sex benefits package. According to the spokesperson, no human rights cases have been filed against the company. Family support programs include extended maternity leaves, and corporate employees can apply for flexible working hours.

Progressive Staff: Scott Paper spends more than 1% of its payroll budget on staff training, a level reflecting serious concern about maintaining skill levels. All employees qualify for tuition refunds that range from 50% to 100% of total course costs, depending on the grade earned. All sites offer an Employee Assistance Program, which includes counselling for substance abuse, retirement, and stress management. To assist with career advancement, Scott Paper conducts "Succession Planning" for all employees, but only salaried employees receive rewards for incentives. The company's employee newsletter, *Dialogue,* is distributed on a quarterly basis. Scholarship funds for both employees and their children help with educational costs.

Sourcing and Trade: The company has no international operations, and reports no policies on sourcing.

Environmental Management and Performance: Scott Paper follows an environmental code (written in 1991 and updated in 1997), and an Environmental Audit Committee (EAC) at the Québec and B.C. plants monitors compliance with regulations. Every other year, special teams of internal personnel and external consultants check compliance during comprehensive facility audits. The EAC also trains personnel on environmental management techniques. The spokesperson reported that monthly environmental health and safety reports by internal management are sent to the company's board. While an environment officer works at each business unit, no employee assumes full-time environmental responsibilities. The company reportedly spends $2 to 3 million each year on environmental waste and energy investments. Scott Paper's Crabtree, Québec facility reported no major chemical releases or waste generation to the NPRI. In 2001, the spokesperson reported that the company runs energy resource conservation, waste reduction, and commodity recycling programs, but provided no statistics. Recycling programs recover material used in packaging, manufacturing processes, and workplace activities. No elemental chlorine is used at the New Westminster pulp mill, so effluents contain neither dioxins nor furans.

Genetically Modified Ingredients: The company reports that none of its products use GM ingredients.

> **Recycled Fibres in Tissue Paper:** Scott Paper is one of Canada's largest sanitary paper recyclers, because it makes and uses recycled fibers in its products, and processes 130,000 tonnes of waste paper annually. To minimize tree harvests and solid waste output, and maximize economic efficiency, the company uses a recycling formula that combines three different fibre types for paper. In the 1990s, Scott Paper opposed using recycled content as the sole selection criterion for the "EcoLogo." Believing that recycled content is an incomplete measure of a product's environmental merit, the company instead proposed a broad set of criteria to evaluate sanitary tissue.

Community Responsibilities: Some discretion for donations is given to individual business units. Although no coordinated Canadian program exists, the company began reviewing its corporate donations policies in 2001. Scott Paper is not pledged to the Imagine Campaign. In the mid 1990s, donations of cash and product declined from $180,000 (1994) to $73,000 (1995). Throughout the 1990s, the company gave paper products to communities affected by natural disasters (1998 Québec ice storm, 1997 Manitoba flood, 1996 Québec floods). A gift-matching program supports the Juvenile Diabetes Foundation every time an employee donates money. Since 1982, the company has sustained the Scott Tournament of Hearts, an annual national curling championship for women. In 2000, it began supporting the Sandra Schmirler Foundation for families with children living with life-threatening problems. Between 1990 and 1995, the company established a $50,000 preservation fund for the Trumpeter Swan of Eastern Canada and added other proceeds from product rebates and toy swan sales.

www.scottpaper.ca

Sifto Salt

Based in Mississauga, Ontario, Sifto Salt mines processes, packages, and markets salt and a magnesium-based line of de-icers. Sifto operates a rock salt mine and evaporation plant in Goderich, Ontario; evaporation plants in Amherst, Nova Scotia and Unity, Saskatchewan; as well as a warehouse in Montreal. The mine in Goderich, which has operated for many decades, was incorporated in 1989 as an operational unit of Domtar, the company that owned Sifto's assets until 1990. Ownership changed in 1997, when a merger between IMC Global Inc. and Harris Chemical Group (HCG) converted Sifto to an indirect subsidiary of HCG, which operates itself as a subsidiary of IMC.

Annual Revenues: No information
Grocery Store Sales: Less than 5%
Brands: Sifto
Corporate Status: Wholly-owned subsidiary of U.S.-based company.
Candor: In 1998 and 2002, a spokesperson at the American parent company responded in the late stages of the research process. Candor is 14%.

Ethical Management and Consumer Relations: Ethics policies are derived from Harris Chemical Group's *Vision, Goals and Guiding Principles* document, introduced in 1997 as part of the parent company's Vision 2000 program. Although this program and its components aren't specifically modified for Canadian operations, employees receive training on it. In the early 1990s, Sifto fought allegations that it misled consumers under the advertising rules established by the Competition Act and the Trademark Act. After Sifto printed a label which claimed that its product was the "purest possible" soda, its competitor, Church & Dwight claimed that its baking soda was represented, by implication, as an impure product. Specifically, C&D argued that its Cow Brand could be misconstrued as containing unnatural substances. Sifto supported its claims by arguing that its product came from a natural deposit, nahcolite, thereby justifying the assertion that it was the only "naturally occurring baking soda on the market." The court did not rule against Sifto, but the judge commented that the science underlying Sifto's claims was based on fine points of technical difference. Sifto settled the civil suit out of court.

2002 Employees Canada: No information   **1998 Employees Canada:** 631

Employee Relations: Of 631 Sifto employees, 75 work at the Goderich plant. Ninety per cent of Goderich employees belong to either the Energy and Chemical Workers or the Canadian Operating Engineers Unions. No strikes or lockouts, unjust dismissals or decertification cases have occurred in the last ten years. When HCG bought Sifto, it took over an operation that according to a 1997 union spokesperson suffered "terrible" union-management relations at the Goderich plant. From his perspective, communications were managed badly, the plant was undercapitalized, and staff reductions led to "employee burn-out." The HCG corporate spokesperson commented that relations had improved under its tenure, adding that the "specific areas of concern" at each location were "being addressed each day."

The corporate spokesperson said that HCG was investing $5.5 million in increased production capacity, including a fully automated packaging system. The union spokesperson also expressed concern about management's introduction of an alcohol and drug-testing program in 1996. In response, the company claimed, "this initiative was implemented at all production facilities of Harris Chemical Group," including Sifto, "to help ensure safety in the workplace." But the union spokesperson said that substance abuse problems among Canadian workers did not warrant testing. The company added, "testing is used both for pre-employment screening and whenever an accident occurs." Even though the program included some counselling, the union spokesperson believed that "the Goderich workers found it degrading." No comment on drug-testing or changes in union-management relations was given in 2002.

Equity and Family: No information was reported.

> **Health and Safety:** Joint Health and Safety Committees are active at all sites. No lost-time or medical injuries occurred at the Goderich site between 1994 and 1998, earning the plant an award from the Salt Institute for 400,000 safe work hours. The Unity, Saskatchewan site achieved 350,000 hours without an accident, and also earned a Salt Institute award. A number of internal safety incentives recognize safe work and accident reduction. The union spokesperson described one cash award given on a yearly basis: all employees are eligible to receive a set amount of money at the start of a year, and with every safety infraction, a portion of the bonus gets deducted. In 1996, after three minor incidents, each worker took home $435. In 1998, Sifto had won four safety awards from the Salt Institute and the Mine Accident Prevention Association of Ontario.

Progressive Staff: No gainsharing programs are offered, although a retirement matching plan, based on corporate financial performance, is extended to all staff. A union-sponsored scholarship goes to employees who take courses outside the company, and the children of employees can compete for two HCG Harris Chemical Group scholarships: one for $4,000, the other worth $16,000. Within the community, students from Goderich District Collegiate can compete for a $350 award from Sifto.

Environmental Management and Performance: In 1998, a full-time manager handled environmental matters at both the Goderich mine and plant. Environmental operating expenditures, including the monitoring and testing of equipment, totaled between $25,000 and $30,000 in 1996 (the last year for which data was available). Sifto does not submit chemical releases and transfers data to the National Pollutant Release Inventory, though PCB storage facilities (at the mine and plant sites) are maintained, monitored, and reported on regularly. For recycling materials, an outside contractor collects paper, cardboard, cans, glass, wood, and plastic bags. An estimated 92% of all waste from plastic bags and film was recycled in 1997. Sifto works to conserve resources and convert byproducts in specific areas. For example, water consumed at the evaporation plant originates at a Sifto well, eliminating its draw on the host town's supply. Used oil is disposed by outside contractors, and old gypsum byproducts are used on agricultural land as a soil conditioner. After struggling with compliance problems in the late 1980s, the Goderich mine introduced pollution abatement controls, and reduced process effluent discharges to zero. Remaining discharges come from mine groundwater seepage that flows to the Maitland River under a certificate of approval. Well water and condensed water vapors from the evaporation process are also certified for discharge into the river. Like many major industrial producers, Sifto is required to monitor wastewater for more than 200 contaminants. Suspended solids and salt particles are recycled to brine wells, which settle out the solids, concentrate the brine, and allow the residue to go back into the product.

Community Responsibilities: No current information on community giving or engagement is reported. In the 1990s, Sifto gave to local civic, health care and youth groups, including the United Way, the Boy Scouts, and the Children's Aid Society.

www.siftocanada.com

Sun-Rype Products Ltd

Based in Kelowna, British Columbia, Sun-Rype Products Ltd. has grown into a major manufacturer of apple-based food and beverage products. The company was established as a member-owned cooperative in 1946 so farmers could expand the commercial possibilities of process-grade apples. It became known for its flagship product, Blue Label Apple Juice. Sun-Rype operates in Canada only, as a publicly traded company that processes apple juice, juice blends, citrus juices, cocktails, nectars, apple sauce, fruit snacks, and fruit energy bars. While its beverage products are found primarily in Western Canada, the food products are sold nationally. Sun-Rype's ownership structure changed in 1996, when it was transformed from a co-operative into a public company with shares trading on the TSX. In 2002, the Great Pacific Capital Corp., a wholly owned subsidiary of The Jim Pattison Group of Companies, held 19.7% of the company, and McElvaine Investment Management Ltd. held 13.8%.

Annual Revenue: $101 million

Grocery Store Sales: 86% grocery, 14% mass merchandisers/club stores

Brands: Blue Label, Sun-Rype

Corporate Status: Publicly-traded Canadian company.

Candor: Sun-Rype has typically been one of the most candid firms EthicScan reviews. Its candor is 65%.

Ethical Management and Consumer Relations: With no formal code of ethics, Sun-Rype relies on a "Statement of Purpose & Philosophy" to address stakeholder concerns about issues like diversity, mutual respect, and honest behaviour. Specific polices deal with the placement of products on store shelves and assurance of privacy for employee records. Sun-Rype's product recall system, consumer safety assurance, and advertising guidelines were not explained in detail.

2002 Employees Canada: 475   **1998 Employees Canada:** 376

Employee Relations: Currently, 327 employees belong to unions (compared with 274 in 1998). Between 1995 and 1996, six salaried and ten unionized employees were laid off, followed by another five between 1997 and 2001. Staff levels rose with the acquisition of Okanagan Dried Fruits in 1997. Sun-Rype has not implemented a formal policy to handle redeployment and retraining in the event of downsizing. When necessary, it provides counselling services and assistance with severance and outplacement. No strikes or lockouts have occurred since minor stoppages in 1988 and 1991. In the last decade, only two grievances— the annual average is 50—have reached final stage arbitration. Employee turnover is high at 17% annually, and is monitored by the union. In 2000, training expenditures of $200,000 ($454 per employee) went primarily toward conferences and training, a five-year increase from $109,000 ($436 per person) in 1995.

Equity and Family: No women sit on the board of directors, but one works among four senior managers. Currently, the company does not document information on the advancement of designated groups. An anti-sexual harassment policy receives sign-off from employees, but is not audited nor supported by training. Male employees can take a paternity leave, but it comes without pay.

Health and Safety:
2000 lost-time accidents: 42
1994 lost-time accidents: 253
Injury rates at Sun-Rype declined dramatically through the 1990s (in 1999, there were 36 lost-time accidents compared with 39 in 1997). The Union spokesperson credits the improved performance to better cooperation between workers and management. Joint efforts to produce solutions for problems such as repetitive strain injury have helped drop the incident rate. The company also employs a full-time Health and Safety Coordinator.

Progressive Staff: Kelowna employees have access to Employee Assistance Plan (EAP) referrals to a range of professionals, including psychologists, social workers, and family counsellors for any personal, family, or workplace problems. Employees at other branches are eligible for re-imbursement whenever they need similar services. No retirement planning or eldercare assistance programs exist, but services for children with special needs are part of the EAP. The company has no health promotion plan. Employees receive a 100% refund for any courses taken. Approximately 2% of employees are on some kind of flexible schedule. When share purchases were first offered in 1994, employees were allowed to buy them for a one-time discount price (40% below the market share valuation), and 10% of the workforce bought stock. In the regular stock option plan, Sun-Rype pays 35% of the market price for the shares purchased by senior executives. While the company has an ad-hoc profit sharing program for staff members, the collective agreement calls for a Gain Sharing Program provision for union employees. In response to questions about the ratio of top executive salaries to plant workers salaries, the spokesperson noted that the CEO and President's compensation is based on a comparison with the salaries of CEOs and Presidents of similar companies.

Sourcing and Trade: The spokesperson said that, generally, all Sun-Rype apples come from Canadian suppliers. When needed, additional apples will be sourced from the United States. For other products, fruit ingredients like oranges must come from southern climates, such as the United States. No details were provided on source countries, or international standards governing human rights. In 2001, the spokesperson reported that Sun-Rype no longer had an interest in a facility located in the Pudong economic development zone of China. The spokesperson stated that EthicScan's ethical sourcing criteria were not applicable to the company.

Environmental Management and Performance: Sun-Rype's environmental code requires a sign-off from its environmental committee but not from employees. Basic information is distributed in an employee handbook, but otherwise they receive no formal training. External auditors, Morrow Environmental Consultants, conduct yearly inspections of Sun-Rype operations, and the environmental committee reports performance results internally to the board of directors. A part-time coordinator receives assistance from an eight person

Environmental Committee of employees. Externally, the company works closely with three industry associations. Emission reduction targets are incorporated into product design, but the company mentions nothing about targets for processes. Energy conservation programs target areas such as steam, solid waste, natural gas, effluent, and electricity. Sun-Rype subscribes to the Canadian Industry Program for Energy Conservation (CIPEC) and the Office of Energy Efficiency (OEE), but no other international protocols. In 1995, the company spent $2,000 for waste reduction initiatives such as Powersmart, a highly efficient fruit concentrator requiring one-third the amount of steam needed by comparable equipment. Sun-Rype supplied no information on chemical releases or transfers to the National Pollutant Release Inventory. The company reports no violations, fines, or awards. The spokesperson explained that Sun-Rype's choice of packaging, the tetra brik, has a comparatively low impact package considering its requirements for energy consumption, transportation, and raw material usage. Within the workplace, three recycling programs cover paper, tetra brik, and glass. Sun-Rype also contributes to a Crown Packaging recycling facility that is funded by packaged goods companies.

Genetically Modified Ingredients: The company gave the following statement: "Sun-Rype participates, through Canadian Food Associations and Regulatory Agencies, in the process of developing a standard for foods derived from biotechnology. [This process should produce] a workable definition and acceptable guidelines for all Canadian food products derived from genetic engineering. There is presently no definition of 'GMO-free' in Canada and the Canadian Standards board has struck a committee that will arrive at a standard for foods. Until such time that there is a legal definition in Canada of 'GMO' and 'GMO free, [SunRype] will not participate in voluntary labelling of food [derived] 'from' or 'not [derived] from' biotechnology. In the absence of generally accepted guidelines or definitions [voluntary labelling process] end[s] up with opinions. As a company, Sun-Rype cannot certify opinions."

Community Responsibilities: Sun-Rype's charitable contributions reached 1% of pre-tax profit, when calculated on a three-year average, and donation guidelines are published on the company's web site. Half of annual corporate giving comes as cash, with the other half as product donations. Sun-Rype has committed itself to promoting healthy active living, and initiatives that bring together children and families. The Sun-Rype Active Kid Challenge, the company's primary community involvement (a $300,000 commitment), works with local groups in communities from B.C. to Ontario, staging active programs such as obstacle courses, product samples, and prize giveaways. A work program helps students with career preparation, and a scholarship fund assists students at Okanagan University College and the B.C. Institute of Technology. The company also gives to the Children's Hospital.

www.sunrype.com

Tetley Canada Inc.

Tetley Canada belongs to Britain's Tetley Group Ltd., the international tea business that holds the worldwide rights to the Tetley brand. Founded in 1969 in Toronto, Tetley Canada has no manufacturing plants in Canada, but distributes tea bags from England, along with a range of iced tea products made at different licensed manufacturers (including Lassonde, McCain, and Super Pufft).

Revenues: No information
Grocery Store Sales: No information
Brands: Lyons, Tetley
Corporate Status: Wholly-owned subsidiary of U.K.-based company.
Candor: In 1998, many of EthicScan's questions were answered. In 2002, this wasn't the case and the candor quotient is 25%.

Ethical Management and Consumer Relations: No formal ethics code or support programs is reported. Advertising and promotion budgets range between $2 and $5 million per year, but Tetley has no toll-free consumer phone line and reported no consumer assurance process.

2002 Employees Canada: 10

Employee Relations: Globally, the Tetley Group employs 1,100 people. Tetley Canada's staff of ten receives support from 250 representatives who provide marketing and distribution services. In 2001, the company spent $2,000 on training per employee ($20,000 in total), an expenditure that has remained consistent over each of the last five years.

Equity and Family: In Canada, four of ten staff are women. At the parent company, zero of seven directors are women. No information is reported on equity or anti-harassment policies. Flexible scheduling is offered for religious, family, and cultural reasons. No formal Employee Assistance Plan is offered, although informal individual referrals exist. Internal communications at the parent company include newsletters, bulletins, and briefing sessions. Tuition costs for external courses are refunded (between 50-100%), and the spokesperson reported that the company offers reward incentives, but did not provide details.

Sourcing and Trade: Despite the fact that the parent company has operations in 40 countries worldwide and procures tea that originates in developing nations, no information regarding sourcing, fair wage, or procurement policies was reported. Tetley is a founding member of the UK Tea Sourcing Partnership whose objective is the ethical sourcing of tea.

Environmental Management and Performance: Tetley Canada follows the parent's environmental policies distributed through a *Good Environmental Practice* booklet sent to all global operations. Since no manufacturing or processing occurs in Canada, no audits take place. No information was available about standards applied at licensed manufacturers.

Despite the fact that Tetley distributes its products in tetra paks, cartons, and plastic—packages that either go to landfill or recycling—no information was provided on initiatives to improve packaging materials.

Genetically Modified Ingredients: The company's products are neither organic nor certified GMO-free.

Community Responsibilities: The company reported no information on current charitable donations. It is not committed to the Imagine Campaign, which encourages a minimum of 1% of pre-tax earnings to be donated to charity. Sponsorships include Cash for Kids, which funds a program for children who have special needs. Other donations go to food banks, and the Canadian Breast Cancer Foundation.

www.tetley.ca

Unilever Canada Limited

Unilever Canada is a subsidiary of the world's largest consumer packaged goods company. The diversified Canadian subsidiary's interests include Unilever Canada - Foods, Unilever Canada Home & Personal Care, Good Humor-Breyers, Unilever Bestfoods Foodservice Canada, Loders Croklaan, Unilever Cosmetics International (Canada), and Bertolli Canada. The parent company started with the production of William Lever's Sunlight soap in 1888. Since 1903, when the company's first plant opened in Toronto, Lever-Ponds (and now Unilever) had continuously produced soap and consumer products at the same site on the Don River. In 2002, the company announced that it would close the plant by mid-2003 after an unsuccessful attempt to sell it as an operating facility. Internationally, Unilever companies make and sell over 1000 brands in 150 countries and employ more than 279,000 people in approximately 90 countries. In 1930, Unilever was formed when Margarine Unie of The Netherlands merged with the British-based Lever Brothers. The parent company's main interests are in food, detergents, and personal products. When Unilever acquired Ben & Jerry's, Slimfast, and BestFoods in 2000, it became one of the world's largest food companies, with revenues of approximately US$49 billion in 2001. As part of its integration of BestFoods, Unilever announced in June 2001 that it would sell 15 North American brands as it reduced core brands by 75%.

> **2000 Revenues:** $1.5 billion
> **Grocery Store Sales:** No information
> **Brands:** Becel, Bertolli, Breyers, Degree, Dove, Hellman's, Imperial, Klondike, Knorr, Lipton, Maille, Pears, Popsicle, Q Tips, Ragu, Red Rose Tea, Salon Selectives, Skippy, Slim-Fast, Sunlight, ThermaSilk, Vaseline, Vim
> **Corporate Status:** Wholly-owned subsidiary of U.K.-based parent company.
> **Candor:** A public relations consultant provided a detailed response to 34% of questions on behalf of Unilever.

Ethical Management and Consumer Relations: Unilever Canada's ethical guidance comes through the global parent's *Code of Business Principles*, which deals with key issues like conflict of interest, corporate conduct, donations, political involvement, fair competition, business partnerships, and product safety and security. Compliance is formally reported to the Board of Directors. Assurance of compliance is to be given and monitored annually, and is subject to review by the Board, supported by an Audit Committee and a Corporate Risk Committee. The *Code of Business Principles* provides assurance that the Board may not criticize management for any loss of business resulting from adherence to the code, as well as providing whistleblower protection. Individual policies cover product placement on store shelves, business gift exchange, and procurement from repressive regimes. Although the company has an Ethics Ombudsperson function, it is staffed internally (Vice-President, Legal & External Affairs), not independently. The only other consumer assurance policy or procedure reported was a toll-free consumer service number. In 2000, the parent company tested a framework to evaluate and manage its CSR performance, and produced *Unilever's Approach to CSR: Social Review 2000*. In the process, Unilever operating companies in nine countries - Canada, the Netherlands, the United Kingdom, Brazil, Turkey, Ghana, India, Poland, and Vietnam - representing over 25% of total business completed self-assessment manuals designed to measure, benchmark, and critically assess performance. Unilever expects to roll out this approach to monitoring CSR performance worldwide by 2003.

2002 Employees Canada: 3,100   **1998 Employees Canada:** 4,000

Employee Relations: Approximately 30% of the Canadian workforce is unionized. At a company as large as Unilever regular acquisitions, divestitures, and restructurings mean that employees are constantly being absorbed and let go. According to the *Social Review 2000*, Unilever provides all employees leaving the company with counselling on financial management, training, and career skills. In February 2001, Unilever plc announced it was cutting 25,000 jobs as it integrated new companies and reduced brands. In April 2001, the company said it would eliminate 8,000 jobs and close 30 plants in North America, Latin America, and Europe (exact locations were not yet disclosed). In February 2002, the company announced the closure of a Toronto plant affecting 330 employees by mid-2003, after an unsuccessful attempt to sell it as an operating plant. The 2002 spokesperson said that Unilever usually sells operations rather than closing them outright. In 1995, the Canadian company laid off 166 non-unionized manufacturing workers from Cheseborough-Pond's Markham plant (which made Q-Tips, Pears, and Vaseline), citing excess capacity and poor profitability. Downsized workers received job search counselling, training, and education assistance, and any worker who remained with the company until the day the plant closed received a "generous severance." Marketing and sales staff did not lose their jobs. Two strikes during the 1990s hit Monarch Fine Foods, when workers demanded that the company keep its Etobicoke plant open (1992). In 2000, Unilever reported that its accident frequency rate (lost time injuries plus restricted work injuries per 100,000 worker hours) had dropped from 1.4 in 1996, to 0.45 in 1999.

Equity and Family: More women work in senior management today (36%) than in 1998 (20%), but the number of board directors (zero) has not changed. In 1998, women held 46% of total workforce positions. Unilever Canada "maintains a broad base hiring practice," but has no formal programs or targets to address imbalances. In 2002, the spokesperson stated that since Unilever is a diversified multinational company, the company does not write policy on this matter, but rather it hires the best people for each job. Promotions come mainly from within, and the company has a system of internal job postings that is available to employees around the world. All forms of harassment are addressed in a formal company statement. Extended maternity and paternity leaves, and three discretionary floater holidays constitute the company's family support programs.

Progressive Staff: Employee skills development is boosted through 100% tuition reimbursement, and scholarship funds for both employees and their children. A fund disburses $5,000 per year to grant five university entrance scholarships. Mental and physical health programs include counselling for stress, substance abuse, and retirement planning, and each employee receives an annual fitness subsidy of $300. Financial planning counselling is also offered to middle to senior managers. Newsletters and electronic bulletins are published, and people can make suggestions through formal and informal networks, including employee climate surveys. In 1996, Unilever spent $1.4 million ($700 per employee) to train its Canadian staff. Since 1995, all employees have been able to join a stock purchase plan administered through payroll deductions, and participate in individual reward plans. The company has made three employee stock offerings in seven years. A stock option plan as part of senior managers' compensation package has been streamlined to include upper and middle managers.

Sourcing and Trade: This multinational is so large that its annual revenues are greater than the gross domestic products of some countries. The parent company has operations in 90 countries worldwide. Asian operations are often joint ventures, such as the company's Shanghai, China toothpaste factory (Unilever holds 60% of this operation, while an Asian partner holds 40%). The parent company reports that it fully complies with the ILO standard for Minimum Work Age. A regional sourcing policy exists within North America, as does a global policy dealing with procurement from repressive regimes. No other details were reported.

Environmental Management and Performance: All companies and divisions operate under the parent company's environmental code, which sets out a commitment to conduct business in an environmentally sound and sustainable manner through continuous improvements in environmental performance. The parent focuses on achieving its sustainability goals through increased efficiency, innovation, and three sustainability initiatives in agriculture, fish, and water. Unilever has a strategy development body, the Unilever Environment Group (UEG) composed of representatives from the company's Business Groups, chaired by the Corporate Development Director. The UEG also meets twice yearly with five external advisors. A Safety and Environmental Assurance Centre provides expertise and advice on safety and environmental matters, hazard analysis, risk assessment, and life cycle assessment. A Safety, Health, and Environment Action Committee is responsible for developing and implementing Unilever's environmental management system, training, and auditing. Audits are carried out at least once every three years by Unilever staff external to the particular site. In 2000, 103 of Unilever's operations were ISO 14001 certified - including five in Canada - and the company plans to have all lead operations certified by 2003. ISO 14001 certified sites are audited annually by the certifying body. Depending on the operation, each business unit's environmental affairs are managed by either a full-time or part-time staff member, and in 2000, 96% of Unilever's sites worldwide had a trained environmental manager. In 1995, the British parent released its first global environment report. The most recent *Environment Performance Summary Report* was produced in 2001, and the company maintains a section of its website with detailed information and updates on its environmental management and performance. In the mid-1990s the then Lever Pond's (now Unilever Home and Personal Care) factory spent over $500,000 on new dust collectors, filters, and operating expenses, while the former Lipton (now part of Unilever Food) devoted $600,000 on capital expenditures and $326,000 on operating expenses. Unilever Canada did not provide the National Pollutant Release Inventory with information on its chemical releases and transfers. Unilever Canada recycles shrink-wrap, foil, cores, powder, chemicals, water, plastic bottle resins and polystyrene, paper, cardboard, cans, glass, wood pallets, packaging, plastics, fibre, and food wastes. From 1995 to 1996, the former Lever Pond's reduced non-hazardous waste to landfill (from

240 tonnes to 100 tonnes). A waste reduction award was given to Lipton by the City of Etobicoke after the company diverted 89% of its non-hazardous waste stream from landfill. When dealing with suppliers, the company sets standards for materials, relies on a database that assesses product life cycle, and develops new ingredients and processes.

Animal Testing: Unilever states that it is trying to eliminate animal testing on its products and ingredients, even though in some cases these tests are demanded by federal regulators to ensure product safety. The parent company has published reports stating that 95% of safety clearance procedures do not require the use of animals, and that the company spends over $1 million annually on alternative testing and claims. In 2002, the company stated that as of October 2000, it no longer tests any finished home or personal care products on animals, but that where required for safety reasons, limited testing would continue on ingredients and food products.

Genetically Modified Ingredients: Unilever decided to discontinue its use of GM ingredients in food sold in the United Kingdom. The parent company supports the use of modern biotechnology within the framework of effective regulatory control and provision of information about its use. The company also supports accessibility to information on biotechnology via toll-free consumer lines, in-store leaflet distribution, product information websites, and labelling of products. Unilever's operating companies are responsible for decision-making regarding the use of genetically modified ingredients but must take into account national food legislation, local custom, product requirements, cost of alternative ingredients, and local customer and consumer views. The policy specifies that only ingredients derived from genetically modified crops approved by regulatory authorities and Unilever's clearance procedures may be used.

Community Responsibilities: The company is now pledged to the Imagine Campaign, and in 2002 launched the Unilever Canada Foundation to disburse 1% of pre-tax profits (just over $1 million). The Unilever Canada Foundation focuses upon youth - particularly through a partnership with Invest in Kids - and the environment, in the area of clean water stewardship. Unilever employees donate time to charitable work; for example, as part of its National Meeting in 2001, Unilever organized a volunteer afternoon in which 650 employees donated a combined total of 2,600 hours to over 20 charities. In the past, the company had supported national groups and organizations in communities where it operates, focusing on the areas of health, cultural, educational, and aboriginal needs. Specific recipients have included the Heart and Stroke Foundation, the Montreal Heart Institute, the Invest in Kids Foundation, the Boys and Girls Clubs, Project Jingle, Camp Trillium, and the United Way. In 2001, Unilever endowed two scholarships in York University's Faculty of Environmental Studies. In 2000, Unilever became Toronto's first "River Partner", as part of a "Living City Campaign," by pledging $210,000 over three years to the program. Lever Ponds designed and funded several environmental education programs for junior and senior high school students across Canada, including "EcoVoyageurs," which Unilever Canada still supports. Partnerships include the World Wildlife Fund, Invest in Kids, and in the past included Friends of the Earth, and the Harmony Foundation, among other groups working in the cities where operations are located.

www.unilever.ca

Pfizer Canada
(Consumer Products division - formerly Warner Lambert)

Warner Lambert was one of North America's biggest confectionery, consumer, and health products companies. The origin of its flagship product line, Adams gum, extended back to Thomas Adams, who is reputed to have invented chewing gum in 1886. In June 2000, Warner Lambert was acquired by Pfizer Inc., the world's largest pharmaceutical company. Pfizer has four operating groups: Pharmaceuticals, Global Research and Development, Animal Health, and Consumer. The Pfizer Consumer Group is the group into which the acquired Warner Lambert product lines were integrated, and it represents consumer health care products, Adams confectionery products, and Schick shaving products. Pfizer's first Canadian operations opened in Montreal in 1953. Today, Pfizer Canada has facilities in: Kirkland, Quebec; Scarborough, Toronto, Mississauga, and Arnprior, Ontario; and Calgary, Alberta.

2001 Revenues: US$32.2 billion

Grocery Store Sales: No information

Brands: (Consumer Healthcare Division)   Reactine, Benadryl, Benilyn, Actifed, Sinutab, Sudafed, Neosporin, Polysporin, Zantac 75, Rolaids, Combantrin, Lubriderm, BenGay, Desitin, Zincofax, Trosyd, Anusol, Nix lotion, Unisom, Gynecure, Plax dental rinse, Efferdent, Listerine (Adams division) Chiclets, Trident, Dentyne, Freshen Up, Bubblicious, Bubbaloo, BodySmarts, Halls, Clorets, Certs (Schick division) Schick razors, Wilkinson Sword blades

Corporate Status: Wholly-owned by U.S. parent.

Candor: The company has a 23% candor quotient.

Ethical Management and Consumer Relations: Pfizer's ethics code, last updated in 2001, is translated into languages spoken at its operations. The Warner Lambert "Creed" addresses specific interests of internal and external stakeholders, and among other things, it establishes guidelines for the placement of product on store shelves. In 2000, media articles reported that Warner Lambert opposed a shareholder resolution calling for a restraint on the increase of drug prices. The company responded that the information used as the basis for the shareholder resolutions was false and misleading in some areas. Brand name consumer and health care product makers often justify high drug prices by arguing that they, and not generic drug makers, must invest heavily on research to innovate new treatments. However, critics of the drug industry point out that more money is often spent on advertising and promotion. In 1996, for example, Warner Lambert's advertising and promotion budget for more than 140 countries (for both consumer and health care divisions) was US$1.6 billion, more than twice than the company's typical R&D budget (about $672 million in 1997).

Employees Canada (Pfizer and Warner Lambert): 2,300

Employee Relations: No Canadian employees are unionized. The spokesperson said that during the 1990s net employment in Canada increased despite consolidation, because new manufacturing lines were introduced. In 1993, the parent company began a global restructuring plan that closed seven drug manufacturing plants and cut 2,000 employees. The company offers advance layoff notice as a regular practice, but no other details were mentioned. A share option purchase plan is available, though the spokesperson did not specify for which employee groups.

Equity and Family: One woman sits on an 11 member executive committee in Canada. Between 1986 and 1992, the representation of women working in field sales increased from 9.6% to almost 15%. In manufacturing, women's participation grew from 42% to 46% (strong compared with most other companies in this book), and at the executive level, the balance rose from 17% to 19% over the same period. Most of these figures are about average for companies in this book. Employment equity policies have guided hiring and promotion since 1976, and are supported by a diversity taskforce that targets minorities, women, and disabled workers. An anti-harassment policy also covers issues related to equity, sexuality, race and disability. Family support policies include maternity, paternity, and adoption leaves, as well as daycare referral. In the 1990s, the company was fined $5,000 by the B.C. Human Rights Council for discriminating against an employee who proved that her pregnancy had an impact on the assignment of promotions at the Parke Davis facility in Vancouver.

Progressive Staff: Warner Lambert offers a substance abuse counselling program called HELP, which can be extended to employees' family members, along with flex-scheduling and telecommuting options. Health promotion includes health club membership subsidies, and a fitness club at the head office. Employee newsletters communicate internal information, and the company conducts independent surveys of employee opinion.

Sourcing and Trade: The parent company operates in 75 countries worldwide, but no program to screen supply chain relations for human rights or environmental concerns was reported.

Environmental Management and Performance: No information on environmental policies or staff was reported, and no progress data is published for external stakeholders. The company has introduced energy efficient systems through voluntary programs such as Green Lights and Energy Star Showcase Buildings, and the company is now saving $1.3 million per year in total energy costs. In the U.S., the parent company expects to save an additional $200,000 per year by participating in the Environmental Protection Agency's Energy Staff computers program. To reduce packaging waste, Warner Lambert has reduced the thickness of its gum wrapper, removed the inner foil from its Trident package, and invested money in new packaging technology. Warner Lambert did not provide the National Pollutant Release Inventory with information on its chemical releases and transfers. In 1996, Warner Lambert was listed as 16th on Environment Canada's list of Top 25 polluters in the Great Lakes area. However, no wastewater discharge exceedances or environmental prosecutions have been reported for any of the three Ontario facilities.

Community Relations: The Canadian company gave $500,000 worth of cash and goods in kind in 1997 (the last year information was reported). Typically, it contributes more than 1% of pre-tax earnings to charity, focusing on health and medical areas, which account for approximately 30% of total donations. Educational support includes nine university scholarships, professional training and research awards to university-based programs in dentistry, dental hygiene, and pharmacy. During the floods that ravaged the west and Québec between 1996 and 1997, the company assisted by donating products to residents in need. During the 1998 ice storm affecting Québec and eastern Ontario, the company's Brockville plant donated food, batteries and clothing, while employees gave their time and financial support.

www.pfizer.ca
www.warner-lambert.com

GRADING TABLE

Company Name:	Corporate Governance	Ethical Management	Employee Relations	Equity & Family	Progressive Staff Policies	Sourcing & Trade	Environmental Management	Environmental Performance	Community Responsibilities	Candor
ADM Agri-Industries	F	F	F+	F	F	F	F+	F	F	11
Alberto Culver Canada Inc.	D-	B	E-	E+	B-	E-	E-	F	F+	46
Alcan Inc.	A-	A	B	D+	A+	A+	B+	D-	B	86
Bayer Inc.	F	C-	C-	B	A-	F	C	D	D	56
Cadbury Beverages Canada Inc./Motts	F+	F+	F+	E-	C-	F	F+	F	D-	20
Campbell Soup Company Ltd.	F	C-	A-	B-	A-	F+	E-	D-	E	68
Canada Bread Company Limited	F+	C+	C+	C-	D+	F	E+	F+	E-	48
Canadian Salt Company Ltd	F	F+	F	F+	E+	F	F+	F	F	12
Canbra Foods Ltd	F	F	F+	E-	D+	F	F+	F	F	19
Cargill Ltd	F	D	E-	E+	B-	E+	D	F+	D+	37
Cavendish Farms Ltd	F	E-	F	F	E+	F	E-	F	F	12
Church & Dwight Ltd	F	F	F+	F	F+	F	E-	E-	F	18
Clearly Canadian Beverage Corporation	F	F+	E+	E-	C-	F	F+	F+	F+	26
Clorox Company of Canada Limited	F	B-	E	D-	B+	F	E+	E+	F+	29
Coca-Cola Bottling Company	F	A+	C-	D	A-	F	D+	D-	E+	58
Colgate-Palmolive Canada Inc	F+	C-	F+	F	D+	E	D-	F+	F+	32
ConAgra Grocery Products	F	F	E-	F+	F+	F	F+	F+	F+	23
Cott Corp.	F	F	F	F	F	F	F	F	F+	11
Cuddy International Corp	F	F	F	F	F	F	F	F	F	16
Culinar Inc.	F	F	F	F	E-	F	F+	F	F+	12
Dare Foods Limited	F	F	E	F	D	F	F+	F+	F	38
Dial of Canada	F+	F	F+	F	F	F	F+	F	F+	18
Dover Industries Limited	F	F	E-	F+	D	F	F+	F	E-	29
E.D. Smith & Sons Ltd.	F	E-	F+	F	F+	F	F	F	F	27
Effem Foods Ltd.	F	F	F	E-	F+	F	F	F	F	10
Energizer Canada Inc.	F	F	F	F	F	F	F	F	F	12

Company Name:	Corporate Governance	Ethical Management	Employee Relations	Equity & Family	Progressive Staff Policies	Sourcing & Trade	Environmental Management	Environmental Performance	Community Responsibilities	Candor
Gay Lea Foods Co-operative Limited	E	E-	B-	E	C+	D-	F+	E	F+	75
General Mills Canada Corp.	F	C-	D+	A	A	E-	E-	F+	D-	49
George Weston Limited	E+	D	F	F+	E	F+	D	F	E-	40
Gerber Canada	F	F+	F	F	D-	F	F	F+	F	18
Gillette Canada Inc.	D+	C+	D+	D+	C+	F+	C-	D-	E+	73
GlaxoSmithKline Inc	F	F	F	F	E+	F	E+	F+	F+	14
Goudas Food Products and Investments Ltd.	F	F	F	F	F	F	F	F	F	11
Heinz Company of Canada, H.J.	F	E	B-	E+	B+	E+	E	E+	F+	62
Hershey Canada Inc.	F	E-	F+	F+	B-	F	E+	E-	F+	25
High Liner Foods Incorporated	A	B-	C	D	A-	B+	C-	D-	D	84
Hostess Frito Lay Co.	F	D+	D+	E	A-	F+	E	E-	F	36
Humpty Dumpty Snack Foods Inc.	D	E-	F	F+	E-	F	F+	E-	F	28
Imperial Tobacco Canada Limited	F+	C-	A	E	A-	E	C	D-	B+	81
Johnson & Johnson Inc.	F	F+	F	F+	F+	F	D+	F+	F+	13
JTI-Macdonald Corp.	F	F+	F	F+	C	F	F+	F	F	26
Kellogg Canada Inc.	F	A+	C+	C+	A+	F+	D+	D	D-	70
Kraft Canada Inc.	F	C-	E	D-	B+	E-	C+	F+	E-	39
Lantic Sugar Limited/Rogers Sugar	F	F	F+	F+	C	F	D-	F+	F+	18
Lassonde Industries Inc. / A Lassonde Inc.	E	D-	C+	C	C+	F+	D-	F	F+	52
Loblaw Brands Limited (Private Label)	D-	E	D	E+	C+	F	C+	E-	E	69
Maple Leaf Foods Inc.	E	B+	E+	D-	A-	F	D-	E-	E+	51
Maple Lodge Farms Ltd.	F	F	F	F	E-	F	E+	F+	E-	20
McCain Foods Limited	F	E	D-	E-	B+	F	D-	E-	E-	36
McCormick Canada	F	D+	C	C	A-	F+	D-	E-	E-	43
Melitta Canada Inc.	F	D	E-	F+	D+	E	E-	E-	E-	31
Metro Inc. (Private Label)	E+	E	F+	F	F	F	F+	F+	F	26

Company Name:	Corporate Governance	Ethical Management	Employee Relations	Equity & Family	Progressive Staff Policies	Sourcing & Trade	Environmental Management	Environmental Performance	Community Responsibilities	Candor
Nestle Canada Inc.	F	E+	F+	E+	C-	F	D+	D	E	29
Ocean Fisheries Ltd.	F	E-	E+	E	B-	C-	D-	E+	E-	44
Old Dutch Foods Limited	F	F+	D	F	E+	E-	F	E	F+	46
Parmalat Canada	F	C+	C-	F+	A-	F+	F+	F	E-	50
Pepsi Bottling Group (Canada), Co.	F	A+	D	B	A+	E-	C	D+	F+	47
Playtex Limited (Canada)	F	E-	F+	F+	C	F	F+	F+	F+	23
Procter & Gamble Inc.	F	B-	C-	C	A+	E-	D+	B	D	57
Quality Meat Packers Limited	F	E-	E-	E+	B	E+	F+	E+	F+	73
Redpath Sugars	F	F+	E-	F	E+	F	E	F	F	22
Robin Hood Multifoods Inc.	F	F	D-	E+	D-	F	F+	F	F+	26
Rothmans Inc.	F+	F	F+	F	F+	F+	F+	F	F	24
S.C. Johnson & Son Limited	F	C	C	B	A	F	B	D-	C-	48
Saputo Inc	F	F	E-	F	F	E-	F+	F	F	24
Sara Lee Corporation of Canada Ltd.	F	F+	F+	F	E+	F+	F+	F	E-	13
Schneider Corporation	E+	B	C-	D+	A+	C-	C	C	C-	74
Scotsburn Co-operative Services Ltd	F	F	F+	E-	D-	E-	E	F	E-	18
Scott Paper Limited	F	E-	D-	E+	B	F	C	D-	F+	47
Sifto Salt	F	F+	F+	F	F+	F	F+	F	F	14
Sobeys (Private Label)	F	F	F+	F	E+	F	E+	F+	F+	36
Sun-Rype Products Ltd.	D	E	C+	D-	B-	F	D+	E-	E+	65
Tetley Canada Inc.	F	F	E-	F	E	F	F+	F	F	25
Unilever Canada Limited	F	E	E+	F+	C-	F	D+	F+	E-	34
Warner Lambert (Pfizer Consumer Product division)	F	D-	F	D-	B	F	F	F+	E-	20

TAKING ACTION

OPTIONS FOR ACTION

If the marketplace does not seem to change fast enough for your liking, you can help shape the future. Individuals and organizations can take a number of initiatives to raise awareness and enhance corporate responsibility. To help you identify strategies, we present options according to: actions as individuals, groups, and communities.

ACTIONS AS INDIVIDUALS

Tell the Company What You're Doing and Why

A number of readers of our earlier books (*The Ethical Shopper's Guide*, 1992, and *Shopping with a Conscience*, 1996) said that these books helped them make decisions to purchase certain products but avoid others. In far too many cases, however, they wrote us to question whether such individually responsible decisions were effective. If you are going to influence the behaviour of large companies, it may not be enough simply to avoid a particular product. We strongly urge you to write to the company and tell it what you are doing, and why. In this way, you'll educate corporate Canada much more directly about the limits you are willing to exert to put your principles on the line.

In other words, vote with your pocketbook, but let companies know what you're doing, when and why. What is it about their operations, or advertising, or product selections that make you change your mind about shopping? What recycling or staff policies or equal opportunity behaviour will it take to get you to patronize that corporation's shops, or use it products and services?

Share Your Actions With the Media

When you decide to act, let others know what you are doing. Write a letter to a newspaper or on-line information source. Discuss your decision at work, with community groups, or with your church, mosque, or synagogue. Use the Action Report in this book to alert EthicScan to what you are doing. We'll add your Action Report to EthicScan Canada's database.

Invest With a Conscience

Many of the companies reviewed (or their parents) are publicly traded. You may want to invest in them as an expression of your confidence in their business practices, or avoid their stock because you are not pleased with what they are doing. Today a growing number of financial counsellors understand the basic ideas behind socially responsible portfolios or ethically screened funds. Many sources of information detailing the relationships between returns on financial investment and investing with values are now available. Find a broker who can explain these ethical funds or personally-directed investments and how they work, including what research sources and screens are used.

ACTIONS IN GROUPS

Apply Values at Organizations Where You Work, Volunteer, and Live

Do not minimize the potential power of ethical action. You are not limited by what you consume within your household. You have significant clout or leverage through your workplace or family business, your volunteer activities, and your charitable contributions. If you operate a small business, you can reassess the financial institution you patronize. If you work for a company, you may want to raise questions about its corporate procurement practices for consumables such as computers, furniture, office supplies, and telecommunications equipment. You can ask questions about the business practice standards of vehicle leasing companies, retail gas chains, courier services, and other suppliers.

Ethical Partnering and Pensions

If you work as a teacher or a public servant, you may want to apply rigorous questions about which private sector organizations your employer partners with. As well, if your employer has a sizable, jointly-trusteed pension fund, you can try to promote more responsible investment policies and shareholder activism.

Influencing Industry Associations

Industry associations are also forces for change. They can set ethical standards for members, provide public complaints mechanisms, arbitrate disputes between members, and discipline bad corporate actors. They can also set fair competition, environmental privacy, safety, and other standards. Some industry associations have no ethical agenda in terms of business practice standards as a condition of membership. Others, in attempting to be inclusive, reduce standards for members to the lowest common denominator. Still others, however, are effective, responsive, and willing to act responsibly for the public good in order to forestall or lessen calls for cumbersome government regulations.

Set Your Organization's Standards Higher Than Legal Compliance

One cornerstone to ethical behaviour at work is to seek to improve something rather than merely minimize harm. This often means setting standards that not only encompass but also move beyond mere compliance with the letter of the law. What is legal may often bring social or environmental benefits, and it may even conflict with an individual's sense of what is ethical or moral. Legally sanctioned behaviour is important, but rarely the best standard. A particular law may not exist, may be hopelessly outdated, or may serve as a poor standard for calibrating worthiness or scientific risk. The letter of the law is an important standard, but we need higher goals than compliance to form a basis for personal and corporate responsibility or ecological sustainability.

Promote the Idea of an Ethics Audit at Work

As companies engage in repeated cycles of downsizing and ignore markets except those in which they will dominate, there is a danger of "corporate anorexia." Corporate executives can become fixated on repeated cycles of layoffs. The consequences for communities in terms of job losses, slower retail sales, and plant closings are well known. The internal consequences—low morale, reduced productivity, and withered corporate loyalty—are only starting to be appreciated.

As a change agent within a company or a not-for-profit organization, you may want to advocate that senior management conduct an ethics audit. Such a review goes by many names, including social audit or triple bottom line audit. It may be conducted inside the organization or by an independent audit firm.

While a financial audit examines an organization's books—its finances, profitability, and performance—a social or ethics audit reviews staff morale, dilemmas at work, and any gaps between espoused corporate values and actual practices. They are a low-cost means to enhance morale and allow companies to refine, clarify, and act on their mission statements.

ACTIONS IN COMMUNITIES

Support Organizations Who Act as Positive Forces for Change

A number of organizations are listed in the Sources for Action section of this book. You can write to them for information. You can support some of the advocacy groups with a financial contribution.

Cooperate

Buyers' clubs, cooperatives, and other member-owned organization provide ways to promote local economic development. They create clout through numbers. Such co-ops and consumer groups have been successful for years in such areas as housing, food distribution, investment, and other activities.

Engage in an Information Campaign or Consumer Boycott

You can take direct action together with others to oppose an irresponsible company. Discussions with management in advance of annual meetings about shareholder resolutions are an effective means of promoting change. They alert management and shareholders at publicly traded companies to issues, and can result in distribution of literature to shareholders. Votes at the annual meeting on such resolutions, or fear of same, can evoke changes in management practices.

Financial institutions, utilities, and other regulated service sector companies can be required to put consumer and public interest issues in monthly statements or billings. You can engage in a publicized letter writing campaign or consumer boycott where you join with like-minded others to highlight public attention to an issue and force a specific change in a company's behaviour..

SOURCES FOR ACTION

Independent Standards for Corporations

	Website Address
Advertising Standards Canada	www.canad.com
Canadian Broadcast Standards Council	www.cbsc.ca
Canadian Radio-Television Telecommunications Commission	www.crtc.gc.ca
Canadian Standards Association	www.csa.ca
International Code of Ethics for Canadian Business	www.uottawa.ca/hrrec/busethics/codeint.html
Ontario Employment Standards Act	www.gov.on.ca/lab/es/ese.htm
International Organization for Standardization	www.iso.ch/iso/en/ISOOnline.openerpage
Redefining Progress: Genuine Progress Indicator	www.rprogress.org
Watson Wyatt: Human Capital Index	www.watsonwyatt.co/homepage/services/hci

Human Rights and International Sourcing

	Website Address
Africa Watch	www.africawatch.com/index2.htm
Amnesty International	www.amnesty.org
Canadian Human Rights Tribunal	www.chrt-tcdp.gc.ca
Clean Clothes Campaign	www.cleanclothes.org
FairTrade Labelling Organisation International (FLO)	www.fairtrade.net
Human Rights Watch	www.hrw.org
International Centre for Human Rights and Democratic Development	www.ichrdd.ca
Maquila Solidarity Network	www.maquilasolidarity.org
TransFair Canada	www.transfair.ca

Ethical Investing & Shopping

	Website Address
Domini 400 Social Index	www.domini.com
Ethical Funds Inc.	www.ethicalfunds.com/index.html
Ethical Investment Association	www.eia.org.au/default.html
Ethical Trading Action Group	www.etag.org
Ethical Trading Initiative	www.ethicaltrade.org
EthicScan Canada	www.ethicscan.ca

Investor Responsibility Research Centre	www.irrc.org
Social Investment Organization	www.socialinvestment.ca
SRI World Group: Social Funds	www.socialfunds.com
The Ethical Investment Consultancy	www.profitwithprinciple.co.uk
The Ethical Investor	www.ethicalinvestor.com.au
Responsible Shopper	www.responsibleshopper.org

Business Corporate Social Responsibility Initiatives	**Website Address**
Canadian Council of Chief Executives	www.ceocouncil.ca
Business for Social Responsibility	www.bsr.org
Canadian Business for Social Responsibility	www.cbsr.bc.ca
Canadian Chemical Producers' Association: Responsible Care	www.ccpa.ca
Canadian Industry Packaging Stewardship Initiative Forest Stewardship Council of Canada	www.fsccanada.org
World Business Council for Sustainable Development	www.wbcsd.ch

Academic	**Website Address**
Caledon Institute of Social Policy	www.caledoninst.org
Centre for Applied Ethics at University of B.C.	www.ethics.ubc.ca
Centre for Business Ethics, Bentley College	campus.bentley.edu/dept/cbe
Clarkson Centre for Business Ethics	www.mgmt.utoronto.ca/CCBE
Graduation Pledge of Social and Environmental Responsibility	www.manchester.edu/academic/programs/departments/Peace_Studies
Human Rights Research and Education Centre at University of Ottawa	www.uottawa.ca./hrrec/busethics/busmain.html
Institute for Business and Professional Ethics at DePaul University	www.depaul.edu/ethics
The Responsive Community	gwis.circ.gwu.edu/~ccps/rcq

Canadian Corporate Social Responsibility Activism	**Website Address**
Canadian Centre for Ethics and Corporate Policy	www.ethicscentre.com

Canadian Council for International Cooperation	fly.web.net/ccic
Ethics Practitioners' Association of Canada	www.epac-apec.ca
The Conference Board of Canada	www.conferenceboard.ca
International Ombudsman Institute	www.law.ualberta.ca/centres/ioi
International Development Research Centre	www.idrc.ca
The North South Institute	www.nsi-ins.ca
Voluntary Challenge and Registry	www.vcr-mvr.ca
CCAF-FCVI Inc.	www.ccaf-fcvi.com/entrance.html
Democracy Watch: Corporate Responsibility Campaign	www.dwatch.ca/camp/corpdir.html
Ethics in Action	www.ethicsinaction.com
KAIROS (formerly the Taskforce on the Churches and Corporate Responsibility)	www.web.net/~tccr

Environment and Sustainable Development	**Website Address**
Canadian Council of Ministers of Environment	www.ccme.ca
Coalition of Environmentally Responsible Economies CERES Principles	www.ceres.org
Commission for Environmental Cooperation	www.cec.org
Earthscan	www.earthscan.co.uk
Energy Probe	www.energyprobe.org/energyprobe/index.cfm
Environment Canada - CEPA Environmental Registry	www.ec.gc.ca/CEPARegistry
Friends of the Earth	www.foe.co.uk
Friends of the Environment Foundation	www.fef.ca
National Roundtable on the Environment and the Economy	www.nrtee-trnee.ca
Pollution Probe	www.pollutionprobe.org
SustainAbility	www.sustainability.co.uk
Sustainable Business On-Line Magazine	www.sustainablebusiness.com
Valdez Principles	www.ceres.org
Environmental Choice Program	www.environmentalchoice.com
Clean Edge	www.cleanedge.com

Government of Canada

	Website Address
Canadian Competition Tribunal	www.ct-tc.gc.ca/english/casetype.html
Canadian Environmental Assessment Act	laws.justice.gc.ca/en/C-15.2
Canadian Environmental Assessment Agency	www.ceaa.gc.ca
Accelerated Reduction/Elimination of Toxics (ARET)	www2.ec.gc.ca/aret/homee.html
National Pollutant Release Inventory (NPRI)	www2.ec.gc.ca/pdb/npr/ npri_home_e.cfm
Development and Use of Voluntary Codes	strategis.ic.gc.ca/SSG/ca00880e.html
Patented Medicines Prices Review Board	www.pmprb-cepmb.gc.ca
Office of Consumer Affairs: Consumer Connection	consumerconnection.ic.gc.ca
The Export Development Act	laws.justice.gc.ca/en/E-20/index.html
Workplace Hazardous Materials	www.hc-sc.gc.ca/ehp/ehd/ psb/whmis.htm

Charity and Philanthropy

	Website Address
Canadian Centre for Philanthropy: Imagine Campaign	www.ccp.ca
Charity.ca	www.charity.ca
National Society of Fund Raising Executives	www.nsfre.org
United Way - Centraide Canada	www.unitedway.ca/english

American and European Corporate Social Responsibility Activism

	Website Address
Corporate Social Responsibility Europe	www.ebnsc.org
European Business Ethics Network	www.eben.org
European Foundation for Management Development	www.efmd.be
Institute of Business Ethics	www.ibe.org.uk
Business Ethics Magazine On-Line	www.business-ethics.com/index.html
Catalyst	www.catalystwomen.org
Corporate Watch	www.corpwatch.org
Ethics Officer Association	www.eoa.org
Ethics Resource Centre	www.ethics.org/businessethics.html
New Economics Foundation	www.neweconomics.org
The Ombudsman Association	www.ombuds-toa.org
The Society for Business Ethics	www.luc.edu/depts/business/sbe

Corporate Accountability, Governance and Ownership	Website Address
Democracy and Corporate Accountability Commission	corporate-accountability.ca
Institute of Social and Ethical Accountability	www.accountability.org.uk
Mills Garthson & Associates	www.millsgarthson.ca
Corporate Governance	www.corpgov.net
Consumer Boycott	www.rainforestweb.org
Social Accountability International	www.sa-intl.org
Transparency International Canada Inc.	www.transparency.ca
Capital Ownership Group	www.the-esop-emplowner.org
Infact	www.infact.org
National Center for Employee Ownership	www.nceo.org

International Corporate Social Responsbility Activism	Website Address
Global Reporting Initiative	www.globalreporting.org
Global Sullivan Principles	www.globalsullivanprinciples.org
Business Charter for Sustainable Development	www.iccwbo.org/home/environ-ment/charter.asp
International Crisis Group	www.intl-crisis-group.org
Business and Social Initiatives Database	oracle02.ilo.org/vpi/welcome
OECD Guidelines on Multinational Enterprises	www.oecd.org/daf/investment/guide-lines
The Caux Round Table: Caux Principles	www.cauxroundtable.org
The United Nations Global Compact	www.unglobalcompact.org
UNEP: Statement by Financial Institutions on Environment and Sustainable Development	www.unitednations.org
World Corporate Social Responsibility	www.worldcsr.com

Employee Development and Protection	Website Address
Banana Link	www.bananalink.org.uk
Bakery, Confectionery and Tobacco Workers International Union	www.bctgm.org
Canadian Autoworkers (CAW) Union	www.caw.ca
Canadian Industrial Relations Board	www.cirb-cri.gc.ca/decisions/index_e.asp
Canadian Labour Congress	www.clc-ctc.ca

Communications, Energy and Paperworkers Union of Canada	www.cep.ca
Sustainable Harvest Coffee	www.fairtrade.com
Union of Needletrades, Industrial Textile Employees (UNITE)	www.uniteunion.org
United Food and Commercial Workers	www.ufcw.ca
United Steelworkers of America	www.uswa.org
Workers Rights Consortium	www.workersrights.org

Alternative Media	Website Address
Adbusters	www.adbusters.org
Article Z	www.articlez.fr/english/index.asp
Business Ethics Magazine	www.business-ethics.com/index.html
Commercial Alert	www.commercialalert.org
Corporate Watch	www.corpwatch.org
Democracy Now	www.pacifica.org/programs/ democracy_now
Fairness and Accuracy In Reporting	www.fair.org
Global Dimensions	www.globaldimensions.net
Independent Media Centre	www.indymedia.org
Le Monde Diplomatique	www.monde-diplomatique.org
Lycos Environmental News	ens.lycos.com
Multinational Monitor	www.essential.org/monitor
Rabble	www.rabble.ca
Responsibility Inc. – CSR news	www.responsibilityinc.com
The Straight Goods	www.straightgoods.com
The Center for Science in the Public Interest	www.cspinet.org
The Media Channel	www.mediachannel.org
The Corporate Ethics Monitor	www.ethicscan.ca

ACTION REPORT

REPORT YOUR ACTIONS

The "Options for Action" section discussed initiatives that individuals and organizations can take to enhance corporate responsibility, both on their own and at the organisations where they work or volunteer. This "Report Your Actions" section can serve as your own record of action and can help communicate these initiatives to others. We suggest you use one Action Report per company. EthicScan will put all such Action Reports sent to us on file, in the EthicScan Canada's Corporate 1500 DataBase.

Your name: _____

Your address: _____

Company(ies) contacted and when _____

1. I communicated with the company by

☐ mail   ☐ e-mail   ☐ telephone   ☐ facsimile   ☐ other

2. I communicated on behalf of

☐ myself   ☐ my family   ☐ an advocacy group   ☐ a social group   ☐ other

3. The concern or issue I raised was

4. I did the following

☐ complimented the company on some aspect of its behaviour
☐ told the company why I was going to shop elsewhere
☐ asked for certain information about the company's operations
☐ told the company what changes I wanted before I would again shop there
☐ other

5. A copy of my communication is attached: ☐ Yes   ☐ No

6. Did the company respond?   ☐ Yes   ☐ No

7. What did you think of the company's response?
(circle one: 1 least satisfactory, to 5 most satisfactory)

overall satisfaction	1	2	3	4	5
timeliness	1	2	3	4	5
quality of information	1	2	3	4	5
quantity of information	1	2	3	4	5
met my concerns	1	2	3	4	5
candour	1	2	3	4	5

8. Other comments _____
_____

Send this form or a copy to
EthicScan, P.O. Box 54034, Toronto, ON Canada, M6A 3B7.

COMMENT AND ORDER FORM

1. Overall, I would rate this guide, *Conscious Consumption*, as

☐ excellent   ☐ very good   ☐ good   ☐ fair   ☐ poor

2. The guide's biggest strength is _____

_____

3. Its most serious weakness is _____

_____

4. I recommend that the following companies be profiled in the next edition

_____

5. Please send the following *Corporate Ethics Monitor* reprints ($5 each; any six $25)

☐ Select Technology Hardware Companies
☐ Select Aerospace Equipment Companies
☐ Select Technology Software Companies
☐ Oil & Gas Services Companies
☐ Biotechnology Companies
☐ Real Estate Companies
☐ Management Holding Companies
☐ The Canadian Banking Sector
☐ Life Insurance Industry
☐ Publicly Traded Investment Firms

6. Please send more information about how my organization can sell copies of this book as a fundraiser to the following official _____

7. Reserve a copy of *Shopping With A Conscience*: 2003 Edition, EthicScan's forthcoming retailer guide ☐

Name _____

Address _____

Postal Code _____ Phone Number (_____) _____

E-Mail _____

Please send this form, with your cheque or money order,
to EthicScan Canada, Box 54034, Toronto, M6A 3B7

INDEX

Hot Rods, Schneider Foods, 238
HP Sauce, E.D. Smith & Sons, 122
Humpty Dumpty Chips, Humpty Dumpty, 158
Humpty Dumpty Snacks, Humpty Dumpty, 158
Hungry Jack, Robin Hood Multifoods, 228
Hunt's, ConAgra Grocery Products, 109
Hy's, McCormick Canada, 184
Iams, Procter & Gamble, 220
IGA, Sobeys, 218
Impact, Clorox Company of Canada, 98
Imperial, Unilever Canada, 258
Inner Science, Procter & Gamble, 220
Interbake Foods, George Weston Limited, 133
Irish Mead, Sara Lee Corporation of Canada, 235
Irish Spring, Colgate-Palmolive Canada, 106
Its Clear, Its Cool ... Its Endless Summer, Cott, 111
Its Cott to be Good, Cott Corp., 111
Ivory, Procter & Gamble, 220
Jack's Snacks, Humpty Dumpty, 158
Javex, Colgate-Palmolive Canada, 106
Jell-o, Kraft Canada, 174
Jets, Clorox Company of Canada, 98
Jewel of the Indies, Goudas Food Products, 145
Jimmy Dean, Sara Lee Corporation of Canada, 235
Jos. Louis, Saputo, 233
Juiced-Up Candies, Dare Foods Limited, 116
Juicy Jumbos, Schneider Foods, 238
Just Right, Kellogg Canada, 170
Kal Kan Foods for Cats, Effem Foods, 124
Kellogg's Nutri-Grain Cereal Bars, Kellogg Canada, 170
Kellogg's Pop Tarts, Kellogg Canada, 170
Ken-L-Ration, Heinz Canada, 146
Kent, Schneider Foods, 238
Kibbles 'n Bits, Heinz Canada, 146
Kik, Cott Corp., 111
Kingsford, Clorox Company of Canada, 98
Kit Kat, Nestle Canada, 199
Kitchen Bouquet, Clorox Company of Canada, 98
Kiwi, Sara Lee Corporation of Canada, 235
Klondike, Unilever Canada, 258
Knechtel, Sobeys, 218
Knorr, Unilever Canada, 258
Kogenate FS, Bayer , 69
Kool-Aid, Kraft Canada, 174
Kraft Cheese, Kraft Canada, 174
Kraft Dinner, Kraft Canada, 174
KY Jelly, Johnson & Johnson, 164
L'Eggs, Sara Lee Corporation of Canada, 235
Lactantia, Parmalat Canada, 209
Lakeland, Canbra Foods, 84

Landmark Feeds, Maple Lodge Farms, 191
Lantic, Lantic/Rogers Sugar, 177
Lassonde, Lassonde Industries, 179
Lauentis, Sara Lee Corporation of Canada, 235
Le Menu, Campbell Soup Company, 76
Lea & Perrins, E.D. Smith & Sons, 122
Lean Cuisine, Nestle Canada, 199
Lemon Blaster, Cott Corp., 111
Lentilino, Goudas Food Products, 145
Lestoil, Clorox Company of Canada, 98
Li'l Cravings, Saputo, 233
Lifestyle, Schneider Foods, 238
Light Tonight, High Liner Foods, 152
Lipton's Iced Teas, Pepsi Bottling Group, 212
Liquid Dial, Dial of Canada, 118
Liquid Gold, Canbra Foods, 84
Liquid Plumber, Clorox Company of Canada, 98
Listerine, Pfizer Canada, 262
Lite n' Fruity, E.D. Smith & Sons, 122
Liz Claiborne, Sara Lee Corporation of Canada, 235
Loblaws Supermarkets, Loblaw, 218
Loblaws, George Weston Limited, 133
Lofood, Empire/Sobeys, 219
Loneys, Dare Foods Limited, 116
Lubriderm, Pfizer Canada, 262
Lucky Charms, General Mills Canada, 130
Lumsden Brothers, Empire/Sobeys, 219
Lunch Buckets, Dial of Canada, 118
Lunch Tyme, Schneider Foods, 238
Lunchables, Kraft Canada, 174
Lunchmate, Schneider Foods, 238
Lyons, Tetley Canada, 257
M&M's Plain & Peanut, Effem Foods, 124
Mach 3 Turbo, Gillette Canada Inc, 138
Mach 3, Gillette Canada Inc, 138
Macrolon, Bayer, 69
Magic Moments, Kraft Canada, 174
Maier's, George Weston Limited, 133
Maille, Unilever Canada, 258
Maine Coast Kettle Chips, Humpty Dumpty, 158
Maltesers, Effem Foods, 124
Mama Thekla, Goudas Food Products, 145
Mamma Lucia, Goudas Food Products, 145
Manwich, ConAgra Grocery Products, 109
Maple Leaf Medallion, Maple Leaf Foods, 187
Maple Leaf Prime Naturally, Maple Leaf Foods, 187
Maple Leaf, Maple Leaf Foods, 187
Maple Lodge, Maple Lodge Farms, 191
Maplehurst, George Weston Limited, 133
Marché Richelieu, Metro Richelieu, 218